SON OF
GOD TO
SUPER
STAR

SON OF GOD TO SUPER STAR

Twentieth-Century Interpretations of Jesus

JOHN H. HAYES

Nashville, Tennessee   Abingdon Press

Son of God to Superstar

Copyright © 1976 by Abingdon Press

Library of Congress Cataloging in Publication Data

Son of God to Superstar.
  Bibliography: p.
  1. Jesus Christ—History of doctrines—20th century. I. Hayes, John
Haralson, 1934-
BT198.S645   232   75-30603

ISBN 0-687-39091-5
ISBN 0-687-39092-3 pbk.

MANUFACTURED BY THE PARTHENON PRESS AT
NASHVILLE, TENNESSEE, UNITED STATES OF AMERICA

ACKNOWLEDGMENT

Acknowledgment is made to the following for permission to use copyrighted material:

Abingdon Press for excerpts from "Primitive Christian Kerygma" by Rudolph Bultmann, which appeared in *Historical Jesus and Kerygmatic Christ*, copyright © 1964 by Abingdon Press.

Andover Newton Quarterly and the Reverend Joseph A. Johnson for excerpts from "Jesus: The Liberator."

Bantam Books for permission to quote excerpts reprinted from *The Passover Plot* by Dr. Hugh J. Schonfield; copyright © 1965 by Hugh Schonfield.

George Allen & Unwin, Ltd. for extracts from *Jesus of Nazareth* by Joseph Klausner.

Adam and Charles Black for extracts from Albert Schweitzer's *The Quest of the Historical Jesus*.

Bobbs-Merrill Publishing Company for permission to reprint excerpts from *The Man Nobody Knows* by Bruce Barton, copyright 1925 by The Bobbs-Merrill Company, Inc., 1952 by Bruce Barton.

James Brown Associates, Inc., Agents, and the author, for permission to reprint excerpts from "Sexuality and Jesus," by Tom Driver, copyright © 1965 by Union Theological Seminary in the City of New York.

Cambridge University Press for permission to quote materials from *The Background of the New Testament and its Eschatology* by T. W. Manson.

Collins Publishers for permission to use excerpts from *The Founder of Christianity* by C. H. Dodd.

Doubleday & Co. for permission to reprint excerpts from *The Sacred Mushroom and the Cross*, copyright © 1970 by John M. Allegro.

Fortress Press for permission to reprint excerpts from *Reimarus: Fragments*, ed. Charles H. Talbert, tr. Ralph S. Fraser, copyright 1970, Fortress Press, Philadelphia, Pa., in the Lives of Jesus Series, ed. Leander Keck.

Victor Gollancz, Ltd. for excerpts from *The Secret Gospel* by Morton Smith.

Son of God to Superstar

For my wife
SARAH
w'm kwl shpr' chkm' sgy' 'mh'
(Genesis Apocryphon XX 7)

PREFACE

The purpose of this volume is to introduce the interested reader to a spectrum of twentieth-century interpretations of the historical Jesus. The enormous number of published studies of Jesus during the past three quarters of a century makes any comprehensive and inclusive survey impossible. This volume attempts to present a representative selection of interpretations ranging from the most traditional to the most radical but with emphasis placed on those studies published during the last twenty-five years.

As far as possible, the interpreters of Jesus have been allowed to present their views in their own words. This explains the extensive use of quotations. Summaries of others' views tend to interpret more than does the use of direct quotes, and summations almost always lose the color and impact of the originals.

No assessment or critique of the individual presentations has been offered. The various studies of Jesus and the diversity of approaches do tend to offer indirect critiques of each other.

Internal footnoting has been used throughout the work. Full bibliographical information is given in the bibliography at the end of the book.

A special word of thanks is due Madeline Hawley, who has worked so diligently typing the manuscript for this volume.

J.H.H.
Candler School of Theology
Interdenominational Theological Center

CONTENTS

1. JESUS: THE HISTORICAL FIGURE

> And Jesus went on with his disciples, to the villages of
> Caesarea Philippi; and on the way he asked his disciples,
> "Who do men say that I am?" And they told him, "John the
> Baptist; and others say, Elijah; and others one of the
> prophets." And he asked them, "But who do you say I am?"
> Peter answered him, "You are the Christ."—Mark 8:27-29

   The search for the outline and character of the historical
life of Jesus has, since the Age of Enlightenment, occupied
and fascinated many of the academic minds of the western
world as have few other historical problems. At times, this
so-called "quest of the historical Jesus" has moved outside
the confines of academic circles and engaged the attention of
the average man, sometimes enraging and occasionally
traumatizing him. As a historical endeavor, the quest has not
been limited to members or exponents of the Christian faith.
Many in the Christian church have, in fact, denounced the
quest as either irrelevant to the Christian faith or as
destructive of genuine belief. Others have proclaimed the
effort to be an indispensable requirement and an aid to
understanding the pristine character of the Christian religion
or as the means to recover a faith beyond the structures of
Christian orthodoxy which would be relevant to and
believable by modern man.

SOME ISSUES IN THE QUEST

In very general terms, it may be said that four primary aspects of the life of Jesus have been the focus of concern throughout the modern phase of the quest. In the first place, there has been a concern to understand Jesus within the context of his place in history, that is within the context of the Jewish community as part of the Roman Empire of the first century. Geographical, religious, cultural, and economic issues of first-century Judaism have been explored as avenues toward a comprehension of the historical Jesus. It is true that this concern for the historical context and sociocultural locale was not a dominant issue in the earliest discussions; however, with the passage of time it has assumed a greater role. This is due on the one hand to the greatly increased knowledge of the period through the influence of archaeological exploration and the discovery and study of ancient documents. On the other hand, this focus has been influenced by the stress on historical causation and sociological conditioning which has characterized historical, cultural, and psychological studies, especially in the area of biographical research. Every man is a child of his time and in some respects a mirror of his age.

It has been assumed therefore that a delineation of the contours of first-century Palestinian Judaism would allow the observer a glimpse if not a complete picture of the historical Jesus. What were the general conditions of life in Palestine at the time? What was the religious situation? What classes and divisions of society existed? What traits and characteristics of Palestinian life may have been dominant influences in his life? To what groups and classes of society may he have belonged, and how may these have influenced the course of his life? These are some of the types of questions which scholars have explored in their attempt to outline the features of the historical Jesus.

Out of this area of concern have come the assumptions that any portrayal of the Jesus of history must understand him in the context of first-century Palestinian Judaism and that the failure to do so renders any such portrayal suspect.

14

A second area of concern in the quest centers on the teachings of Jesus. What was the content of his message? What did he preach? What antecedents and frames of reference were available to his audience through which they could understand his message? What was the central concern of his teaching and preaching? Did he offer a new understanding of religion, a new approach to life, a new vision of social order, a new sense or understanding of God, and/or a new interpretation of the course of history? Or in his teaching and preaching did he offer merely a new synthesis of faith and ethics adapted from his contemporaries? Was the message of Jesus obscured, transformed, or merely transmitted by the early church? These are the types of questions explored in the concern to discover the content and message of the preaching and teaching of the historical Jesus.

Out of this area of concern has come the conclusion that any adequate understanding of the Jesus of history must present the content of his vision of life whether this vision was ethically, socially, religiously, and/or politically oriented.

A third concern of this area of research centers on the death of Jesus. A rather firm fact concerning the life of Jesus is that he was put to death during the rule of Pontius Pilate who was Roman procurator or *praefectus* over Judaea during the years A.D. 26–36. Why was Jesus put to death? What was there in his life and preaching that would have stirred the Jewish leaders and/or the Romans to seek his execution? Was his death the culmination of his life and career? Was it due to a misunderstanding or a miscarriage of justice? What role and influence did Jesus have in his own death? How did Jesus understand and face up to his death? These are the types of questions about his death explored in various interpretations of Jesus.

Out of this area of concern has come the conclusion that any portrait of the historical Jesus must take seriously the death of Jesus and seek to understand what actions and/or teachings in his life led to his crucifixion.

A final concern in research on Jesus centers on the origins of the church. Why did Jesus' ministry attract a following?

What was there in his life that could have given the impetus to the birth of the Christian community? What in his life and death could have become the ground of the primitive Christian faith? Why were his followers willing, if not compelled after his death, to carry on the movement which he had begun? Is it possible to understand the life and faith of Jesus? Is there any unbridgeable gap or continuity between the preaching and teaching of Jesus and that of the early church? These are the types of questions discussed by those concerned with the relationship of the life and faith of the early church to the life and faith of the historical Jesus.

Out of this area of concern has come the conviction that any historical depiction of the life and teachings of Jesus must explain what there was in his career which could account for the birth of the Christian community.

Before examining representative twentieth-century recon-structions of the Jesus of history, it will be helpful to review a spectrum of earlier interpretations of Jesus and then ask how it is possible to interpret the historical Jesus in such diverse ways.

SOME PRE-TWENTIETH-CENTURY LIVES OF JESUS

Prior to the eighteenth century, no one had examined the New Testament with the aim of reconstructing the historical outline of Jesus' life apart from faith in the Christ of Christian theology. This does not mean that the church had not been concerned with historical questions concerning Jesus' life and ministry. In some respects, the quest is as old as the church itself. The author of the Gospel of Luke, in his prologue (1:1-4), states that his purpose in writing was to present an "orderly account," implying that this had not been the case for the "many who have undertaken to compile a narrative of the things which have been accomplished among us." The selection of four Gospels as the canonical sources for the life of Jesus and the repudiation of the more than fifty so-called apocryphal Gospels by the church certainly reflect discrimination about which sources were to be accepted as primary for understanding Jesus.

Late in the second century, Tatian hoped to replace the four Gospels with a single version, a single portrait of Christ. His harmony of the life of Christ, called the *Diatessaron*, combined the materials in the Gospels generally following the outline of Matthew for the events prior to the trial and crucifixion of Jesus; for the latter Tatian followed the account found in John. His harmony eliminated the duplications in the Gospel traditions. His work manifests an element of critical analysis: where the Gospel accounts differed, he gave the account which to him appeared most probable. The *Diatessaron* was in use in the Syriac church until the fifth century and was translated into several other languages, although Tatian himself was declared a heretic.

The use of harmonies of the Gospels to present a unified picture of the life of Jesus was employed by Eusebius and St. Augustine in the fourth century. Part of the purpose behind such harmonies was to oppose the idea that the four Gospels were contradictory in many places—an idea which had been around and sometimes used against Christians since the second century. The belief in the divine inspiration of the Gospels stifled any serious critical appraisal of them, although Augustine was fully aware of the differences between them. Augustine sought to explain away these differences so that in the last analysis everything in all four Gospels was accurate and historical. Augustine was willing, unlike Tatian, to see the doublets in the Gospels as reflecting genuine historical events; Jesus performed similar acts and spoke identical or similar sayings on more than one occasion.

During the Middle Ages, poetic presentations of Jesus (beginning in the fourth century) and harmonies of the Gospels were used for teaching and devotion. Beginning in the sixteenth century, a proliferation of Gospel harmonies occurred among both Catholics and Protestants, including a new pattern which presented the Gospel traditions in parallel columns—what might be called the "synopsis" pattern. Behind these harmonies lay both the desire to present within one volume the total material on Jesus and the aim to combat skeptics who might criticize the Gospels because of their contradictions and differences. The number of harmonies during this period may reflect the renewed interest in the Bible, the influence of the moveable-type printing press, the budding "science" of historical research or all of these.

Probably the most influential harmony of the Gospels was that by Osiander (1498–1552) published in 1537. Its methodology is illustrated in its title which translates as: *Greek and Latin Gospel Harmony in four books, in which the gospel story is combined according to the four evangelists, in such a way that no word of any one of them is omitted, no foreign word added, the order of none of them disturbed, and nothing is displaced, in which, however, the whole is marked by letters and signs which permit one to see at a first glance the points peculiar to each evangelist, those which he has in common with the others, and with which of them.* Osiander adhered to the principle that if an action or saying of Jesus was reported two or three times in slightly differing form or in a different order then Jesus must have spoken the saying or accomplished the action two or three times over. Thus the daughter of Jairus was raised from the dead on three different occasions; Jesus cleansed the temple on three separate occasions; identical sayings found in different contexts were repeated by Jesus at different times in his career, and so on.

The Protestant Reformation produced no critical analysis of the Gospels, although both Luther and Calvin were aware of the differences between the Gospels and their sequence of events and the variations between events and sayings within the Gospels. Luther's verdict on this matter was not intended to encourage investigation into such matters: "The Gospels follow no order in recording the acts and miracles of Jesus, and the matter is not, after all, of much importance. If a difficulty arises in regard to the Holy Scriptures and we cannot solve it, we must just let it alone." Here his doctrine of the divine inspiration of scripture seems to have precluded any need for evaluative and critical judgment. This is not totally what one would have expected from Luther who elsewhere could criticize the book of James, which he described as a "right strawy epistle," and the book of Revelation for which he had little use.

Calvin, who differed with Osiander and refused to assume that the sequence of events and teachings in each gospel were historical, wrote a commentary on a harmony of the gospels. In this work, Calvin argued that "no fixed and distinct order of dates was observed by the evangelists in composing their narratives. The consequence is that they disregard the order of time and satisfy themselves with presenting in a summary manner, the leading transactions in the life of Christ."

The first thorough attempt to present a study of Jesus apart from the church's confessional and orthodox faith in Jesus as the divine son of God was made by Hermann Samuel Reimarus (1694–1768). His discussion of Jesus is contained in his *magnum opus,* a manuscript of over four thousand pages, which circulated during his lifetime in anonymous form. After his death, parts of his work were published— beginning in 1774—by the philosopher Lessing. In his "The Intention of Jesus and his Teaching," published in 1778, Reimarus argued that an absolute distinction must be drawn between the faith of the early church and what Jesus proclaimed and taught during his lifetime. He tried to outline the process by which the Gospels had come into existence, and he set the first three Gospels over against the fourth. For his reconstruction of Jesus' ministry, he tended to set aside the Fourth Gospel as more doctrinal than historical. Reimarus sought to understand Jesus within the context of first-century Judaism and claimed that Jesus had no desire to do away with Jewish religion and replace it with another. Jesus' preaching of the kingdom of heaven assumed the typical Jewish beliefs about the hope of a coming messianic kingdom which would free the Jews from foreign domination and political oppression. Jesus believed that under his leadership the kingdom of the messiah was about to dawn. In this coming kingdom, a new and deeper morality, which would fulfill and supercede the old law, would come into being. Jesus sent out his disciples to rally the Galileans to a popular uprising, and in Jerusalem he called for an open revolt against the Jewish leaders. No such uprising or revolt occurred, and Jesus' aim to establish an earthly kingdom and deliver the Jews from oppression failed, and he was put to death. Jesus performed cures but no miracles which would have rallied the people to his cause. After Jesus' death the disciples adopted a spiritualized interpretation of the messianic kingdom—an interpretation also borrowed from Judaism—and proclaimed that the messiah must appear twice, once in lowly human form and again in triumph. The disciples stole the body of Jesus, hid it, and after fifty days proclaimed his resurrection and the nearness of his second coming as the messiah triumphant.

Reimarus' portrayal of Jesus represented a radical break with Christian orthodoxy, and numerous refutations of it were published. How can one explain such a radical interpretation of Jesus within the context of eighteenth-century thought? In the first place, radical interpretations of Jesus had been earlier proclaimed however without the historical concerns of Reimarus. Socinus (1525–62) and Servetus, who was burned at the stake in Calvin's Geneva in 1553, had both denied the divinity of Jesus and regarded him as a human prophet and the founder of a religion. This is not to say that Reimarus was familiar with their thought but only to note that some aspects of his radical presentation were not without precedence. Secondly, interest in the origin of the Gospels and their relationship to each other was beginning to dawn. The recognition that the first three Gospels were not independent accounts of the career of Jesus but were interdependent was a significant development in New Testament studies. This understanding of the Gospels was just beginning to emerge at the time of Reimarus. For example, J. G. Herder (1744–1803), a younger contemporary of Reimarus, published investigations on the Gospels (1796–97) in which he argued that the first three Gospels were Palestinian and historical in origin while the Fourth Gospel was not historical but doctrinal in character. The common basis for the first three Gospels was an oral Aramaic gospel proclaimed by the earliest apostles (so also Lessing). Mark was, according to Herder, the oldest of the Gospels. Thirdly, rationalism, represented by the German Christian Wolff and English Deists such as Toland, Collins, Chubb, and Woolston and the Frenchman Voltaire, had begun to challenge the miraculous element in the Gospel traditions and to argue for religion within the bounds of reason. The miracles of Jesus were rationalized—for example, the dead were not raised but only awakened from a lethargic sleep—and Jesus' resurrection was understood as a phantom appearance seen by visionaries and dreamers if not an outright invention. The rationalists saw in Jesus a prophet and the founder of a more perfect form of "natural religion." Even Rousseau (in 1769) argued that Jesus' aims were to free the Jews from Roman rule and introduce them to true freedom. Fourthly, Reimarus was a creative, radical free-thinker, an advocate of rational religion, and was obviously intent upon an attack on the church's faith. Schweitzer describes Reimarus' work in the following statement: "Seldom has there been a hate so eloquent, so lofty a scorn; but then it is seldom that a work has been written in the just consciousness of so absolute a superiority to contemporary opinion" (*The Quest of the Historical Jesus*, 15).

Reimarus was the harbinger of things to come, although his work did not itself receive very widespread circulation nor exert an immediate or far reaching influence. To illustrate the developing interests in the Jesus of history, several representative interpretations will be noted.

During the nineteenth century, a number of authors produced studies of Jesus and his teachings based on the principles of philosophical rationalism. Rationalism argued that no more of religion can be accepted than is amenable to human intellect and logic and can justify itself at the bar of reason. Therefore full blown rationalism eliminated every-thing supernatural from the arena of belief. This meant that the life of Jesus must be exorcised of all things supernatural, either through outright denial or through reinterpretation. The rationalists believed that the desupernaturalization of the gospel traditions would provide the world with a Jesus whose life and teachings were acceptable to natural religion and reason and more relevant to contemporary man. The rationalists of course had no desire to do away with religion but merely to free it from supernaturalism so that it would more adequately mirror acceptable beliefs. In the United States, Thomas Jefferson reflected this concern, and his version of the New Testament eliminates all the miracles and concludes the Gospels with the death of Jesus.

A classic expression of this rationalistic interpretation of Jesus is the 1828 work by H. E. G. Paulus (1761–1851). For Paulus, Jesus was the supreme example of purity and serene holiness whose character was genuinely human and capable of imitation and emulation by all mankind. Much of his discussion is related to and an explanation of the Gospel miracles. Paulus does not doubt that the biblical writers intended to ascribe miracles to Jesus and that Jesus' disciples understood certain events in his life as miraculous. However, he argued that this was due to either their misunderstanding of certain events or their failure to recognize secondary causes which lay behind the so-called miracles. Paulus argued that the miracles of healing were performed by Jesus either through the exertion of his spiritual power over the nervous system of the sufferer or else through the use of curative medicines known only to him. The nature miracles are understood as reflections of the disciples' misunderstanding or are otherwise open to rational explanation. Jesus did not walk upon the water; he walked along the shore and in the mist surrounding the lake the disciples thought he walked upon the lake's surface. He did not still the storm; the ship at the moment of Jesus' awakening entered the shelter of a hill, and the disciples ascribed to him power over wind and sea. Jesus did not multiply the loaves and fishes; when Jesus began to distribute the food and share it, those present with provisions followed his good example and shared their supplies. The transfiguration was the result of an interview of Jesus with two dignified-looking men whom his disciples, only half awake in the early morning sunlight, thought were

Elijah and Moses. Raisings from the dead were deliverances from premature burial. Jesus' death on the cross was a death-like trance and the surface wound of the spear, the unguents, the cool grave, the storm, and the earthquake resuscitated him. Upon resuscitation, Jesus removed his burial clothes and dressed in a gardener's clothes. After this, he appeared to his disciples for forty days, and then accompanied by the same two men who appeared at the so-called transfiguration (actually secret followers), he bid farewell to his disciples on the Mt. of Olives and disappeared behind a cloud after which his two friends addressed the disciples. Afterward, Jesus died without this being known by his followers.

The rationalists gave extensive consideration to many of the teachings of Jesus stressing the moral and ethical elements. Often the sayings of Jesus were interpreted, restated, or paraphased. For example, the beatitude, "Blessed are the mourners for they shall be comforted," is restated by one rationalist (J. J. Hess, 1741–1828) as: "Happy are they who amid the adversities of the present make the best of things and submit themselves with patience; for such men, if they do not see better times here, shall certainly elsewhere receive comfort and consolation."

A number of nineteenth-century writers produced what may be called imaginary or fictionalized accounts of Jesus' life and ministry. A basic characteristic of practically all of these works is their attempt to discover the true plot of Jesus' life lying behind the disconnected episodes of the gospel accounts. As a rule, these lives of Jesus assume the existence of a secret society to which Jesus belonged or by whom he was controlled. Generally this secret society is identified with the Essenes who are described most fully in the writings of the first-century Jewish historian Josephus but who are not mentioned in the New Testament or the Jewish Talmud.

Examples of this type of approach are the works of K. F. Bahrdt (1741–1792); F. W. Ghillany (1807–76), who wrote under the pseudonym of Richard von der Alm; and Ludwig Noack (1819–85). Bahrdt's work, which was the earliest fully developed specimen, can serve to illustrate the approach. Bahrdt found the clue to his explanation of Jesus' life in the characters of Nicodemus and Joseph of Arimathea. Why, he asked, should these wealthy members of the Jewish upper class make their brief and enigmatic appearances in the New Testament? His answer was that they were Essenes, members of a secret society. This society, whose members had infiltrated practically all ranks and organizations in Judaism, had as its goals the desire to rescue the Jews from their nationalistic and sensuous messianic hopes and the aim of leading the Jews to a higher knowledge of spiritual truths. To do this, they set out to present to the nation a claimant of messiahship who would destroy these false and misleading messianic expectations. Jesus, shortly after his birth, fell under the control of this society which taught him about the falsity of the priesthood, the horror of Jewish sacrifices, and introduced him to the Greek philosophers Plato and Socrates. Upon hearing of the death of Socrates, Jesus as a lad resolved to emulate his heroic death. By the time he was twelve, Jesus' instruction by the society was far advanced.

Jesus' ministry was clearly planned from the beginning. He and John the Baptist, along with various Essene characters whom Bahrdt introduced into the story, in consultation, planned their public careers. Jesus had acquired medical skills from a Persian and Luke, the physician. In order to find some acceptance, Jesus, under the direction of the society, appeared as a messianic figure with many of the characteristics of the expected Jewish messiah—always, of course, with the purpose of freeing the Jews from their gross messianic beliefs. The miracles of Jesus were well orchestrated events which the gospel writers who were not members of the inner circle of the Essenes assumed to be miraculous. For example, the feeding of the five thousand was executed through the help of the society which had filled a cave with bread and passed it out to Jesus for distribution.

Contact with the Essene community was preserved throughout Jesus' career—his departure to secret places for prayer involved meetings in caves with the Essene leaders of which all his disciples were unaware. Jesus taught in two different ways—in simple terms for the general audience and in esoteric and mystic form for the initiates. The Gospel of John has preserved an expression of the latter.

Jesus' "death" was well planned by the community. He did not die but was only drugged. After three days his wounds were healed, and he could walk. Members of the Essene community played the role of angels in the resurrection stories. From his seclusion with the Essene community, he made later appearances, even to Paul on the way to Damascus. He continued to share in the life of the secret Essene community until his death.

Somewhat similar to these imaginary or fictionalized versions of the life of Jesus is Ernest Renan's *Life of Jesus* published in 1863. Renan (1823–92) was, however, a scholar of repute and was much more bound to the biblical text—although his imagination and literary artistry were given full expression. Renan was a Catholic, one of the first to offer a systematic treatment of the life of Jesus, and his work was addressed to a popular audience. The book was given an enthusiastic reception; it sold sixty thousand copies in the first six months and went through twenty-three editions during his lifetime. Renan's Jesus stands out as the embodiment of an idyllic humanity whose career centered on the common folk of Galilee, who are idealized almost beyond recognition by the sentimentalization of the author. In other words he produced a historical novel about Jesus. Schweitzer, speaking in sarcastic tones because Renan's vision of Jesus differed so radically from his own, wrote: "Renan's *Vie de Jesus* . . . is Christian art in the worst sense of the term—the art of the wax image. The gentle Jesus, the beautiful Mary, the fair Galilaeans who formed the retinue of the 'amiable carpenter,' might have been taken over in a body from the shop window of an ecclesiastical art emporium" (182). The ministry of Jesus is placed amid the blue skies, gentle breezes, seas of waving grain, the gleaming lilies, and the vibrant landscapes of Galilee. Even Renan's Jesus stoops to trickery in the raising of Lazarus, a miracle staged by Jesus to encourage the faltering faith of his disciples in him. In describing the scene in the Garden of Gethsemane, Renan wrote: "Did he recall the clear fountains of Galilee where He might have refreshed himself; the vineyard and the fig-tree under which he might have been seated; the young maidens who might perhaps have consented to love Him? Did He curse his bitter destiny, which had forbidden to him the joys conceded to all others? Did he regret his too lofty nature, and, the victim of his own grandeur, did he weep because he had not remained a simple artizan of Nazareth?" (*The Life of Jesus*, 318). In a final summation of the work of Jesus, Renan wrote:

This sublime person, who each day still presides over the destinies of the world, we may call divine, not in the sense that Jesus absorbed all divinity, or was equal to it (to employ the scholastic expression), but in this sense that Jesus is an individual who has caused his species to make the greatest advance towards the divine. Humanity as a whole presents an assemblage of beings, low, selfish, superior to the animal only in that their selfishness is more premeditated. But in the midst of this uniform vulgarity, pillars rise towards heaven and attest a more noble destiny. Jesus is the highest of these pillars which show to man whence he came and whither he should tend. In him is condensed all that is good and lofty in our nature. He was not sinless; he conquered the same passions which we combat; no angel of God comforted him, save his good conscience; no Satan tempted him, save that which each bears in his heart. And as many of the grand aspects of his character are lost to us by the fault of his disciples, it is probable also that many of his faults have been dissembled. But never has any man made the interests of humanity predominate in his life over the littlenesses of self-love as much as he. Devoted without reserve to his idea, he subordinated everything to it to such a degree that towards the end of his life, the universe no longer existed for him. It was by this flood of heroic will that he conquered heaven. . . . He lived only for his Father, and the divine mission which he believed it was his to fulfil.

As for us, eternal children, condemned to weakness, we who labor without harvesting, and shall never see the fruit of what we have sown, let us bow before these demi-gods. They knew what we do not know: to create, to affirm, to act. Shall

26

originality be born anew, or shall the world henceforth be content to follow the paths opened by the bold creators of the ancient ages? We know not. But whatever may be the surprises of the future, Jesus will never be surpassed. His worship will grow young without ceasing; his legend will call forth tears without end; his sufferings will melt the noblest hearts; all ages will proclaim that among the sons of men there is none born greater than Jesus (375-76).

The first extensive interpretation of Jesus written by a Jew was the work of Joseph Salvador published in Paris in 1838. Salvador's work treats not only the historical Jesus but also the history of the church to the end of the first century. A number of Salvador's emphases are noteworthy. He argued that Jesus never taught a single idea nor laid down any precept that was not to be found in the Jewish scriptures or the writings of the sages contemporary with Jesus. The Sermon on the Mount for example was traced back to influence from the book of Ben Sirach. The tone of Jesus' teaching however differed from that of the Pharisaic Judaism of his day. Pharisaic Judaism, he argued, placed its emphasis on preparing men for earthly life and the transformation of the life of society. Jesus, on the other hand, stressed the religious and ethical life of the individual in terms of an orientation to the future life, and he therefore adopted a negative attitude toward civilized life and disregarded the existing social order. The Pharisees were concerned to lay down prescribed ceremonial laws and practices to preserve and insure national persistence as a people. The laws were a means of guarding Jewish nationalism. Jesus gave however no thought to and was unconcerned about such matters.

Salvador claimed that much of what is written in the Gospels was inserted or created in order to depict the life of Jesus as the fulfillment of Old Testament scriptures. Much of what was said about Jesus' birth, death, and resurrection were derived from Oriental and Greek mythology. Salvador defended the trial of Jesus against the charge of its illegality often claimed by Christians. He compared the early church with pagan religious corporations of Jesus' day.

Another view of Jesus which came to vogue in Germany near the end of the century denied the Jewish origin of Jesus. This view did not arise as a counter to the interpretation of Jesus by Jews but is merely mentioned at this point for the sake of convenience. It was an outgrowth of liberal interpretations of Jesus combined with a racist theory of the superiority of the Aryan peoples. Part of the concern of the studies reflecting this belief in the non-Semitic origin of Jesus was the desire to justify the Aryan nations' acceptance of Christianity. The view was espoused by Houston Stuart Chamberlain, Ernst Häckel, and others. Interestingly enough, some who advocated this view adopted the argument of the Jewish legend found in the Talmud which claimed that Jesus' father was a Roman soldier named Pandera. The theory of Jesus as an Aryan survived to become a dogmatic principle in Adolph Hitler's Nazism.

The work which perhaps had the greatest influence on the academic study of the historical Jesus was *The Life of Jesus Critically Examined* by David Friedrich Strauss (1808–74), published in two volumes (1835–36). Because of one of its special emphases, his presentation has been categorized as mythological. Strauss' work was thorough and scholarly and dealt with practically all the important issues which still haunt and fascinate New Testament research. Strauss gave detailed attention to the question of the New Testament sources for the life of Jesus and challenged the historical value of the Gospel of John. The first three Gospels he saw as composite structures created out of diverse narratives and discourses which made it impossible to use them to establish a fixed chronological order for the life of Jesus. The Gospels contain various strata of legend and narrative with John being the most dominated by apologetic and dogmatic purposes.

For Strauss, the messianic consciousness of Jesus was a historical fact in the sense that Jesus believed that after his earthly life was over he would be taken to heaven from which he would return to bring in his kingdom, a kingdom to be established by the supernatural intervention of God. Thus, for Strauss, the ministry of Jesus was oriented to futuristic events; that is, it was eschatologically conditioned.

Many of the events ascribed to the career of Jesus were myths, according to Strauss. In making such a declaration, Strauss opposed equally the supernaturalistic interpretation which accepted the miraculous events as narrated as historical occurrences and the rationalistic interpretation which sought to explain the events as either due to the misunderstanding of the disciples or to the operation of secondary causes. For Strauss, myth was "the clothing in historic form of religious ideas, shaped by the unconsciously inventive power of legend, and embodied in a historic personality" (Schweitzer, 79). It was a form of expression of religious faith. The mythological character of much of the Gospel tradition meant that the Gospels must be taken as primarily religious documents and not as biographical history.

The question of the origin and character of the Gospels, the eschatological orientation of Jesus' ministry and preaching, and the problem of the role of mythological thought in the portrayal of Jesus are Strauss' legacy to the subsequent course of New Testament studies, although in many ways he was continuing the work of Reimarus.

The nineteenth century saw the rise of thoroughgoing skepticism with regard to Jesus which went to the point of denying his historicity. Bruno Bauer (1809–82) was one of the first and most influential representatives of such a position. Bauer did not begin his studies with his skeptical view formulated; it was the product of his literary studies on the Gospels and other New Testament writings published between 1840 and 1877. Bauer began his studies on the Gospels with an investigation of the Gospel of John. The Fourth Gospel he concluded was the product of the creative reflection of its author who presented his theological views through the utilization of the *logos* concept. Bauer's subsequent investigations of the other Gospels led to a similar skepticism. The Gospels—even Mark which he considered the earliest—were literary products of their authors who projected back into a historical form the Christ of the Christian community. Many of the Gospel stories embody reflections of the early church's experiences and contain the church's explanations of its life and character. The Jesus of the Gospels was thus the product of the church and the Gospel writers' imagination, not the creator of Christianity. Bauer, in his last work, sought to explain the origin of the church by placing its beginning in the early days of the second century through the confluence of influences from Judaea, Greece, and Rome. It owed its origin to numerous factors: Stoicism, Neo-Platonism, the general resignation which characterized the Roman Empire in the second half of the first century, the Roman philosopher Seneca, and the Neo-Roman Jews, Philo and Josephus. Behind the Gospels' depiction of Jesus can be seen the shadowy influence of Seneca, Philo, and Josephus.

The nineteenth century saw numerous presentations of the historical Jesus, which may be designated liberal lives of Jesus. In some respects, these liberal lives of Jesus represent a continuation of the interests of the earlier rationalists. That is, their aim was to present a version of the life and teachings of Jesus which would be acceptable to modern man and at the same time challenge man's religious and ethical consciousness. Liberal scholars accepted the assumption that the Gospels are basically nonhistorical in their present form. However, liberalism felt that through a rigorous application of historical-critical study to the Gospels it was possible to discover the basic outline of the life of Jesus and the basic content of his teachings. On the basis of these, a reconstruction of the historical Jesus could be developed which could be distinguished from the Christ of faith. Liberal versions of the life of Jesus reached their apogee at the end of the nineteenth and the beginning of the twentieth century. An important contribution to this approach was the theological position of Albrecht Ritschl and his followers. Ritschl had argued that the concept of the kingdom of God which Jesus utilized in his preaching referred to the final and ideal goal of human life, a social goal which could be attained by moral and ethical endeavor and heroism on the part of mankind.

A classic example of the liberal presentation of Jesus is found in Adolf Harnack's *What Is Christianity?* Harnack argued that one must study the Gospels and Jesus in order to discover something useful for us in our age. In such a study, the basic aim is to distinguish "what is permanent from what is fleeting, what is rudimentary from what is merely historical." The essence of the preaching of Jesus, Harnack argued, has to be separated from the shell in which Jesus preached it. That is, the abiding Gospel must be separated from the eschatological and other-worldly language of Jesus which belongs to that which is merely historical. When this is done, Harnack concluded that "the Gospel in the Gospel is something so simple, something that speaks to us with so much power, that it cannot easily be mistaken" (15). This something so simple—the essentials of the teachings of Jesus—could be understood in terms of the kingdom of God and its coming, God the Father and the infinite value of the human soul, and the higher righteousness and the commandment of love. Speaking of these essentials, Harnack wrote:

To our modern way of thinking and feeling, Christ's message appears in the clearest and most direct light when grasped in connexion with the idea of God the Father and the infinite value of the human soul. Here the elements which I would describe as the restful and restgiving in Jesus' message, and which are comprehended in the idea of our being children of God, find expression. I call them *restful* in contrast with the impulsive and stirring elements; although it is just they that are informed with a special strength. But the fact that the whole of Jesus' message may be reduced to these two heads—God as the Father, and the human soul so ennobled that it can and does unite with him—shows us that the Gospel is in nowise a positive religion like the rest; that it contains no statutory or particularistic elements; *that it is, therefore, religion itself.* It is superior to all antithesis and tension between this world and a world to come, between reason and ecstasy, between work and isolation from the world, between Judaism and Hellenism. It can dominate them all, and there is no factor of earthly life to which it is confined or necessarily tied down (68-69).

DIFFICULTIES IN RECONSTRUCTING THE LIFE OF JESUS

How is it possible for conscientious, academically trained scholars, working with the same material and presumably seeking the same objectives, to arrive at such diverse interpretations of the historical Jesus and the content of his preaching and teaching? What were and are the problems which seem to make it impossible for academicians and scholars to reach a consensus on the nature and character of the historical life of Jesus? The problems seem to fall into three basic categories. First, there are the problems associated with the extent and character of the source materials. Second, there are the problems associated with the attempts to develop a methodology for approaching the issue of reconstructing the historical Jesus. And third, there are the problems involved in the presuppositions and objectives of the researcher.

The primary source material for any knowledge of the historical Jesus is of course the New Testament. There are some scattered references to the early church and to Jesus in ancient non-Christian sources. These include references found in Seutonius, Pliny, Tacitus, Josephus, the Talmud, and the Koran. Nothing of a historical value about Jesus can be gained from the first two. Tacitus who lived about A.D. 60-120 notes, in discussing the persecution of Christians under Nero, that the founder of the sect was Christus who "was executed at the hands of the procurator Pontius Pilate in the reign of Tiberius" (*Annales,* xv. 44). The authenticity of references in Josephus to Jesus is questioned since in one passage (*Antiquities,* xviii 63-64) he gives a good Christian confession about Jesus. Most scholars suspect a Christian interpolation. In the Slavonic version of Josephus' account of the Jewish war with Rome, several long passages appear which are not found in the Greek text (see below, pp. 154-55). The evidence about Jesus in the Talmud has been summarized in the following fashion by Joseph Klausner:

There are reliable statements to the effect that his name was Yeshu'a (Yeshu) of Nazareth; that he "practised sorcery" (*i.e.* performed miracles, as was usual in those days) and beguiled and led Israel astray; that he mocked at the words of the Wise; that he expounded Scripture in the same manner as the Pharisees; that he had five disciples; that he said that he was not come to take aught away from the Law or to add to it; that he was hanged (crucified) as a false teacher and beguiler on the eve of the Passover which happened on a Sabbath; and that his disciples healed the sick in his name.

There are statements of a tendencious or untrustworthy character to the effect that he was the bastard of an adulteress and that his father was Pandera or Pantere; that for forty days before his crucifixion a herald went out proclaiming why Jesus was to be put to death, so that any might come and plead in his favour, but none was found to do so; that there was doubt whether Jesus had any share in the world to come (*Jesus of Nazareth*, 46).

The Koran which dates from the seventh century A.D. contains several references to Jesus. In Islam, Jesus was accepted as one of the greatest of the prophets but not on an equal footing with Muhammad. The Koran accepted the tradition of the virgin birth but denied that Jesus was crucified. In Muslim tradition, someone else was put to death while Jesus was raised to heaven, a view held by some unorthodox groups in early Christianity.

There are numerous nonbiblical Christian traditions about Jesus. Over fifty different apocryphal Gospels are known or are referred to by the early church fathers. Most of these have survived, if at all, only in fragmentary form or in quotations. Some of the episodes about Jesus in these Gospels describe him as a miracle working child at the age of four and five or as a teacher of secret sayings. As a rule, these Gospels attempted to expand the traditions about Jesus or else to portray him as teaching a form of Christianity different from the orthodoxy of the second and third centuries.

When one turns to the New Testament, there are surprisingly few references to the historical career of Jesus outside of the four Gospels (see Galatians 1:19, 4:4; Romans 1:3; I Corinthians 7:10-11, 9:5, 14, 11:23-26, 15:4-8). A cursory reading of the four Gospels easily suggests the great differences which exist between Matthew, Mark, and Luke (the so-called Synoptic Gospels) on one hand and the Gospel of John on the other hand. In the synoptics, Jesus teaches in parables and short sayings; in John, he teaches in long allegorical speeches. In the synoptics, Jesus does not proclaim himself as messiah; in John, Jesus preaches himself as the messiah from the beginning of his ministry. In the synoptics, Jesus begins his career in Galilee after the arrest of John the Baptist; in John, he carries on a simultaneous ministry with the Baptist in Judah. In the synoptics, Jesus cleanses the temple during the last week of his career; in John, this event takes place at the beginning of his ministry. In the synoptics, Jesus was crucified on what is now called Good Friday; in John, the crucifixion occurs on Thursday. In the synoptics, Jesus goes to Jerusalem only once during his ministry; in John, he is in and out of Jerusalem on several occasions. In the synoptics, Jesus' ministry appears to be rather short; in John, it lasts for over three years. Much of the material in the synoptics has no parallel in John and vice versa. In other words, it is very difficult to reconcile the two portrayals of Jesus.

Even within the synoptic traditions, numerous differences exist. To take one example: All three Gospels report a visit to the tomb early one Sunday morning. In Mark 16:1-8, Mary Magdalene; Mary, the mother of James; and Salome go to the tomb, find the stone rolled away and a young man sitting in the tomb who tells about the resurrection. In Matthew 28:1-10, Mary Magdalene and Mary go to the tomb, an earthquake occurs, an angel descends and rolls away the stone, the guards tremble and fear, and the angel reports the resurrection. In Luke 24:1-11, Mary Magdalene; Joanna; Mary, the mother of James; and other women come to the tomb, find the stone rolled away, and two men in the tomb announce the resurrection to the women.

Study of the Synoptic Gospels has led to the conclusion that Mark was the first Gospel written and that Matthew and Luke are both dependent upon Mark plus a sayings source (referred to as "Q") not used by Mark. In addition, Matthew and Luke both contain some material unique to each Gospel. Thus the vast majority of scholars assume that behind the synoptics are four "sources" of which Mark and the sayings source are the most important.

The basic problem concerning the Gospel sources for the reconstruction of the historical Jesus centers on their character and reliability. Are the Gospels historical documents? Or biographical? How much influence have the individual authors and church tradition contributed to the portraits of Jesus in the Gospels? John 20:31 states that the Gospel was written to create belief in Jesus; that is, the Gospels were written as documents of faith or to stimulate faith and not to report mere historical facts. Luke, in the prologue, states that the Gospel was written with a particular perspective, to present "an orderly account." The author of Luke also notes that he is dependent upon previously written accounts as well as church tradition. The basic issues here are (1) how much the individual authors of the Gospels who wrote a generation or so after Jesus have utilized material or perhaps formulated traditions to support their individual purposes and (2) how much influence the church and its faith has had on the shape, content, and character of the traditions about Jesus.

Given the nature and character of the Gospels, is it possible to develop a methodology or approach which will allow one to reconstruct something of the outline of Jesus' career and his teaching? Is it possible, in other words, to determine what in the Gospels reflects the actual life of Jesus? Two extreme approaches to this question have been proposed. Some scholars argue that the Gospel traditions—events and sayings—should be accepted as authentically historical unless it is impossible to reconcile diverse traditions or unless there are overwhelming reasons to doubt a tradition. Others conclude that nothing should be accepted as authentic unless good reasons can be given to establish authenticity. Numerous variations, of course, exist between these two polar approaches. For the first position, the basic problem centers on the reconciliation of the differences between the

Gospels. For the latter position, the problem consists of developing criteria by which authenticity can be established. In attempting to establish authentic traditions, scholars have sought for "pillar passages"—that is, for passages whose historicity and genuineness seem assured. Some of the criteria which have been used are: appearance in more than one of the Gospel sources, occurrence of a saying in more than one form, reflection of an Aramaic linguistic background, reflection of Palestinian conditions, lack of any parallel in either Judaism or the early church, and various combinations of these.

The diversity in reconstructions of the historical Jesus are not only due to the character of the source materials and the methodological questions but also to the presuppositions and objectives of the researcher. Research without presuppositions is of course impossible. One's scientific assumptions about the world, for example, will influence the way in which the miracle stories are understood. If one assumes that nature is a closed continuum of cause and effect, this will certainly determine the manner in which the miraculous is evaluated. However, if one believes the universe to be open to the intervention of divine activity, this will color the treatment of the miraculous.

The religious convictions of the investigator are obviously a factor in one's research on the historical Jesus. A scholar who takes a decidedly antichurch attitude, as many of the earlier investigators did, will present a picture of Jesus quite different from one who seeks to support the church's faith through research.

One's sociocultural background and context can influence one's research. Frequently, current philosophical interests and cultural issues provide clues and approaches which scholars utilize in investigating the life of Jesus. Portraits of Jesus sometime seem to be a reflection of a present cultural or philosophical fad.

Even the personality and ego of the researcher may influence his investigations. Much research is based on the hope and excitement of new discovery and new perspectives.

Perhaps this drive to reveal the unknown is a greater factor in much historical research than we realize and more important to the personality and ego of the researcher than he imagines.

Many people have argued that the presuppositions and dispositions of researchers are the dominant factors in research on Jesus. Do all men find in Jesus what they wish to find or create him in their own image? This has frequently been proposed, but it certainly is an overstatement of the influence of one's convictions and presuppositions. Few scholars have taken such cavalier freedom with their treatments of the historical Jesus. For many, study of the historical Jesus has been not a support of their beliefs but a serious trial of their faith.

2. JESUS: THE CHRIST
OF ORTHODOXY

Lord Jesus Christ, the only-begotten Son of God, begotten of
the Father before all the ages, Light of Light, true God of true
God, begotten not made, of one substance with the Father,
through whom all things were made; who for us men and for
our salvation came down from the heavens, and was made
flesh of the Holy Spirit and the Virgin Mary, and became
man, and was crucified for us under Pontius Pilate, and
suffered and was buried, and rose again on the third day
according to the Scriptures, and ascended into the heavens,
and sitteth on the right hand of the Father, and cometh again
with glory to judge living and dead, of whose kingdom there
shall be no end. —*The Nicene Creed* (A.D. 325)

Throughout the centuries, Christian orthodoxy has held
that the Jesus of history, the Christ of Christian faith, and the
presentations of Jesus in the Gospels are, for all practical
purposes, identical. The two works to be discussed in this
chapter, though separated by decades and radically different
in approach, reflect this position.

David Smith, in the preface to his widely popular work *The
Days of His Flesh*, states that his two aims in discussing the
historical Jesus were (1) "to vindicate the historicity of the
evangelic records and adduce reason for believing, in
opposition to an influential school of modern criticism, that
they present Jesus as He actually lived among men, and not
as He appeared to a later generation through a haze of
reverence and superstition" and (2) "to justify the church's
faith in Him as the Lord from Heaven." In these aims, one
can see the faith and ambition of an orthodox interpretation
of Jesus and the Gospels.

Smith's book opens with a discussion of the Gospels as
sources for the life of Jesus. The preservation and transmis-

sion of the traditions about Jesus are related to the process by which rabbinical teachings were preserved and passed on through oral transmission. Reference is made to the efforts of the rabbis "directed to the immaculate transmission of the Oral Law" in which "disciples were drilled in the multitudinous precepts of that interminable tradition until they had them by heart. The lesson was repeated over and over till it was engraved upon their memories" (xiii). Among the disciples of the rabbis, "the study of the Law was thus a purely mechanical exercise, and the least disposition to originality would have been fatal to proficiency. The qualifications were a retentive memory and scrupulous adherence to the letter of the tradition. It must be handed on exactly as it had been received, *ipsissimis verbis* . . . and, if a disciple forgot a word . . . it was accounted to him as if he were guilty of death" (xiv). The same method of transmitting traditions was adopted in the early church: "It was at once natural and inevitable that the Apostles, being Jews, should follow it in recording the life and teaching of Jesus" (xv) and "it was the sacred duty of those to whose custody it had been committed to guard it no less faithfully than the Rabbis guarded the traditions of the elders" (xvi).

Between the time of the apostles and the writing of the Gospels, "there was a class of teachers in the primitive church whose function it was to go about instructing the believers in the oral tradition and drilling it into their minds in the fashion of the rabbinical schools. They were named the Catechisers and their scholars the catechumens" (xvii).

Smith describes the writing of the Synoptic Gospels in the following terms:

The oral tradition emanated from the Apostles, being their testimony to the things they had seen and heard. It was preserved and disseminated far and wide by the Catechisers; and when the Evangelists composed their narratives, they simply reduced the oral tradition to writing, each adopting the version of it which was current in his locality. The First Gospel represents the tradition as it circulated in Judaea, and though it was not written as it stands by Matthew, it was certainly derived from him and is stamped with his authority. The Second Gospel represents the tradition as it circulated in the Roman church, and it has this connection with Peter, that Mark was his companion and enjoyed the advantage of hearing his discourses. . . . The Third Gospel, composed by Luke, the physician of Antioch and the companion of Paul, represents the tradition as it circulated in Asia Minor and Achaia, and is pervaded by the spirit of the Apostle of the Gentiles (xvii-xviii).

The Synoptic Gospels thus exhibit close parallels and at times absolute verbal agreement but "each gospel is an independent reproduction of the apostolic tradition, and the differences are such variations as were natural and inevitable in the process of oral transmission" (xviii). The evangelists were therefore not so much authors as editors. In their editorial work, the editors had to omit much of the authentic tradition that was passed along to them. Some of this authentic material later shows up in quotes of the early church fathers and in additions to the Greek texts of the Gospels—although most of the additions to the biblical texts are worthless material and represent originally marginal annotations innocently inserted into the text.

The evangelists were not only forced to omit much of the oral tradition but they were also forced to exercise editorial freedom since in oral transmission, the original tradition had gotten broken up into sections with the chronological sequence being lost. Since the Catechisers repeated only so much of the tradition at a time, the material was generally passed along as "a large assortment of disconnected material. . . . To ascertain the historical sequence was, to a large extent, impossible; nor was it indeed any great matter to the Evangelists" (xx). The editors then arranged the material more topically than chronologically. Examples of this arrangement are the Sermon on the Mount (Matthew 5-7) and the Commission of the Twelve (Matthew 10). Thus the evangelists often introduced *logia* or sayings without the incidents to which they were originally connected or introduced incidents out of chronological order because they illustrated the theme at hand.

Jesus: The Christ of Orthodoxy

The oral transmission and recording of the tradition obviously allowed "sundry mishaps" to befall it. Among these, Smith notes: (1) slips of memory, (2) fusion of similar but really distinct passages, (3) emendation of what was deemed incredible or unintelligible, (4) mutilation of obscure *logia*, (5) modification of the tradition when an Old Testament prophecy found its fulfilment in some incident in Jesus' ministry, (6) confusion due to an erroneous presupposition in the minds of the editors, and (7) editorial comments inserted in the tradition as *logia* of Jesus. Such mishaps, however, are rather easy to detect and rectify (xxvi-xxxiv).

The Fourth Gospel was written to correct some of these mishaps as well as to supplement the Gospels of Matthew, Mark, and Luke. The Fourth Gospel was written by the disciple John who could, therefore, "in the fulness of his personal knowledge" (xxxii) make such corrections and supplementation. For example, John detailed Jesus' Judaean ministry because the synoptic traditions had originally been formulated under the apostles at Jerusalem where the incidents of the Judaean ministry were well known and needed no special mention. Another example is in the story of the cleansing of the temple where the Fourth Gospel has preserved the correct chronology.

The greatest differences among the Gospels are to be found, according to Smith, in the birth stories and the accounts of the resurrection. This is due to the fact that the apostolic tradition encompassed only the ministry of Jesus. The tradition therefore began with the public ministry of Jesus and concluded with the death of Jesus. Thus there were no birth and resurrection accounts in the transmitted tradition. The birth narrative in Matthew goes back to Joseph, a tradition which circulated in Jerusalem and Judaea and thus stressed Bethlehem as the home of Joseph and Mary. Luke's version represents Mary's account of the tradition; in fact Luke may have heard this story from Mary herself during Luke's visit to Jerusalem with Paul (xxxviii).

The diversity in the accounts of the resurrection is due, according to Smith, to three factors. First, "when the tradition took shape, the wonder of the Resurrection was at its height . . . an amazing and overwhelming fact which had happened but yesterday and was fresh in every mind." Second, exposition of the Resurrection in the tradition "was deemed all the more needless for as much as the Lord's Return was believed to be imminent." Third, "the Apostles always speak with a certain reticence about the Resurrection. They proclaim the fact, but they refrain from entering into particulars" (xxxix). Only after time passed and the Lord did not return did John, the last surviving eye witness, yield to the importunities of the believers and write the wondrous story. Therefore, the Gospel of John presented the resurrection narratives accurately thus correcting the synoptics who "agree only in their unfaltering and triumphant proclamation of the fact that Jesus rose and appeared to His disciples" (xl).

Thus the Gospels provide the reader with the apostolic tradition which was passed along in the church through the process of oral tradition with some disturbance and distortion of this tradition, but such as can be corrected. In so far as recovering the *ipsissima verba* of Jesus, however, Smith warns the reader to remember that the evangelists "wrote from memory" and thus "seldom, if ever, is it given us to quote a sentence and say: 'The Lord spoke these words.' The utmost that we can say is: 'He spoke after this manner.'" Yet, "one knows instinctively where Jesus ceases and the Evangelist begins. It is like passing into another atmosphere. . . . The words of Jesus shine on the pages of the Evangelists. It is indeed indubitable that they have suffered some measure of change and are not always written precisely as they came from His lips; but the change is generally inappreciable. As they stand on the sacred page, they attest their originality" (xlvi-xlvii).

Thus does Smith explain the origin of the Gospels and the historical reliability of the traditions.

In his discussion of the life of Jesus, Smith basically accepts as historical the accounts of the Gospels supplementing these with references to historical events contemporary to the time of Jesus and with references to Jewish and other

Near Eastern literature and practices. The preexistence of Jesus is accepted as well as his virgin birth, although Smith notes that Jesus' birth probably took place sometime between April and October, perhaps in 5 B.C. Jesus went through the normal Jewish childhood, was taught by his parents, received instruction in the Jewish elementary school, was taught the trade of carpentry by his father, absorbed much from his days in Nazareth amid his life with his brothers and sisters, and enjoyed "a sweet and happy childhood" (18).

Jesus became aware of his true person and mission during the Passover festival which he attended in Jerusalem at the age of twelve. "Nevertheless He quietly returned to Nazareth and resumed His simple and duteous life. For eighteen years He toiled with hammer and saw, knowing all the while Who He was and wherefore He had come, yet hiding the wondrous secret in His breast and never, until His hour arrived, revealing it by word or sign. . . . All the while He would be brooding over those Sacred Scriptures which spake of Him, foretelling His Advent and prefiguring His Redemption. And He would be looking abroad, with keen eye and sympathetic heart, upon the world which He had come to save" (23-24).

Jesus submitted himself to baptism at the hands of John the Baptist without guilt or fear, and "as John surveyed that serene form and that holy face radiant with the peace of God, his soul bowed in reverence and awe, and, like every mortal who ever came under the gaze of Jesus in the days of His flesh, he realised his own unworthiness" (31). Jesus thus submitted himself to a baptism of repentance just as "in His helpless infancy He endured the rite of circumcision" and later "paid year by year the Temple-tax, though as the Son of God whose House the Temple was, He might have claimed exemption" (31-32). The baptismal vision, experienced by John and Jesus, revealed to John the Baptist that Jesus was none other than the messiah (although John later became possessed of doubt about this).

"Impelled by the Holy Spirit, who had taken possession of Him at His Baptism and thenceforth dwelt in Him 'without measure,' Jesus retired" to the wilderness where he wrestled with the perplexities which crowded upon him (34). Smith explains the temptations in terms of Jesus' psychological struggle with the common expectations and desires of the Jewish people as well as with possible alternative patterns which his ministry might assume. Jesus, however, affirmed what he already knew: "He had not come to be welcomed and honoured but to be rejected and slain, a sacrifice for the sin of the world" (38).

The earliest disciples of Jesus were recruited, as noted in the Fourth Gospel, from the followers of John the Baptist since Jesus would not have chosen men whom he had not tested and approved. Jesus' basic designation for himself was Son of man, a title taken over from current Judaism where the term "sons of man" was employed to refer to "common folk." Smith suggests that this "nickname" was originally used by the people of Jesus as a "contemptuous epithet" and adopted by Jesus "as a continual protest against that secular ideal of the Messiahship which more than anything else hindered His recognition and acceptance; and in assuming it Jesus designed to make men think and perchance discover that the true Messianic glory was not what they conceived—not the glory of earthly majesty but the glory of sacrifice. And He had the further design of identifying Himself with the weak and despised, and thus revealing His grace" (50).

Jesus' public ministry was begun in Jerusalem at the Feast of Passover in A.D. 26. "Ever since His twelfth year He had gone up annually with the train of pilgrims from Galilee, but on this occasion it was not the mere custom of the Feast that took Him hither. He would go up as the Messiah. It was fitting that His public ministry should open in the sacred capital and His first appeal be addressed to the rulers of the Nation" (58). It was on this occasion that he cleansed the temple. This event perplexed the Jewish rulers who subsequently sought from him a sign and later sent their representative, Nicodemus, "to wait upon Him and ask what they [his miracles] meant. Of this much they had no doubt, that Jesus was a God-sent teacher, and they thought it probable that He was indeed the Messiah." Jesus did not answer directly but sought to show Nicodemus that the kingdom of God was "a spiritual order invisible to the eye of sense" and that "the Jews should be required to enter the Kingdom of Heaven by that door of humiliation [regeneration], on the self-same terms as the despised Gentiles" (65). Like the Jewish leaders, Nicodemus did not understand or could not accept the idea and "would go away in utter bewilderment. Yet the good seed had been sown in his heart, and after many days it sprang up and bore rich and abiding fruit" (68).

Jesus' first phase of ministry in Jerusalem ended with the arrest of John the Baptist and Jesus' desire not to precipitate at that time his final crisis with the Jewish leaders. Smith affirms, following the Gospel of John, a Samaritan ministry of Jesus, early in his career, that is, on his return to Galilee.

In discussing the miracles of Jesus, Smith accepts their historicity (with the exception of the story of the coin in the fish's mouth [Matt. 17:24-27], an incident in which he merely engaged in a little raillery with Peter). However, in discussing Jesus' exorcism of demons, he points out that Jesus did not believe in demons, yet "with gracious condenscension He accomodated Himself to the ignorance of men, but He did not share it" (108). To have shared the idea of demonical possession would have involved Jesus with the passing opinions of his day, and "He never entangled His teaching with contemporary ideas; He never made a statement which has been discredited by the progress of human knowledge" (106). "Jesus dealt with the demoniacs after the manner of a wise physician. He did not seek to dispel their hallucination. He fell in with it and won their confidence" (108).

The opposition to Jesus by the Jewish leaders was based on a number of factors: his actions on the Sabbath, his usurpation of the role of God, his identification of himself with God in the forgiveness of sin, and his association with the outcasts of society.

Smith understood the Sermon on the Mount, while recognizing that all this material was not spoken on one occasion, as part of the ritual of Jesus' ordination of the twelve instructing them on "how they should comport themselves as the heralds of His Kingdom." He was thus "not enunciating a general code of Christian ethics" nor setting out general rules of conduct for "literal and universal application" but outlining for the disciples "a loftier goodness" since "their vocation imposed upon them a peculiar necessity for self-abnegation and self-effacement" (161-62).

In sending out the Twelve, Jesus' instructions that they were to go only to the lost house of Israel, implies, according to Smith, that Jesus understood his ministry as inclusive of the Gentiles. Otherwise, why the instruction since "no Jew would have dreamed of preaching to Gentiles or Samaritans, and the idea would never have entered into the Apostles' minds had not Jesus, by His sympathy with aliens, set them the example" (217). Jesus' apparently harsh response to the Phoenician woman (Mark 7:24-30) was in actuality his proverbial response to her proverbial retort and in no way must be understood as reflecting Jesus' limitation of his ministry and teaching to the Jews (250-51).

The final confrontation between Jesus and the Jewish leaders which led to his arrest, trial, and crucifixion was due to the Sanhedrin's fear that such miracles as the raising of Lazarus "must procure Jesus a vast access of popularity; and, knowing the jealous surveillance which Rome exercised over turbulent Palestine, they dreaded the consequences, should the multitudes rally round Him and acclaim Him the Messianic King of Israel" (374). It was a question of removing Jesus rather than risk the national tragedy that might follow such popular acclamation.

Judas' betrayal of Jesus was due to disillusionment.

He was a disappointed man. He had attached himself to Jesus because he deemed Him the Messiah and expected reward and honour in the Messianic Kingdom. [Although Jesus had taught his disciples about the form his ministry must take and had predicted his resurrection, they, like

Judas had not understood.] Gradually the truth had come home to him, and he had discovered the vanity of expectation. His disillusionment was complete when he realised that what awaited Jesus was not a crown but a cross. He perceived that he had embarked on a ruinous enterprise, and to his worldly judgment it appeared the wisest policy to come out of it on the best possible terms. It may be also that he was actuated by a desire to be avenged on the Master who, as he deemed, had fooled him (436-37).

Jesus had, however, from the time of his call of Judas known of his ultimate betrayal and had seen in him a vehicle of the divine purpose.

For Smith, the trial of Jesus before the Sanhedrin was illegal, "a succession of flagrant illegalities" (469). Insufficient and disagreeing witnesses were used, the capital case was heard on a single day, and no written votes were cast: all acts prohibited by Jewish law regulated by the Talmudic tractate *Sanhedrin* (472). Pilate did the best he could under the conditions, but "when his position is understood, it appears that he was to a large extent the victim of circumstances, and may even claim a measure of pity" (477).

Over half a century of serious and critical New Testament study separates David Smith's *The Days of His Flesh* from Ethelbert Stauffer's *Jesus and His Story*. Nonetheless, Stauffer's view of the historical Jesus agrees with the confession embodied in the title to Smith's volume: "God himself had become man, more human than any other man in the wide expanse of history" (195).

Stauffer begins his discussion by agreeing with the opinion of many critical scholars concerning the New Testament Gospels upon which any reconstruction of the historical Jesus must draw.

Today we know that the theological and church-oriented bias in the traditions is much older than the Gospels themselves. Twenty-five years ago a prominent Protestant theologian [Hans Lietzmann] wrote: "The Passion of Jesus, as it unfolds before our eyes in the Gospels, must be counted among the most tremendous creations of religious fiction." Today we must ask ourselves whether this same verdict does not apply to everything the Gospels have to say about Jesus (vii-viii).

In spite of such a negative affirmation about the historical nature of the Gospel materials, Stauffer argues that it is still possible to provide a portrait of the historical Jesus although not in the sense envisioned by many of the nineteenth-century efforts.

The nineteenth-century ideal was a *biography* of Jesus—that is to say, a representation of the psychological development of Jesus, of his mind and his activities, rendered with narrative vividness, analytic insight, and plausibility. Whether this was a legitimate ideal is a moot question. At any rate, we know today that it was unattainable. What, then, may our ideal be, what ideal am I entitled to set up? I reply: a *history* of Jesus. By this term I mean something extremely modest. I mean a strict clarification of those facts which can be ascertained, possibly of a series of events, perhaps too of a number of casual relationships (xiii).

Stauffer's ambition is a "presentation of facts and casual relationships." In establishing such a presentation, Stauffer argues that the "Evangelists' interpretation of Jesus, the interpretation offered by the dogmas of the church, and even my personal interpretation of Jesus are barred" (xiii).

If the Gospel interpretation, church dogma, and researchers' bias are to be eliminated, how is it possible to isolate the "historical facts from the dogmatic bias" (viii). How can one go beyond "lives" of Jesus based solely on the Bible or on imaginative techniques and arrive at a pragmatic history of Jesus? How does one discover "Jesus' own interpretation of himself" (xiii)? His answer to this question is: "To open new sources unaffected by Christian tendencies" (viii).

In speaking of such sources, Stauffer divides them into indirect and direct sources. The indirect sources are those which provide the "contemporary testimony on the conditions, events, and personalities that played a part in the story of Jesus. In such testimony there is no mention of Jesus himself. For the most part, the authors of these documents knew nothing whatsoever about the existence of Jesus. Consequently, these writings are quite free of religious fiction or dogmatic bias" (viii). Stauffer is here speaking about those documents and remains which provide information about Palestinian conditions and Roman governmental administration and activities during the time contemporary with Jesus: "on personalities, Jewish politics, Palestinian geography, jurisprudence, taxation, penal code, familial law, religious law, liturgy, expectation of the Messiah, astronomy, and astrology" (6). Of special importance in this cateogry are "the Jewish legal provisions concerning heretics and the rules of trials. . . . When we train the rays of legal history upon the Gospels, we obtain a historical X-ray photograph. Upon it stands revealed the clear outline of the life of Jesus" (viii-ix). These indirect sources are of special importance, according to Stauffer, in arriving at a chronological synchronization of the life of Jesus.

The direct sources are those ancient sources which contain direct statements about Jesus. Some of these sources are Jewish, mentioning Jesus by name or under a code name. "Most of these texts are the work of the rabbinical authorities; a few spring from the movement that grew up around John the Baptist. There are not many; they are all very short, in many cases camouflaged and muddled; and in these texts, also, truth and fiction are closely intertwined." However, "in these brief notices lie concealed many an old tradition concerning Jesus, traditions perhaps reaching back to the days of Caiaphas, and at any rate back to the first and second centuries" (ix).

According to Stauffer, these Jewish sources, generally critical and polemical in nature, and the Christian Gospels as well, were the products of the early Jewish-Christian conflict. Both the Jewish texts on Jesus and the Christian Gospels were the products of "a passionate controversy centering around the interpretation and the meaning of Jesus of Nazareth. . . . The oldest and most important function of the traditions was polemical. They originated in the conflict over Jesus. . . . Out of these struggles emerged the Gospels and the rabbinical or Baptistic documents concerning Jesus" (xii). The origin of these conflicts Stauffer places back into the life of Jesus but it was the shape of the conflict after

Jesus' death that produced the final form of the traditions. "On the one side there were the groups around Peter, James, Matthew, Luke, and John. On the other side stood the scribes, the anti-Roman partisans, the desert sects, the disciples of John the Baptist, and the Samaritans" (xii). Stauffer argues that in these polemical Jewish and Christian texts there is testimony and countertestimony concerning Jesus. In these texts, one frequently finds that the "facts are employed in the one case to sustain faith in Christ, in the other to attack that faith." When such a "confrontation of witnesses yields statements that agree on some points, then these points must represent facts accepted by both sides" (x). These facts, according to Stauffer, provide the hope for writing a history of Jesus.

The direct Christian sources about Jesus are dated, according to Stauffer, in the following order: the speeches of Peter in Acts, the Epistles of Paul, the *Logia* (or Q) reconstructed from Matthew and Luke, the Synoptic Gospels which adhered most faithfully to the language of Jesus, the Fourth Gospel which clarified the chronology in the story of Jesus, Jewish-Christian books (apocryphal traditions) which have survived in fragmentary form and in quotations by early church fathers. Non-Christian sources include, in addition to the Roman authors, Josephus and the rabbinic traditions; the medieval Mandaean texts stemming from the oldest community of the followers of John the Baptist; Islamic texts including the Koran and the eleventh century writings of Al Ghazzali, which contain some material going back to an ancient Judao-Christian tradition; and two Chinese lives of Jesus written around A.D. 640 at the insistence of Emperor Tai-Tsung, which are based, according to Stauffer, on ancient Syrian traditions, some going back to non-Christian sources (3-5).

In outlining his "pragmatic history of Jesus," Stauffer stresses the importance of chronology. Confronted with the problem of the synoptic chronology which envisions a ministry of Jesus of about a year and a half, according to Stauffer (in Mark 2:23 it is springtime and in Mark 14:1 it is spring again), and the Gospel of John which has Jesus' ministry span four years, Stauffer argues: "There is no fitting the chronological structure of the Gospel of John within the narrow span of the Synoptic account. But it is possible to fit the Synoptic frame into John's structure. This is important as evidence for the correctness of the Johannine chronology." Thus chronologically, "the Fourth Evangelist corrects and integrates the Synoptic account and treats the entire period of Jesus' ministry, the early phase under the Baptist, and the concluding, climactic phase" (7). Dating the beginning of the ministry of John the Baptist to A.D. 28 (see Luke 3:1-2), Stauffer arrives at the following chronology for the ministry of Jesus:

Spring of 28: Baptism of Jesus. Passover of 29: cleansing of the Temple. November 29: northward journey through Samaria. December 29 to the autumn of 30: ten quiet months. Autumn of 30: arrest of John the Baptist. October 30: Feast of Tabernacles in Jerusalem. Late autumn of 30: fresh beginning in Galilee. Spring of 31: Passover in Galilee. October 31: Feast of Tabernacles in Jerusalem. Passover of 32: Passover of death (8).

Was Jesus a son of David? To this question Stauffer can answer an assured yes since Joseph was a member of this family line. Support for this premise is deduced not from the New Testament evidence but from other traditions. Firstly, Jewish evidence from the time shows that many Jews preserved lists of Jewish families which were officially supervised and "were of the highest importance in legal matters concerning marriage, property, occupation and religion" (14). Secondly, Stauffer points to the fact that

Domitian, in connection with his persecution of the former Jewish royal dynasty, called to Rome two great-grandsons of Joseph (grand-nephews of Jesus) by the names of Zachariah and James, because they had been denounced to him as Davidites. The two "confessed" their Davidic origins without ifs or buts, but were released on the grounds that they were completely non-political. Under Trajan, however, the aged

Bishop Simeon (cousin of Jesus and successor of James the Just) was condemned to death as a "Davidite and Christian" (14-15).

"In both the major Gospels (Matthew and Luke) Jesus is accounted the son of the Virgin Mary. Is the miraculous birth of Jesus a historical fact" (15)? Stauffer answers yes and then adduces his evidence both from Christian and anti-Christian testimony which agree on the matter and therefore substantiate the fact. Stauffer finds a belief in the virgin birth of Jesus in all four Gospels and the earlier *Logia*. At the marriage festival in Cana where Jesus turned the water into wine (John 2:1-11), John reports the incident so that "with Mary already counting upon Jesus' power to work miracles, he [the author] appears to take it for granted that the mother knows from the beginning the secret of her son" (16). In the *Logia*, Jesus' opponents berate him for being a glutton and drunkard, a particular insult which was "flung at a person born of an illegitimate connection who betrayed, by his mode of life and his religious conduct, the stain of his birth. This was the sense in which the Pharisees and their fellows employed the phrase against Jesus. Their meaning was: he is a bastard" (16). In Mark 6:3, the countrymen of Jesus refer to him as "son of Mary," as do the Samaritan, Mandaean, and Koranic texts, a practice followed only when the father was unknown. A rabbinic tradition, dated as before A.D. 70 by Stauffer, speaks of Jesus as "the bastard of a wedded wife" while later Jewish texts claimed he was the illegitimate son of the Roman Panthera. All these lines of evidence are asserted as proof of Jesus' virgin birth. "Jesus was the son of Mary, not of Joseph. That is the historical fact, recognized alike by Christians and Jews, friends and adversaries" (18).

Other facts associated with Jesus' birth which are authenticated, according to Stauffer, by direct and indirect sources, are his birth at Bethlehem (Matthew 2:1-5, Luke 2:4), the census reported by Luke (Luke 2:1-5), the miraculous star (Matthew 2:2-11), and the massacre of the children by Herod (Matthew 2:16). Jesus' membership in the

Davidic family, whose ancestral home was Bethlehem, and the fact that Jewish writings never deny his birth there, while later playing down any connection of the messiah with Bethlehem, lead Stauffer to affirm the conclusion of the ancient church historian Origen: "Jewish polemicists could not deny the birth of Jesus at Bethlehem and therefore expurgated any mention of Bethlehem [see Micah 5:2] in connection with Messianic prophecies, in order not to foster belief in Jesus, the child of Bethlehem" (20).

Since D. F. Strauss, many scholars have argued that the census referred to in the Lucan infancy narrative was the census taken in A.D. 6/7 when the Romans took direct control over Judaea after Archelaus, the son of Herod the Great, was deposed. Josephus, the ancient Jewish historian refers to a census at this time but not to one during the reign of Herod which would be required by the Lucan text if Jesus was born before the death of Herod in 4 B.C. Stauffer argues that a "wealth of inscriptions, papyri, and other original documents on ancient taxation laws has come to light" which refutes Strauss' conclusions (22). Stauffer draws from Egyptian papyri and other references reflecting Roman taxation practices, inscriptional references to Quirinius, and the fact that King Herod came under Augustus' displeasure in 8 B.C. to argue the following: "In the autumn of 12 B.C. Quirinius took charge of Oriental affairs and commenced the census in the Roman East. In 8 B.C. Herod the Great was demoted. In 7 B.C. the *apographa* [a systematic listing of all taxable persons and property] in Palestine began. At this time Joseph probably journeyed to Bethlehem with Mary. In A.D. 7 the work of the census was completed with the *apotimesis*" [the official assessment of taxes] (31). Josephus' reference to a census during this time is therefore to the final phase. Stauffer realizes that there is no definite reference to the 7 B.C. *apographa* but argues that all the circumstantial evidence supports Luke at this point. Thus Jesus was born in 7 B.C. and began his public ministry at the age of about thirty-three. Stauffer declares Luke 3:13, which states that Jesus began his ministry at about thirty years of age, to be

useless for purposes of chronology since thirty was considered in antiquity as the "age when a man stood at the peak of
his powers," and anyway Luke only says he was *about* thirty
years old (7).

In the seventeenth century, the astronomer "Kepler
ascribed the star of Bethlehem to the unique orbit of the
planet Jupiter in the year 7 B.C." During this year, there was a
conjunction of Jupiter and Venus in the spring, and in the
summer and autumn, the planet "encountered the planet
Saturn in the Sign of the Fishes—this being the extremely
rare Great Conjunction that takes place in this form only
once every 794 years" (32). Stauffer argues that throughout
the ancient world, the year 7 B.C. was predicted by
astronomers, on the basis of astronomical calculations, to be
a very propitious and apocalyptic year. Stauffer notes the
Berlin Planetary Tablet, the Celestial Almanac, and the
tradition associating Jupiter with Augustus as pointing to this
expectation. The Berlin Planetary Tablet from Egypt (copied
in A.D. 42) lists the movements of the planets for the years 17
B.C. to A.D. 10, while the Celestial Almanac, a cuneiform
tablet from Sippar, "The Greenwich of Babylonia," predicts
the positions of the planets for the year 7 B.C. and notes in
particular the conjunction of Saturn and Jupiter in the
Fishes. In Rome, "Augustus was regarded as Jupiter in
human form. . . . Venus was considered the star of the Julian
family, and Saturn the symbol of the Golden Age. In these
circumstances the extraordinary path of Jupiter in 7 B.C.
could only be taken as referring to the career of the Emperor
Augustus" (34). Thus the world was anticipating the
phenomenal year 7 B.C. In the East, "Saturn was considered
to be the planet of Palestine. . . . Jupiter was regarded as the
star of the ruler of the universe, and the constellation of the
Fishes as the sign of the last days. . . . The clay tablet of
Sippar may be regarded as the astronomical pocket-almanac
with which the wise men set out from the East" (33-34).
Thus the Eastern Magi set out for Jerusalem and witnessed
the star of Bethlehem as a historical fact.

The historicity of Herod's massacre of the innocents is

confirmed for Stauffer on the basis of Matthew 2, references to the characters of Herod and Augustus, and passages from Josephus and the apocalyptic work called the *Assumption of Moses* (dated by Stauffer to A.D. 6–15). The passage in the *Assumption of Moses* (chapter 6) speaks in a prophecy after the event (or a "diatribe . . . in the nature of a literal report" [38]) of a ruler (Herod) who would follow the Hasmonaeans (whose reign ended in 63 B.C.) and who would slaughter the old and young without mercy as was done at the time of the Exodus in Egypt. Stauffer relates this reference to a passage by Josephus which, in describing the slaughter of the babies in Egypt at Moses' birth, spoke of the announcement of a king to be born among the Hebrews following which the pharoah issued his edict to destroy every male child. The testimony to Herod, Augustus' brutality, and especially Herod's numerous exterminations of family and enemies in the year 7 B.C. convince Stauffer that "Herod's massacre of the innocents is a historical fact, no matter what fable-making was at work" (41).

Although Stauffer admits that we are told very little about Jesus' life from 7 B.C. to A.D. 27, he accepts as historical the flight to Egypt and the trip to the temple for Passover at the age of twelve, in A.D. 6, the year Archelaus was deposed—when the "occupation troops of the Roman procurator were marching through the streets of the city for the first time" (54). From Jewish sources describing Palestinian life and religion, Stauffer seeks to fill in the hidden years of Jesus stressing his education in the law and holy scriptures and his knowledge of the apocryphal materials—in their preedited form—and especially texts dealing with martyrology. Jesus read the Bible like any of his Jewish contemporaries, but he read them knowing—like a son—the love of God the father. Jesus spoke Aramaic and Greek and knew Hebrew and Latin as well.

On the basis of Jewish texts, Stauffer is able to describe Jesus' physical appearance. "In rabbinical theory, the reflection of the divine presence could descend only upon a man of tall and powerful stature. Evidently Jesus was able to meet this physical standard, for otherwise his adversaries would surely not have missed the chance to attack him on such grounds" (59). "His voice must have had a unique resonance, and his manner of speech a unique gracefulness" (60). The long years of waiting

"may have been years of temptation, for Jesus and his mother. . . . The excitement that had surrounded his birth had to remain concealed in order not to cast suspicion upon the grown man and bring down upon him the bloodhounds of Herod [Antipas] and the Romans. Jesus, too, held his peace. He could only wait. It was as if the millennial expectations of mankind and of all creation, the ancient hopes of the people of Israel, were concentrated and raised to their peak in those decades that Jesus of Nazareth spent in waiting" (62).

Jesus' public ministry was inaugurated with his baptism by John the Baptist, whom he had known from childhood. For a time he had functioned as a member of the movement of John—a fact recognized by rabbinical and Mandaean sources—where he engaged in baptizing respondents and was "considered by the public, and by the disciples of John as well, to be no more than the Baptist's favorite disciple, the most successful of his messengers" (65). Jesus was aware of his divine sonship, as was his mother, and after the wedding in Cana, the "disciples guessed it" (66). Jesus performed miracles as his opponents during his lifetime recognized and as later rabbinical sources admitted; in fact, "Jesus himself considered it of the greatest importance that his miracles should be observed, checked, and confirmed by outsiders and opponents" (9).

Jesus' cleansing of the temple was an "absolute rigorous application of the rabbinical precepts" against priestly corruption, and "since Jesus was as concerned with preserving the holiness of the temple as the most scrupulous Pharisee . . . he even had many sympathizers in the ranks of the Great Sanhedrin" (67). The cleansing of the temple won Jesus the enmity of the higher priesthood and the Sadducees; his disregard of the Sabbath laws and customs won him the enmity of the rabbinate and the Pharisees.

Following the Passover of A.D. 31, Jesus was placed under close scrutiny by his adversaries and a "new swarm of emissaries from the Sanhedrin arrived in Galilee. There were signs of intensified counter-propaganda. Curses were called down upon the head of the blasphemer" (84). "Lawyers from Jerusalem were already arriving in Capernaum to look into Jesus' miracles on the spot" (85). Jesus was judged to be preaching apostasy and performing demonic miracles, and for a time it appeared that the whole city of Capernaum might be officially declared a "seduced city"—guilty of apostasy (see Deuteronomy 13:12-18).

The events following the beginning of this open opposition between Jesus and the religious establishment have to be seen, according to Stauffer, in the light of Jewish law regarding heretics which provides an objective tool to reconstruct the subsequent events, since it was the "provisions against heresy which dictated each successive phase in the prosecution of Jesus" as a violator of the Torah and a preacher of apostasy. This "inevitable conflict that had to end in a verdict of death" explains "Jesus' early conviction that death would be his lot; . . . the attitude of Judas, the fears of Jesus' mother, his kindred, his disciples, and sympathizers; . . . and the rigid consistency of the Great Sanhedrin" (77). Jesus became a fugitive. The Sanhedrin set out to arrest and convict this heretic.

The basic charge of the Sanhedrin against Jesus was his use of the expression "I am He," an expression originating in the Old Testament where it is a formula used by the deity in speaking of himself. It was thus a theophanic formula and in using it and calling for a "confession of faith in this 'I am He' as the prerequisite for the forgiveness of sins" (91), it "was the purest, the boldest, and the profoundest declaration by Jesus of who and what he was. . . . This meant: where I am, there God is, there God lives and speaks, calls, asks, acts, decides, loves, chooses, rejects, suffers, and dies. Nothing bolder can be said, or imagined. It was the profoundest declaration" (194). The Sanhedrin took action to remove this heretical apostate.

The first effort to excommunicate Jesus by the Sanhedrin failed because of the opposition of Nicodemus. The Sanhedrin later "came to the unanimous decision to excommunicate anyone who . . . declared his faith in Jesus" (92). Jesus' sermon about himself as the good shepherd at the Festival of Dedication (Hanukkah) in December, 31 (John 10:22-39), greatly angered the Sanhedrin, and they sought to arrest him, but he escaped. "There are sundry indications that stones were already flying through the air as Jesus escaped the fanatics like a bird fleeing the nets of the fowler" (98). Jesus fled from Judaean territory taking refuge in Transjordan. After Jesus raised Lazarus from the dead, the Sanhedrin took definite action: "The result was that the Great Sanhedrin decided to condemn Jesus to death. A proclamation of outlawry was issued, reminding all Jews faithful to the Torah of their obligation to denounce the criminal" (103). Stauffer sees in the Talmudic statement that before Jesus was crucified on the eve of the Passover a herald had gone forth and announced the sentence and called for witnesses for forty days, a confirmation of this verdict of the Sanhedrin. The forty days are to be taken as an approximately correct round figure, but the "passage enables us to date the proclamation of outlawry mentioned in John 11:57— sometime in February of A.D. 32" (104).

Jesus withdrew from his pursuers and returned north for a short time, only leaving his hiding place to return later to Jerusalem. Why did he follow this course: "Jesus wished to die on the Passover" (105). After Jesus' return to and entry into Jerusalem, it was only a matter of time before the Sanhedrin would arrest him; but it had to pick its time, since "it was impossible to capture Jesus in the midst of his massed bodyguards" (111). The Sanhedrin sought to arrest Jesus and execute him before Passover so that peace and public order might be preserved as far as possible. But the Sanhedrin needed help, for it was hard to find and seize Jesus. "The final struggle between Jesus and Caiaphas must have been in actuality far more dramatic than the accounts of the Evangelists suggest" (112). Here Judas enters the picture since it was he who betrayed the Master and offered the Sanhedrin its opportunity. But why did Judas do this deed: "It may be that Judas, the non-Galilean, had for months been a secret agent of the Jerusalem Sanhedrin assigned to work among the Galilean's disciples. At any rate, he regarded the capture of the man who had been proclaimed a blasphemer and pseudo-prophet as his bounden duty. For he took an oath pledging himself to commit the betrayal—an oath that may well have included a curse upon himself should he fail to carry out the task he had undertaken" (112).

The trial of Jesus by the Sanhedrin ended in a unanimous vote against the blasphemer who in his trial had again used the theophanic formula "I am" (Mark 14:62). Since the Sanhedrin had been deprived in A.D. 30 of its jurisdiction over capital crimes (209), the Sanhedrin had to secure a condemnation and execution from Pilate. Before Pilate, Jesus was indicted on political charges as "instigator of unrest, a partisan, a messianic king" (128). Pilate wished to avoid the execution but was pushed by Caiaphas the high priest and "on the eve on the Passover Jeshu of Nazareth was executed" as the rabbinical texts say and the Fourth Gospel states (143).

The story of the empty tomb is historical—"even Jesus' opponents reluctantly—and therefore all the more credibly—bear witness to the fact of the empty tomb" (144). Stauffer supports this claim not only by the New Testament witness but by rabbinical claims that the disciples stole the body or the gardener removed it. Further confirmation is found in a Roman inscription discovered in Nazareth in 1878 and published in 1930. This inscription is a summary of an imperial edict directed against the robbery of corpses and the desecration of graves. "Perhaps it is based upon a rescript of Emperor Tiberius, and may possibly be the Emperor's reply to Pontius Pilate's report on Jesus, the empty tomb, and the rumors that the body had been stolen" (146).

The appearances of the risen Christ are historical events. The absence of any reference to the women as recipients of appearances from Paul's list in I Corinthians 15 is due to that fact that according to Jewish law "women were not qualified to bear witness" (151). The later Jewish opponents did not seek to deny the resurrection and the appearances, they merely sought to discredit the account. "They contended that Jesus had always practiced magical raisings from the dead, and that his own 'resurrection' was nothing but a necromantic trick" (152).

3. JESUS: THE APOCALYPTIC VISIONARY

As of old Jacob wrestled with the angel, so German theology wrestles with Jesus of Nazareth and will not let Him go until He bless it—that is, until He will consent to serve it and will suffer Himself to be drawn by the Germanic spirit into the midst of our time and our civilisation. But when the day breaks, the wrestler must let Him go. He will not cross the ford with us. Jesus of Nazareth will not suffer Himself to be modernised. As an historic figure He refuses to be detached from His own time. —Albert Schweitzer, *The Quest of the Historical Jesus* (p. 312)

The Quest of the Historical Jesus by Albert Schweitzer has to be considered one of the most influential books of the twentieth century. Insofar as New Testament scholarship is concerned, it probably has to be classified as the most important work of modern times. The book, like the man himself, has cast its shadow across our times, a shadow not confined to the academic world, a shadow touching directly or indirectly every intellectual attempt to come to grips with the Jesus of history.

In the narrowest sense, the work is a survey of the research on the life of Jesus since the time of Reimarus. Its focus, however, centers primarily on Protestant German scholarship. In page after page, Schweitzer presents scholarly research on the subject interspersed with a sharp, incisive critique of the methodologies employed and the conclusions drawn. But the book is more than a history and a presentation of the research of others. It contains Schweitzer's own understanding of the historical Jesus and his relationship to the twentieth century.

In his delineation of the contours of Jesus research, Schweitzer focused on the three basic either/or problems which had developed in nineteenth-century research. "The first was laid down by Strauss: *either* purely historical *or* purely supernatural. The second had been worked out by the Tübingen school and Holtzmann: *either* Synoptic *or* Johannine. Now came the third: *either* eschatological *or* non-eschatological" (238). In other words, first, was the life of Jesus to be understood in historical terms or in supernatural categories? Was it to be understood in terms of a rigorous historical critical analysis or in terms of a faith acceptance of the supernatural? Secondly, in discussing the historical Jesus, are the synoptic or the Johannine perspectives and traditions to be the basic point of departure? Thirdly, was Jesus' teaching and life dominated by and oriented to the eschatological future?

Before moving to an analysis of Schweitzer's portrait of the historical Jesus, we should note two works published just prior to Schweitzer's survey since they pose many of the issues with which he was concerned. The first of these is Johannes Weiss' *The Preaching of Jesus Concerning the Kingdom of God* (1892). The second is Wilhelm Wrede's *The Messianic Secret in the Gospels: A Contribution toward the Understanding of the Gospel of Mark* (1901). The first of these, by Weiss, forced upon scholars the alternative of discounting the eschatological in Jesus and his message or else taking the matter with absolute seriousness. In describing the clarity of Weiss' presentation, which he called "thoroughgoing eschatology," Schweitzer wrote:

In passing . . . to Johannes Weiss the reader feels like an explorer who after weary wanderings through billowy seas of reed-grass at length reaches a wooded tract, and instead of swamp feels firm ground beneath his feet, instead of yielding rushes sees around him the steadfast trees. At last there is an end of "qualifying clause" theology, of the "and yet," the "on the other hand," the "notwithstanding"! The reader had to follow the others step by step, making his way over every footbridge and gang-plank which they laid down, following all the meanderings in which they indulged, and must never let go their hands if he wished to come safely through the labyrinth of spiritual and eschatological ideas which they supposed to be found in the thought of Jesus.

In Weiss there are none of these devious paths: "behold the land lies before thee" (238).

The basic theses of Weiss' book are the following: (1) All modern ideas read into the concept of the kingdom of God must be eliminated. (2) The kingdom of God was for Jesus a transcendental reality, without political expectations, and still in the future and was spoken of as present only as a cloud may be said to be present by casting its shadow upon the earth. (3) Jesus did not establish the kingdom; he only proclaimed its coming and waited its establishment by supernatural means. (4) As Jews under the kingdom, penitence was necessary for the kingdom's coming, but since sufficient penitence did not show itself, Jesus offered his own death as the ransom price. (5) Jesus died believing that he would return again in splendor and glory after his death. (6) The ministry of Jesus and that of John the Baptist differ only in Jesus' consciousness of being the messiah—that is, his consciousness that he would exercise the messiahship in the future beyond death at his return. (7) The ethic of Jesus was an ethic to set men free from the world so they might be prepared to enter unimpeded into the kingdom. Schweitzer saw in Weiss the first scholar since Reimarus who had taken seriously the eschatology in the preaching of Jesus.

For Schweitzer, Wrede represented what he called "thoroughgoing skepticism." Wrede challenged the opinion, commonly held at the time, that Mark, the earliest Gospel, provided the means to arrive at a historical view of Jesus. The Marcan motif of the messianic secret was for Wrede unhistorical, and its dominance in the Gospel shows that the Gospel is a product of the church's faith, a chapter in the history of dogma rather than an historical representation of the life of Jesus. The narrative of Mark arose from the impulse of the church to give a messianic form to the otherwise nonmessianic earthly life of Jesus. Thus the structure and interconnections between the individual units in Mark were attributed to a secondary development and were not a reflection of the historical ministry of Jesus. Schweitzer summarizes the implications of Wrede in the following terms:

Formerly it was possible to book through-tickets at the supplementary-psychological-knowledge office which enabled those travelling in the interests of Life-of-Jesus construction to use express trains, thus avoiding the inconvenience of having to stop at every little station, change, and run the risk of missing their connexion. This ticket office is now closed. There is a station at the end of each section of the narrative, and the connexions are not guaranteed (333).

Schweitzer accepted the positions of Weiss in his emphasis on the eschatological form of Jesus' message. Wrede's arguments were partially adopted. Schweitzer agreed that the Gospel of Mark could no longer be used as was common in nineteenth-century research—that is, as a reliable foundation document in reconstructing the historical life of Jesus.

In formulating his version of the historical Jesus, Schweitzer worked with the following general overall assumptions. (1) In spite of critical and skeptical study of the Gospels, these documents still reflect the historical Jesus and the course of his career in a sufficient form to warrant a reconstruction of this history. This is especially the case with the Gospel of Matthew and to a lesser degree the Gospel of Mark. "The Life of Jesus cannot be arrived at by following the arrangement of a single Gospel, but only on the basis of the tradition which is preserved more or less faithfully in the earliest pair of Synoptic Gospels" (394). (2) Not only Jesus' preaching but also his teaching and the actual course of his ministry were eschatologically or apocalyptically determined. (3) The secret of the messiahship of Jesus was truly a secret. Jesus understood himself as the messiah but sought to guard this belief from his followers and disciples.

For Schweitzer, the ministry of Jesus lasted perhaps for one year at the most. His contact with John the Baptist probably occurred during one Passover season—the following Passover he was dead. It was a year dominated by Jesus' belief in his own messiahship in which Jesus' acted on the basis of this dogmatic belief concerning his messiahship. The erratic character of the Gospel traditions is due to the erratic dogmatic actions of Jesus and not to the church's reconstruction of his actions. "His life . . . was dominated by a 'dogmatic idea' which rendered Him indifferent to all else" (353).

"The chaotic confusion of the narratives ought to have suggested the thought that the events had been thrown into this confusion by the volcanic force of an incalculable personality, not by some kind of carelessness or freak of the tradition" (351). The dogmatic element is thus not the faith of the church which was imposed upon the traditions, the dogmatic element goes back to Jesus himself. Even the closest disciples of Jesus did not understand the incoherent shape of his life.

Even its most critical moments were totally unintelligible to the disciples who had themselves shared in the experiences, and who were the only sources for the tradition. They were simply swept through these events by the momentum of the purpose of Jesus. That is why the tradition is incoherent. The reality had been incoherent too, since it was only the secret Messianic self-consciousness of Jesus which created alike the events and their connexion. Every life of Jesus remains therefore a reconstruction on the basis of a more or less accurate insight into the nature of the dynamic self-consciousness of Jesus which created the history (395).

Jesus' public ministry centered on his pronouncement of the immediacy of the eschatological, supermundane kingdom of God. Jesus did not understand himself as a teacher. When a successful and happy work as a teacher opened itself to him, Jesus abandoned at that moment the people anxious to learn and eager for salvation.

His action suggests a doubt whether He really felt Himself to be a "teacher." If all the controversial discourses and sayings and answers to questions, which were so to speak wrung from Him, were subtracted from the sum of His utterances, how much of the didactic preaching of Jesus would be left over?

But even the supposed didactic preaching is not really that of a "teacher," since the purpose of His parables was, according to Mark iv. 10-12, not to reveal, but to conceal, and of the Kingdom of God He spoke only in parables (Mark iv. 34). . . . Jesus, whenever He desires to make known anything further concerning the Kingdom of God than just its near approach, seems to be confined, as it were by a higher law, to the parabolic form of discourse. It is as though, for reasons which we cannot grasp, His teaching lay under certain limitations. It appears as a kind of accessory aspect of His vocation. Thus it was possible for Him to give up His work as a teacher even at the moment when it promised the greatest success (353-54).

Behind Jesus' hesitancy to be a teacher lay the influence of the idea of predestination. Jesus did call for repentance on the part of the people and understood their repentance as forcing the kingdom of God or taking it by force; but Jesus also believed and proclaimed that "many are called, but few are chosen." The Beatitudes, for example, are not to be understood as exhortations or admonitions "but as a simple statement of fact: in their being poor in spirit, in their meekness, in their love of peace, it is made manifest that they are predestined to the Kingdom. By the possession of these qualities they are marked as belonging to it. In the case of others (Matt. v. 10-12) the predestination to the Kingdom is made manifest by the persecutions which befall them in this world. These are the light of the world, which already shines among men for the glory of God (Matt. v. 14-15)" (355).

If Jesus' function was not that of a teacher, how then does one explain the Sermon on the Mount? It was a special ethic, an interim ethic, applicable only to the time between the proclamation of the coming kingdom and its arrival. "There is for Jesus no ethic of the Kingdom of God, for in the Kingdom of God all natural relationships, even, for example, the distinction of sex (Mark xii. 25 and 26), are abolished. Temptation and sin no longer exist. All is 'reign,' a 'reign' which has gradations—Jesus speaks of the 'least in the

Kingdom of God'—according as it has been determined in each individual case from all eternity, and according as each by his self-humiliation and refusal to rule in the present age has proved his fitness for bearing rule in the future Kingdom" (365-66).

In proclaiming the apocalyptic end of history, Jesus spoke of the mystery of the kingdom of God. What was the mystery of the kingdom?

It must consist of something more than merely its near approach, and something of extreme importance; otherwise Jesus would be here indulging in mere mystery-mongering. The saying about the candle which He puts upon the stand, in order that what was hidden may be revealed to those who have ears to hear, implies that He is making a tremendous revelation to those who understand the parables about the growth of the seed. The mystery must therefore contain the explanation why the Kingdom must now come, and how men are to know how near it is. For the general fact that it is very near had already been openly proclaimed both by the Baptist and by Jesus. The mystery, therefore, must consist of something more than that (355-56).

The mystery or secret of the kingdom was its analogical and temporal connection with the harvest. In Matthew 9:37-38, Jesus spoke of the harvest as plentiful and the laborers as few. This reference to the harvest was, according to Schweitzer, directly related to the actual harvest at hand in the Palestinian fields. In the parables of the kingdom, Jesus compared the kingdom to the sowing and planting and the ultimate harvest. The initial fact in the parable is the sowing. The point of importance is not the sower but the fact that the sowing has taken place. The sowing was present or already past—it had taken place in the "movement of repentance evoked by the Baptist and now intensified by His own preaching. . . . That being so, the Kingdom of God must follow as certainly as harvest follows seed-sowing. . . . Any one who knows this sees with different eyes the corn growing in the fields and the harvest ripening, for he sees the one fact in the other, and awaits along with the harvest the heavenly, the revelation of the Kingdom of God" (356). In other words, Jesus believed the coming of the kingdom would occur in conjunction with the harvest already ripening in the fields. "The harvest ripening upon earth is the last" (357). This was the true secret of the kingdom.

Jesus' actions and his expectations regarding the coming of the kingdom, Schweitzer finds reflected in Matthew 10-11. "Without Matt. x. and xi. everything remains enigmatic" (360). These two chapters contain Jesus' commissioning of his disciples, his sending them forth to proclaim the coming kingdom, and narratives about Jesus' actions in their absence. How and why are these two chapters so important in understanding the course of Jesus' ministry?

Jesus expected the coming of the kingdom at harvest time. Before sending out his disciples, Jesus "charged" them. "He tells them in plain words (Matt. x. 23), that He does not expect to see them back in the present age. The Parousia of the Son of Man, which is logically and temporally identical with the dawn of the Kingdom, will take place before they shall have completed a hasty journey through the cities of Israel to announce it. That the words mean this and nothing else, that they ought not to be in any way weakened down, should be sufficiently evident. This is the form in which Jesus reveals to them the secret of the Kingdom of God" (358-59). The disciples went forth and preached but the prediction was not fulfilled, the kingdom of God had not arrived, the Son of man had not come! "The disciples returned to Him; and the appearing of the Son of Man had not taken place. The actual history disavowed the dogmatic history on which the action of Jesus had been based. An event of supernatural history which must take place, and must take place at that particular point of time, failed to come about. That was for Jesus, who lived wholly in the dogmatic history, the first 'historical' occurrence, the central event which closed the former period of His activity and gave the coming period a new character" (359).

In order to understand the significance of this failure of the arrival of the kingdom for Schweitzer's view of the reconstruction of the course of Jesus' life, it is necessary to point to a few other elements in Matthew 10 and how Schweitzer interpreted these in terms of Jesus' apocalyptic expectations. It should, in this respect, be emphasized that Schweitzer viewed the discourse in Matthew 10 as "historical as a whole and down to the smallest detail" (363).

In his discourse, Jesus spoke of the suffering which would confront the disciples in their mission and the disrupted relationships which would result—it would be a sword not peace that Jesus' coming would bring (Matthew 10:34). These sufferings were the messianic woes which were immediately to precede the arrival of the kingdom. In conjunction with their mission, Jesus believed, the Spirit of God would be given, fulfilling Joel 3:13, and the disciples would be granted divine knowledge to make known the mystery of the kingdom.

A kind of supernatural illumination will suddenly make known all that Jesus has been keeping secret regarding the Kingdom of God and His position in the Kingdom. This illumination will arise as suddenly and without preparation as the spirit of strife.

And as a matter of fact Jesus predicts to the disciples in the same discourse that to their own surprise a supernatural wisdom will suddenly speak from their lips, so that it will be not they but the Spirit of God who will answer the great ones of the earth (362).

In other words, Jesus believed that the coming of the Son of man—the arrival of the kingdom—would take place in the midst of the disciples' mission, and the suffering and gift of the Spirit would fulfill the requirements of the messianic dogma about the suffering events preceding the end. According to Schweitzer, Jesus believed that he would be the Son of man. During the preaching mission of the disciples, he believed that he would be revealed as the heavenly Son of man. "That Jesus of Nazareth knew himself to be the Son of Man who was to be revealed is for us the great fact of His self-consciousness" (367).

The nonoccurrence of the kingdom's arrival divided Jesus' ministry into two halves. The first half was oriented to the coming of the kingdom at that year's harvest time; the second half was characterized by Jesus' actions in light of the failure of this apocalyptic vision. The significance of this failure for the course of Jesus' ministry is hard to overemphasize in Schweitzer's reconstruction.

The whole history of "Christianity" down to the present day, that is to say, the real inner history of it, is based on the delay of the Parousia, the non-occurrence of the Parousia, the abandonment of eschatology, the progress and completion of the "de-eschatologising" of religion which has been connected therewith. It should be noted that the non-fulfilment of Matt. x. 23 is the first postponement of the Parousia. We have therefore here the first significant date in the "history of Christianity"; it gives to the work of Jesus a new direction, otherwise inexplicable (360).

The second half of Jesus' career must not be seen however as a time in which Jesus was no longer acting on his beliefs concerning the eschatological end. The nonrealization of the kingdom's arrival reoriented some elements in his views, but he still acted as the apocalyptic visionary on the basis of his messianic and kingdom dogmas. From beginning to end, "Jesus' purpose is to set in motion the eschatological development of history, to let loose the final woes, the confusion and strife, from which shall issue the Parousia, and so to introduce the supra-mundane phase of the eschatological drama" (371). Neither Jesus nor John the Baptist were borne along by the current of an external eschatological movement or enthusiasm.

They themselves set the times in motion by action, by creating eschatological facts. . . . The Baptist appears, and cries: "Repent, for the Kingdom of Heaven is at hand." Soon after that comes Jesus, and in the knowledge that He is the coming Son of Man lays hold of the wheel of the world to set it moving on that last revolution which is to bring all ordinary history to a close. It refuses to turn, and He throws Himself upon it. Then it does turn; and crushes Him. Instead of bringing in the eschatological conditions, He has destroyed them. The wheel rolls onward, and the mangled body of the one immeasurably great Man, who was strong enough to think of Himself as the spiritual ruler of mankind and to bend history to His purpose, is hanging upon it still. That is His victory and His reign (370-71).

Before we examine Schweitzer's discussion of Jesus' final effort to turn the wheel, we should note his discussion of the messianic secret, which Jesus had not intended to reveal, and how this came to be known in the days following the first delay of the Parousia.

Two events are of special importance with regard to this question—the Transfiguration (Mark 9:2-13) and the confession of Jesus as the messiah by Peter at Caesarea Philippi (Mark 8:27-33). How are these to be understood? In the first place, Schweitzer argues that although Jesus acted through-out his ministry with the full knowledge that he was the messiah, "He had never had the intention of revealing the secret of His Messiahship to the disciples. Otherwise He would not have kept it from them at the time of their mission, when He did not expect them to return before the Parousia" (386). The secret was discovered by the inner circle of three disciples at the Transfiguration and revealed to the others by Peter at Caesarea Philippi. Here it should be noted that Schweitzer rearranges the order of these events. In the Gospels, the confession of Peter precedes the Transfiguration. Schweitzer argues that for them to be understood properly, the order must be reversed.

After the return of the disciples from their mission, Jesus' overwhelming desire was to get away from the people. He and his disciples withdrew to Bethsaida (Mark 8:22), and it is this context to which the Transfiguration belongs. The Transfiguration was, in fact, "the revelation of the secret of the Messiahship to the three who constituted the inner circle of the disciples. And Jesus had not Himself revealed it to them; what had happened was, that in a state of rapture common to them all, in which they had seen the Master in a glorious transfiguration, they had seen Him talking with

Moses and Elias and had heard a voice from heaven saying, 'This is my beloved Son, hear ye Him.' . . . Even at the transfiguration the 'three' do not learn it from His lips, but in a state of ecstasy, an ecstasy which He shared with them" (385-86).

At Caesarea Philippi, the secret of Jesus' messiahship was made known to the other disciples by Peter. So Jesus did not reveal to his disciples and certainly never to the general public that he was the messiah. "Jesus did not voluntarily give up His messianic secret; it was wrung from Him by the pressure of events" (386). Jesus did however reveal to his disciples, at Caesarea Philippi, the secret of his forthcoming suffering.

Jesus' journey to Jerusalem was undertaken "solely in order to die there" (391). Why did Jesus choose this course? Jesus had "placed his Parousia at the end of the pre-Messianic tribulations" at the time of the disciples' mission (388). After the suffering and his Parousia did not occur, Jesus reached the conclusion that he must undergo the tribulation and suffering himself; it would not begin of itself. "That was the new conviction that had dawned upon Him. He must suffer for others . . . that the Kingdom might come" (389). Jesus then came to associate the suffering of the messianic prelude to the coming of the kingdom with an historic event, with his own death: "He will go to Jerusalem, there to suffer death at the hands of authorities. . . . He no longer speaks of the general tribulation" (388). Jesus was now to force the kingdom and undergo the suffering; "another of the violent must lay violent hands upon the Kingdom of God. The movement of repentance had not been sufficient" to force the kingdom (389). Jesus must die for the many who were predestined for the kingdom and in his death compel its coming. Jesus had reached this last conclusion on the basis of the prophecy of the suffering servant spoken of in the book of Isaiah (see especially Isaiah 53). So "for Jesus the necessity of His death is grounded in dogma, not in external historical facts" (392). Schweitzer interpreted Jesus' understanding of the death of the suffering servant in the following manner: "The mysterious description of Him who in His humiliation was despised and misunderstood, who, nevertheless bears the guilt of others and afterwards is made manifest in what He has done, points, He feels, to Himself. And since He found it there set down that He must suffer unrecognised, and that those for whom He suffered should doubt Him, His suffering should, nay must, remain a mystery" (390). Thus Jesus felt no obligation nor need to make clear his understanding of his death, in fact, he felt exactly the reverse.

Jesus' activity in Jerusalem was calculated to bring about his suffering and death. In the events which led up to his death, according to Schweitzer, Jesus was the "sole actor" intent upon the "deliberate bringing down of death upon Himself." He "thinks only how he can so provoke the Pharisees and the rulers that they will be compelled to get rid of Him. That is why He violently cleanses the Temple, and attacks the Pharisees, in the presence of the people, with passionate invective" (392).

In Jerusalem, no one except Jesus and the disciples knew the secret of his messiahship. "The entry into Jerusalem was . . . Messianic for Jesus, but not for the people" (394). Then the High Priest suddenly showed himself in possession of the secret. The finger pointed to Judas as the betrayer of the secret.

For a hundred and fifty years the question has been historically discussed why Judas betrayed his Master. That the main question for history was *what he betrayed* was suspected by few and they touched on it only in a timid kind of way. . . .

In the betrayal . . . there were two points, a more general and a more special: the general fact by which he gave Jesus into their power, and the undertaking to let them know of the next opportunity when they could arrest Him quietly, without publicity. The betrayal by which be brought his Master to death, in consequence of which the rulers decided upon the arrest, knowing that their cause was safe in any case, was the betrayal of the Messianic secret. Jesus died because two of His disciples had broken His command of silence: Peter when he made known the secret of the

Messiahship to the Twelve at Caesarea Philippi; Judas Iscariot by communicating it to the High Priest (396).

In Jesus' trial before Pilate, the multitude was there only to ask for the release of a prisoner according to the custom. But they were a threat to the priests who had hoped to have Jesus crucified before anyone knew what was happening. They might have asked for Jesus' release, since they considered him an honored prophet. The priests however went among the crowd "telling them why he was condemned, by revealing to them the Messianic secret" (397).

That makes Him at once from a prophet worthy of honour into a deluded enthusiast and blasphemer. That was the explanation of the "fickleness" of the Jerusalem mob which is always so eloquently described, without any evidence for it except this single inexplicable case.

At midday of the same day—it was the 14th Nisan, and in the evening the Paschal lamb would be eaten—Jesus cried aloud and expired. He had chosen to remain fully conscious to the last (397).

Schweitzer had no doubt about the ability to discover the historical Jesus. He also had no doubt about the liberals' reconstructed historical Jesus' irrelevance for modern man.

Those who are fond of talking about negative theology can find their account here. There is nothing more negative than the result of the critical study of the Life of Jesus.

The Jesus of Nazareth who came forward publicly as the Messiah, who preached the ethic of the Kingdom of God, who founded the Kingdom of Heaven upon earth, and died to give His work its final consecration, never had any existence. He is a figure designed by rationalism, endowed with life by liberalism, and clothed by modern theology in an historical garb.

This image has not been destroyed from without, it has fallen to pieces, cleft and disintegrated by the concrete historical problems which came to the surface one after another, and in spite of all the artifice, art, artificiality, and violence which was applied to them, refused to be planed down to fit the design on which the Jesus of the theology of

74

the last hundred and thirty years had been constructed, and were no sooner covered over than they appeared again in a new form (398). . . .

The study of the Life of Jesus has had a curious history. It set out in quest of the historical Jesus, believing that when it had found Him it could bring Him straight into our time as a Teacher and Saviour. It loosed the bands by which He had been riveted for centuries to the stony rocks of ecclesiastical doctrine, and rejoiced to see life and movement coming into the figure once more, and the historical Jesus advancing, as it seemed, to meet it. But He does not stay; He passes by our time and returns to His own. What surprised and dismayed the theology of the last forty years was that, despite all forced and arbitrary interpretations, it could not keep Him in our time, but had to let Him go. He returned to His own time, not owing to the application of any historical ingenuity, but by the same inevitable necessity by which the liberated pendulum returns to its original position (399).

If such negative results for theology result from the study of the historical Jesus, this did not mean the end of Christianity for Schweitzer. If the Jesus of history could not be brought with meaning into the present, the same could not be said for "Jesus."

Jesus of Nazareth will not suffer Himself to be modernised. As an historic figure He refuses to be detached from His own time. He has no answer for the question, "Tell us Thy name in our speech and for our day!" But He does bless those who have wrestled with Him, so that, though they cannot take Him with them, yet, like men who have seen God face to face and received strength in their souls, they go on their way with renewed courage, ready to do battle with the world and its powers (312). . . .

We are experiencing what Paul experienced. In the very moment when we were coming nearer to the historical Jesus than men had ever come before, and were already stretching out our hands to draw Him into our own time, we have been obliged to give up the attempt and acknowledge our failure in that paradoxical saying: "If we have known Christ after the flesh yet henceforth know we Him no more" [II Corinthians 5:16]. And further we must be prepared to find that the historical knowledge of the personality and life of Jesus will not be a help, but perhaps even an offence to religion.

But the truth is, it is not Jesus as historically known, but Jesus as spiritually arisen within men, who is significant for our time and can help it. Not the historical Jesus, but the spirit which goes forth from Him and in the spirits of men strives for new influence and rule, is that which overcomes the world.

It is not given to history to disengage that which is abiding and eternal in the being of Jesus from the historical forms in which it worked itself out, and to introduce it into our world as a living influence. It has toiled in vain at this undertaking. As a water-plant is beautiful so long as it is growing in the water, but once torn from its roots, withers and becomes unrecognisable, so it is with the historical Jesus when He is wrenched loose from the soil of eschatology, and the attempt is made to conceive Him "historically" as a Being not subject to temporal conditions. The abiding and eternal in Jesus is absolutely independent of historical knowledge and can only be understood by contact with His spirit which is still at work in the world. In proportion as we have the Spirit of Jesus we have the true knowledge of Jesus.

Jesus as a concrete historical personality remains a stranger to our time, but His spirit, which lies hidden in His words, is known in simplicity, and its influence is direct. Every saying contains in its own way the whole Jesus. The very strangeness and unconditionedness in which He stands before us makes it easier for individuals to find their own personal standpoint in regard to Him (401). . . .

He comes to us as One unknown, without a name, as of old, by the lake-side, He came to those men who knew Him not. He speaks to us the same word: "Follow thou me!" and sets us to the tasks which He has to fulfil for our time. He commands. And to those who obey Him, whether they be wise or simple, He will reveal Himself in the toils, the conflicts, the sufferings which they shall pass through in His fellowship, and, as an ineffable mystery, they shall learn in their own experience Who He is (403).

4. JESUS: THE CONSTANT CONTEMPORARY

So often we have added to the word, "he was in the world," the seemingly pious and proper theological conclusion, "but he was not of the world," that we have actually come to believe it. So we have looked for someone who was not there and missed the one who was. —Morton S. Enslin, *The Prophet from Nazareth* (p. 7)

A number of studies on the historical Jesus have sought to focus on the permanent relevance of the historical Jesus. Many of these works have been thoroughly historical and critical in their approach to the sources for a life of Jesus but have attempted in the process to lay hold of some distinctive feature or features in the life and teachings of Jesus which will address and challenge modern man. There is, in other words, no mere interest in the historical Jesus simply for the sake of antiquarian information about this person in the past. This perspective, of course, embodies one of the fundamental interests of the rationalistic lives of Jesus without being directly influenced by any particular rationalistic reconstruction. Simultaneously, the search for a historical Jesus relevant to modern man embodies the ambitions of the nineteenth-century liberal quest. It should be noted that frequently when the nineteenth-century liberal scholars and their twentieth-century counterparts sought for a Jesus relevant to their times, they were not necessarily thinking of relevance only with regard to the church and Christians. The search was for a Jesus relevant to modern man whether Christian or otherwise. And in fact, some of these portraits of the historical Jesus have frequently appealed to many who would not and perhaps could not describe themselves as Christian. Other scholars within the same general stream sought for a historical Jesus who could form the ground of Christian faith over against the orthodox Christ confessed and preached by the church. Thus they sought to construct an alternative route to Christian faith different from traditional expressions.

Various aspects or features in the life of the historical Jesus have occupied the concerns of scholars searching for a Jesus relevant and contemporary to modern man. Some have pointed to the life of Jesus as a pattern or paradigm of human existence to be imitated in the present. Others have pointed to the personality of Jesus or the person of Jesus as a basis of faith. Still others have focused on the inner life of Jesus as the ground and basis for communion with God. Some have pointed to the religious life of Jesus, and others focused on his theological understanding of God. Many had examined the teachings of Jesus as the embodiment of a style of life or an approach to existence.

In this chapter, we shall examine three studies which, although not representing every perspective, display a representative selection of approaches.

The first work is the book by Bruce Barton entitled *The Man Nobody Knows*. This volume, described by its publisher as the "most popular and successful religious book of our age," has experienced a wide distribution having sold over 600,000 copies in hardcover form.

The intent and interest of the author in writing this book can be seen in his introduction. He describes his feelings of repulsion when as a lad he was presented by the church and Sunday school with a Jesus who was a "pale young man with no muscle and a sad expression" and red whiskers. Jesus was encountered as a sissified lamb of God, a physical weakling, a kill-joy, a man of sorrows, and as a nonfighter in the battle of life.

Barton then set out to present a true picture of the historical Jesus based on a reading of the New Testament Gospels which would counter and offer an alternative to this typical Jesus of Sunday school theology. In painting his portrait of Jesus, Barton wishes to "take the story just as the simple narratives give it—a poor boy, growing up in a peasant family, working in a carpenter shop; gradually feeling His powers expanding, beginning to have an influence over His neighbors, recruiting a few followers, suffering disappointments, reverses and finally death. Yet building so solidly and well that death was only the beginning of His influence" (19).

Barton begins with what he calls the "eternal miracle" which happens to all men of power; that is, the "awakening of the inner consciousness of power" (20). When did Jesus become aware of this power and become conscious of his divinity? When did he realize that "he was larger than the limits of a country town, that his life might be bigger than his father's?" One cannot be certain but the "consciousness of His divinity must have come to Him in a time of solitude, of awe in the presence of Nature. . . . Somewhere, at some unforgettable hour, the doing filled his heart. He knew He was bigger than Nazareth" (21). Perhaps at his baptism by John, Jesus realized that "He was going to do the big things which John had done; He felt the power stirring in Him: He was all eager to begin" (22). Jesus' enthusiasm soon was clouded with doubt, and he struggled to affirm his initial feeling. "In the calm of that wilderness there came the majestic conviction which is the very soul of leadership—the faith that His spirit was linked with the Eternal, that God had sent Him into the world to do a work which no one else could do, which—if He neglected it—would never be done. . . . The youth who had been a carpenter stayed in the wilderness; a man came out. . . . Men who looked on Him from that hour felt the authority of one who has put his spiritual house in order and knows clearly what he is about" (23-24).

Jesus' basic characteristics of leadership which gave him power over men were threefold. (1) He possessed the quality of conviction which begets loyalty and commands respect. (2) He possessed the powerful gift of picking men and recognizing hidden capacities in them. "He had the born leader's gift for seeing powers in men of which they themselves were often almost unconscious" (27). He brought together an unknown group of men who had never accomplished anything—a "haphazard collection of fishermen and small-town businessmen, and one tax collector"— and out of them built an organization. Take Matthew, for example: the "crowd saw only a despised taxgatherer. Jesus saw the potential writer of a book which will live forever" (28). (3) In training his organization, Jesus manifested an unending patience. For three years he struggled to teach them, to lead them to an understanding knowing "that the way to get faith out of men is to show that you have faith in them" (29).

In leadership qualities Jesus was successful, whereas John was a miserable failure.

John the Baptist . . . could denounce, but he could not construct. He drew crowds who were willing to repent at his command, but he had no program for them after their repentance. They waited for him to organize them for some sort of effective service, but he was no organizer. So his followers drifted away, and his movement gradually collapsed. The same thing might have happened to the work of Jesus. He started with much less than John and a much smaller group of followers. He had only twelve, and they were untrained, simple men, with elementary weakness and passions. Yet because of the fire of His personal conviction, because of His marvelous instinct for discovering their latent powers, and because of His unwavering faith and patience, He molded them into an organization which carried on victoriously. Within a very few years after His death, it was reported in a far-off corner of the Roman Empire that "these who have turned the world upside down have come hither also." A few decades later the proud Emperor himself bowed his head to the teachings of this Nazareth carpenter, transmitted through common men (30-31).

Jesus must be understood as having been physically strong. When he spoke of building a house upon a rock he knew what he was talking about. His fellow townsmen had frequently "seen Him bending His strong clean shoulders to deliver heavy blows; or watched Him trudge away into the woods, His ax over His shoulders, and return at nightfall with a rough-hewn bean" (36). When he cleansed the temple he showed the stuff he was made of. "As His right arm rose and fell, striking its blows with that little whip, the sleeve dropped back to reveal muscles hard as iron. No one who watched Him in action had any doubt that He was fully capable of taking care of Himself. The evidence is clear that no angry priest or money-changer cared to try conclusions with that arm" (35). When Jesus spoke to the sick man upon his pallet, his command and his appearance solicited confidence.

"Walk!" Do you suppose for one minute that a weakling, uttering that syllable, would have produced any result? If the Jesus who looked down on that pitiful wreck had been the Jesus of the painters, the sick man would have dropped back with a scornful sneer and motioned his friends to carry him out. But the health of the Teacher was irresistible; it seemed to cry out, "Nothing is impossible if only your will power is strong enough." And the man who so long ago had surrendered to despair, rose and gathered up his bed and went away, healed—like hundreds of others in Galilee—by strength from an overflowing fountain of strength (39).

Something of the person of Jesus can be seen in the fact that whereas men followed him, "women worshiped Him" (40).

The important, and too often forgotten, fact in these relationships is this—that women are *not* drawn by weakness. The sallow-faced, thin-lipped, so-called spiritual type of man may awaken maternal instinct, stirring an emotion which is half regard, half pity. But since the world began, no power has fastened the affection of women upon a man like manliness. Men who have been women's men in the finest sense have been vital figures of history (41). . . .
All His days were spent in the open air—this is the third outstanding testimony to His strength. On the Sabbath He was in the synagogue because that was where the people were gathered, but by far the greater part of His teaching was

done on the shores of His lake, or in the cool recesses of the hills. He walked constantly from village to village; His face was tanned by the sun and wind. Even at night He slept outdoors when He could—turning His back on the hot walls of the city and slipping away into the healthful freshness of the Mount of Olives. He was an energetic outdoor man. The vigorous activities of His days gave His nerves the strength of steel. As much as any nation ever, Americans understand and respect this kind of man (43).

When Jesus stood before the Roman procurator, "in the face of the Roman were deep unpleasant lines; his cheeks were fatty with self-indulgence; he had the colorless look of indoor living. The straight young man stood inches above him, bronzed and hard and clean as the air of His loved mountain and lake." Surely no painter could ever have produced a truer picture than the words that "dissipated cynical Roman cried: 'Behold the man!' " (45).

Christian theology has done Jesus tremendous harm in failing to stress that he was a very sociable man. "The friendliest man who has ever lived has been shut off by the black wall of tradition from those whose friendship He would most enjoy. Theology has reared a graven image and robbed the world of the joy and laughter of the Great Champion" (46-47). Jesus loved a crowd. He was the type of man whom you would have chosen as a companion on a fishing trip. "No other public figure even had a more interesting list of friends. It ran from the top of the social ladder to the bottom" (53).

Jesus' message of God portrays God as a great companion. It announced a "happy God, wanting His sons and daughters to be happy" (56).

That was the message of Jesus—that God is supremely better than anybody had ever dared to believe. Not a petulant Creator, who had lost control of His creation and, in wrath, was determined to destroy it all. Not a stern Judge dispensing impersonal justice. Not a vain King who must be flattered and bribed into concessions of mercy. Not a rigid Accountant, checking up the sins against the penances and striking a cold hard balance. Not any of these . . . nothing like these; but a great Companion, a wonderful Friend, a kindly indulgent, joy-loving Father (61-62).

Jesus hoped through the instrumentality of his small band of disciples to carry his message to the world. Soon his organization would succeed, and his message would conquer. "It conquered not because there was any demand for another religion but because Jesus knew how, and taught His followers how, to catch the attention of the indifferent, and translate a great spiritual conception into terms of practical self-concern" (71).

Jesus was a master teacher, always complete master of the situation. His teaching in parables avoided the unattractive generality. His teachings were marvelously condensed, simple ("all the great things in human life are one-syllable things"), with sincerity illuminating every word, every sentence he uttered, and they are repeatable.

And whoever feels an impulse to make his own life count in the grand process of human betterment can have no surer guide for his activities than Jesus. Let him learn the lesson of the parables: that in teaching people you first capture their interest; that your service rather than your sermons must be your claim on their attention; that what you say must be simple and brief and above all *sincere*—the unmistakable voice of true regard and affection (99).

In Jesus' works and his relations with people, one can see his philosophy which Barton summarizes in three prepositions:

1. Whoever will be great must render great service.
2. Whoever will find himself at the top must be willing to lose himself at the bottom.
3. The rewards come to those who travel the second, undemanded mile (109).

One of the final tests of man's life is how he bears up under disappointment. In this test, Jesus shows his true greatness. Jesus' hometown turned against him, his brothers deserted him, his best friend died doubting him, the people forsook him, his disciples fled from him, and yet when Jesus was dying upon the cross he "so bore Himself that a crucified felon looked into His dying eyes and saluted him as King" (133).

Morton Enslin, in his *The Prophet from Nazareth,* provides a search for the "real Jesus" of history and for a Jesus who "was never placed in any tomb, but has lived in the hearts and lives of the millions of men and women to whom he is endlessly calling, demanding that they follow with him to the only goal" (217).

The basic theses of Enslin's book are:

(1) All who heard Jesus understood him. His enemies sent him to the cross, not because they did not know what he meant but because they did. His first followers braved the same opposition which had cost him his life and sounded his word at home and abroad because they knew what he had meant and had accepted it as the very word of God. (2) While we cannot write a biography, we can know the man, can see him engaged in a life-and-death struggle, in the midst of real men, enemies and friends alike, not lifeless puppets seeming to move on the silver screen of an altogether-other Cinerama *in vacuo theologico.* (3) Far from being dispensable, a figure cavalierly to be dismissed as inconsequential then, irrelevant now, he stands ever demanding from his followers the same commitment and devotion to their tasks which he brought to his (14).

What can be known about this real Jesus? Enslin suggests that the material about the early life of Jesus—the birth narratives and the story of his visit to the temple at the age of twelve—are "charming stories," a "lovely part of the Christian tradition," perhaps "closer to poetry than to unedited prose." They, especially the stories of the virgin birth, reflect a class of stories like those told of "many heroes who have achieved fame in the past, as Romulus, the elder Scipio, Augustus, Sargon, Cyrus, Alexander the Great, Pythagoras, and Plato. It was as natural to the ancient world to explain unusual prowess or achievement as due to a divine parent as it is to us to style one superlatively great of 'more than human clay' " (38). Nevertheless something may be said of Jesus' early life: "With confidence, we must ascribe his birth, as well as early years, to the little Galilean town of Nazareth" (39).

Enslin sees selected verses from the synoptics (Luke

4:17-21, 7:39; Mark 1:15, 6:3, 12:37, 14:55, 15:15) as revealing the "basic facts in the story" of Jesus.

And these facts, when set down simply are: a man completely convinced that God had revealed to him that at long last the promised time of triumph was at hand, the period of testing and trial was momentarily to pass, the new age to dawn. Convinced himself, he was able to convince others, and they gladly harkened. To those in positions of authority and power the man and his message were alike an outrage and a menace and had to be suppressed at any cost. And with little difficulty they were able to convince the resident governor of the necessity of quenching the blaze before it was too late (37).

What triggered the public ministry of Jesus? "What led one who had hitherto been a Galilean carpenter to assume the role of a prophet of God?" (41). It was perhaps not the activity of John the Baptist, since the two were probably never associated and the "two movements were originally quite unrelated." Jesus first became associated with John the Baptist in church tradition which "sought to bring a later generation of followers of the Baptist into their ranks by the claim that John had been but the conscious forerunner of their crucified Lord and that his one function had been to designate his greater successor" (42). Why Jesus suddenly began his career can no longer be determined, but Enslin argues that it may have been triggered by one of the altercations between the Jews and Pilate or some local Galilean episode.

For Enslin, Jesus was a prophet not unlike the Old Testament prophetical figures. He was the herald of the new age about to dawn, and, as a prophet, he announced the will of God which had been supernaturally revealed to him. In announcing the nearness of the kingdom, Jesus was declaring that God's purpose and intent are inevitable.

The kingdom comes of itself. It is in consequence of God's initiative. It is not that Jesus brings it. Instead, God has appointed him to announce its approach. . . . To that extent it may be said that the kingdom has brought Jesus. It comes of

itself, unobserved, impossible to detect by outward signs or
clues, and quite apart from man's efforts. In soberest reality it
is the act of God, not the deed of any man (74). . . .

Thus few things would seem more certain than that Jesus
believed passionately in the near approach of the universal
sovereignty of God, which, as he viewed it, was the
apocalyptic "age to come." This was the good news which he
so insistently proclaimed (79).

In his proclamation, Jesus was clearly understood by his
audience, attracted common people who heard him gladly,
and it was this acceptance of the proclamation of Jesus that
lived on in spite of his later death. One must see this
confidence which his followers had that he was indeed a
prophet sent by God as the basis of the later missionary work
of the church.

Had not his companions become convinced—perhaps more
deeply than some of them at the moment realized—of the
rightness of his claim to be a prophet sent by God, it is highly
improbable that they would have seen him on the Easter
morning. . . . The later conventional stories of the
Resurrection—supernatural appearances, resuscitated body,
empty tomb—were the *result* of this all-central confidence,
not its *cause*. To fail to see this is to strip Jesus of his true
significance and to make of him but one more puppet in an
otherworldly drama (91).

Jesus' proclamation of the coming kingdom with its note of
radical change, economically and otherwise, attracted the
economically oppressed and the religiously scorned, the
common people. "In a word, to those at the bottom of the
wheel, whichever way the wheel were to turn, it could not fail
to bring an improvement" (108). But this aroused the
establishment, the wealthy and those in positions of power.
Jesus' apocalyptic views aroused the suspicions of the
educated for whom the law embodied true religion. "The way
his word was accepted," by the humble, poor, and uneducated, "led to his appearing the understanding and sym-
pathizing 'friend of publicans and sinners,' the caustic and
unsympathetic foe of those in positions of wealth and power"
(110).

Jesus: The Constant Contemporary

In his preaching, Jesus was no exponent of social change. The demands he laid upon his hearers and would-be followers were "for the sake of the man himself, not for the alleviation and betterment of society and the world at large" (123). The ethics which Jesus proclaimed demanded a sort of conduct which would continue after the coming of the new world and the new age. "It may very well be that in the eyes of Jesus there was nothing radically new in such a way of life. Rather, it was the way men have lived in their earlier innocence before they had allowed themselves by their new traditions to vitiate and change the ways ordained by God" (125). "In the last analysis, it would seem that for Jesus the ideal life, which God had ordained from the beginning and which would be demanded by his final judge at the coming Final Judgment, was the sort of life and conduct which appealed to him personally" (126). In other words, the words of Jesus on the ideal life "come from a man who is accustomed to a direct and common-sense view of what is 'obviously' fair and sensible and who is equally accustomed to express himself in the homeliest and simplest way" (127).

Part of the attractiveness of Jesus—both to his contemporaries and to moderns—was the fact that Jesus lived up to what he taught as the ideal. It was his "personality"—"that amazing and babbling congeries of gifts and abilities"— which convinced many (128).

The qualities, essence, or whatever other terms be used to attempt to classify and interpret "personality," quite elude the scales and camera. But it is they which constitute the real person, and it is they which constituted the real Jesus. And *this* was not put into any grave. It had been built by that strange alchemy of life into those with whom he had been in contact. Had this not been the case, it is highly unlikely that they would have "seen" him in the days following Easter (129).

Enslin argues that behind some of the miraculous cures and exorcisms attributed to Jesus may lie a kernel of historical truth. "Granted the belief that the word was freighted with power, there is little ground for wonder that on occasion the effect was realized" (152). Most of the miracles are not to be rationalized nor stripped of their miraculous quality to reveal some historical nucleus. Such "explanations which are harder to credit than the difficulties which they seek to explain are to most academic disciplines suspect, even if to the theologian they are attractive and convincing" (158). Many of the miracle stories were the result of reading Old Testament texts and episodes and applying these to Jesus by creating events which reflect the text. For example, probably behind the story of the stilling of the storm lie such Old Testament passages as Psalms 107:23-30; 89:9.

When Jesus went to Jerusalem—to continue his work—his fate was sealed. "Rumors of the rabble-rousing, demon-possessed prophet with his message of the overthrow of law and order—exaggerated and garbled rumors and their credence by those in authority are no invention of the modern world—had preceded him" (173). For the religious leaders, "Jesus' easy pronouncements and judgments . . . were . . . the insolent and outrageous mouthings of an ignorant and untrained peasant, who not only was unforgivably destitute of the knowledge which God himself had enjoined upon all men as their chief duty, but who also blindly attacked them for doing what they knew was in strictest accord with God's clearly revealed will" (176). The clash, in other words, partially centered on the issue of a simple, common sense, prophetic approach versus a religious system founded on the strict observance of the law and its interpretation as the final will of God. Simultaneously, the actions of Jesus confirmed to the religiously and educationally elect that he was a friend of sinners. "His careless hobnobbing at table with publicans and harlots gained for him the name, 'a gluttonous man and a winebibber' [Matthew 11:19], that is, he ate too heartily, drank too freely, and kept very disreputable company" (176).

Jesus' actions in cleansing the temple was an "enacted parable" reflecting his disgust with the religious life of the temple.

Surely the sweating hosts of pilgrims surging through its courts, the lowing and bellowing of terrified cattle in the pens and on the slabs for slaughter; the billowing clouds of smoke and the nauseous stench from burning fat and meat; the cries of hawkers and money-changers—all this might have seemed to an even less sensitive observer than the prophet from Nazareth, little accustomed to such tumult and superficial piety, a strange answer to the age-old query of a Micah [see Micah 6:6-8]. . . .

To the outraged eyes of the prophet from Nazareth he was but once more joining the ranks of the host of the earlier prophets whom God had raised up, as he uttered his blasts against this sorry perversion of Israel's greatest obligation and privilege (180).

The prompt action by the religious leaders against Jesus and his speedy trial and condemnation were "occasioned by Jesus' passionate avowal that the axe was already laid at the root of the tree and that the end of the present order was at hand, for this in the eyes of the authorities was a direct attack upon both state and temple. And the fact that he was no remote or solitary figure—no voice of one crying in the wilderness—but had come, as they were convinced, with a throng of followers to Jerusalem for the express purpose of inciting the mob of pilgrims to violence, only added to their fears and fury" (182). "That Jesus was arrested and speedily remanded to the Roman governor for condemnation and execution as a man whose words and actions were dangerous to the state would seem as certain as the elaborating details are obscure" (200).

So Jesus was condemned, crucified, and buried. But his movement and message did not die. It found continued embodiment in the Easter experience. But how is this experience to be understood?

The usual—to many the natural—understanding of the Easter hope . . . is in terms of a changed Jesus. To me there appears a far profounder change, without which our hopes would be dead: Not a changed Jesus, but changed disciples. Jesus was the same. He had sown his seed, had lived his life, had built himself into the lives of those with whom he had lived and worked. . . . The change was not in any physical transformation of the body he had tenanted, but in the outlook and convictions of the men and women whom he had touched (209-10).

His followers realized that the one they had followed could not but yet be alive for he was even then living in them. "The real Jesus was not the flesh and blood and the bone and the skin, but that something which had the power to reproduce itself in them, that lived in them" (212). Like to his first century companions so to us in the modern world, "there stands the figure of the Prophet from Nazareth, who by his life has left us both the proof that men, however heedless, however blind they may be, do have sufficient of the divine insight to see in such a life the very impress of God himself, and the challenge to do in our day an equivalent of what he did in his" (216). "Not the body which walked the Palestinian hills, but that essence of the divine that made Jesus Jesus; that quality which drew men to him, which transformed them, which enabled them to see aright the kind of life God wished them to live—that still lives. Jesus is not dead, can never die" (217).

In *Jesus on Social Institutions*, Shailer Mathews provides an interpretation of Jesus and argues for the relevancy of his life and teachings for modern man. For Mathews, Jesus and his teachings must be viewed and understood against the revolutionary spirit of his time. The background and context of Jesus' ministry must be viewed through the means of social psychology and particularly the psychology of revolution.

All revolutions are preceded by and spring from the same social attitudes. A new class consciousness is evoked by a sense of political, economic, and social inequality; propaganda arouses a spirit of revolt; a sense of injustice breeds the desire for revenge; an enthusiasm for some abstract ideal provokes a series of outbreaks that attempt to realize the hopes and avenge the wrongs of an oppressed group (13).

The Roman Empire which had brought many advances to ancient men had, in the process of its domination, suppressed nationalism. For many, this provided no real problem, but the Jews, in spite of the derived blessings received and the special religious privileges granted them, were the one people who refused to be repressed and nurtured within their culture a revolutionary spirit.

Instead of the peace and municipal growth, the Jews could see only the policeman and the soldier. Instead of prosperity, they could only see the tax collector. Instead of freedom of worship, they could see only the Temple guard of Roman soldiers who kept them from religious massacres. Instead of cities like Caesarea, and Samaria, Tiberias, and those of the Decapolis, they could see only the standards of the foreign power. Their suppressed nationalism turned to the praise of their past, the glorification of David, and the hope for the reëstablishment of a Davidic dynasty through the aid of their God. This was revolution in the making (16).

Only a small segment of Jewish society directly profited from Roman rule. The masses were subjected to extreme taxation, economic inequality, and political repression. These pent-up frustrations and surging hopes produced a revolutionary eschatological hope, a messianic expectation.

Its really significant elements are simple: (1) the defeat of Satan by God; (2) the defeat of the Romans by God's aid given to the Jews; (3) the complete establishment of the will of God in the Jewish people by observance of the Mosaic law, as a preparation for the divinely established Jewish kingdom; (4) the reliance upon force, violence, and massacre to being about this social order (28).

It is against this background that one must understand the teachings of Jesus. In such revolutionary thoughts and hopes "lay human values that needed to be reinterpreted rather than opposed. To accomplish this proved to be the task and opportunity of Jesus" (28). "For, without leading revolt, he was to live and teach in the atmosphere of revolution, use the language of revolution, make the revolutionary spirit the instrument of his message, and organize a movement

composed of men who awaited a divinely given new age"
(12).

Jesus' mission was that of reshaping the "revolutionary
hopes in the crucible of his own individuality" (32).

Jesus found in his own experience a censor of the
psychology which he shared and to which he appealed. He
looked to God as the ultimate basis of all future blessing, and
God he knew as a father rather than a king. This conviction,
born of the study of the prophets and reënforced by his own
experience, prevented his full acceptance of the revolutionary hopes of those who followed him. The defeat of Satan
could be shown in cures, but the reign of God was to be
established by God himself. Human effort would not bring it
in. Ideals need not be adjusted, therefore, to social processes.
The passionate desire on the part of the people for a better
social order with better institutions and better authority could
be analyzed by Jesus because he felt within himself the spirit
of the Heavenly Father. All elements in the hopes of his times
that were inconsistent with this filial experience he rejected
(38).

Jesus repudiated the role of violence in bringing about the
kingdom of God—the perfect order of society. In fact, "He
was not seeking to establish the kingdom of God but to
prepare men to enter it" (60). He sublimated the social
passion of the revolutionary hopes transforming the "revolutionary spirit into a new moral attitude pregnant with social
implications" (42). "God's will will not be done on earth, until
men love their enemies and are determined rather to be just
than to oppress, to be brothers rather than masters" (39).
"Jesus was far less interested in the rights than in the
obligations of men." "His gospel was not a new Declaration of
Rights but a Declaration of Duties" (73).

The essential content of the teaching of Jesus is described
by Mathews in a number of ways: "love as a dominating force
in nature and history," "sacrificial social-mindedness,"
"heroic sacrifice," "social coöperation in which the coöperat-
ing parties treat each other as persons," "brotherliness," and
"social goodwill." Although Jesus anticipated the speedy
arrival of the kingdom, his ethical imperatives were not

anchored in this eschatological perspective but rather in the character and will of God. "In the character of God lies the justification of goodwill and love on the part of those who await the kingdom" (51). "Love, as the characteristic of God, was the indispensable characteristic of those who would enjoy his reign" (37-38).

Jesus was a revolutionary and an agitator, but he did not set out to destroy the established institutions and create new ones. "He was endeavoring to inculcate attitudes in the individual soul rather than to organize a n ?w state or to urge political reform" (107). Nonetheless, the effort of the individual to express goodwill and love in society would lead to the transformation of society and its institutions. Jesus was not a legislator; therefore he proposed no legislation as the means to transform society; he was no economist, so he offered no economical system for men preparing for the kingdom; but he was an "expounder of attitudes for the group preparing for the kingdom" (84).

Jesus taught that love is a practicable basis upon which to build human relations. Once let humanity actually believe this and the perspective of values will be changed. Giving justice will replace fighting for rights; the democratizing of privilege will replace the manipulation of social advantages; the humanizing of necessary economic processes will replace the exploiting of human life in the interests of wealth or pleasure (155).

5. JESUS: THE JEW
FROM GALILEE

Jesus was not a Christian: he was a Jew. He did not proclaim a new faith, but taught men to do the will of God. According to Jesus, as to the Jews, generally, this will of God is to be found in the Law and the other canonical Scriptures.
—Julius Wellhausen, *Einleitung in die drei ersten Evangelien* (p. 113)

The twentieth century has witnessed a sharp upsurge of interest in Jesus by Jews. Literary discussions of Jesus by Jewish writers are now commonplace. One element in this Jewish concern with Jesus is the renewed interest in recovering the Jewish past fostered by the existence of the Israeli state in Palestine. A second factor is the more ecumenical atmosphere existing worldwide between Jews and Christians. Sympathetic treatments of Jesus by several Jewish scholars, especially that by Martin Buber, have encouraged open and frank discussion of the issues.

This Jewish interest in Jesus has been described in the following way by Rabbi David Polish: "Ever since new Israel began, a special interest in Jesus has been manifested. This does not indicate, as some Christian theologians have wishfully stated, a turning toward Christianity. It does, however, show that in the free atmosphere of Israel, a new approach towards Jesus, removed from the realm of polemics or interpretation common to medieval Judaism, is taking place. It is to be expected that in the land where Jesus lived and from which the Christian message went forth, a deep interest should be stirred among Jews" (*The Eternal Dissent,* 207).

Some analogies between the life and fate of German Jews during World War II and that of Jesus have been noted as a factor contributing to this interest in Jesus. "The Nazarene's fervour, his love of his country and people and his tragic death have endeared him particularly to Jewish thinkers of the Auschwitz generation" (Pinchas E. Lapide, *Journal of Theology for Southern Africa,* V [Dec., 1973] 51).

The sense of kinship with Jesus can be seen in this evaluation by Martin Buber contained in the preface to his *Two Ways of Faith:* "Since early youth I have sensed in Jesus my great brother. That Christendom considers him God and Saviour, I always deemed a fact of supreme importance which I must seek to comprehend for his sake and for my own. . . . I am more certain than ever that he deserves a place of honour in the religious history of Israel, and that this place cannot be defined by any of the customary categories." In his recent book, *Brother Jesus,* Schalom Ben-Chorin has written: "For this our brother Jesus has been dead for us, and has now come back to life." Of this kinship with Jesus, Buber has written further: "We Jews know Jesus in a way—in the impulses and emotions of his essential Jewishness—that remains inaccessible to the Gentiles subject to him" (*Werke,* III, 957).

Several Jewish authors have written novels about Jesus, among them Scholem Asch, Ahoron A. Kabak, and Max Brod. Asch's book, *The Nazarene,* met with rather mixed Jewish reaction partially due to its highly favorable portrait of Jesus and partially due to its portrayal of the Jewish role in the death of Jesus.

Courses on Jesus and Christianity are now offered at the Hebrew University in Jerusalem and other Israeli institutions of higher learning where they enjoy popularity. But instruction about Jesus is not limited to the upper educational levels. Exposure to the life and teachings of Jesus is now a commonplace for the average Israeli student.

In assessing the importance of this Jewish interest in Jesus, Pinchas E. Lapide has written: "One may say that while the Israeli books on Jesus of one or two decades ago merely expressed academic or historic curiosity, those since the late '60's show a growing self-identification of their authors with the life, thought and fate of their Galilean compatriot. At a time when Christianity's Christ is being demoted by Paul Tillich to 'essential manhood in existence;' when Gerhard Ebeling obfuscates him into 'the basic situation of man as word-situation;' when Rudolf Bultmann and his school seem bent on demythologizing him out of all reality, it is refreshing to see the Jesus of Judaism take on new substance and credibility in the literature of his native land" (*Journal of Theology for Southern Africa,* 56).

In this chapter, we can discuss at length only two major Jewish treatments of Jesus—the first major scholarly study of the twentieth century and the most recent presentation. However, two other works on Jesus should be mentioned at this point: the first is David Flusser's *Jesus* published in 1969. Flusser says he wrote his book primarily "to show that it is possible to write the story of Jesus' life." For Flusser, Jesus was a religious genius whose personality makes it impossible to explain him purely on the basis of the psychological and cultural influences exerted upon him. Jesus was the great preacher, unique in Jewish thought, whose call to unconditional love went beyond anything found in the contemporary Judaism of his day.

Israeli Supreme Court Justice Haim Cohn has written a book, *The Trial and Death of Jesus,* which explores the issue most troubling to Jewish-Christian relationships throughout the centuries. Cohn argues that the Gospel accounts which depict a trial and condemnation of Jesus by the Sanhedrin on the night before the crucifixion cannot be historical. Cohn concludes that many factors argue against the historicity of the trial as depicted. (1) It is doubtful if the Sanhedrin would have undertaken any investigation on behalf of the hated Pontius Pilate. (2) A trial after sundown is most unlikely especially on the eve of Passover when Jews would have been busy with ritual preparations for the celebration. (3) Any condemnation would have required two truthworthy witnesses. Cohn contends that the Jewish leadership was not interested in securing Jesus' death. "There can, I submit, be only one thing in which the whole Jewish leadership of the day can have been, and indeed was, vitally interested: and that was to prevent the crucifixion of a Jew by the Romans, and, more particularly, of a Jew who enjoyed the love and affection of the people" (115). The high priest and the Sadducean Sanhedrin set out, according to Cohn, to support and save the widely popular Jesus from the Romans in order to help salvage their own sagging reputations among the people. Thus the Sanhedrin's actions with Jesus were intended to save him. It first examined witnesses to find men who could testify in his favor before the Romans. Finding none, it sought to persuade Jesus to plead not guilty before Pilate, but he refused. When Jesus refused to cooperate and bow to the authority of the Sanhedrin, there was nothing that could be done to prevent the Roman trial from taking its course and Jesus from being condemned for the political crime of sedition.

The first major objective, scholarly study of Jesus by a Jewish academian was Joseph Klausner's *Jesus of Nazareth: His Life, Times, and Teaching*, first published in Hebrew in 1922. The English translation appeared in 1925. His statement of the purpose in writing the book is worth quoting in part.

Above all things, the writer wished to provide in Hebrew for Hebrews a book which shall tell the history of the Founder of Christianity along the lines of modern criticism, without either the exaggeration and legendary accounts of the evangelists, or the exaggeration and the legendary and depreciatory satires of such books as the *Tol'doth Yeshu.* . . . Of the necessity for such a book it is needless to speak at length: it is enough to say that there has never yet been in Hebrew any book on Jesus the Jew which had not either a Christian propagandist aim—to bring Jews to Christianity, or a Jewish religious aim—to render Christianity obnoxious to Jews (11).

Klausner first provides a thorough examination of all the ancient sources about Jesus—Jewish, Roman, Christian—analyzing them in terms of bias and historicity. He examines their origin, their nature, and intent. Just as he notes the Christian tendencies and theologizing in early Christian traditions about Jesus, so he points out the tendencies and unreliability of much in the Jewish references, and especially so in the medieval Jewish accounts and narratives about Jesus.

The author's survey of the history of the study of the life of Jesus is an admirable historical essay. Though briefer than that of Schweitzer, it is more comprehensive in the number of scholars surveyed, especially with regard to Jewish writings about Jesus, an area almost totally neglected by Schweitzer.

Klausner then surveys the political, economic, religious, and intellectual conditions of the period from Pompey's conquest of Jerusalem till the destruction of the temple (63 B.C.–A.D. 70). It is a survey still worth the reading.

In describing the childhood and youth of Jesus, Klausner argues that "Jesus was as legitimate as any Jewish child in Galilee . . . [and] there is scant support for the theory . . . that Jesus may have been of Gentile origin" (232-33). Klausner was refuting the idea widely discussed in German literature at the turn of the century, namely, that Jesus was of Aryan extraction and therefore Gentile. The genealogical references in Matthew and Luke, Klausner argues, were the product of the church's desire to claim that Jesus was the messiah from the stock of Jesse. The virgin birth stories are the product of the later church's desire to present Jesus as the divine Son of God. Although his father died when Jesus was still young, Klausner claims "that his father's memory was more precious to him than his living mother, who did not understand him and whom he turned away when she and his brothers came to take possession of him" (235).

The natural environment of Galilee and Nazareth exerted the first great influence on Jesus.

Jesus: The Jew from Galilee

There, cut off by mountains from the great world, wrapped up in natural beauty, a beauty tender and peaceful, sorrowful in its peacefulness, surrounded by peasants who tilled the soil, with few necessities in life—there, Jesus could not help being a dreamer, a visionary, whose thoughts turned not on his people's future (he was far removed from their political conflicts), nor on the heavy Roman yoke (which had scarcely touched him); his thoughts turned, rather, on the sorrows of the individual soul and on the "Kingdom of Heaven," a kingdom not of this world. ... This Nazareth, tightly enclosed within its hills, hearing but a faint, distant echo of wars and conflicts, a charming corner, hidden away and forgotten, could create only a dreamer, one who would reform the world not by revolt against the power of Rome, not by national insurrection, but by the kingdom of heaven, by the inner reformation of the *individual* (236-37).

A second influence on the youthful Jesus was the Hebrew scriptures.

His was an active mind and a fervid imagination, and the study (by his own reading or from the lips of others) of the books of the Prophets set his spirit aflame. The stern reproofs of the "First Isaiah," the divine consolations of the "Second Isaiah," the sorrows of Jeremiah, the soaring vision and stern wrath of Ezekiel, the sighs and laments of the Psalms, the promises foreseen in Daniel (and, perhaps, the *Book of Enoch*), together with those portions of the Pentateuch, full of the love of God and the love of man—all moved him to rapture and enthusiasm, penetrated his soul and enriched his spirit (237).

A third influence on Jesus was the life of the Galileans. Following the death of Herod and the census of Quirinius, Galilee became a "boiling cauldron of rebels, malcontents and ardent 'seekers after God.'" As the result of taxation, rebellions, and disease the people lived a hard life. They looked forward to the messianic age when there would be an end to all sorrows and pains, all servitude and ungodliness.

Jesus, who was one of the people and lived among them, knew their distress and believed too in the prophetic promises and consolations, certainly meditated much on present conditions, and his imagination pictured for him in glowing colours the redemption, both political and spiritual.

As one of the "meek upon earth," the prevailing element with him was the spiritual side of the messianic idea, that of redemption (237).

At the baptism—the most decisive event in his life—Jesus came to believe he was the messiah. "Was there any reason why he, great and imaginative dreamer that he was, he who felt himself so near to God, he who was so filled with the spirit of the prophets, he who felt with his every instinct that what above all things was wanted was repentance and good works—was there any reason why *he* should not be the imminent Messiah? Perhaps his very name 'Jesus,' 'he shall save,' may have moved this simple villager to believe that he was the redeemer" (252).

Certain differences separated Jesus, the Galilean itinerant, from the Rabbis and homilists of his day. (1) The main purport of his teaching was the near approach of the messiah and the kingdom of heaven. For them, this was secondary. (2) The Pharisees taught the observance of the ceremonial laws. Jesus taught scarcely anything beyond the moral law and this generally in parables. (3) Jesus relied but slightly on scriptures in his teaching, whereas for the Pharisees, the basic teaching method was exposition of the scriptures and their interpretation. (4) Jesus was a worker of miracles; for him teaching and miracles possessed equal importance (264-67).

Jesus always called himself the "Son of man," that is, "simple flesh and blood." Jesus did, in using this term of himself, partially divulge his messiahship, especially for those who were familiar with the Son of man passages in Daniel and Enoch (256-57).

The miracles of Jesus are divided by Klausner into five types: (1) "Miracles due to a wish to fulfil some statement in the Old Testament or to imitate some Prophet"; (2) "Poetical descriptions which, in the minds of the disciples, were transformed into miracles"; (3) "Illusions;" (4) "Acts only apparently miraculous"; and (5) "The curing of numerous 'nerve cases' " (267-71).

In his life, "Jesus remained steadfast to the old *Torah:* till his dying day he continued to observe the ceremonial laws like a true Pharisaic Jew" (275). "Although Jesus never ventured wholly to contradict the Law of Moses and the teaching of the Pharisees, there yet was in his teaching the nucleus of such a contradiction" (248). The activity of Jesus and his disciples did, however, raise some doubt about his total obedience to the demands of the Torah. "The Pharisees and the local authorities were ... displeased by his consorting with 'publicans and sinners,' and by his disciples' abstention from fasting and their frequenting the publicans' banquets" (277). His healing on the Sabbath when life was not endangered was an "important landmark in Jesus' career." The Pharisees, the leaders of Jewish democracy, viewed such action with disfavor and "instilled into the people a dislike for Jesus" (279).

Jesus selected close disciples, first four (260) and then perhaps twelve to be associated with him. His sending out of the disciples to preach the coming of the kingdom and the need for repentance and good works was due to the fact that his enemies had become numerous and "Jesus felt the fatigue of constant teaching" (285).

Jesus' final break with the Pharisees came when he taught his disciples that there is nothing from without that could defile a man. "Thus Jesus would abrogate not only fasting, and decry the value of the washing of hands in the 'tradition of the elders' or in current traditional teaching, but would even permit (though he does this warily and only by hints) the foods forbidden in the Law of Moses" (291). The Pharisees came to view Jesus as a "sorcerer, a false prophet, a beguiler and one who led men astray (as the *Talmud* describes him), and it was a religious duty to put him to death. He was compelled to escape" (293).

In withdrawal, at Caesarea Philippi, Jesus' made known his messiahship to his disciples but taught them that he must suffer. He realized his coming suffering because he had seen the fate of John the Baptist, because he was presently being persecuted and opposed, and because he must undergo the messianic pangs. The idea of a messiah who should be put to death was incomprehensible to the Jews and to Jesus; therefore Jesus may have spoken of his sufferings to the disciples but not of his death. He went to Jerusalem where he believed "he should suffer greatly but would, in the end, be victorious and be recognized by the crowds of people who had come up to the Passover, as the Messiah" (302). The final revelation of his messiahship must "be done in Jerusalem, the Holy City, where the greatest publicity was possible, and not in an out-of-the-way corner such as Upper Galilee" (303).

Jesus revealed himself as the messiah in the gates of the city in his entry into Jerusalem and sought a dramatic means to reveal his messiahship within the city. "What public-religious deed could better secure publicity than some great deed in the Temple, the most sacred of places, which now, in the days immediately before the Passover, was crammed with Jews from every part of the world? Jesus resolves, therefore, to purify the Temple" (313). In doing so, Jesus was forbidding much of what the Mishnah forbade when it denounced using the temple as a shortcut; in other words, his act had some legal basis. "Both the act and the sentiment gained the approbation of the people; but the priests were enraged" (315). When Jesus and his disciples left Jerusalem after cleansing the temple, they "were satisfied with what they had accomplished in, or near the Temple: they had aroused popular indignation against their leaders, they had won popular approval and created an impression" (316).

Jesus, however, was shortly to lose his popular support. How? In his response to the question of paying tribute to Caesar, Jesus convinced the people that he "was not their expected redeemer who would free them from the Roman-Edomite yoke" (318). In other words, he failed to fulfill the political expectations of messiahship.

It was Judas' disappointment with Jesus and his desire to

turn the "deceiver" over to his just reward that led him to betray Jesus. As Klausner describes Judas' sentiments, these seem to be a reflection of the rejection of Jesus by the general population intensified by Judas' repudiation of his previous commitments.

He was gradually convinced that Jesus was not always successful in healing the sick; that Jesus feared his enemies and persecutors, and sought to escape and evade them; that there were marked contradictions in Jesus' teaching. One time he taught the observance of the Law in its minutest detail, ordaining the offering of sacrifices and submitting to priestly examination, and so forth; while at other times he permitted forbidden foods, paid little respect to Sabbath observance and the washing of hands, and hinted that "the new wine must be put in new bottles." One time he deferred to public opinion and paid the Temple half-shekel, and refused to countenance or discountenance the payment of tribute to Caesar; while another time he inveighs against the Temple and the best of the nation and the nation's rulers. One time he says, "Whosoever is not against us is for us," and another time, "Every one who is not with me is against me." One time he ordains, "Strive not against evil," while another time he himself rises up against the traffickers and moneychangers in the Temple and takes the law into his own hands. One time he says that a man must give all his goods to the poor, and another time he allows himself to be anointed with oil of myrrh, worth three hundred dinars.

What was more, this "Messiah" neither would nor could deliver his nation, yet he arrogated to himself the role of "the Son of man coming with the clouds of heaven," asserting that he should sit at the right hand of God in the Day of Judgment, daring to say of the Temple, the most sacred place in the world, that not one stone of it should remain upon another and, actually, that he would destroy it and in its place raise up another after three days!

Judas Iscariot became convinced that here was a false Messiah or a false prophet, erring and making to err, a beguiler and one who led astray, one whom the Law commanded to be killed, one to whom the Law forbade pity or compassion or forgiveness. Till such time as Jesus divulged his messianic claims to the disciples at Caesarea Philippi, Judas had not thought to find in Jesus more than might be found in any Pharisaic Rabbi or, at the most, in a Jewish prophet. But after this revelation to the disciples at Caesarea, and to the entire people at Jerusalem, Judas expected that in the Holy City, the centre of the religion and the race, Jesus would demonstrate his claims by mighty works, that he would destroy the Romans and bring the Pharisees and Sadducees to naught; then all would acknowledge his messianic claims and all would see him in his pomp and majesty as the "final saviour."

But what, in fact, did Judas see? No miracles (Matthew alone tells how Jesus healed the blind and lame in the temple, matters unknown to Mark), no mighty deeds, no one is subdued by him, the mighty Messiah escapes nightly to Bethany; except for "bold" remarks against the tradition of the elders and vain arrogance, Jesus reveals no plan by which he will effect the redemption. Was it not, then, a "religious duty" to deliver up such a "deceiver" to the government and so fulfil the law: Thou shalt exterminate the evil from thy midst [Deut 13:2-12] (324-25).

The death of Jesus took him by surprise. He had no foreknowledge of his impending death and did not anticipate it. He sensed he needed armed protection against his enemies and thus "prepared himself and his disciples for armed opposition in the time of need" (see Luke 22:36-38). "He dreaded suffering and persecution and like everyone of delicate susceptibilities he had a deeply disturbing premonition of impending trouble" (331). When the attempt at armed resistance in the garden failed to do more than wound one of the police, the disciples were seized with fear and fled. Jesus was taken to the high priest for "trial."

The trial of Jesus before the Sanhedrin, according to Klausner, was not a trial proper but only a preliminary examination which led to his being turned over to Pilate for trial. This hearing was conducted by only a few of the priestly caste—the aristocratic Sadduccees—and much of their action was taken out of fear of Pilate. Being practical politicians they took into account the national danger involved in not turning over Jesus.

There was no real justice in the case: neither the Sanhedrin nor Pilate probed deeply enough to discover that Jesus was no rebel; and a Sadducaean Court of law would not pay scrupulous regard to the fact whether or not Jesus was a "blasphemer," or "false prophet," or an inciter to idolatry, in the Biblical or *Mishnaic* sense. But when or where *has* ideal justice prevailed!

Of the two charges which the Sanhedrin brought against Jesus—blasphemy and Messianic pretensions—Pilate took account of the second only. Jesus was the "King-Messiah" and so, from Pilate's standpoint (since he could have no notion of the spiritual side to the Hebrew messianic idea), he was "king of the Jews." This was treason against the Roman Emperor for which the *Lex Juliana* knew but one punishment—death; and the prescribed death of rebel traitors was—crucifixion (350).

How does one explain the empty tomb and the resurrection appearances? Certainly deception on behalf of the disciples is no answer. The church was not founded on trickery and fraud. Klausner explains the events as follows:

Deliberate imposture is not the substance out of which the religion of millions of mankind is created. We must assume that the owner of the tomb, Joseph of Arimathaea, thought it unfitting that one who had been crucified should remain in his own ancestral tomb. Matthew alone tells us that the tomb was new, hewn out of the rock specially for Jesus the Messiah (just as the ass's colt on which Jesus rode was one on which none other had ever sat). Joseph of Arimathaea, therefore, secretly removed the body at the close of Sabbath and buried it in an unknown grave; and since he was, according to the Gospels, "one of the disciples of Jesus," or "one who was looking for the kingdom of God," there was some measure of truth in the report spread by the Jews, though it was, in the main, only the malicious invention of enemies unable to explain the "miracle."

The fact of the women going to anoint the body is proof that neither they nor the other disciples expected the resurrection, and that Jesus had not told them beforehand that he would rise again. Mark, the oldest of the Gospels, says that the women were *afraid* to say that they had found the tomb empty and that an angel had appeared to them. It should also be remembered that one of those who saw the angel was Mary Magdalene "from whom Jesus cast out seven devils," *i.e.*, a woman who had suffered from hysterics to the verge of madness. In the end she could not restrain herself and told what she had seen.

Then the Apostles, with Peter at their head, remembered Jesus' words, that "he would go before them to Galilee." Judas Iscariot, of course, had left them. Matthew reports that he repented his treachery, returned the thirty pieces of silver, and, like Ahitophel, hanged himself. Another account tells how he did not commit suicide but died a horrible death "at the hands of heaven.". . .

After his death, and after the women had, at last, related the vision which they had seen, first Peter and then the other disciples also saw Jesus in a vision (as did Paul later), when they went to the appointed mountain in Galilee. . . . It is impossible to suppose that there was any conscious deception; the nineteen hundred years' faith of millions is not founded on deception. There can be no question but that some of the ardent Galilaeans saw their Lord and Messiah in a vision. That the vision was spiritual and not material is evident from the way Paul compares his own vision with those seen by Peter and James and the other apostles. . . . Consequently the vision seen by the disciples, a vision which Paul deliberately compares with his own, was a spiritual vision and no more. This vision became the basis of Christianity; it was treated as faithful proof of the Resurrection of Jesus, of his Messiahship, and of the near approach of the kingdom of heaven. But for this vision the memory of Jesus might have been wholly forgotten or preserved only in a collection of lofty ethical precepts and miracle stories.

Could the bulk of the Jewish nation found its belief on such a corner-stone? (357-59).

Klausner concludes his work with a discussion of the teachings of Jesus and why Christianity was found unacceptable to the Jews of his day. Klausner stresses the fact that Jesus was always a "Jew to his fingertips." His mission was only to Jews. His teachings were Jewish. "In all this Jesus is the most Jewish of Jews, more Jewish than Simeon ben Shetah, more Jewish even than Hillel" (374). Yet in Jesus, one finds an exaggerated Judaism, a stress on the moral ideals in the form of such an extremist and individualistic ethic that neither society nor nation could endure their implementation. Jesus' attitude toward the ceremonial laws was such as to make them of secondary importance and almost to nullify them. But no people, no nation can endure without them. "The nation as a whole could only see in such public ideals as those of Jesus, an abnormal and even dangerous phantasy." Jesus' teachings in this exaggerated form—this radicalization of ethics—would have had the effort of negating "everything that had vitalized Judaism; . . . it brought Judaism to such an extreme that it became, in a sense, *non-Judaism*. . . . Judaism brought forth Christianity in its first form (the teaching of Jesus), but it thrust aside its daughter when it saw that she would slay the mother with a deadly kiss" (376).

Secondly, Jesus possessed an exaggerated sense of nearness to God which gave the impression that there was one man with whom God was exceptionally intimate beyond any other. Such a view of intimacy with God by one man Judaism could not accept. In addition, Jesus spoke of God as if all—good and evil—are of the same worth in God's sight. Such a view destroys the idea of God as a God of justice, as a God of history. This Judaism could not accept.

Judaism is a national life, a life which the national religion and human ethical principles (the ultimate object of every religion) embrace without engulfing. Jesus came and thrust aside all the requirements of the national life; it was not that he set them apart and relegated them to their separate sphere in the life of the nation; he ignored them completely; in their stead he set up nothing but an ethico-religious system bound up with his conception of the Godhead.

In the self-same moment he both annulled *Judaism* as the *life-force* of the Jewish nation, and also the nation itself as a nation. For a religion which possesses only a certain conception of God and a morality acceptable to *all* mankind, does not belong to any special nation, and, consciously or unconsciously, breaks down the barriers of nationality. This inevitably brought it to pass that his people, Israel, rejected him. In its deeper consciousness the nation felt that then, more than at any other time, they must not be swallowed up in the great cauldron of nations in the Roman Empire, which were decaying for lack of God and of social morality (390).

Finally there was the "self-abnegation" taught by Jesus. Jesus was not an ascetic like John the Baptist, but he adopted, after the beginnings of his persecution by the Pharisees and the Herodians, a negative attitude toward the life of this present world. But Judaism assumed a life-affirming attitude. Jesus' belief in the nearness of the end led to this extremist ascetic system. "He cared not for reforming the world or civilisation" (397). To adopt such a negating attitude would have led Judaism to remove itself from the whole sphere of ordered national and human existence, to give up its national world outlook. Judaism could not accede to such a monastic, ascetic ideal which to it has ever been foreign. Klausner concludes with a positive appreciation of Jesus' ethical teachings and of him as a teacher.

Jesus is, for the Jewish nation, *a great teacher of morality and an artist in parable.* He is *the* moralist for whom, in the religious life, morality counts as—everything. Indeed, as a consequence of this extremist standpoint his ethical code has become simply an ideal for the isolated few, a "Zukunfts-Musik," an ideal for "the days of the Messiah," when an "end" shall have been made of this "old world," this present social order. It is no ethical code for the nations and the social order of to-day, when men are still trying to find the way to that future of the Messiah and the Prophets, and to the "kingdom of the Almighty" spoken of by the *Talmud,* an ideal which is of "this world" and which, gradually and in the course of generations, is to take shape in this world.

But in his ethical code there is a sublimity, distinctiveness and originality in form unparalleled in any other Hebrew ethical code; neither is there any parallel to the remarkable art of his parables. The shrewdness and sharpness of his proverbs and his forceful epigrams serve, in an exceptional degree, to make ethical ideas a popular possession. If ever the day should come and this ethical code be stripped of its wrappings of miracles and mysticism, the Book of the Ethics of Jesus will be one of the choicest treasures in the literature of Israel for all time (414).

Professor Geza Vermes, in his *Jesus the Jew,* has developed a rather new approach to the question of Jesus' relationship to the Judaism of his day and to the issue of the typological category most useful in understanding Jesus within the Jewish life and culture of his day. Scholars have seen Jesus as a Rabbi, a Pharisee, a Prophet, an Essene, a Zealot, a Teacher, an apocalyptic visionary, or as a member of the *am-ha-aretz*—the people of the land. For Vermes, Jesus did not belong among the Pharisees, Essenes, Zealots, or Gnostics, but was one of the holy miracleworkers of Galilee. In other words, Jesus is best seen and understood against the background of a charismatic Judaism of the first century. "Everything combines, when approached from the viewpoint of a study of first-century A.D. Galilee, or of charismatic Judaism, or of his titles and their development, to place him in the venerable company of the Devout, the ancient Hasidim" (223). For Vermes then three lines of approach contribute to this view of Jesus: the character of first-century Galilean life and culture, the resemblances between the words and works of Jesus and those of some of the Hasidim, and the titles which were most likely applied to him during his lifetime either by himself or others.

First, how does Jesus fit into the context of first-century Galilean life from which he came? Galilee, in the period before the destruction of the temple, was a territory *sui generis*. "Not only did it have its own peculiar past, but its political, social and economic organization also contributed to distinguish it from the rest of Palestine. The conflict between Jesus and the religious and secular authority outside Galilee was at least in part due to the fact that he was, and was known to have been, a Galilean" (43-44).

Geographically, Galilee, the northernmost district of Palestine, was a "little island in the midst of unfriendly seas." It was basically an "autonomous and self-contained politico-ethnic unit" surrounded by Gentiles and heathen on the East, North, and West and separated from Judaea on the south by the Samaritans and the Hellenistic territory of Scythopolis, a Greek city-state of the Decapolis. Galilee's overwhelming Jewishness was a recent historical phenomenon. Only after the final triumph of the Maccabeans at the end of the second century B.C., were the Galileans annexed to the Jewish state and issued an ultimatum to "be circumcised and to live in accordance with the laws of the Jews" (44).

Governmentally, Galilee at the time of Jesus was still ruled by a descendant of Herod and was spared the humiliation of direct rule by the Romans. Galilee was reasonably populous and wealthy with a "self-sufficiency which, with the legacy of its history and the unsophisticated simplicity of its life, is likely to have nourished the pride and independence of its inhabitants" (46).

Galilee was also a hotbed of revolutionary and rebel movements. The struggle against the Roman Empire was a "full-scale Galilean activity in the first century A.D." (47). The major Jewish revolts against the Romans were led by Galileans but in particular by the members of one Galilean family, that of Ezekias who first led a revolt against Herod's rule in about 47 B.C. and whose descendants were prime movers in the revolt of A.D. 66. Thus in the first century, the word "Galilean" had taken on the dark connotation of revolutionary. In addition to being strong nationalists, the Galileans were "quarrelsome and aggressive among themselves" but were ones who "preferred honour to financial gain" (48).

In rabbinical sources, the portrait of a northerner— Galilean—shows him "as a figure of fun, an ignoramus, if not both" (52). The Galilean did not speak correct Aramaic, was generally a religiously uneducated person, and was rather loose in his attitudes toward such matters as temple sacrifices and offerings, levitical laws of cleanness and uncleanness, and to the rabbinic code of proper behavior. Pharisees were not a dominant element in Galilee, and in fact it seems that the Pharisaic presence and impact on Galilee postdates the first century or at least the time of Jesus' ministry. The Pharisees with whom Jesus is shown in conflict must therefore have been foreign—that is, Judaean. Thus Jerusalem and southern opposition to Jesus was due to the fact that as a Galilean he was a political suspect and a religious nonconformist; that is, he was a victim "to a sentiment of superiority on the part of the intellectual *élite* of the metropolis towards unsophisticated provincials" (57). Could anything good come out of Galilee?

Secondly, how is Jesus related to the charismatic Judaism of his day? Vermes analyzes the texts which discuss two such charismatic holy men—Honi, called the Circle-Drawer by the rabbis and the Righteous by Josephus, a first century B.C. saint, and Hanina ben Dosa who lived before the fall of Jerusalem in A.D. 70. Both of these were probably Galilean; the first not absolutely for sure but the latter undoubtedly.

Honi was a man to whom tradition and his contemporaries ascribed power over natural phenomenon; he possessed among other things, the power to cause rain. Hanina was a holy man possessed by the power to cure, even from a distance, to deliver people in physical peril, and to influence natural phenomena. Hanina gave expression to the Hasidic piety with its detachment from possessions, a lack of interest in legal and ritual affairs, and an exclusive concentration on moral questions. These Hasidim spoke of their relationship to God in terms of father-son and could be and were called sons of God. They were also understood as prophetic figures, heirs to an ancient prophetic tradition possessing powers which came from their immediate contact with God. As authoritative figures, they were addressed as "lord." As popular figures, the "image of the charismatic was inseparable from the figure of Elijah."

That a distinctive trend of charismatic Judaism existed during the last couple of centuries of the Second Temple is undeniable. These holy men were treated as the willing or unsuspecting heirs to an ancient prophetic tradition. Their supernatural powers were attributed to their immediate relation to God. They were venerated as a link between heaven and earth independent of any institutional mediation.

Moreover, although it would be forcing the evidence to argue that charismatic Judaism was exclusively a Northern phenomenon because Jesus, Hanina ben Dosa, and possibly Abba Hilkiah were Galileans, this religious trend is likely to have had Galilean roots. It is, in any case, safe and justifiable to conclude that the unsophisticated religious ambiance of Galilee was apt to produce holy men of the Hasidic type, and that their success in that province was attributable to the simple spiritual demands of the Galilean nature, and perhaps also to a lively local folk memory concerning the miraculous deeds of the great prophet Elijah (79-80).

The longest section of Vermes' book is a discussion of the titles applied to Jesus in the Synoptics Gospels in light of the use of these titles in first-century Judaism and particularly in a Galilean milieu. The object of this effort is to determine what Jesus' contemporaries thought of him and perhaps what Jesus thought of himself. The title "prophet," which is frequently applied to Jesus in the Synoptics, is considered an authentic title ascribed to Jesus during his ministry: "It seems to have been the description he himself preferred" (99). "The belief professed by his contemporaries that Jesus was a charismatic prophet rings so authentic, especially in the light of the Honi-Hanina cycle of traditions, that the correct historical question is not whether such an undogmatic Galilean concept was ever in vogue, but rather how, and under what influence, it was ever given an eschatological twist" (90). The eschatological twist is related, by Vermes, to the expectation of a prophetic revival hinted at in I Maccabees (4:46; 14:41) and Josephus, to the belief in the return of the prophet Elijah, and to the expectation of a coming prophet like Moses (Deuteronomy 18:18). Jesus' celibacy is explained on the basis of the general incompatibility between prophecy and marriage, a factor referred to in several rabbinic texts. The title prophet with regard to Jesus was not developed very intensively in early Christianity, in spite of its authenticity with reference to Jesus' career, because it could not be exploited in dogmatic terms and secondly because of the great number of pseudoprophets who appeared in conjunction with the first Jewish revolt against Rome.

The term "lord" is also assumed to be authentic in light of its usage in Aramaic sources. In fact, it appears to have been a frequent title utilized in the earliest Christian traditions. "In Jewish Aramaic the designation, '(the) lord,' is appropriate in connection with God, or a secular dignitary, or an authoritative teacher, or a person renowned for his spiritual or supernatural force" (121). "The title primarily links Jesus to his dual role of charismatic Hasid and teacher, and if the stress is greater in the earlier strata of the tradition, that is no doubt due to the fact that his impact as a holy man preceded that of teacher and founder of a religious community" (127).

Of the title "messiah" as applied to Jesus, Vermes writes: "Since the figure of the Messiah appears not to have been central to the teaching of Jesus, and since no record has survived of any hostile challenge concerning his Messianic status before his last days in Jerusalem; since, moreover, he deliberately withheld his approval of Peter's confession and, in general, failed to declare himself to be the Christ, there is every reason to wonder if he really thought of himself as such" (149). Such an argument does not deny that "Jesus' denial of Messianic aspirations failed to be accepted by his friends as well as his foes" (154). Vermes understands the early church's emphasis on Jesus as the messiah as due "to its psychological and polemical value in the Jewish-Christian debate" (155).

The importance of the title "Son of man" has dominated New Testament scholarship for generations. Vermes' analysis of the evidence offers a radical departure from previous research.

To sum up, there is no evidence whatever, either inside or outside the Gospels, to imply, let alone demonstrate, that "the *son of man*" was used as a title. There is, in addition, no valid argument to prove that any of the Gospel passages directly or indirectly referring to Daniel 7:13 may be traced back to Jesus. The only possible, indeed probable, genuine utterances are sayings independent of Daniel 7 in which, in accordance with Aramaic usage, the speaker refers to himself as the *son of man* out of awe, reserve or humility. It is this neutral speech-form that the apocalyptically-minded Galilean disciples of Jesus appear to have "eschatologized" by means of a midrash based on Daniel 7:13 (185-86).

Thus, according to Vermes, Jesus did not understand himself as nor refer to a Son of man figure who would appear as the apocalyptic judge or as a redemptive suffering one.

The use of the term "Son of God" in the Old Testament and rabbinic literature shows a wide range of usage: of angels, of the Israelite king, of Israelites or the people as a whole, of just men, and of the messiah as an epithet. Thus Vermes argues that there is no reason to deny the title to the historical Jesus but there, it "derives from his activities as a miracle-worker and exorcist, and from his own consciousness of an immediate and intimate contact with the heavenly Father" (211).

Thus for Vermes, Jesus was a first century Galilean Hasid, a miracle-worker, healer, and exorcist, who was referred to and known as a prophet, lord, and son of God. But he was more than an ordinary charismatic Hasid: "no objective and enlightened student of the Gospels can help but be struck by the incomparable superiority of Jesus" (224).

Second to none in profundity of insight and grandeur of character, he is in particular an unsurpassed master of the art of laying bare the inmost core of spiritual truth and of bringing every issue back to the essence of religion, the existential relationship of man and man, and man and God.

It should be added that in one respect more than any other he differed from both his contemporaries and even his prophetic predecessors. The prophets spoke on behalf of the honest poor, and defended the widows and the fatherless, those oppressed and exploited by the wicked, rich and powerful. Jesus went further. In addition to proclaiming these blessed, he actually took his stand among the pariahs of his world, those despised by the respectable. Sinners were his table-companions and the ostracised tax collectors and prostitutes his friends (224).

6. JESUS: THE PROCLAIMER CALLING TO DECISION

> The earliest Church resumed the message of Jesus and through its preaching passed it on. So far as it did only that, Jesus was to it a preacher and prophet. But Jesus was more than that to the Church: He was also the Messiah; hence that Church also proclaimed him, himself—and that is the essential thing to see. He who formerly had been the *bearer* of a message was drawn into it and became its essential *content. The proclaimer became the proclaimed.*—Rudolf Bultmann, *Theology of the New Testament*, Volume I (p. 33)

The most influential school in German New Testament scholarship during the twentieth century has centered around Rudolf Bultmann and his students. Bultmann repudiated the quest of the historical Jesus declaring it historically an impossibility and theologically an irrelevancy. However, out of Bultmann's circle of students there developed, during the 1950s, a so-called new quest of the historical Jesus. In this chapter, we will examine Bultmann's position as well as that of the new quest by the so-called post-Bultmannians.

In order to understand and appreciate Bultmann's position, several developments in New Testament studies and in philosophy and theology need to be noted since these form a background for Bultmann's approach.

The first of these is the development of New Testament form criticism. As a discipline, modern form criticism developed near the end of the nineteenth century, being first applied to classical and Germanic literature and then to the Old and New Testaments. Form criticism is an attempt to classify and study literature on the basis of genre analysis. That is, literary materials, on the basis of their form, structure, mood, and content, are divided into various genres and analyzed with regard to their use and function. Behind and involved in the concerns of genre analysis is the question of the genres' use and employment within the community which preserved them.

With regard to the New Testament Gospels, the following conclusions were drawn from the results of form critical studies: (1) The traditions in the Gospels originally circulated in the church as independent and unconnected units. Therefore the connections between the units (with the possible exception of the passion story) are not indigenous to the earliest form of the traditions. (2) The traditions that now make up the Gospels were preserved because they could be utilized by the church in its preaching, teaching, worship, and dialogue with non-Christians. (3) The traditions have been influenced by and are expressive of the faith of the early church in Christ the risen redeemer. (4) In the process of transmission, the traditions were sometimes molded, changed, and transformed by the faith of the church or the Gospel writers. (5) Traditions were sometimes created by the church or borrowed from non-Christian sources and baptized into the church's tradition. Bultmann was not only influenced by form critical studies but was also one of the main participants in development of the movement and methodological approach to the Gospels. His work, *The History of the Synoptic Traditions*, published in its first edition in 1921, represents in many ways the culmination of form critical study of the Gospels.

A second development reflected in Bultmann's approach was the revival of Reformation theology which is generally designated with the rubrics, neo-orthodoxy or dialectical theology. Karl Barth, the Swiss theologian, is generally considered the father of this theological movement and was certainly its most significant exponent. The rise of neo-orthodoxy is frequently associated with the publication of Barth's commentary on Romans published in 1919 against the background of World War I in Europe. In several ways, many of the conclusions concerning the historical Jesus which have characterized the neo-orthodox position were already articulated by Martin Kähler in a book published in Germany in 1892 and translated into English with the title *The So-Called Historical Jesus and the Historic, Biblical Christ.* Kähler argued against the possibility of rediscovering the Jesus of history and thus attacked and repudiated the nineteenth-century quest. Among other reasons, he argued that the kerygmatic nature of the Gospels, that is their preaching and confessional character, made it impossible to use the materials for biographical purposes. In this he anticipated the later conclusions of form criticism. Secondly, Kähler argued that the proper object of Christian faith is not the Jesus of history but the Christ of faith as preached in the church. Thirdly, he contended that to try to construct Christian faith around the historical Jesus or a Jesus reconstructed on the basis of a historical-critical study of the Gospels was to attempt to base faith on historical facts, a denial of the Reformation principle of salvation or justification by faith alone. Faith based on the historical Jesus would not be Christian faith but a Jesusology indistinguishable from idolatrous hero worship.

A third development was the rediscovery of the eschatological-apocalyptic orientation of Jesus' life and preaching. Johannes Weiss and Albert Schweitzer among others stressed the central importance of this perspective for any interpretation of the historical Jesus and his message. Bultmann took this emphasis seriously and sought to interpret the eschatological dimension in terms relevant to his understanding of modern man.

A fourth factor which contributed to Bultmann's interpretation of the New Testament was the rise of existentialist philosophy. The origin of existentialism is generally traced back to the thought of the Danish theologian Søren Kierkegaard. Bultmann was directly dependent, however, upon the thought of the German existentialist philosopher Martin Heidegger. Existentialist philosophy stresses man's need to affirm his authentic existence through decision and commitment by abandoning all security in an unreserved openness to the future. Bultmann claimed that existentialist philosophy and the New Testament are in this regard saying the same thing independently.

Bultmann's *Jesus and the Word* was originally published in Germany in 1926 but reflects an approach to Jesus which Bultmann has continued to hold throughout his teaching and preaching career. Being primarily an exposition of the teachings of Jesus, this work contains little discussion of the historical Jesus. So we shall turn to some other of Bultmann's writings for his statements about the historical Jesus.

Behind the kerygmatic Christ of the Gospels—the Christ of faith—stands a "concrete figure of history—Jesus of Nazareth. His life is more than a mythical event; it is a human life which ended in the tragedy of crucifixion" ("New Testament and Mythology," 34). If one asks Bultmann what might be known about the activity of the historical Jesus, he responds: "With a bit of caution we can say the following concerning Jesus' activity: Characteristic for him are exorcisms, the breech of the Sabbath commandment, the abandonment of ritual purifications, polemic against Jewish legalism, fellowship with outcasts such as publicans and harlots, sympathy for women and children; it can also be seen that Jesus was not an ascetic like John the Baptist, but gladly ate and drank a glass of wine. Perhaps we may add that he called disciples and assembled about himself a small company of followers—men and women" ("The Primitive Christian Kerygma," 22-23). How Jesus may have understood events in his own life is not open for our understanding. For example, the "Gospels furnish us with no biographical data on the basis of which one can decide what was in Jesus' mind when he went to his death" ("Is Jesus Risen as Goethe?" 233).

Why was Jesus drawn to Jerusalem at the end of his career? If the assumption is correct that "first and foremost his journey to Jerusalem was undertaken in order to confront the people there, in the holy city, with the message of the kingdom of God, and to summon them at the eleventh hour to make their decision"; if it is correct that "only on the journey with his followers to Jerusalem and the temple did Jesus seek the final decision," then he scarcely reckoned on execution at the hands of the Romans, but only on the imminent appearing of the kingdom of God. But these are all assumptions. What is certain is merely that he was crucified by the Romans, and thus suffered the death of a political criminal. This death can scarcely be understood as an inherent and necessary consequence of his activity; rather it took place because his activity was misconstrued as a political activity. In that case it would have been—historically speaking—a meaningless fate. We cannot tell whether or how Jesus found meaning in it. We may not veil from ourselves the possibility that he suffered a collapse ("The Primitive Christian Kerygma," 24).

To attempt an understanding of how Jesus may have viewed his death represents, for Bultmann, an illegitimate psychologizing of Jesus. Nonetheless, Bultmann does say in regard to the death of Jesus that "he knew himself to be sent by God and therefore also understood his destiny as determined by God" ("Is Jesus Risen as Goethe?" 233).

"Events" associated with Jesus, such as the virgin birth and the resurrection, must be understood as legendary. The virgin birth is the "legendary expression for faith's claim that the source of the meaning of the person of Jesus is not to be seen in his natural this-worldly origin. . . . The divine sonship of Christ consists in the fact that Jesus, in obedience to God as the Father . . . and in authority, proclaimed the Word of God which still encounters us today as his Word" ("Is Jesus Risen as Goethe?" 230). With regard to the resurrection, Bultmann says: "Both the legend of the empty tomb and the appearances insist on the physical reality of the risen body of the Lord," but a "corpse cannot come back to life or rise from the grave" (*Myth and Christianity*, 60). "An historical fact which involves a resurrection from the dead is utterly inconceivable" ("New Testament and Mythology," 39). "The reports of a bodily resurrection of Jesus are legends. But with that it is by no means said that the resurrection of Jesus is only the legendary concretization of an idea. The resurrection reports are the legendary concretization of the faith of the first Christian community in the risen Lord, the faith that God has exalted the crucified one as Lord" ("Is Jesus Risen as Goethe?" 237). "The real Easter faith is faith in the word of preaching which brings illumination. If the event of Easter Day is in any sense an historical event additional to the event of the cross, it is nothing else than the rise of faith in the risen Lord, since it was this faith which led to the apostolic preaching" ("New Testament and Mythology," 42). "Jesus is risen in the message of the church" ("Is Jesus Risen as Goethe?" 238).

Bultmann suggests that Jesus did not believe himself to be the messiah, but he considered this to be a matter of "secondary importance." "When we are dealing with the life and portrait of Jesus, we can only say of his preaching that he doubtless appeared in the consciousness of being commissioned by God to preach the eschatological message of the breaking-in of the Kingdom of God and the demanding but also inviting will of God. We may thus ascribe to him a prophetic consciousness, indeed, a 'consciousness of authority'" ("The Primitive Christian Kerygma," 23). "Jesus' preaching had 'kerygmatic' character. He did not appear as a teacher or rabbi, but as a prophet with an eschatological message, though he may also have made use of the doctrine and forms of rabbinic teaching for an interpretation of the will of God, the proclamation of which is intimately connected with the eschatological message" (27). Jesus' preaching however is not identical with the early kerygma of the church. Jesus did not preach the Christ-kerygma. Jesus' preaching must therefore be understood within the context of Judaism.

Over against the reproach that I conceive of Jesus as a Jew and assign him to the sphere of Judaism I must first of all simply ask: Was Jesus—the historical Jesus!—a Christian? Certainly not, if Christian faith is faith in him as the Christ. And even if he should have known that he was the Christ ("Messiah") and should actually have demanded faith in himself as the Christ, then he would still not have been a Christian and ought not to be described as the subject of Christian faith, though he is nevertheless its object (19).

In his book, *Primitive Christianity in its Contemporary Setting,* Bultmann discussed the proclamation of Jesus as a part of his discussion of Judaism.

Bultmann has described the preaching of Jesus in the following terms: "The preaching of Jesus is the eschatological message of the coming—more, of the breaking-in of the Kingdom of God. . . . For Jesus the eschatological proclamation goes hand in hand with the proclamation of the will of God, with the call to radical obedience to God's demands culminating in the commandment of love" ("The Primitive Christian Kerygma," 16).

Bultmann claims that for the early church's kerygma, only the "that" of the historical Jesus was of any importance. With this Bultmann's theology is in agreement. That is, the historicity of Jesus is of importance but not in terms of a portrait of or reconstructed Jesus of history.

Paul and John, each in his own way, indicate that we do not need to go beyond the "that." Paul proclaims the incarnate, crucified, and risen Lord; that is, his kerygma requires only the "that" of the life of Jesus and the fact of his crucifixion. He does not hold before his bearer's eyes a portrait of Jesus, the human person, apart from the cross (Gal. 3:1), and the cross is not regarded from a biographical standpoint but as saving event. . . . The eschatological and ethical preaching of the historical Jesus plays no role in Paul. John gives all due emphasis to the humanity of Jesus, but presents none of the characteristics of Jesus' humanity which could be gleaned, for example, from the Synoptic Gospels. The decisive thing is simply the "that" ("The Primitive Christian Kerygma," 20).

The really decisive thing is the *that* of Jesus' coming, not the *what,* that is, not the historical verifiable data of his life and work. Now it is uncontestable that in Paul and in the rest of the New Testament, except in the Synoptic Gospels, only the *that,* and not the *what,* plays a role. In the assertion of the *that,* the paradox is maintained that a historical figure, the person of Jesus of Nazareth, is at the same time the eschatological figure, the Lord Jesus Christ ("Is Jesus Risen as Goethe?" 231).

In Bultmann, one can see the full acceptance of three basic conclusions which had slowly developed out of the New Testament research and the quest for the historical Jesus in the nineteenth and the early part of the twentieth century as these found expression in critical scholarship. These general conclusions were: (1) The Gospel materials are kerygmatic, not biographical in nature; they have been influenced by and reflect the post-Easter faith of the early church. Therefore no biography or real presentation of the historical Jesus is possible even if this should be desirable. (2) The eschatological orientation of the early church and the preaching of Jesus cannot be ignored but must be confronted head on. Bultmann sought to preserve this eschatological emphasis but in terms of an existentialist reinterpretation. In the preaching of the word (the kerygma), man is confronted with the decisive eschatological event in the radical call to decision and authentic existence. "The proclamation of the church is an eschatological phenomenon in which Christ encounters us as present, and as final if this proclamation encounters us for the last time" ("Is Jesus Risen as Goethe?" 238). (3) Much of the New Testament is mythological reflecting an outmoded world view and a cosmological eschatology. To meet this issue, Bultmann proposed a hermeneutical approach called "demythologization." Such a methodology sought to preserve the kerygmatic message by interpreting the mythology in existential terms. "Whereas the older liberals used criticism to *eliminate* the mythology of the New Testament, our task today is to use criticism to *interpret* it" ("New Testament and Mythology," 12). The following statements illustrate Bultmann's view of myth, its importance, and its reinterpretation.

The cosmology of the New Testament is essentially mythical in character. The world is viewed as a three-storied structure, with the earth in the centre, the heaven above, and the underworld beneath. Heaven is the abode of God and of celestial beings—the angels. The underworld is hell, the place of torment. Even the earth is more than the scene of natural, everyday events, of the trivial round and common task. It is the scene of the supernatural activity of God and his angels on the one hand, and of Satan and his daemons on the other. These supernatural forces intervene in the course of nature and in all that men think and will and do. Miracles are by no means rare. Man is not in control of his own life. Evil spirits may take possession of Him. Satan may inspire him with evil thoughts. Alternatively, God may inspire his thought and guide his purposes. He may grant him heavenly visions. He may allow him to hear his word of succour or demand. He may give him the supernatural power of his Spirit. History does not follow a smooth unbroken course; it is set in motion and controlled by these supernatural powers. This aeon is held in bondage by Satan, sin, and death (for "powers" is precisely what they are), and hastens towards its end. That end will come very soon, and will take the form of a cosmic catastrophe. It will be inaugurated by the "woes" of the last time. Then the Judge will come from heaven, the dead will rise, the last judgment will take place, and men will enter into eternal salvation or damnation (1-2). . . .

The real purpose of myth is not to present an objective picture of the world as it is, but to express man's understanding of himself in the world in which he lives. Myth should be interpreted not cosmologically, but anthropologically, or better still, existentially (10). . . .

The importance of the New Testament mythology lies not in its imagery but in the understanding of existence which it enshrines (11). . . .

To de-mythologize is to deny that the message of Scripture and of the Church is bound to an ancient world-view which is obsolete (*Jesus Christ and Mythology*, 36).

Now to return to Bultmann's *Jesus and the Word*. As we have seen, Bultmann claimed that the preaching of Jesus centered in his eschatological message of the coming and breaking-in of the kingdom of God and his proclamation of the will of God. In *Jesus and the Word*, Bultmann discusses Jesus' message in terms of his teachings on the coming of the kingdom, the will of God, and God the remote and the near. By the message of Jesus, Bultmann was referring to what he called "the oldest layer of the synoptic tradition." This oldest layer is reached, according to Bultmann, by peeling away the later tradition. "Everything in the synoptics which for reasons of language or content can have originated only in Hellenistic Christianity must be excluded as a source for the teaching of Jesus." This brings one to the "Aramaic tradition of the oldest Palestinian community," but here again there are layers of traditions which reflect the interests of the church and its later development which must be removed to expose the oldest tradition. But here again some uncertainty remains, since one cannot be absolutely certain how far that tradition and "community preserved an objectively true picture of him and his message." However, "no sane person can doubt that Jesus stands as the founder behind the historical movement whose first distinct stage is represented by the oldest Palestinian community" (13).

As Bultmann expounds the teaching of Jesus on the kingdom of God, his emphasis fell upon the inauguration of the kingdom. "His message is based on the certainty: *the Kingdom of God is beginning, is beginning now!*" (30). Thus Bultmann does not accept the thoroughgoing eschatology of Weiss and Schweitzer in which the kingdom for Jesus was an event still entirely future though absolutely imminent.

The future Kingdom of God . . . is not something which is to come in the course of time, so that to advance its coming one can do something in particular, perhaps through penitential prayers and good works, which become superfluous in the moment of its coming. Rather, the Kingdom of God is a power *which, although it is entirely future, wholly determines the present*. It determines the present because it now compels man to decision; he is determined thereby either in this direction or in that, as chosen or as rejected, in his entire present existence. Future and present are not related in the sense that the Kingdom begins as a historical fact in the present and achieves its fulfillment in the future; nor in the sense that an inner, spiritual possession of personal attributes or qualities of soul constitutes a present hold on the Kingdom, to which only the future consummation is lacking. Rather the Kingdom of God is genuinely future, because it is not a metaphysical entity or condition, but the future action of God, which can be in no sense something given in the present. None the less this future determines man in his present, and exactly for that reason is true future—not merely something to come "somewhere, sometime," but destined for man and constraining him to decision.

The coming of the Kingdom of God is therefore not really an event in the course of time, which is due to occur sometime and toward which man can either take a definite attitude or hold himself neutral. Before he takes any attitude he is already constrained to make his choice, and therefore he must understand that just this necessity of decision constitutes the essential part of his human nature. Because Jesus sees man thus in a crisis of decision before God, it is understandable that in his thought the Jewish Messianic hope becomes the absolute certainty that in this hour the Kingdom of God is coming. If men are standing in the crisis of decision, and if precisely this crisis is the essential characteristic of their humanity, then every hour is the last hour, and we can understand that for Jesus the whole contemporary mythology is pressed into the service of this conception of human existence. Thus he understood and proclaimed his hour as the last hour (51-52).

The kingdom confronts man with the ultimate either-or and calls man to repentance and readiness for self-sacrifice in which every other interest disappears before the exclusiveness of the demand of God. The kingdom is proclaimed as eschatological deliverance. In his preaching, Jesus rejected the whole content of apocalyptic speculation, the calculation of the time and the watching for signs. For Jesus, the coming of the kingdom was for the benefit of the Jewish people though he stressed that the Jew as such has no claim before God.

Jesus was not only an eschatological prophet of the kingdom of God, he *"actually lived as a Jewish rabbi,"* teaching in the synagogue, gathering around him a circle of pupils, disputing along the same lines as Jewish rabbis, using the same methods of argument and the same turns of speech, and coining proverbs and parables (58). Jesus, in teaching the will of God, "conceived radically the idea of obedience" (73) and "demanded obedience without any secondary motive," such as rewards (79).

The will of God is then for Jesus as little a social or political program as it is either an ethical system which proceeds from an ideal of man and humanity or an ethic of value. He knows neither the conception of personality nor that of virtue; the latter word he does not even use, it is found first in Hellenistic Christianity. As he has no doctrine of virtue, so also he has none of duty or of the good. It is sufficient for a man to know that God has placed him under the necessity of decision in every concrete situation in life, in the here and now. And this means that he himself must know what is required of him, and that no authority and no theory can take from him this responsibility (108). . . .

Jesus thought of love neither as a virtue which belongs to the perfection of man, nor as an aid to the well-being of society, but as an overcoming of self-will in the concrete situation of life in which a man encounters other men. Hence Jesus' requirement of love cannot be more nearly defined in content, or be regarded as an ethical principle from which particular concrete requirements can be derived, as would be possible with the humanistic command of love, which depends on a well defined ideal of humanity. *What* a man must do in order to love his neighbor or his enemy is not stated. It is assumed that everyone can know that, and therefore Jesus' demand for love is no revelation of a new principle of ethics nor of a new conception of the dignity of man (112-13).

Jesus as the eschatological prophet proclaimed the coming kingdom and called for repentance and decision. Jesus as the Jewish rabbi preached radical obedience to the will of God. "How is the preaching of Jesus concerning the will of God related to his proclamation of the coming of the Kingdom? Or, as it could be phrased, how are Jesus the rabbi and Jesus the prophet related?" (120-21). Bultmann provides the following answer to this question, an answer which illustrates his existentialist interpretation of Jesus' message:

The one concern in this teaching was that man should conceive his immediate concrete situation as the decision to which he is constrained, and should decide in this moment for God and surrender his natural will. Just this is what we found to be the final significance of the eschatological message, that man *now* stands under the necessity of decision, that his "Now" is always for him the last hour, in which his decision against the world and for God is demanded, in which every claim of his own is to be silenced. Since, then, the message of the coming of the Kingdom and that of the will of God point men *to the present moment as the final hour* in the sense of the hour of decision, the two do form a unity, each is incomplete without the other (131).

In describing what he was doing in *Jesus and the Word*, Bultmann has said: "If I desire an encounter with the Jesus of history, it is true that I must rely on certain historical documents. Yet the study of those documents can bring us to an encounter with Jesus only as a phenomenon of past history. That was the aim and method of my *Jesus and the Word*. The Jesus of history is not kerygma, any more than my book was. For in the kerygma Jesus encounters us as the Christ—that is, as the eschatological phenomenon *par excellence*. . . . I am deliberately renouncing any form of encounter with a phenomenon of past history, including an encounter with the Christ after the flesh, in order to encounter the Christ proclaimed in the kerygma, which confronts me in my historic situation" ("A Reply," 117). Bultmann thus does here, as in other of his writings, admit some possibility of knowledge about the historical Jesus but denies anything beyond the "that" of Jesus to be of any significance for Christian faith. "It is therefore illegitimate to go behind the kerygma, using it as a 'source,' in order to reconstruct a 'historical Jesus' with his 'messianic consciousness,' his 'inner life' or his 'heroism.' That would be merely 'Christ after the flesh,' who is no longer. It is not the historical Jesus, but Jesus Christ, the Christ, preached, who is the Lord" ("The Historical Jesus and the Theology of Paul," 241).

Accepting such hypotheses, the Bultmann circle engaged in no quest for the historical Jesus until the mid-1950s. In 1953, Ernst Käsemann delivered a lecture in which he called

127

for a renewed interest in the earthly Jesus arguing that this was not only possible but also necessary if the church was to avoid finding itself committed to a mythological lord unrelated to the historicity of Jesus. For him, the issue is the question of whether there was continuity between the preaching of Jesus and the preaching faith of the early church.

Out of the obscurity of the life story of Jesus, certain characteristic traits in his preaching stand out in relatively sharp relief, and . . . primitive Christianity united its own message with these. The heart of our problem lies here: the exalted Lord has almost entirely swallowed up the image of the earthly Lord and yet the community maintains the identity of the exalted Lord with the earthly. . . . The question of the historical Jesus is, in its legitimate form, the question of the continuity of the Gospel within the discontinuity of the times and within the variation of the kerygma ("The Problem of the Historical Jesus," 46).

Käsemann thus stresses the continuity of the preaching of Jesus with the preaching of the early church—thus a point of contact between the kerygma of the early church and that of Jesus.

Ernst Fuchs suggested a second line of approach to the problem of the continuity between the earthly Jesus and the Christ of faith. Fuchs claims that in the actions of Jesus as well as in his message, Jesus' conduct manifests implicitly his own eschatological understanding of his person which became explicit in the preaching of the church. The church's kerygma and faith thus made explicit what was already implicit in Jesus' actions and words.

The first major study of the historical Jesus emanating from the Bultmann circle was Günther Bornkamm's *Jesus of Nazareth*. Bornkamm recognizes the difficulty of penetrating the Gospel traditions to discover something of the historical Jesus. "We possess no single word of Jesus and no single story of Jesus, no matter how incontestably genuine they may be, which do not contain at the same time the confession of the believing congregation or at least are embedded therein. This makes the search after the bare facts of history difficult and to a large extent futile" (14).

In spite of this interblending of the church's faith in the narration of Jesus' history, Bornkamm argues that two apparently conflicting characteristics are to be seen in the Gospels: "an incontestable loyalty and adherence to the word of Jesus, and at the same time an astonishing degree of freedom as to the original wording" (17). The degree of freedom exercised by the Gospel writers is evident in their "believing interpretation of the history and person of Jesus." The words of Jesus "spoken while he was here on earth . . . soon took on a post-Easter form." In addition, "words spoken by the Risen Christ" originally "declared to the Church by her inspired prophets and preachers" have been read back into the tradition and "became words of the earthly Jesus" (19). The task of the interpreter is "to seek the history *in* the Kerygma of the Gospels, and in this history to seek the Kerygma" (21). In spite of the formation of the traditions in the light of the post-Easter faith, the Gospels show an interest in the pre-Easter Jesus for the church "made herself contemporary with her earthly pre-Easter Lord. . . . She made herself one with those who did not already live by faith, but who at the beginning were called to obedience and faith by the word of Jesus" (23-24). In telling the story of Jesus in brief anecdotes, the church gave expression to the person and history of Jesus in each unit. Understood as expressive of the person and history of Jesus, the "primitive tradition of Jesus is brim full of history" (26).

Bornkamm can proceed to speak of the "historically indisputable traits" and the "rough outlines of Jesus' person and history" (53). The birth narratives cannot be used as the basis for historical assertions. Jesus' home was semipagan, despised Galilee. His native town was Nazareth. His family belonged to the Jewish part of the population of Galilee. Jesus' father was a carpenter, and possibly he was himself. We know the names of his parents and his brothers who were not originally believers. Jesus' mother tongue was Aramaic. As a Jewish rabbi, Jesus was certainly acquainted with

Hebrew, and he and his disciples may have had some knowledge of Greek. His baptism by John the Baptist is "one of the most certainly verified occurrences of his life." Jesus began his work in Galilee, like John, as a prophet of the coming kingdom of God, but unlike John did not practice baptism but relied on "spoken word and helping hand." There is no certainty about the length of his ministry. People flocked to him; disciples followed him; and enemies arose to oppose him. The last decisive turning point in his life was the "resolution to go to Jerusalem with his disciples in order to confront the people there with his message in face of the coming kingdom of God. At the end of this road is his death on the cross." Bornkamm recognized the meager character of this outline but suggested that "it contains most important information about the life story of Jesus and its stages" (53-55).

Bornkamm considers Jesus' activity and preaching under the rubrics "rabbi" and "prophet." Jesus however superceded the normal category of prophet since he "never speaks of his calling, and nowhere does he use the ancient, prophetic formula" (Thus says the Lord) (56). Jesus was also a rabbi "who proclaims the divine law, who teaches in synagogues, who gathers disciples, and who debates with other scribes in the manner of their profession and under the same authority of scripture" (57). But Jesus differed from the ordinary rabbi in that he taught not just in synagogues, had followers who differed from ordinary rabbinic disciples, and taught with an immediacy and authority to which nothing in contemporary Judaism corresponds. Jesus' directness and authority were part of the mystery of his personality and influence, the mystery of making present the reality of God which signifies the end of the world in which it takes place.

Was Jesus the messiah, and did he so understand himself? In confronting this issue, Bornkamm says "Jesus does not directly make this claim, but lets it be absorbed in his words and works without justifying either in virtue of some office well known to his hearers, and without confirming the authority which the people are willing to acknowledge in him" (170). "There is in fact not one single certain proof of Jesus' claiming for himself one of the Messianic titles which tradition has ascribed to him." "We should, therefore not speak about Jesus' non-Messianic history before his death, but rather of a movement of broken Messianic hopes, and of one who was hoped to be the Messiah, but who not only at the moment of failure, but in his entire message and ministry, disappointed the hopes that were placed in him" (172). Bornkamm claims "that the Messianic character of his being is contained *in* his words and deeds and *in* the unmediatedness of his historic appearance." "The secret of his being could only reveal itself to his disciples in his resurrection" (178). With regard to whether Jesus understood himself as the Son of man, Bornkamm writes: "Although the historical Jesus spoke most definitely of the coming Son of man and judge of the world in the sense of the contemporary apocalyptic hope, and did so with the amazing certainty that the decisions made here with regard to his person and message would be confirmed at the last judgment, nevertheless he did not give himself the title Son of man. Also we can hardly assume that the earthly Jesus saw himself as destined to be the heavenly judge of the world" (177).

Jesus' basic preaching centered on the kingdom of God. The proclamation of the kingdom announced that God will reign—a message which Jesus preached with authority. Was this kingdom conceived of as present or future? "For Jesus calls: the shift in the aeons is here, the kingdom of God is already dawning." "It is happening now in Jesus' words and deeds" (67). "God's victory over Satan takes place in his words and deeds, and it is in them that the signs of this victory are erected" (68). Jesus proclaimed a call to repentance "to lay hold on the salvation which is already at hand, and to give up everything for it" (82). This preaching of the kingdom and the call to repentance manifest Jesus' prophetic function.

As a rabbi, Jesus taught the will of God. In his teaching, Jesus assumed an attitude of freedom over against the law.

"For Jesus, . . . the will of God is present in such immediate fashion that the letter of the law may be gauged by it" (100). The will of God, as preached by Jesus, demanded "obedience right in the heart of the actual deed itself" (106) that is, concrete obedience. His commandment to love "puts the other person in the centre" (112).

Jesus' disciples must be distinguished as a more intimate group from his followers in the wider sense. Bornkamm accepts the historicity of the twelve disciples who were "scarcely the creation of the post-Easter Church" (150).

For Bornkamm, the turning-point in Jesus' life was the decision to go to Jerusalem. For Bornkamm, the purpose of this decision is clear.

The reason why Jesus sets out with his disciples on his journey to Jerusalem cannot be doubted. It was to deliver the message of the coming kingdom of God in Jerusalem also, Jerusalem which Jesus himself calls the city of God, "the city of the Great King" (Mt. v. 35). As for every Jew, Jerusalem is also for Jesus not only the capital, but also the place which is in a special way connected with Israel's destiny. . . . The sources do not tell us clearly at what moment his readiness to accept death—a readiness which Jesus, as we know, demanded from his disciples too—turned into the certainty of his imminent end. We may, however, assume that first and foremost his journey to Jerusalem was undertaken in order to confront the people there, in the holy city, with the message of the kingdom of God, and to summon them at the eleventh hour to make their decision (154-55).

Jesus' last supper took place near the time of the Passover festival, but, according to Bornkamm, it is doubtful that this supper was itself held as a Passover meal. Many of the elements which made up the Passover celebration ritual are missing from the accounts, and Paul no where associates the Lord's Supper and Passover. The association of the two goes back to the early Christians and the first three Gospel writers (162).

The fixed point concerning Jesus' trial is the fact that he was put to death by the Romans and crucified, an act which was the exclusive right of the Roman court and by a form of death which was instituted for political crimes. Pilate's portrayal as an involuntary instrument of the public may reflect authentic tradition. "It is most probably authentic and not the invention of later poetic imagination that Pilate tried to extricate himself by offering to pardon Jesus, but that the incited people insisted upon the liberation of the Zealot Barabbas instead of Jesus—Barabbas who was rightly sentenced for the crime of which Jesus was wrongly accused" (164).

Speaking of the resurrection, Bornkamm says "there would be no gospel, not one account, no letter in the New Testament, no faith, no church, no worship, no prayer in Christendom to this day without the message of the resurrection of Christ" (181). "The miracle of the resurrection does not have a satisfactory explanation in the inner nature of the disciples, nor . . . does it have an analogy in the eternal dying and rebirth in nature" (185). "According to the interpretation of the early church, Easter is above all else God's acknowledgement of this Jesus, whom the world refused to acknowledge, and to whom even his disciples were unfaithful. It is at the same time the intervention of God's new world in this old world branded with sin and death, the setting up and beginning of his kingdom" (184). However, "the event of Christ's resurrection from the dead, his life and his eternal reign, are things removed from historical scholarship. History cannot ascertain and establish conclusively the facts about them as it can with certain other events of the past. The last historical fact available to them is the Easter faith of the first disciples" (180).

7. JESUS: THE MESSIANIC SUFFERING SERVANT

The historian is dealing in the end with an historical figure fully conscious of a task which had to be done, and fully conscious also that the only future which mattered for men and women depended upon the completion of his task. The future order, which it was the purpose of Jesus to bring into being, depended upon what he said and did, and finally upon his death. This conscious purpose gave a clear unity to his words and actions, so that the actions interpret the words and the words the actions.

Jesus acted as he did act and said what he did say because he was consciously fulfilling a necessity imposed upon him by God through the demands of the Old Testament. He died in Jerusalem, not because the Jews hounded him thither and did him to death, but because he was persuaded that, as messiah, he must journey to Jerusalem in order to be rejected and to die. —Edwyn Hoskyns and Francis Noel Davey, *The Riddle of the New Testament* (pp. 172, 115)

In this chapter, we shall examine the dominate description of the historical Jesus as he has been depicted in what may be called the mainstream of British and American scholarship from the 1930s until the 1960s. Among the many scholars who would fit within this mainstream are T. W. Manson, William Manson, C. H. Dodd, Vincent Taylor, A. M. Hunter, W. D. Davies, and J. W. Bowman. In German academic circles, Joachim Jeremias and Oscar Cullmann and to a lesser degree W. G. Kümmel and Eduard Schweizer are counterparts to this strand in English language scholarship.

A number of characteristics are held in common by most of the above named scholars. First of all, these scholars make a rather reserved use of form criticism especially with regards to the conclusions to be drawn about the importance of the church in the formation and transmission of the traditions. In much German New Testament study, deductions drawn from the results of form critical studies have frequently produced radical doubts about the historicity, chronology, and order of many of the Gospel traditions. In English scholarship, this has seldom been the case. If one compares Rudolf Bultmann's *History of the Synoptic Tradition* with Vincent Taylor's *The Formation of the Gospel Tradition,* this difference in perspective and in the conclusions drawn becomes immediately obvious. In the preface to his work, Taylor has written: "If in the hands of Professor Bultmann Form-Criticism has taken a skeptical direction, this is not the necessary trend of the method; on the contrary, where its limitations are recognized, Form-Criticism seems to me to furnish constructive suggestions which in many ways confirm the historical trustworthiness of the Gospel tradition" (vi). This more cautious assessment of form criticism is admirably reflected in the following statements by T. W. Manson.

After thirty years it is possible at least to attempt a rough appraisal of Form-Criticism; and it may perhaps be suggested that it has by now done about all that it could do, and more than it ought. Strictly speaking the term "form-criticism" should be reserved for the study of the various units of narrative and teaching, which go to make up the Gospels, in respect of their form, and that alone. It is concerned with the structure of these units; and it is certainly interesting to learn that there are a number of anecdotes in Mark, Matthew, and Luke, in which a brief statement of time and place leads up to a short conversation between Jesus and someone else, which is terminated by a dogmatic pronouncement from our Lord. It is interesting but not epoch-making. So far as structure goes, similar stories can be found in Boswell's *Life of Samuel Johnson* and elsewhere. We can list these stories in the Gospels. We can label them, and other units, when we are agreed about the terminology of the science. But a paragraph of Mark is not a penny the better or the worse as historical evidence for being labelled "apophthegm" or "pronouncement story" or "paradigm." In fact if Form-Criticism had been confined to this descriptive activity, it would probably have made little stir. We should have taken it as we take the forms of Hebrew poetry or the forms of musical composition. But Form-Criticism got mixed up with . . . the *doctrine* of the *Sitz im Leben*. . . .

The *Sitz im Leben* introduces a new set of considerations, which again have little or nothing to do with Form-Criticism in the strict sense of the word. It is undoubtedly a good thing that the Gospels should be studied in the context—so far as we can know it—of the interests, problems, and practical needs of the people who first used them. No doubt the stories and sayings were useful to missionary preachers of the first century. No doubt they gave guidance to the early communities on questions of faith and conduct. But we shall be travelling much too far and far too fast if we infer from that that they were created by the community to serve these ends or to meet these needs. In most cases it is equally possible, and a good deal more likely, that the tasks, problems, and needs of the first-century Church affected the selection, and in some cases the interpretation, of what went into the Gospels out of a much larger mass of available material. But even that may not be the whole truth of the matter. It is at least conceivable that one of the chief motives for preserving the stories at all, and for selecting those that were embodied in the Gospels, was just plain admiration and love for their hero. It is conceivable that he was no less interesting, *for his own sake,* to people in the first century than he is to historians in the twentieth ("The Life of Jesus," 212-14).

A second characteristic of this approach is its high regard for the transmission process through which the traditions of Jesus were passed on in the church. The stress falls on the reliability of the transmission process rather than the creativity of the church in using the materials to meet new life situations. The function of the church was the preservation not the creation of tradition. This approach argues that the intention in the collection and transmission of the tradition was always to hand on what Jesus himself taught, and to bring this home to the hearers or readers. Dodd has written the following about the Synoptic Gospels and their reflection of the "corporate memory" which handed down the traditions:

When all allowance has been made for ... limiting factors—the chances of oral transmission, the effect of translation, the interest of teachers in making the sayings "contemporary," and simple human fallibility—it remains that the first three gospels offer a body of sayings on the whole so consistent, so coherent, and withal so distinctive in manner, style content, that no reasonable critic should doubt, whatever reservations he may have about individual sayings, that we find reflected here the thought of a single, unique teacher (*The Founder of Christianity,* 21-22).

The question, how far this or that story may be taken as an accurate account of what happened on this or that occasion is one upon which judgments will vary. Some, as they stand, may be found more credible than others. One or the other may be felt to be not in character. But taken together, these stories, told from many different points of view, converge to give a distinct impression of a real person in action upon a recognizable scene (36).

A third interest evidenced in this approach is reflected in the stress laid on the historical references contained in the kerygma. The biblical materials are recognized as serving a preaching or kerygmatic concern but within this concern lies a devotion to the facts of the historical Jesus. C. H. Dodd stressed, in his influential study *The Apostolic Preaching and its Developments,* that there was an "immense range of variety in the interpretation that is given to the *kerygma*" but argued "that in all such interpretation the essential elements of the original *kerygma* are steadily kept in view" (74). The implications of the consistency of the kergymatic portrayal of Jesus have been drawn by T. W. Manson.

The nerve of the argument is that when we examine the early Christian convictions, which may be supposed to have shaped or even created the story of Jesus, we find a single and consistent story of Jesus in brief. We have abstracts of the propaganda speeches of the earliest Christians in Acts; and when we compare these with similar passages in the Pauline Epistles, we find a singular unanimity. It is natural to infer that such close agreement between men as different as Peter and Paul is the result neither of accident nor of design; that their claims for Jesus Christ tally because they are founded on facts. Whatever may be said about this or that detail in the Gospels, there was a total impression made by Jesus on those who came nearest to him and knew him best; and it is that total impression that is embodied in the *kerygma* ("The Life of Jesus," 215-16).

A fourth characteristic of this approach is a great respect for the Marcan outline and order of the life of Jesus. Although

Wrede, Schmidt, and German form critics in general were suspicious of the order and structure of the Gospel of Mark, this suspicion has not been characteristic of British scholarship. Dodd wrote of Mark that "he appears to have reproduced what came down to him with comparatively little attempt to write it up in his own way. . . . In Mark, within a very broad general scheme, there is a certain freedom and looseness of arrangement, and in his rather rough and informal style we seem often to overhear the tones of the living voice telling a story. We are probably near to the 'original eyewitnesses and servants of the gospel' " (*The Founder of Christianity,* 24). T. W. Manson is more emphatic about the value of the Gospel of Mark even when only speaking of the teachings of Jesus which are very slim in the Gospel. "We have in Mark only an outline and we have to apply to the other sources for fuller information at almost every point. But—and this is the crux of the matter—it is an outline which we can trust: and if we wish to frame a comprehensive picture of the teaching as a whole, as it developed during the course of the ministry, it is this Marcan outline which we must make the foundation" (*The Teaching of Jesus,* 26-27).

An emphasis on the realized aspects of eschatology as opposed to a futuristic interpretation has been a fifth characteristic. Dodd was the prime and most significant spokesman for "realized eschatology."

From . . . many . . . passages it is surely clear that, for the New Testament writers in general, the *eschaton* has entered history; the hidden rule of God has been revealed; the Age to Come has come. The Gospel of primitive Christianity is a Gospel of realized eschatology (*The Apostolic Preaching,* 85).

While, however, the New Testament affirms with full seriousness that the great divine event has happened, there remains a residue of eschatology which is not exhausted in the "realized eschatology" of the Gospel, namely, the element of sheer finality. . . . Thus the idea of a second coming of Christ appears along with the emphatic assertion that His coming in history satisfies all the conditions of the eschatological event, *except* that of absolute finality (93).

This school of interpreters claims that the stress on the realized character of the kingdom represents not only the interpretation of the early church—it goes back in origin to Jesus who saw in his own life and work the coming of the kingdom.

A final characteristic of this group of scholars is their willingness to utilize the Gospel of John as a source for the historical Jesus. Such a use of the Gospel nowhere approaches the utilization made of it by such scholars as David Smith and Ethelbert Stauffer. Much of Dodd's research during his last years focused on the Fourth Gospel and the traditions lying behind it. In commenting on the usage of the Fourth Gospel in discussing the historical Jesus, Dodd has written:

The "set pieces" of the Fourth Gospel, composed with great art, are comparable with the Greek philosophical dialogue. Yet dispersed among these elaborate literary compositions, or even embedded in them, there are sayings which stand out because they have the familiar ring. Some indeed are recognizably identical with sayings reported in the other gospels, though the wording may differ because the writer has his own linguistic habits, and sometimes he gives what seems to be a different translation of the same Aramaic original. In addition, on a closer examination of the dialogues and discourses it often turns out that the writer is only spelling out, in his own idiom of thought, what is already implicit in sayings reported in the other gospels. All this encourages the belief that the writer drew from the same general reservoir of tradition. That reservoir, we may be sure, contained more than has come through in our written gospels. There are sayings of Jesus recorded only in the Fourth Gospel which seem to bring into relief aspects of his teachings slenderly represented, if at all, in the others, and these may be of importance to complete the picture. It would be unwise to neglect them, though to make use of them in a strictly historical investigation calls for some critical tact (*The Founder of Christianity*, 22-23).

The two representative examples of an interpretation of Jesus as the messianic suffering servant which we will now examine are by T. W. Manson and John W. Bowman. At points, these scholars' arguments will be augmented by statements of others who share a similar perspective.

Integral to this presentation of Jesus is the fundamental conviction that Jesus understood himself as the Jewish messiah, but that he understood his role and function in this capacity in terms radically different from those of contemporary Judaism.

The typical Jewish belief in the messiah centered on a victorious political leader who would serve as the agent for the fulfilment of God's plan and the establishment of God's kingdom. Jesus' ministry did not conform to this widely expected pattern. Nonetheless, Jesus was the messiah who in a creative fashion understood his role by interpreting and combining several concepts borrowed from the Old Testament. This creative interpretation which understood and redefined messiahship in terms of a suffering and dying messiah was the characteristic interpretation of the early church, but it had its origin in the depths of Jesus' own spirit. The pattern of Jesus' life is to be understood, at least partially, as his refusal to fit the pattern of the typical Jewish messianic expectations.

The central violent contradiction between the primitive Christian *kerygma* and the Jewish Messianic hope is that which sets the crucified Messiah of Christian experience over against the triumphant hero of Jewish fancy. Now it is easy to see that the notion of a crucified Messiah is a stumbling-block to the Jews (I Cor. i. 23): to complete the picture we have also to realise that the Jewish hope of a successful Messiah was equally a stumbling-block to Jesus. It is from this point of view of the fundamental contradiction between the Jewish Messianic hope and Jesus' convictions concerning his own Ministry that the Gospel story becomes, in its main lines, an intelligible piece of history (T. W. Manson, *The Servant-Messiah*, 36). . . .

The whole Ministry—the teaching of Jesus, his acts, and finally the Cross, are a standing denial of the current beliefs and hopes (50).

Jesus' understanding of his life and ministry seems to have bypassed the typical Jewish concepts of his day and to have been based on a fresh understanding of the Old Testament prophets. "Jesus simply bypassed all contemporary Jewish groups, going back to the prophetic Scriptures for what stimulus he required, and . . . set before himself a reconstructed image of Messiahship, one of a highly spiritual and moral type, universalistic and so nonracial in character" (Bowman, *Which Jesus?*, 144).

The dominant pattern in Jesus' understanding of his ministry resulted from his combination of the messianic office with that of the figure of the suffering servant depicted in several passages in the book of Isaiah. In these passages, the servant is described as "one who has been given and has accepted a calling from God, and devoted himself body and soul to his service, bearing witness to the truth of God, enduring many sufferings, and in the end laying down his life for the sake of others" (Dodd, *The Founder of Christianity*, 103-4). It was Jesus and he alone, so it is argued, who was responsible for the creative fusion of these two concepts which had prior to his time remained separate and isolated.

The traditions of the baptism of Jesus give expression to this view of messiahship which it became Jesus' intention to fulfil.

The evangelists are united in their testimony that from this moment [his baptism] the Holy Spirit of prophecy came upon Jesus in a unique way and that that Spirit remained with him to direct and teach throughout his ministry. Moreover, the voice of his Father spoke to him saying, "Thou art my Son, the Beloved one; with Thee I am well pleased." It is probable, as Mk implies, that none but Jesus heard the voice speaking to him out of heaven. For it is characteristic of the voices of scripture that they are heard only by those prepared to receive them (cf. Jn 12:27-30; Ac. 22:7-9). And yet this voice, though spoken only to Jesus himself, is clearly indicated as being an objective one; it is the voice of the eternal Father speaking to his eternal Son. It quotes, moreover, from two passages of scripture—Ps. 2:7 and Isa. 42:1. The former of these is from a coronation psalm, wherein is narrated the coronation of the reigning messiah by the Lord God himself. In the psalm the words "Thou art my Son" form the first part of the coronation formula which serves to constitute the reigning king of Israel or Judah as the Lord's current viceroy. Equally, in the latter quotation is to be found the ordination formula of the Suffering Servant of Yahweh pronounced by the Lord himself. As used of Jesus, accordingly, these combined formulae serve at once to declare him Messiah and Suffering Servant of the Lord (Bowman, "The Life and Teaching of Jesus," 734-35).

The temptations of Jesus are to be understood as Jesus' repudiation of various other forms which his messiahship might have taken. T. W. Manson has written "that what Jesus rejects in the Temptations are methods of 'bringing in' the kingdom of God: (a) the economic . . .; (b) the game of political intrigue backed by military force; (c) propaganda which would eventually create an artificial nimbus for the national leader. All three were familiar phenomena in the life of the time" (*The Servant-Messiah*, 56-57). In other words, if the baptism "may be regarded as the announcement of God's choice and appointment of Jesus as Messiah, the [temptations] may equally be regarded as our Lord's deliberate choice of God as the sole object of his loyalty, trust and obedience, that is, as his King. In all his work the Father is to be the paramount chief and the paramount interest: everything that he does is to be done for God, with God, and under God. He is to be in the most complete sense the Servant of the Lord, the perfect subject of a perfect King" (*The Teaching of Jesus*, 197).

This unique understanding of his ministry in terms of a suffering-servant messiah meant that Jesus' ministry was to possess a certain character—a character which did not overtly encounter his audience with a claim to messiahship. Thus there was, in a certain sense, a messianic secret which goes back to the historical life of Jesus.

Jesus at no time would have been found "in character" had he stepped out into the marketplace or the Temple and shouted out: "Look at me! I am the Messiah, the Son of Man, the Suffering Servant," or any like title for himself. Rather, by word and deed, everything he ever said and did simply added up to what these words may mean. Of this he was always cognizant; so as he went about as Mediator of the Kingdom of God to men, he did not have to be continually stating his case; he had merely to go on *being* these things, thereby challenging all his contemporaries in one way or another to *see* them for themselves and to make the *believing response* they were calculated to inspire (Bowman, *Which Jesus?*, 139-40).

The miracles or mighty works of Jesus were an integral part of his public ministry. They were the means by which he carried out the implications of his preaching "in the form of philanthropic work calculated to ameliorate man's distresses at every level of his life" (Bowman, "The Life and Teaching of Jesus," 737). Jesus' miracles were not performed to startle his audience or to produce wonder and awe in his power.

It is true that Jesus would perform no *sign* of an unmistakably supernatural kind such as his enemies constantly demanded of him (Mk 8:11f.) To have complied with such a request would have been quite out of character on the part of Jesus who by all accounts never set out merely to prove anything about his person or mission. It was characteristic of him rather that he looked for that spiritual insight in men with which they could very well pass their own judgments (737).

The mighty works of Jesus were therefore not performed primarily to produce faith, they were basically the natural expression of his person. They were performed for humanitarian reasons to meet the temporal needs of man. "In a very real sense, therefore, Jesus' miracles were 'memorial signs' for those who possessed the spiritual insight to discern in them the sovereignty of God at work in the midst of his people; they were, so to speak, 'acted parables,' demonstrating the presence of the kingdom of God as having arrived in and through Jesus." Some of the so-called nature miracles are to be understood, as they now appear in the text, as the result of a mistranslation of some Greek idiom (walking on the seashore not the sea), as miracles of divine providence (the stilling of the storm), or as acted parables (the feeding of the multitudes) (737).

In his ministry of words—teaching and preaching—"Jesus assumes the role of the Gospel Herald who declares that the epoch referred to in the writing of the prophet [Isaiah] has now arrived; Jesus' contemporaries stand upon the very threshold of the Kingdom's inauguration" (Bowman, "The Life and Teaching of Jesus," 739). Thus Jesus' words and works supplemented each other and pointed to the nearness and arrival of the kingdom. Jesus' message of the kingdom was eschatologically oriented. The word "kingdom" is an abstract word meaning sovereignty or lordship. In the preaching of Jesus, references to the kingdom of God as near at hand meant "for Jesus that God's lordship is about to be realised in some sense in human experience."

Before Peter's confession at Caesarea Philippi, Jesus spoke of the Kingdom of God as *something that was about to come* and . . . after the confession his message was "The Kingdom has now come. Come in." . . . Accordingly, the Kingdom will have come, in Jesus' meaning of the term, with the confession of Peter. For to acknowledge God's Messiah (his viceroy) will be the same as to acknowledge God's lordship itself. When a man does this, then the Kingdom has come in his experience. . . . The Kingdom was, therefore, in the teaching of Jesus, in the first instance an individual experience of God's lordship over the life of the disciple who acknowledged the same. But there can be no doubt that Jesus also had in view a group, the prophetic remnant composed of his little band of disciples, in whose corporate experience of fellowship with one another and with Jesus as their Lord and Master the Kingdom was realised. . . . Finally, Jesus also no doubt looked forward to the final consummation of the Kingdom of God at the end of history and on more than one occasion expressed himself after this fashion (Mk 8:38, 13, 14:62) (739).

Thus the kingdom of God was proclaimed in the preaching of Jesus as God's lordship, as near at hand, as realized in a man or group's submission to this lordship, and as something to be consummated at the end of history.

The call of an intimate circle of followers was an important and deliberate activity of Jesus.

His aim was to constitute a community worthy of the name of a people of God, a divine commonwealth, through individual response to God coming in his kingdom. . . . Those who accept his kingdom "like a child" enter in, and so by act of God himself, which is especially exhibited in the forgiveness of sins, his people is formed within the old Israel, ready to emerge in due time (Dodd, *The Founder of Christianity,* 90-91).

For Bowman, Jesus' call of twelve disciples is a special, symbolic, and actual move to create a new Israel, a new people of God. Behind such action lies the biblical concept of a faithful group—a remnant—within the community as a whole, which was loyal and submissive to God. In Jesus' function as the suffering-servant messiah, he embodied within himself the true remnant. With the selection of twelve, Jesus began to build up a new assembly of God's people, starting from the Twelve as a remnant to form the new people of God, what in later times was termed the church. Bowman argues however that the decisive move of Jesus to create a new remnant only occurred after Jesus was rejected by his own people when he preached in the synagogue in Nazareth (Luke 4:16-30). "Jesus' appointment of the Twelve is somehow to be related to his rejection from the assembly of his people." After this event, "Jesus never again darkens the door of a synagogue" (*Which Jesus?,* 146). *"It would seem that Jesus considered the Nazareth incident as a definite symbol of his 'extirpation' from the congregation of the Old Israel."*

Taken together, these data seem to tell us that as Jesus was in the course of being ejected from among the people of God, he was at the same time taking steps to raise up a new Israel—a "remnant" of the old. The old congregation had condemned itself in judging its Messiah as unworthy to have a place within its ranks. So he turned to the task of gathering a new and worthier congregation about his own person as its center and obvious leader (Bowman, *The Intention of Jesus,* 217).

In preparing the disciples as the remnant of a new people of God, Jesus gave special instruction and training to the twelve. Thus the emphasis in the Gospels on Jesus' special private instruction to his disciples reflects a true historical element in the ministry of Jesus. "The culmination of this period of activity comes as Jesus turns his feet toward Caesarea Philippi at the foot of Mount Hermon with a view to a quiet time of retreat with his disciples away from the multitudes" (Bowman, "The Life and Teaching of Jesus, 740). This withdrawal of Jesus from the crowds and the subsequent events at Caesarea Philippi mark the watershed of the ministry of Jesus dividing it into two distinct phases. At Caesarea, Peter acknowledged Jesus as the messiah, and Jesus' instruction of his disciples became more serious and pointed.

It is here that we have the great turning point in the Ministry marked by Peter's recognition of Jesus as the expected Messiah. And here the clash between the two messianic ideals is manifest. What does Peter mean when he says, "You are the Messiah?" And how does Jesus receive the statement? Mark's answer to the latter question is that Jesus forbade the disciples to speak to anyone about himself. The context requires us to add the words "as Messiah." As for the former question the answer is given almost immediately in Mark, when Peter indignantly repudiates the idea that the messianic destiny can be anything but glory and success. Jesus is equally uncompromising in maintaining that the task of the Son of Man is of another kind and that its glory and success will be very different from the gaudy triumphs on which the hearts of Peter and the other disciples are set.

With that the calling of the disciples begins all over again. The terms of discipleship are made terribly plain: he who swears fealty to me makes his compact with scorn and derision, defeat and death. From this point onwards three themes are closely linked in Mark's narrative: the relentless claims of Jesus on his disciples, the stubborn hopes and ambitions of the disciples themselves, and the repeated predictions of the Passion of the Son of Man (Manson, *The Servant-Messiah,* 71-72).

In the Caesarea episode, Jesus is said to have told the disciples that the Son of man must suffer many things, be rejected by the elders, chief priests, and scribes, be killed, and after three days rise again (Mark 8:31). The third important title—in addition to messiah and suffering servant—here enters the picture. How does this particular strand of interpretation understand the term "Son of man" and Jesus' employment of that title in his self-understanding?

T. W. Manson has written the following concerning the interpretation of the title Son of man in the Gospels:

"Son of Man" in the Gospels is the final term in a series of conceptions, all of which are found in the Old Testament. These are: the Remnant (Isaiah), the Servant of Jehovah [Yahweh] (II Isaiah), the "I" of the Psalms, and the Son of Man (Daniel). . . . It is the idea of the Remnant which is the essential feature about each of these: . . . Son of Man in the Gospels is another embodiment of the Remnant idea. In other words, the Son of Man is, like the Servant of Jehovah, an ideal figure and stands for the manifestation of the Kingdom of God on earth in a people wholly devoted to their heavenly King . . . [Jesus'] mission is to create the Son of Man, the Kingdom of the saints of the Most High, to realise in Israel the ideal contained in the term. This task is attempted in two ways: first by public appeal to the people through the medium of parable and sermon and by the mission of the disciples: then, when this appeal produced no adequate response, by the consolidation of his own band of followers. Finally, when it becomes apparent that not even the disciples are ready to rise to the demands of the ideal, he stands alone, embodying in his own person the perfect human response to the regal claims of God (*The Teaching of Jesus*, 227-28).

Thus the Son of man title reflects, according to Manson, a collective or corporate meaning which refers to the obedient saints of God—the true remnant—and an individual meaning, the ideal obedient Israelite which Jesus used in understanding himself and his ministry.

Sometime shortly after the Caesarea Philippi episode, Jesus left Galilee for the south and ultimately Jerusalem. Why did Jesus go up to Jerusalem? In discussing this issue, Manson has written:

The question has often enough been asked already, and we have a good many answers to choose from. The older lives of Jesus, written from the standpoint of dogmatic orthodoxy, were ready with an answer in terms of orthodox dogmatics [that is, Jesus went up to die]. More rationalising studies tended to make the death of Jesus a regrettable incident like the death of Socrates. Jesus goes up to Jerusalem to give a course of lecture-sermons on the Fatherhood of God and the Brotherhood of Man, and then becomes the victim of an unfortunate miscarriage of justice. Thoroughgoing eschatology tends to make the Cross an unsuccessful gamble, something like what happens when a chess-player sacrifices his queen in the hope of forcing a mate, and it does not come off (*The Servant-Messiah*, 75-76).

We must ask, not, Why did Jesus go up to Jerusalem?, but rather, Is "going up to Jerusalem" an adequate description of what Jesus did when he left Galilee for the last time? I venture to think that it is not. No doubt Jerusalem is the ultimate goal of the journey; but I think it would be more in keeping with what we know about the mind of Jesus, and also truer to the facts, to say that Jesus left Galilee to continue in the south, that is in Judaea and Peraea, the same kind of Ministry that he had begun in the north (77).

Jesus' Jerusalem ministry was carried out, according to Bowman, with a spirit of assurance and with Jesus totally in command of the situation.

This spirit of assurance never leaves him to the end. Everything happens as he wills that it shall happen and at the time which he has determined for it. And yet, throughout all this confident activity, Jesus in act and word exhibits a gracious redemptive purpose. It is with this purpose that he successively challenges the nation and its ruling classes, the city of Jerusalem and its multitudes, to exhibit faith in himself as the moral and spiritual leader whom God has appointed for them. Amid this week's rapidly shifting scenes, one gains the impression that Jesus sees his ministry drawing to a focus. His "hour" has at last arrived. And he will see it through in masterful fashion ("The Life and Teaching of Jesus," 742).

Jesus' assurance of his messiahship and his understanding of the form of that messiahship brought him into the final conflict with Israel and Rome.

Every day it becomes clearer to the Messiah Jesus, if to nobody else, that the kingdom of God does not come, cannot come, by defeating the kingdoms of the world at their own game; that the Messiah is not, and cannot be, the latest, loudest, and most successful of a long line of international gangsters; that Israel is not to be, and rightly understood cannot be, just another and a greater Rome. But neither Israel nor Rome can see that. Jewish hopes and Roman suspicions are concentrated on the same object, an object far removed from the thoughts of Jesus (Manson, *The Servant-Messiah*, 76).

Except for the crucifixion, the two dominating events in Jesus' ministry in Jerusalem are the triumphal entry and the cleansing of the temple. In entering the city, according to well-laid plans, Jesus was "consciously fulfilling the prophecy of Zech. 9:9 with a view to challenging the capital city to see in him God's true Messiah. But neither the city nor Jesus' own disciples discern his purpose and they give him merely the reception accorded to the usual pilgrim band coming up to Jerusalem from the ends of the earth to worship at the feast [of Passover]" (Bowman, "The Life and Teaching of Jesus," 743). Jesus' cleansing of the temple was directed against the trading and selling, in themselves legitimate, which took place in the court of the Gentiles. Jesus' objections to this practice were "(a) that it offended against the principle of universalism at the heart of all true religion, and (b) that the type of control involved was debasing the practices of religion to a materialistic level" (Bowman, "The Life and Teaching of Jesus," 743).

This challenge to the Jewish leaders and the assumption that he made exalted claims for himself eventually led to his arrest and crucifixion. The trial—or preliminary hearing—before the Sanhedrin and the trial before Pilate focused on Jesus as a threat to peace and stability—that is on the issue of his messiahship. Condemned by both, Jesus was crucified.

[Pilate] was not greatly impressed by the case. His private opinion seems to have been that the whole affair arose out of the malice and ill-will of the Jewish authorities, and that he was being used for their purposes. There his judgement was sound. He also came to the conclusion, after seeing Jesus and questioning him, that he was harmless. . . . There was a case of sorts; and even if Jesus was practically harmless alive, he would be quite harmless dead. So sentence was passed and execution followed without delay. By sunset on Friday it was over; and Jesus, with all the hopes and fears he had aroused, was buried in the rock tomb.

And most of the people who had been concerned doubtless went to bed that night with fairly easy consciences. Pilate had earned another day's salary as Procurator of Judaea; and his province was quiet and peaceful—at any rate on the surface. The Temple authorities could feel that they had made things secure against untimely reforming zeal—for the time being at least. Patriotic Jews could tell themselves that it had been a mistake ever to imagine that Jesus was the kind of leader they were looking for—and in that they were not mistaken. Devout Jews could reflect that such an end as that which had overtaken Jesus was hardly to be wondered at, after the way in which he had flouted the scribes and even criticised the provisions of the Law itself. We might almost say that Jesus was crucified with the best intentions; and that those who sent him to the Cross believed that they were doing their plain duty by the Empire or the Temple or the Law or the hope of Israel. Doubtless many, perhaps most, of them did so believe. . . . In Pilate, Caiaphas, and the rest the lesser loyalties united against the kingdom of God incarnate in Jesus the Messiah; and so Jesus went to the Cross—and made it his everlasting throne (Manson, *The Servant-Messiah*, 87-88).

But the story does not end here for the disciples encountered the risen Lord. The stories of the resurrection appearances and the empty tomb are difficult, if not impossible to harmonize, but they all point to the essential truth: *"Christians do not inherit their task from Christ, they share it with him.* We are not the successors of Jesus, but his companions" (*The Servant-Messiah*, 98).

8. JESUS: THE POLITICAL REVOLUTIONARY

The iconolaters have never for a moment conceived Jesus as a real person, who meant what he said, as a fact, as a force like electricity, only needing the invention of suitable political machinery to be applied to the affairs of mankind with revolutionary effect. Thus it is not disbelief that is dangerous in our society; it is belief. The moment it strikes you (as it may any day) that Jesus is not the lifeless, harmless image he has hitherto been to you, but a rallying centre for revolutionary influence, which all established States and Churches fight, you must look to yourselves, for you have brought the image to life, and the mob may not be able to stand that horror. —George Bernard Shaw, *Androcles and the Lion* (preface)

Throughout the course of research on the historical Jesus, the view that Jesus was a revolutionary who sought the overthrow of the Jewish-Roman establishment of his day has been frequently considered and occasionally expounded. Recently the thesis has been proposed anew and has attracted academic and popular concern—both support and repudiation.

Reimarus was the first to propose that Jesus' ministry was a call to political revolt. In discussing Jesus' sending out of the disciples to announce that the kingdom of heaven was at hand Reimarus wrote:

He knew that if the people believed his messengers, they would look for a worldly king, and would attach themselves to him with the conviction that he was this king; because, unless they received further and better instruction, they could have no other conception of the kingdom of heaven or kingdom of God, or of any faith in the same, than that which they had learned according to the popular meaning of the words, and to the prevailing impression of them. . . . But Jesus did not convey to them any better idea of himself. . . .

Jesus then must have been well aware that by such a plain announcement of the kingdom of heaven, he would only awaken the Jews to the hope of a worldly Messiah; consequently, this must have been his object in so awakening them. . . . In sending such missionaries, he could have had no other object than to rouse the Jews in all parts of Judea, who had so long been groaning under the Roman yoke, and so long been preparing for the hoped-for deliverance, and to induce them to flock to Jerusalem.

With this intention the rest of the acts agree. ("Concerning the Intention of Jesus and His Teaching," 136-38).

Jesus and John the Baptist had actually arranged the course of their ministry and their preaching toward the end of political revolt: "Neither John nor Jesus could have had any other object than that of awakening the people to a speedy arrival of the long-hoped-for deliverer, and of making them eager for his coming" (141). When the Jews sought to make Jesus king, "Jesus slipped away from them and escaped to a mountain. It is remarkable that he did not seize this opportunity of reproving the people, of assuring them that they were mistaken, and that he had come for a very different purpose. This would have been most necessary if Jesus really had had another object in view, and wished the people to think so" (142). Jesus refused on that occasion to be made king, not because he opposed the idea but because the setting and timing were not correct.

It was not his intention to allow himself to be made a king in a desert place, and by a common rabble, such as then surrounded him. Neither the time nor the place suited him. His thoughts were bent upon a grand entry into the city of Jerusalem, at the Passover, a time when all Israelites throughout Judea would be assembled there, and when it would be conducted in a festive manner, and when, by the united voices of the populace he would be proclaimed King of the Jews (142-43).

Jesus chose his hour, laid his plans, and rode into Jerusalem on an ass to appear as the king spoken of in Zechariah 9:9. The crowds welcomed him enthusiastically, and the town was thrown into a state of excitement. "This extraordinary public procession, which was not only tolerated by Jesus, but had been diligently encouraged by him, could not have been aimed at anything but a worldly kingdom. He wished that all the people of Israel who were there gathered together should unanimously proclaim him king" (146). Jesus failed to receive the support of the nation; only the common rabble accepted him. His scheme crumbled and Jesus lost courage.

He ordered some swords to be procured to defend himself with in case of attack, but was uneasy, lest even one of his own disciples should divulge his place of retreat. He began to quiver and quake when he saw that his adventure might cost him his life. Judas betrayed his hiding-place, and pointed out his person. . . . He ended his life with the words, *"Eli Eli, lama sabachthani? My God, my God, why hast thou forsaken me?"* [Matt 27:46]—a confession which can hardly be otherwise interpreted than that God had not helped him to carry out his intention and attain his object as he had hoped he would have done. It was then clearly not the intention or the object of Jesus to suffer and to die, but to build up a worldly kingdom, and to deliver the Israelites from bondage. It was in this that God had forsaken him, it was in this that his hopes had been frustrated (150).

This possible political-revolutionary factor in the career of Jesus has been stressed by a wide spectrum of scholars. Julius Wellhausen has written that Jesus sought to free his people "from the yoke of hierocracy and nomocracy. For this purpose he perhaps did not act merely as a teacher but also as an agitator, and inwardly laid claim for himself to messianic authority to rule, or at least give the appearance of doing so. During the cleansing of the temple he did not hesitate to use violence; his disciples had weapons and tried to fight when they were taken by surprise" *(Einleitung in die drei ersten Evangelien,* 83). The idea of Jesus as a social revolutionist was especially attractive to socialist interpreters of Jesus at the turn of the century. The socialist Karl Kautsky wrote in 1908: "The assumption that the execution of Jesus was due to the fact that he was a rebel is . . . not only the sole assumption which can make the indications in the Gospel clear, but it is also completely in accordance with the character of the epoch and of the locality" *(Foundations of Christianity,* 369).

The first full treatment of the subject of Jesus as a political revolutionary was the two volume work of Robert Eisler published in 1929–30 with a Greek title which can be translated "Jesus, a King not Reigning." Eisler's theory was founded upon references in ancient Jewish and Christian sources, including the New Testament, and upon some materials found in the Slavonic, or Old Russian, version of the history of the Jewish war written by Josephus. The passage in Josephus which contributed greatly to Eisler's theory contains the following account of a wonder-worker whom scholars almost unanimously see as Jesus although most do not consider the text to be from Josephus.

At that time there appeared a man, if it is permissible to call him a man. His nature and form were human, but his appearance was something more than that of a man; notwithstanding his works were divine. He worked miracles wonderful and mighty. Therefore it is impossible for me to call him a man; but again, if I look at the nature which he shared with all, I will not call him an angel. And everything whatsoever he wrought through an invisible power, he wrought by word and command. Some said of him, "Our first lawgiver is risen from the dead and hath performed many healings and arts," while others thought that he was sent from God. Howbeit in many things he disobeyed the Law and kept not the Sabbath according to our fathers' customs. Yet, on the other hand, he did nothing shameful; nor did he do anything with aid of hands, but by word alone did he provide everything.

And many of the multitude followed after him and harkened to his teaching; and many souls were in commotion, thinking that thereby the Jewish tribes might free themselves from Roman hands. Now it was his custom in general to sojourn over against the city upon the Mount of Olives; and there, too, he bestowed his healings upon the people.

And there assembled unto him of ministers one hundred

and fifty, and a multitude of the people. Now when they saw his power, that he accomplished whatsoever he would by a word, and when they had made known to him their will, that he should enter into the city and cut down the Roman troops and Pilate and rule over us, he disdained us not.

And when thereafter knowledge of it came to the Jewish leaders, they assembled together with the high-priest and spake: "We are powerless and too weak to withstand the Romans. Seeing, moreover, that the bow is bent, we will go and communicate to Pilate what we have heard, and we shall be clear of trouble, lest he hear it from others, and we be robbed of our substance and ourselves slaughtered and our children scattered." And they went and communicated it to Pilate. And he sent and had many of the multitude slain. And he had that Wonder-worker brought up, and after instituting an inquiry concerning him, he pronounced judgment: "He is a benefactor, not a malefactor, nor a rebel, nor covetous of kingship." And he let him go; for he had healed his dying wife.

And he went to his wonted place and did his wonted works. And when more people again assembled round him, he glorified himself through his actions more than all. The teachers of the Law were overcome with envy, and gave thirty talents to Pilate, in order that he should put him to death. And he took it and gave them liberty to execute their will themselves. And they laid hands on him and crucified him contrary to the law of their fathers (*The Jewish War,* between II., 174-75).

Using this passage and certain New Testament references, Eisler argued that Jesus was reluctantly persuaded by his followers to participate in armed insurrection against the Romans. Eisler placed Jesus squarely within the camp of patriotic Jewish resistance to Roman rule in Palestine. In the cleansing-of-the-temple episode, Jesus led an armed revolt against the Romans, seized the temple, was expelled by the Romans, taken captive, and executed for insurrection.

The theory of Eisler was revived in popular form by the American Jewish writer Joel Carmichael in 1962 in a volume entitled *The Death of Jesus.* Carmichael summarizes his presentation of Jesus in the following terms:

Jesus was the Herald of the Kingdom of God, and he tried to take it by storm. In the strangely blurred and mutilated recollections of his career we can dimly discern the outlines of a visionary who was also a man of action and who attempted to set in motion the machinery of God's will.

He was squarely in the tradition of the Jewish religious patriots, tortured by the crushing weight of the Roman Empire, who arose in Palestine and assaulted the Roman power and its vassals.

We see his enterprise frustrated and himself undone; his followers scattered and his movement, doubtless, drowned in blood. He ended like many others in Israel—in agony and death, a prey to the powers of this world (203).

The most recent thorough attempt to portray Jesus as a political revolutionary is the work by S. G. F. Brandon entitled *Jesus and the Zealots: A Study of the Political Factor in Primitive Christianity.* Brandon begins his investigation with the following statement: "Ironic though it be, the most certain thing known about Jesus of Nazareth is that he was crucified by the Romans as a rebel against their government in Judaea" (1). In order to understand and explain this fact and the character of the historical Jesus which it implies, Brandon examines the revolutionary and political relations between the Romans and the Jews during the years between A.D. 6-73, the Zealots and their philosophy which lay behind many of the altercations with Rome, how the death of Jesus came to be explained in a manner that played down its true character and presented him as a pacifist, and the evidence which might suggest that Jesus was a patriotic rebel against Roman authority.

Brandon dates the origin of the Zealot party in Judaism to the revolt led by Judas the Galilean at the time of the census undertaken by the Roman legate in Syria, P. Sulpicius Quirinius, in A.D. 6 when Archelaus, a son of Herod the Great, was deposed and Judaea placed under direct Roman control. This census was the "cause of the first act of rebellion against their heathen masters and the founding of a party, the Zealots, who were destined some sixty years later to lead their people into the fatal war of independence against Rome" (26). Judas the Galilean was the son of a certain Ezekias, a "brigand chief," who had operated in Galilee during the early governorship of Herod over that area. Herod had executed Ezekias and suppressed his followers (about 47 B.C.), an act for which he was summoned before the Sanhedrin for an explanation. Brandon suggests that this need to make an official explanation implied that Ezekias had a great significance for the Jews who had mourned his death. Judas had his first altercation with the Romans during the unrest which followed the death of Herod in 4 B.C. At that time, "Judas broke into the Herodian palace at Sepphoris in Galilee and seized the property and arms stored there. His exploits caused him to be greatly feared; he is also reported to have aspired to royalty." The uprisings at the time, of which that led by Judas was only one among many, were suppressed by Varus, the Roman governor of Syria, and two legions of troops. "The punishment inflicted on the captured rebels was savage: two thousand of them were crucified" (29).

At the time of the census in A.D. 6, according to Josephus, "Judas incited his countrymen to revolt, upbraiding them as cowards for consenting to pay tribute to Rome and tolerating mortal masters, after having God for their Lord" (*The Jewish War,* II, 367). Josephus then points out that Judas founded a sect of his own in association with Saddok, a Pharisee. Of this "philosophical" sect, Josephus wrote: "Its sectaries associated themselves in general with the doctrine of the Pharisees; but they had an invincible love of liberty, for they held God to be their only lord and master. They showed an indifference toward the fortunes of their parents and friends, in their resolve to call no man master" (*Antiquities,* XVIII, 23). Josephus sought to blame such brigand groups for the war against Rome which led to the destruction of Jerusalem. Since Josephus wrote his history of the war "to commemorate the victories of his imperial patrons" (35) and to argue that the revolt did not reflect the true sympathies of the Jewish people, he played down, according to Brandon, the true attitude of the Zealots and the real support they had among the people. In spite of these desires, "client of the Roman Caesars he was, Josephus could not wholly suppress recognition of the religious motives that had inspired Zealotism" (36-37).

Josephus does not use the name Zealot with regard to Judas' movement although he later traces the Sicarii, who got their name from the Roman *sica* used in assassinations, to the followers of Judas. Brandon explains this lack of the term in the following way:

In the light of this evidence, various and fragmentary though it is, the reason for Josephus' apparent embarrassment over the name "Zealot" becomes clear. The name was an honourable one, proudly assumed by those who, following the example of Phinehas [Num. 25:6-13], uncompromisingly sought to maintain Israel's absolute conformity to the Torah and its complete loyalty to Yahweh as its sovereign Lord. . . . In writing of recent Jewish affairs for his Roman readers, it was obviously more politic for him to represent the Zealots as criminals, who misled the Jewish people into making their fatal challenge to Roman power, than as patriots who sacrificed themselves for their ideal of Israel as a theocracy under Yahweh (46-47).

In light of the theocratic ideal in Judaism and the apocalyptic expectation current at the time, Brandon argues that the Zealot beliefs may have been more than just patriotic fanaticism. "It is, therefore, a necessary inference that Judas and Saddok, when they called upon their people to withstand the Roman demand, also believed that the kingdom of God was at hand. Even Josephus admits that they expected God's succour, and it is likely that, no less vividly than Jesus, they might have envisaged the intervention of twelve legions of angels" (51). Brandon considers it probable that the "Zealots were animated by hopes which passed beyond the freeing of Israel from its servitude to Rome to some concept of world-mastery" (60). For Brandon, "Zealotism was essentially a popular movement, embodying both the religious and social aspirations and resentments of the 'people of the land' " (68). "Zealotism must be recognised as a true and inherently noble expression of Jewish religious faith, and one that was sanctioned and inspired by the example of many revered figures of Israel's heroic past" (63-64).

The offspring of Judas continued to lead uprisings against the Romans. Two of his sons, Jacob and Simon, were crucified by the procurator Tiberius Alexander (c. A.D. 46–48). In the summer of A.D. 66, Menahem, a son of Judas, seized the fortress at Masada. He later marched to Jerusalem "as a king" but was assassinated by the followers of the priest Eleazar. Masada was under the control of another Eleazar, a descendant of Judas, until the Jews holding the massive mountainous fortress chose to commit suicide rather than surrender to the Romans in A.D. 73.

In discussing the Zealots, Brandon sought to demonstrate that the movement was in existence as a powerful force among the Jews throughout the time of the life and career of Jesus. In summarizing the discussion of this political movement, he writes:

The Zealots stood in true succession to the Yahwist prophets of old. They were, like Phinehas, zealous for the God of Israel. Their ideal was the ancient prophetic one of Israel as the Elect People of Yahweh. In their zeal to maintain that ideal they could be cruelly uncompromising and fanatical; but no more so than many of the revered heroes of their sacred tradition. Their tragedy was that, unlike the Maccabees before them in their struggle with the ramshackle empire of the Seleucids, in Rome they had themselves to contend with the greatest power of the ancient world, and, for all their courage and zeal, that power was invincible to them. But, if they could not win, they knew how to suffer for their faith. . . . The cross was the symbol of Zealot sacrifice before it was transformed into the sign of Christian salvation (145).

In a chapter entitled "Israel's Cause Against Rome, A.D. 6–73" (65-145), Brandon surveys the numerous encounters between the Roman authority in Palestine and the Jews. At times these altercations involved the majority of the Jews, as when the emperor Gaius ordered that a statue of Zeus be set up in the temple at Jerusalem, and at other times, they only

involved small groups, often Zealot-led, intent on overthrow-
ing Roman rule.

In seeking to establish a relationship between early
Christians and these Jewish rebellions, Brandon argues that
during the period from the death of Jesus until the fall of
Jerusalem Jewish Christians retained a firm relationship to
Judaism and shared the Zealot ideal. Brandon concludes, on
the basis of the book of Acts and later texts which discuss
early Jewish Christianity, that Jewish Christians held beliefs
greatly different from that of Gentile Christians. Gentile
Christianity, inaugurated by Stephen and given expression
by Paul, tended to break with Judaism and go its separate
way. In describing this Jewish Christianity, Brandon writes:

We have discerned a community of Jews, who, recognising
in Jesus the Messiah of Israel, surmounted the shock of his
death at the hands of the Romans. Convinced that God had
raised him from death, these disciples' faith in his Messiahship was intensified, taking the form of an urgent expectation that he would soon return, with supernatural power, to
fulfil his Messianic task of "restoring the kingdom to Israel."
In anticipation of that glorious event, they believed that it
was their vocation to prepare their fellow-Jews by presenting
Jesus to them as the Messiah, by urging them to repent of
those sins which had caused him to die a martyr's death to
Roman cruelty and Jewish obduracy, and by exhorting them
to be worthy of divine redemption. When faced with the
unexpected and unwelcomed fact of Gentile adherents to
their movement, they required their confirmation to certain
Jewish laws, even seeking to have them circumcised as a
guarantee against Paul's antinomianism. Thus they continued as zealous Jews, distinguished from their compatriots
only by their expectation that Jesus would soon return to
earth as the Messiah. Their movement was given both
dynastic continuity and effective leadership by James, the
brother of Jesus, and on his death, if later tradition is to be
trusted, the succession passed to another relative, Symeon [a
cousin of Jesus]. The reputation of the movement seems to
have stood high in Jewish religious circles, and it attracted
the allegiance of both priests and Pharisees, and its members
merited the description "zealots of the Torah" [Acts 21:20]
(190).

Brandon argues that these Jewish Christians supported and fought in the great Jewish revolt against the Romans. "Indeed, from all our knowledge of them, it would seem that their attitude towards the Romans would scarcely have differed from that of the Zealots" (199). According to Brandon, the Gospel of Matthew was produced by Jewish Christians in Alexandria in Egypt who shared the same faith as those of the mother church in Jerusalem, although written after the pacificist character of Jesus had been developed following the wars with Rome.

Brandon, of course, recognizes that the four Gospels argue that Jesus was innocent of the charge of sedition for which he was crucified by the Romans. "What makes the Christian accounts of the crucifixion specially notable, as records of historical fact, is that they represent Jesus as being innocent of the charge on which he was condemned. Although they vary in some details, the four Gospel accounts agree in showing that Jesus was falsely accused of sedition by the Jewish authorities, and that these authorities forced the· Roman governor, Pontius Pilate, against his better judgment, to condemn and execute him" (1-2). Confronting this fact, Brandon tackles the question of the origin of this apology of innocence, that is, the origin of the oldest Gospel account.

Brandon traces the origin of the idea of Jesus' innocence of the charge of sedition to the writer of the Gospel of Mark, a Gospel which he designates an *Apologia ad Christanos Romanos*. The fact that Mark represents the first written Gospel and was thus a radical innovative development in Christianity demands explanation, according to Brandon. His explanation centers around the idea that Mark was written shortly after the fall of Jerusalem in A.D. 70 as an apology for Gentile readers in Rome where anti-Jewish sentiment was rampant. His general conclusions are:

Faced by the need to explain the Roman execution of Jesus, the author of Mark replaced the original Jewish Christian story of the martyr's death, at the hands of the heathen Romans and their Jewish collaborators, by that of the long-intentioned murder of the Son of God by the Jewish leaders, supported by their people. Seeking to remove any suggestion that Jesus had been implicated in the Jewish freedom movement, Mark presents him as serenely insulated from contemporary political interests and concerns, except that he is shown as endorsing the payment of tribute to Rome. . . .

This abstraction of Jesus from the political life of his time meant also the representing of him as essentially detached from his racial origins and heritage (280).

Brandon draws upon various arguments to support these conclusions. Accepting the ancient tradition which associated the Gospel of Mark with Rome as well as modern scholarly dating of the book to the period A.D. 60-75, Brandon argues that the most likely time for writing was just after the fall of Jerusalem, an event which not only provided the occasion but also the impetus for the work. "In the year 71 popular interest in Jewish affairs was powerfully stimulated in Rome by the magnificent triumph with which the new emperor Vespasian and his son Titus celebrated their conquest of rebel Judaea" (225). Spoils from the victory, including items taken from the temple, and Jewish captives were presented before the Romans in the triumphant processions. Coins were struck showing Judaea humiliated and bearing the inscription *Judaea Capta*. It was a time when interest in and hostility toward Jewish revolutionary activity were widespread. Certainly it was no time to preach Jesus as a Jewish messiah condemned to death by the Romans as a freedom fighter. "A most pressing need, then, existed in the Christian community in Rome at this time for an explanation of Pilate's condemnation and execution of Jesus as a revolutionary against Rome's superiority over Judaea" (247).

A portrayal of Jesus that would separate him from Jewish revolutionary elements and present Jesus as acceptable to Romans in the anti-Jewish atmosphere of the time was achieved by Mark through a number of means. He showed Jesus as one who supported the Jewish payment of tribute to Rome. Mark 12:13-17 would have been so read by a Roman audience. Mark shows Jesus as a predictor of the destruction of the Jewish temple (Mark 13:1-4). The rending of the temple veil (Mark 15:38) signified the obsolescence of Judaism and the temple in the light of Jesus' death. Jesus is depicted not as a Jewish messiah but as the Son of God, in the sense expounded in Paul's version of Christianity, a factor unrecognized by anyone in the Gospel narratives except for the Gentile Roman soldier at the cross (Mark 15:39). Jesus is shown being opposed by his family, misunderstood by his Jewish disciples, and persecuted by the Jewish leaders. In turn, the rejected Jesus is pictured as rejecting his fellow Jews. Mark thus contains a repudiation of the Jews, a defamation of the family of Jesus, and a derogatory presentation of the apostles. Jesus was, in other words, not really a Jew, certainly no freedom fighter for those who misunderstood and abused him. "Jesus, though born a Jew, was never properly appreciated by Jews and . . . implicitly repudiated his racial relationship with the Jews" (265). "Jesus is represented as setting aside any claim that his Jewish nationality might have had on him" (273).

Mark fails to point out that Simon, one of Jesus' disciples, was a Zealot by simply not translating the Aramaic word Cananaean which means "the Zealot." In not providing a translation, Mark broke with his typical pattern of explaining Aramaic terms with their Greek equivalents. The trial of Jesus is presented by Mark in such a way as totally to blame the Jews. The crucifixion was only the culmination of their attitude toward him. The Barabbas episode in which the Jews chose release for Barabbas and crucifixion for Jesus is considered unhistorical by Brandon for two reasons. There is no other attestation to this practice in Jewish or Latin sources in spite of the fact that Josephus was intent on pointing out all privileges granted to Jews by the Romans and such a practice would have hampered effective government in so seething a country as Judaea. In his depiction of Pilate, Mark covers over the actual course of the trial. Pilate is pictured by Mark as a man uncertain of Jesus' guilt but who is forced by the Jewish leaders into pronouncing sentence. Pilate is said to have perceived that it was the envy of the priests which made them push their charges against Jesus. Mark suggests (Mark 15:14) that Pilate privately recognized the innocence of Jesus but does not have the procurator publicly declare such an awkward position. In addition to presenting Jesus' death as an act resultant upon the hatred of the Jewish leaders, Mark ignored the disturbances in Palestine caused by Pilate's rule. Pilate is presented in Mark's Gospel as an indecisive man, but Brandon argues that what we know of him from other sources depict him as a decisive individual prone to over- rather than under-react.

When the other Gospels were produced some ten to fifteen years later with their portraits of Jesus, several changes were made in the traditions. "Their authors utilised traditions not included in Mark; they were not immediately involved with the consequences of the Jewish War and so were not obliged to be so circumspect as the Markan writer; and they elaborated the Markan portrait of Jesus into that of the pacific Christ [who taught acceptance of injury at the hands of others], which became the established tradition of Christianity" (284-85). These developments produced two results: Jesus is presented in several respects as even more unconcerned with actual political realities than in the Gospel of Mark. At the same time, some elements in the Christian tradition which suggest Jesus' political involvement are not so repressed as in Mark. In regard to Matthew's version of the trial, for example, the First Gospel introduces Pilate's wife as testifying to Jesus' innocence and Pilate symbolically washes his hands to disavow any responsibility for the death. The Jews are consequently made even more to blame for Jesus' death: "His blood be on us and on our children" (Matthew 27:24-5). When Jesus is arrested in Gethsemane, Jesus tells his disciple to put away his sword, since those who take to the sword will perish by the sword (Matthew 26:52). Whereas Mark only mentions the temptations of Jesus in the wilderness, Matthew and Luke use these to show that Jesus clearly renounced any claim to "an earthly kingdom and its acquisition by force of arms" (310).

After these lengthy preliminary considerations, Brandon

turns to the New Testament evidence which suggests that Jesus was intentionally put to death by the Romans because Pilate was convinced that he was politically dangerous and that a "bond of common sympathy surely united Jesus and his followers with those who sought to maintain the ideals of Judas of Galilee" (358).

The presence of a Zealot among Jesus' intimate band of disciples suggests, to Brandon, "that Jesus deliberately chose a professed Zealot for an Apostle, which, in turn, indicates that the profession of Zealot principles and aims was not incompatible with intimate participation in the mission of Jesus" (355). The events narrated about Jesus' Jerusalem ministry in the Synoptic Gospels suggest to Brandon the clearest association of Jesus with Zealot and revolutionary principles. In his cleansing of the temple, Jesus was conducting an attack on the trading system of the temple. The selling of sacrificial animals and the money exchange in the temple were controlled by the priestly and aristocratic magnates who directed and profited from its operations. "The organisation and maintenance of the Temple and its cultus were an immense undertaking, involving enormous economic resources and the employment of a great body of officials and servants, control of which was lucrative and conferred great power and influence" (331). "This attack on the Temple trading system constituted, therefore, a most radical challenge to the authority of the sacerdotal aristocracy, and it was a truly revolutionary act, for the high priest held his office and authority from the Romans, and was thus an essential factor of the Roman government in Judaea. To challenge the rule of the high priest was thus, in effect, to challenge the Roman rule" (332). The Gospels depict Jesus making the attack alone, but Brandon considers this highly unlikely since the company of traders, the temple police, and the Roman troops in the fortress of Antonia overlooking the temple precincts could have easily subdued one man. Brandon suggests that the attack "was achieved by the aid of an excited crowd of his supporters and was attended by violence and pillage" (333). This would explain why no action was taken against him for fear of the multitude (Mark 11:18). Perhaps Jesus may also have uttered some threat against the temple since this charge was brought against him in his trial. "By attacking the system which the sacerdotal aristocracy authorised and from which it drew a considerable revenue, and by making some pronouncement of his intention to destroy the present ordering of the temple and replace it by another more pure and holy, Jesus anticipated what the Zealots achieved in A.D. 66" (335).

The cleansing of the temple, according to Brandon, "coincided with an insurrection in the city, in which Zealots appear to have been involved" (339) (Mark 15:6-7) although the relationship between the two events is uncertain. "In the end, it would seem that the movement of Jews and that of the Zealots converged in revolutionary action in Jerusalem" (356). For Brandon, Jesus' attack on the temple may have been only of symbolic character, although he raises the question as to whether or not Jesus and his supporters may not have intended to seize the rest of the temple with its treasury and thus gain control of the greatest source of sacerdotal power. At any rate, Jesus seems to have seen the ranks of the temple and Sanhedrin hierarchy as the major impediment to a reformed people, deserving of God's salvation. "Clearly, while they ruled Israel for Caesar and to their own advantage, the nation could never be made ready for God's kingdom" (338). The sacerdotal aristocracy saw Jesus' attack on the temple "as a declaration of war against them by Jesus," and they moved to seize him (339).

The events surrounding the Last Supper and the arrest in the garden of Gethsemane suggest Jesus' revolutionary associations. The movement of Jesus and his disciples to the garden late at night points to a prearranged meeting "since Judas Iscariot knew of it and was able to inform the Jewish leaders in time to allow their organisation of an arresting force." Brandon suggests that Mark 14:27-8 "may preserve some memory of Jesus' intention of withdrawing to the desert places of Galilee after the failure of his coup in Jerusalem, thus following the Zealot pattern" (340). At the Last Supper,

Jesus checked on the armament of his followers (Luke 22:35-8), and Brandon considers it unlikely that the disciples were only lightly armed. "With how many swords the disciples were armed is immaterial; it is scarcely likely that it was only two" (341). Whether Jesus intended to resist arrest or whether "he had realised that the tide of events was turning against him, and that he was hesitating whether to give up and withdraw to Galilee" cannot be determined. Resistance was offered, but the Gospels speak of only one incident. "They may well be right: except for one of their number who reacted quickly, the disciples may have been confounded by a sudden and determined assault, and Jesus, realising that resistance was hopeless, surrendered himself. The possibility must be allowed, however, in view of the apologetical concern of the Gospel writers, which we have noted, that the resistance was of a more serious nature, even though it proved ineffective" (342).

Is it possible to determine Jesus' attitude toward Roman power which lay behind the sacerdotal aristocracy whom Jesus attacked in the cleansing of the temple? Brandon believes that it is and that several factors provide the clue. The first of these is Jesus' preaching of the kingdom of God. According to Brandon: "Jesus looked forward to the achievement of an apocalyptic situation that necessarily involved the elimination of the Roman government in Judaea" (344). The proclamation of the kingdom's nearness and the belief that Jesus himself was playing a crucial role in preparing for its advent show that Jesus must have known that conflict with the Romans was inevitable. Secondly, Jesus' statement to his disciples that any who would follow him must take up his cross (Mark 8:34) shows that Jesus saw his mission embroiling himself and his followers with the Romans, since crucifixion was the Roman punishment for extreme Jewish patriots.

Brandon argues further that Jesus' reply about tribute money (Mark 12:13-17) was originally stated as a protest against paying tribute to the Romans. "It was, indeed, a saying of which any Zealot would have approved, because . . .

for the Zealot there was no doubt that God owned the land of Israel, not Caesar" (347). Only when the passage is looked at from a Roman perspective does it support the payment of tribute to the Romans.

Luke's specification of the priestly charges against Jesus before Pilate (Luke 23:2,5) notes three accusations: (1) perverting the nation, (2) forbidding payment of tribute to Caesar, and (3) claiming to be a messianic king. Brandon considers these to be the legitimate charges brought against Jesus, charges anchored in the actions and teachings of Jesus, actions and teachings of a dynamic leader not a visionary swept along by forces he unleashed but could no longer control.

Jesus himself may not have been a member of the Zealot movement, but his revolutionary teachings and actions placed him firmly in the philosophy of political and religious revolution which characterized his day. He differed from the Zealots only in the fact that he was more immediately concerned to attack the Jewish sacerdotal aristocracy, and thus the Romans indirectly, than to engage the Romans openly.

The following is Brandon's summary of the course of Jesus' life and his espousal of revolutionary thought which led to his crucifixion by the Romans for sedition:

Believing that the kingdom of God was at hand, Jesus sought to prepare his fellow-Jews morally and spiritually for membership of this kingdom, whose advent would achieve Israel's destiny as the Elect People of God. Two great obstacles stood in the way of the fulfilment of his mission: the Jewish sacerdotal aristocracy and the Roman government. Jesus seems to have been more concerned with the former, probably because its members were Jews and the traditional leaders of Israel. Consequently, he saw their mode of life and abuse of power as constituting a scandalous contradiction of his ideal of a holy people, ready and prepared for the coming of God's kingdom. Their power, therefore, had to be challenged, and perhaps broken. How long Jesus took in coming to this conclusion is not clear; but our sources point to his finally making a decision to go to Jerusalem at the

Passover, for action that he believed would be fateful. He carefully planned an entry into the city, which was designed to demonstrate his Messianic role. This challenging action was quickly followed by his attack on the Temple trading system. The Gospels do not permit us to know whether this "Cleansing of the Temple" was intended to be the prelude to further action against the hierarchy, although this would seem to be its logical implication. So far as our evidence shows, the "Cleansing of the Temple" was not followed by measures designed to prevent the traffic from restarting; yet it appears that the Jewish leaders did not then feel strong enough to arrest Jesus publicly. The operation in the Temple apparently took place about the same time as an insurrection elsewhere in the city, which the Romans suppressed. This rising was undoubtedly instigated by the Zealots, and it is difficult to believe that it was quite unconnected with Jesus' action in the Temple, although the Gospels mention no connection. The Gospel record gives the impression that the action which Jesus had initiated by coming to Jerusalem proved in some way abortive, and that, by the time of the Passover, Jesus had to take precautions against a surprise attack by the Jewish authorities.

What plans Jesus had, when he was arrested, are unknown. The fact that he was taken by night, after his rendezvous had been betrayed to the Jewish leaders by Judas, suggests that he had no intention of surrendering himself voluntarily, as a kind of sacrificial victim, to his enemies. The latter, whose authority had been gravely challenged by him, proceeded, as we have seen, in a manner that is intelligible in terms of their responsibility to the Roman government for Jewish affairs. After his arrest, they examined him to obtain all possible information about his intentions, and probably the identity and strength of his followers, preparatory to delivering him to Pilate as guilty of subversive views and actions. That Pilate sentenced him to death for sedition was the logical sequel to the case submitted by the Jewish authorities—that he also ordered him to be crucified between two . . . , who were probably Zealots, suggests that he connected Jesus with the insurrection that had coincided with Jesus' activities in Jerusalem (350-51).

9. JESUS: THE BLACK MESSIAH

For nearly 500 years the illusion that Jesus was white dominated the world only because white Europeans dominated the world. Now, with the emergence of the nationalist movements of the world's colored majority, the historic truth is finally beginning to emerge—that Jesus was the non-white leader of non-white people struggling for national liberation against the rule of a white nation, Rome. —Albert B. Cleage, Jr., *The Black Messiah* (p. 3)

In recent years, black consciousness has come to expression if not to realization and fulfillment in the United States and throughout much of the world. In the 1950s and 1960s, the movement toward full civil rights for blacks reached a new plateau. In the wake of the civil rights movement, black power was born and, in the shadow of black power, a renascent black theology has grown.

Black theology has been defined by the National Committee of Black Churchmen in the following terms:

For us, Black Theology is the theology of black liberation. It seeks to plumb the black condition in the light of God's revelation in Jesus Christ, so that the black community can see that the gospel is commensurate with the achievement of black humanity. Black Theology is a theology of "blackness." It is the affirmation of black humanity that emancipates black people from white racism thus providing authentic freedom for both white and black people. It affirms the humanity of white people in that it says "No" to the encroachment of white oppression. The message of liberation is the revelation of God as revealed in the incarnation of Jesus Christ. Freedom IS the gospel. Jesus is the Liberator!

Jesus: The Black Messiah

The development of a black theology and a black interpretation of Jesus may be viewed from three different perspectives. On the one hand, black theology arose because "white theology is severely limited in its interpretation of the Christian faith in so far as the non-white peoples of the world are concerned" (Bishop Joseph A. Johnson, Jr., "Jesus: The Liberator," 87). Johnson expounds on the limitations of traditional or white theology in the following manner:

The interpretation of Christian Theology and of Jesus expounded by white American theologians is severely limited. This is due to the simple reason that these white scholars have never been lowered into the murky depth of the black experience of reality. They never conceived the black Jesus walking the dark streets of the ghettos of the north and the sharecropper's farms in the deep south without a job, busted, and emasculated. These white theologians could never hear the voice of Jesus speaking in the dialect of blacks from the southern farms, or in the idiom of the blacks of the ghetto. This severe limitation of the white theologians' inability to articulate the full meaning of the Christian faith has given rise to the development of Black Theology (88).

A second perspective which precipitated the rise of black theology has been the association of traditional Christianity with oppression of the blacks. Again Bishop Johnson gives expression to this factor:

The tragedy of the interpretations of Jesus by white American theologians during the last three hundred years is that Jesus has been too often identified with the oppressive structures and forces of the prevailing society. His teachings have been used to justify wars, exploitation of the poor and oppressed peoples of the world. In His name the most vicious form of racism has been condoned and advocated. In a more tragic sense this Jesus of the white church establishment has been white, straight haired, blue eyed, Anglo-Saxon, that is, presented in the image of the oppressor. This "whiteness" has prevailed to the extent that the black, brown, or red peoples of the world, who have accepted Jesus as Lord and Savior, were denied full Christian fellowship in His church and were not accepted as brothers for whom Jesus died (86-87). . . . White theology has not been able to re-shape the life of the white church so as to cleanse it of its racism and to liberate it from the iron claws of the white racist establishment of this nation. White theology has presented the blacks a religion of contentment in the state of life in which they find themselves. Such an interpretation of the Christian faith avoided questions about personal dignity, collective power, freedom, equality and self-determination. The white church establishment presented to the black people a religion carefully tailored to fit the purposes of the white oppressors, corrupted in language, interpretation and application by the conscious and unconscious racism of white Christians from the first plantation missionary down to Billy Graham.

The white Christ of the white church establishment is the enemy of the black man (90).

The two previously noted perspectives on black theology have possessed a negative connotation. Black theology is however a theology with a positive orientation or, as expressed by James H. Cone, a "theology whose sole purpose is to apply the freeing power of the gospel to black people under white oppression" (*Black Theology and Black Power*, 31). It is a "theology whose sole purpose is to emancipate the gospel from its 'whiteness' so that blacks may be capable of making an honest self-affirmation through Jesus Christ" (32). "The task of Black Theology . . . is *to analyze the black man's condition in the light of God's revelation in Jesus Christ with the purpose of creating a new understanding of black dignity among black people, and providing the necessary soul in that people, to destroy white racism*" (117).

The double focus on black theology has been expressed by Gayraud S. Wilmore in the following terms:

Black theology expresses both affirmation and negation. It affirms the real possibility of freedom and manhood for Black people, and it negates every power that seeks to demean and rob Black people for the determination of their own destiny. Black theology's contribution to the universal knowledge of God does not lie in its being only the reverse side of traditional Christian theology—white theology in Black vesture. . . . Rather, in its illumination of the religious meaning of Black liberation, Black theology breaks with the

172

determinative norms of white theology and unveils the deepest meaning of human freedom for all men (*Black Religion and Black Radicalism,* 297).

Jesus—his life and teachings—occupies an important position in practically all expressions of black theology. "Black Theology . . . takes seriously the historical Jesus. We want to know who Jesus *was* because we believe that that is the only way to assess who he *is.* If we have no historical information about the character and behavior of that particular Galilean in the first century, then it is impossible to determine the mode of his existence now. Without some continuity between the historical Jesus and the kerygmatic Christ, the Christian gospel becomes nothing but the subjective reflections of the early Christian community" (James Cone, *A Black Theology of Liberation,* 201).

Black theologians, in stressing the importance of the figure of Jesus for black theology, have come to speak of a black Jesus or a black messiah. What does such a concept mean and what understanding of the historical Jesus does it imply?

For Albert Cleage, the idea of Jesus as the black messiah means exactly what it says: "Jesus was a revolutionary black leader, a Zealot, seeking to lead a Black Nation to freedom" (*The Black Messiah,* 4). Cleage argues that the traditional form of Christianity and its understanding of Jesus is a radical distortion of Jesus and his message. In a sermon to his congregation, the Shrine of the Black Madonna in Detroit, he expresses this idea in the following way:

I would say to you, you are Christian, and the things you believe are the teachings of a Black Messiah named Jesus, and the things you do are the will of a black God called Jehovah; and almost everything you have heard about Christianity is essentially a lie.

You have been misled. Christianity for you has been misinterpreted. That which you believe to be Christianity, the theology and philosophy of history which you reject, is not Christianity. The Christianity which we see in the world today was not shaped by Jesus. It was put together by the Apostle Paul who never saw Jesus, and given form and shape

during the Middle Ages when most of the hymns were
written, the hymns which for the most part enunciate white
supremacy. "Fairest Lord Jesus." Most of the famous
religious pictures that you see were painted between the
fourteenth and the seventeenth centuries by white artists.
When Dutch artists painted religious pictures, everything
looks just like it all happened in Holland. When French
artists painted religious pictures, the biblical characters look
French.

But we didn't realize this when we looked at our Sunday
School literature as children. When we turned the pages and
always saw a white Jesus, when we saw pictures of a white
God pointing down at creation, we didn't realize that these
were not statements of fact but statements by white men
depicting what they wanted to believe was true. I say, what
they wanted to believe was true, because essentially they
knew that white men did not create Christianity. They
borrowed it, more bluntly, they stole it. In fact, of all the
peoples on earth, the one people who have never created a
religion worthy of the name religion are white people.

All religions stem from black people. Think of them for a
moment. The Muslim religion, the Buddhist religion, the
Jewish religion, the Christian religion, they all come from
parts of the world dominated by non-white peoples (37-38).

In claiming that Jesus was nonwhite, Cleage argues that
the Jewish nation from which Jesus came was nonwhite.
"The intermingling of the races in Africa and the Mediterranean area is an established fact. The Nation Israel was a
mixture of Chaldeans, Egyptians, Midianites, Ethiopians,
Kushites, Babylonians and other dark peoples, all of whom
were already mixed with the black people of Central Africa"
(3).

Abraham was a Chaldean—probably nonwhite—and
Abraham, Moses, and other Israelites married Egyptians.
Thus Israel was closely related to Africans. Upon their entry
into Canaan, the Hebrews intermarried with the local
population and again in captivity, the Israelites mixed with
the people of Babylonia, which was a nonwhite nation.
"Israel was a mixed-blood, non-white nation. What usually
confuses you is the fact that the Jews you see today in
America are white. Most of them are the descendants of

174

white Europeans and Asiatics who were converted to Judaism about one thousand years ago. The Jews were scattered all over the world. In Europe and Russia, they converted white people to Judaism. The Jews who stayed in that part of the world where black people are predominant, remained black" (41).

Jesus came to the Black Nation Israel. We are not talking now about "God the Father." We are concerned here with the actual blood line. Jesus was born to Mary, a Jew of the tribe of Judah, a non-white people; black people in the same sense that the Arabs were black people, in the same sense that the Egyptians were black people. Jesus was a Black Messiah born to a black woman.

The pictures of the Black Madonna which are all over the world did not all turn black through some mysterious accident. Portraits of the Black Madonna are historic, and today in many countries they are afraid to take the ancient pictures of the Black Madonna out of storage so that people can see them. . . . But the Black Madonna is an historic fact, and Jesus as a Black Messiah is an historic fact (42).

Jesus' ministry was directed to the nation of Israel and stood in the line of the Hebrew prophets who sought to build God's kingdom out of the nation Israel. Jesus' preaching of the kingdom was not otherworldly, but totally this-worldly. "Jesus talked of the kingdom of God on earth" (44). During his career, Jesus sought to build Israel into a nation again. He however had to counter the despair of the people which saw no hope for the future.

Each individual was trying to secure his own little individual benefits from his relationship with the Roman oppressor, some little favor, some little special privilege. The Black Nation of Israel had degenerated into total corruption and hopelessness. Black people no longer believed in themselves and black people no longer loved each other. Their lives were molded by what they thought they could get out of the Romans. They loved their oppressors and hated their brothers because their oppressors had power and their brothers were powerless (60). . . .

So no real Nation existed when Jesus began his ministry.

175

He walked from village to village, preaching, teaching, healing, performing miracles, anything to get a group of people together so that he might give him his simple message. "It is necessary that you turn your back upon individualism and join with your brothers to again build a Black Nation of which we can be proud." Jesus called men to a real decision. In all probability his disciples were already committed to the revolutionary struggle as Zealots before they saw Jesus, but when they heard him, they accepted his leadership and followed him (61). . . .

With the death of John the Baptist, Jesus moved into unquestioned leadership of Israel's revolutionary forces, making inevitable the combined opposition of the white oppressor, Rome, and those black collaborators who feared that revolution might destroy their privileged positions. There were the revolutionary Zealots on one side and the collaborating Scribes and Pharisees on the other, but most of the people hesitated to make a decision and refused to support either side (62). . . .

Jesus didn't spend his life waiting to be crucified. A lot of people seem to have the impression that Jesus walked around with his hands folded, waiting for his enemies to nail him to a cross. That's a lie. He was fighting and twisting and turning all of his life, trying to teach and organize, even while he knew that his enemies were working day and night to destroy him and his influence with the people. When Jesus finally came before Pilate and the people screamed "crucify him, crucify him," this was the result of the campaign of vilification that had been carried on against him by the priests, the Scribes, the Pharisees, and the people in power who were afraid that their power would be lost if a Black Nation came into being. There were the friends who said that he was insane, or he wouldn't be risking himself, and there were the enemies who said that he was evil and in league with the devil. These were the people who killed Jesus. Not the white Gentiles, but his own black people (67).

Jesus did not preach an individualistic ethic; he spent his days fighting against an individualistic form of religion. Jesus sought to root out individualism and stressed the importance of the people as a group, as a nation, seeking to lead the people as a whole from oppression and suffering through revolutionary action. Neither was Jesus a preacher of universal love.

Jesus didn't spend all of his time walking around talking about love. He was trying to bring the Nation together. When he said, "Go the second mile, turn the other cheek," he meant inside the Black Nation. When he said, "Don't come to the altar and try to pray unless you've made peace with your brother," he was talking about inside the Nation. When a Gentile woman came to Jesus and said, "My little girl is on the verge of death. Do something for her," he said, "I don't know you. You're not in the Nation. I came to Israel." She fell on her knees and said, "At least give me the crumbs from the table." And he looked at her and said, "You have a lot of faith," and he healed the little girl. But he didn't come to the Gentiles (98). . . .

Christian people have for so many years misunderstood the teachings of Jesus. Turn the other cheek, go the second mile; if a man takes your coat, give him your cloak as well—these are the internal ethics of a people who are struggling to become a Nation. Jesus meant that you should turn the other cheek to your black brother and to your black sister. For Jesus, the whole idea of brotherhood and love had to do with brotherhood and love within the Nation Israel. He was calling black people from a sense of identification with their white oppressor, and telling them that they must turn their backs on a world in which they were relegated to a second-class position. They must accept the fact that their power lay in their unity, in their willingness to forgive each other and to work and fight and struggle together (215).

For Cleage, the significant aspect of Jesus' ministry was his life and teachings—his efforts to insure the salvation and growth of a nation—and not his submissive acceptance of suffering, the cross, and death. The activities of Jesus in Jerusalem were not undertaken to die and thus to fulfill prophecy. His activity in the capital city was undertaken to insure some success for his movement, to rescue the nation from oppression, and to create a new nation.

When he went into Jerusalem, he didn't just go in to meet with Pontius Pilate and Herod and let them make speeches. He went in to confront an enemy. That's the difference. He went in to do battle against an enemy. The first night he got out of sight as quickly as possible. The next day he came back into the city and went to the Temple. The Temple was the center of the corruption that was destroying the Nation. The priests, Scribes, and the Pharisees controlled the power there. But it wasn't real power. It was Uncle Tom power. They depended upon Rome for their very existence, but Rome let them carry on their little rackets. . . . Everything in the Temple had been reduced to a racket, and the rackets were operated by Jews with the connivance of Rome (78-79). . . .

Jesus went through the whole of Holy Week fighting to salvage what he could of his Movement, leaving people something that they could pass on when he was killed. Every day of this climactic week before his crucifixion he tried to do what he could to see that his teachings about the Nation were understood. On Wednesday he went to Bethany with his friends. He made almost a whole day's journey to sit down alone with the people who were to be the nucleus of the Nation. He sat down in the home of Mary and Martha with others who were committed to the revolution, and talked to them all day and far into the night. You remember the woman who came bringing the expensive ointment. "She anoints me for my burial," he said. But he was trying to tell them the things they were to remember.

Then, on Thursday, he went back for the Passover meal with his disciples. He knew that if anything was to be preserved after his death it all depended upon the under-standing of these twelve men. They had heard him. They knew his message. If they couldn't carry it on, it was done, it was lost and his work was finished. So on Thursday he sat down with the twelve and talked to them. He tried to get them to understand that the Nation can come into being only when we are willing to sacrifice and be humble (81).

The importance of the resurrection is not to be found in the resurrection of the physical Jesus; the significance of the resurrection lies in the rebirth of the nation. One must read the stories of the resurrection and realize that these were written many years after the death of Jesus when its true significance had been clouded by later interpretations.

So the Resurrection that we celebrate is not the Resurrec-tion of the physical body of Jesus, but the Resurrection of the Black Nation which he started, the Resurrection of his ideas and his teachings. The immortality which Jesus has lies in the fact that two thousand years later we remember, and two thousand years later we are trying to do the same thing he tried to do with the Black Nation in Palestine. Today, in the midst of corruption, we are drawing people one by one, two by two, into the Black Nation. This task and the faith that it can be done, this is the Resurrection (99). . . .

Jesus undertook the Resurrection of the Nation. This is why the Disciples were not greatly concerned when the women went to the tomb and found that Jesus was not there. They were not primarily concerned with the Resurrection of Jesus as an individual. Jesus had taught that a Black Nation was to come into being out of a people who had ceased to believe in the possibilities of a new Nation and his Disciples had begun to catch a glimpse of this kind of Resurrection (93).

The distortion of the true life and message of Jesus, the black messiah, was primarily the work of the apostle Paul.

During this early period when people were trying to determine the meaning of the life and death of Jesus, the Apostle Paul came on the scene with an entirely new interpretation. He had never seen Jesus in the flesh, but his interpretation dominated the early Church and greatly influenced the Gospels when they were written. So in the Book of Galatians and in the Acts of the Apostles, you have a whole lot of arguing going on between the Disciples and the Apostle Paul. Paul was out in the field moving from city to city, organizing churches. He was a great organizer in the modern sense. He did whatever was necessary to put an organization together. The Disciples and the followers of Jesus back in Jerusalem said, "This man is not organizing the right kind of churches. He has forgotten the things that were important to Jesus." But Paul wrote letters and they wrote nothing. Why were the followers of Jesus critical of the Apostle Paul? Because the Apostle Paul was leaning over backward to convert the Gentiles. "Apostle to the Gentiles" meant Apostle to the white people. Paul was taking the religion of a Black Nation to white people who had no background in religion. But to make it acceptable to them he had to change it (88-89). . . .

The Apostle Paul was a Jew. He went to the Gentiles with a religion about a Black Messiah and immediately he began to change it so that they would be able to accept it. Greece and Rome were heathen nations. They conceived of God in primitive terms as someone who went around throwing thunderbolts at his enemies. . . . So when the Apostle Paul tried to take the religion of Jesus to them, he distorted the Black Messiah to make him fit their primitive conceptions. To understand what paganism did to Jesus, compare the Gospel of Mark with the Gospel of John. That is because the Gospel of John has taken on the pagan, heathen philosophy of the Gentiles and tried to weave it into the life of Jesus. The historic Jesus is completely lost (89).

For some black theologians, the concept of Jesus as the black messiah does not carry the historical implications found in Cleage, implications about the history and nature of ancient Israel out of which Christ came. For example, James Cone can write: "But some whites will ask, Does Black Theology believe that Christ was *really* black? It seems to me that the *literal* color of Jesus is irrelevant, as are the different shades of blackness in America. . . . But as it happens, *he was not white* in any sense of the word, literally or theologically. Therefore, the Reverend Cleage is not too far wrong when he describes Jesus as a black Jew; and he is certainly on solid grounds when he describes him as the Black Messiah" (*A Black Theology of Liberation,* 218). In a somewhat similar vein, J. Deotis Roberts declares: "I do not take the figure of a black Messiah in a literal historical sense. It is rather a symbol or a myth with profound meaning for black people" (*Liberation and Reconciliation,* 130). From these quotes, it appears that Cone stands closer to Cleage than Roberts.

For Cone and Roberts, and for other black theologians, the concept of Jesus as the black messiah is an interpretative concept or symbol which serves both a negative and positive function. On the one hand, it is the means for the repudiation of the traditional portrait and interpretation of Jesus within white Christendom or what has been called "whiteanity." The white messiah of western Christianity has been one in whose name whites have subjected and oppressed the nonwhites of the world. Such a Christ appears as the enemy not the friend and liberator of the oppressed.

The task of explicating the existence of Christ for black people is not easy since we live in a white society that uses

Christianity as an instrument of oppression. The white conservatives and liberals alike present images of a white Christ that are completely alien to the liberation of the black community. Their Christ is a mild, easy-going white American who can afford to mouth the luxuries of "love," "mercy," "long-suffering," and other white irrelevancies, because he has a multi-billion-dollar military force to protect him from the encroachments of the ghetto and the "communist conspiracy." But black existence is existence in a hostile world without the protection of the law. If Christ is to have any meaning for us, he must leave the security of the suburbs by joining black people in their condition. What need have we for a white Christ when we are not white but black? If Christ is white and not black, he is an oppressor, and we must kill him. The appearance of Black Theology means that the black community is now ready to do something about the white Christ, so that he cannot get in the way of our revolution (Cone, *A Black Theology of Liberation,* 198-99).

On the other hand, the idea of Jesus as the black messiah is a means for understanding the central thrust of the life and ministry of the historical Jesus and the means for making Jesus relevant to the struggles of blacks in today's world. For black theologians, a central feature of the historical Jesus was his identity as an oppressed and his identity with the oppressed.

Taking seriously the New Testament Jesus, Black Theology believes that the historical kernel is the manifestation of Jesus as the Oppressed One whose earthly existence was bound up with the oppressed of the land. . . . To understand the historical Jesus without seeing his identification with the poor as decisive is to misunderstand him and thus distort his historical person. And a proper theological analysis of Jesus' historical identification with the helpless is indispensible for our interpretation of the gospel today (202-3).

The stage of his ministry was the streets. His congregation consisted of those who were written off by the established church and state. He ministered to those who needed him, "the nobodies of the world," the sick, the blind, the lame and the demon possessed. He invaded the chambers of sickness and death and hallowed these with the healing words of health and life. He invaded the minds of the demon possessed and in those dark chambers of night he brought light, sanity and order. Jesus ministered to men in their sorrow, sin and degradation and offered them hope and light and courage and strength. He offered comfort to the poor who did not fit into the structure of the world. Jesus comforted the mourner and offered hope to the humble. He had a message for the men and women who had been pushed to the limits of human existence and on these he pronounced his blessedness.

The people who received help from Jesus are throughout the Gospels on the fringe of society—men who because of fate, guilt and prejudices were considered marked men (Johnson, "Jesus: the Liberator," 95-96).

The black Jesus is understood as the liberator, as the one who came to bring redemption from oppression, as the revolutionary political messiah whose goal in living was human freedom. "Jesus' proclamation of the kingdom is an announcement of God's decision about oppressed man. 'The time is fulfilled, and the kingdom of God is at hand,' that is, slavery is about to end, since the reign of God displaces all false authorities" (Cone, *A Black Theology of Liberation,* 207). "Jesus is the Oppressed One whose work is that of liberating humanity from inhumanity. Through him the oppressed are set free to be what they are" (209).

The black messiah is the means for making Jesus relevant to the total struggles of today's blacks.

The Black Christ is he who threatens the structure of evil as seen in white society, rebelling against it, thereby becoming the embodiment of what the black community knows that it must become. Because he has become black as we are, we now know what black empowerment is. It is black people determining the way they are going to behave in the world (216). . . .

In our language today, the oppressed are the people of the black ghettos, the Indian reservations, the Spanish *barrios,* and other places where whiteness has created misery. To participate in God's salvation is to cooperate with the Black Christ as he liberates his people from bondage. Salvation then primarily has to do with earthly reality and the injustice inflicted on those who are helpless and poor. To see the salvation of God is to see these people rise up against their oppressors, demanding that justice become a reality now and not tomorrow. . . . The new day is the presence of the Black Christ as expressed in the liberation of the black community (226-27).

The black Christ liberates and the universal Christ reconciles. The Jesus of the disinherited set us free. The Jesus who breaks through the color line reconciles all men. But all persons must be confronted by Jesus and take seriously his personal claims on their lives and their people before he can become Lord of all. We cannot fully know Jesus in the role of reconciler until we know him in his role as liberator. The way to a knowledge of Christ as reconciler passes through his "liberator role." *Jesus means freedom!* (Roberts, *A Black Political Theology,* 138).

10. JESUS: THE MESSIANIC SCHEMER

> The destined road for Jesus led to torture at Jerusalem on a Roman cross, to be followed by resurrection. But these things had to come about in the manner predicted by the Scriptures and after preliminaries entailing the most careful scheming and plotting to produce them. Moves and situations had to be anticipated, rulers and associates had to perform their functions without realizing that they were being used. A conspiracy had to be organized of which the victim was himself the deliberate secret instigator. It was a nightmarish conception and undertaking, the outcome of the frightening logic of a sick mind, or of a genius. And it worked out.
> —Hugh J. Schonfield, *The Passover Plot* (p. 125)

As a young Jewish college student, Hugh J. Schonfield says he read numerous Jewish and Christian interpretations of Jesus and felt they were partly right and partly wrong. For him, "there was a mystery which called for further explanation" (2). His explanation of that mystery has now been presented in his best-selling book, *The Passover Plot*.

Like many other scholars in the course of the study of the historical Jesus, Schonfield feels that, as the New Testament tells the story, something is missing. A major piece of the puzzle must still be put into its proper place in order to understand the full plot which made up the life of Jesus. Schonfield is not here concerned merely with the fact that the early church overlaid the historical Jesus with its "pagan assessment of his worth in terms of deity" (3). Nor with the traditional portraiture which is so "baffling in its apparent contradiction of the terms of our earthly existence" (2). Nor is he merely referring to the fact that the Gospel writers produced their works with "meager resources of documentation and living recollection. This was because of the Jewish revolt against Rome in A.D. 66 which resulted in the devastation of Palestine and Jerusalem and largely extinguished access to fuller information." This latter problem, like the former ones, can be overcome for, in attempting to understand Jesus, "actually we are better placed now than they were. When the Gospels were composed, legend, special pleading, the new environment of Christianity after the war, and a changed view of the nature of Jesus, gave them a flavour of which we have to be fully conscious when we enlist their essential aid in the quest of the historical Jesus" (6).

The missing element which allows a true understanding of Jesus' career is the recognition that "awareness of being the Messiah meant everything to Jesus" and that "in affirmation of that office, that peculiar and incredibly difficult function, he directed his life, anticipated his execution, and envisaged his resurrection." In other words, the plot of Jesus' life was the plot given to it by Jesus who planned and controlled not only its major contours but contrived to bring to pass those details around which the Christian faith would be built. The "plot" is thus the element "which strikes the keynote of the whole extraordinary undertaking to which Jesus committed himself."

This book reveals him as a master of his destiny, expecting events to conform to the requirements of prophetic intimations, contriving those events when necessary, contending with friends and foes to ensure that the predictions would be fulfilled. Such strength of will founded on faith, such concentration of purpose, such astuteness in planning, such psychological insight as we find him displaying, marks him out as a dominant and dynamic personality, with a capacity for action which matched the greatness of his vision. He could be tender and compassionate, but he was no milk-and-water Messiah. He accepted that authority had been conferred upon him by God, and he exercised it with profound effect, whether favourable or unfavourable, on those who came in contact with him (7).

For Schonfield, the overriding factor in the life of Jesus was his belief that he was the Jewish messiah. This was also the fundamental element in the faith of the early church: "Christianity . . . did not begin as a new religion but as a movement of monotheistic Jews who held Jesus to be their God-sent king and deliverer. Here, in a sentence, is what it is imperative to know about the origins of Christianity" (12).

But behind the man Jesus and the faith of the early church lies an idea upon which they both were founded. "It is often said that Christianity is founded upon a person. That is true. But it is only part of the historical truth. What, so to speak, was the person founded upon? The answer is that he was founded upon an idea, a strange idea current among the Jews of his time, an idea alien to Western thought which many non-Jewish theologians still find very inconvenient, the idea of Messianism" (12).

In order to understand the idea behind the man, Schonfield argues, it is absolutely necessary to realize that Jesus accepted a current interpretation of the messiah and acted on the basis of this interpretation without attempting any reinterpretation of the concept.

We have no right to say that while Jesus accepted the designation of Messiah he did so in a sense quite different from any expectations entertained in his time. It would be unthinkable for him to do this, firstly because being the Messiah meant answering to certain prophetic requirements which for him were divinely inspired, and secondly because he would consciously have been depriving his people of any possibility of acknowledging him: he would be inviting them to reject him as a false Messiah (13).

What elements made up this messianism which Jesus inherited and applied to himself? In the first place, it did not involve any "paganised doctrine of the incarnation of the Godhead with which for Christians it has become intermingled" (13). The messianism of the time in no way identified the messiah with God—a blasphemous concept threatening to Jewish monotheism—so that "Jesus as much as any other Jew would have regarded as blasphemous the manner in which he is depicted, for instance, in the Fourth Gospel" (14). The messianism that was rampant in the days of Jesus focused upon the "establishment of the Kingdom of God on earth, for which the prerequisite was a righteous Israel, or at least a righteous remnant of Israel" (19). The fulfilment of prophetic predictions, such as those in the book of Daniel, led people to believe they were living in the last days just before the end. Various groups, like the Pharisees and Essenes, were aiming at the perfection of the community and the satisfaction of daily life.

Strange imaginings had gripped the Jewish people at this time, the time Jesus came into the world, fed by those who interpreted the Scriptures to them. According to many preachers, the eleventh hour had come, the Last Times had begun, the Kingdom of God was at hand. The world was on the eve of Wrath and Judgment. The Messiah would appear (26).

Jesus was thus born into an environment ablaze with messianic fervor. But how was the messiah conceived? What would be his character? The expected messiah was not understood in terms of a militant warrior. "In fact in references to the Messiah up to the time of Jesus the conception of a Warrior Messiah does not appear" (27). Only among the Palestinian peasantry and the oppressed was any such warrior messiah expected. The general view of the expected messiah saw him as just, holy, the perfect Israelite, the messiah of righteousness, living in close communion with God and obedient to his will. Among the Galilean sectarian groups of which Jesus had some knowledge, there existed an "ancient Israelitish type of religion" (31) in whose thought the righteous king figure·had been combined with the idea of the suffering just one; and the conception of the messiah had been infused with the concept of son of man. So all the material lay at hand for Jesus to appear as the messiah.

The right understanding of Jesus commences with the realisation that he identified himself with the fulfilment of the Messianic Hope. Only on this basis do the traditions about him become wholly intelligible. He was no charlatan, wilfully and deliberately misleading his people, well knowing that his posing as the Messiah was fraudulent. There is not the slightest suspicion of pretence on his part. On the contrary, no one could be more sure of his vocation than was Jesus, and not even the threat of imminent death by the horrible torture of crucifixion could make him deny his messiahship. We have to accept the absolute sincerity of Jesus (33).

How did Jesus come to believe himself the messiah? Schonfield suggests that this must have come to him in his tender years of childhood. It was not something given in a miracle of birth, for "there was nothing peculiar about the birth of Jesus. He was not God incarnate and no Virgin Mother bore him" (42). "He was as completely human as every baby" (44). He may have sensed his messiahship because of some parental hopes associated with a first born child, or due to some external circumstance, or a chance laudatory remark about his future, or perhaps from hearing of the Galilean struggles and hopes. It was, nonetheless, during his early years that Jesus came to his understanding of himself as the messiah, since "the major features of what he had to do were clear to Jesus before he went to be baptised by John" (46).

Of Jesus' youthful years and their impact upon Jesus, Schonfield writes:

So the picture we can form of the young Jesus is of a quiet, dutiful, watchful individual, with an inner life of his own and a deep-seated faith. He had a bright intelligence and was by no means aloof from his surroundings, yet was prone to detach himself from them. He was not at all uncommunicative when it came to finding out what he wished to know; but he was rather a strange boy and something of a puzzle to his parents, not readily drawing attention to himself, and inwardly busy with tremendous imaginings which it was impossible for him to reveal. What some of his cherished thoughts were about we may hazard a confident guess: they were about the world, about God's dealings with Israel, and about the deliverer who had been promised to his people (48).

The form which Jesus understood his messiahship must take was the result of a number of factors. Most dominant of all was his insight into and understanding of the messianic interpretation of the scriptures. On the basis of such texts or oracles and some instruction and insight borrowed from the Galilean sectarians, Jesus developed his understanding of what must befall the messiah. "A prophetic blueprint of the Days of the Messiah was the outcome of his investigations. The Scriptures thus disclosed to him the character of his mission, how his message would be received, his fate, and his subsequent appearance in glory as king and judge of the nations " (59).

Jesus seems also to have possessed what might be called a "father fixation" (53), perhaps developed because of the unexpected early death of his father Joseph. His understanding of his special sonship to God was no doubt influenced by this factor. He may also have obtained from the communities of the sectarian saints some "elements of the healing art cultivated and practised" (57) by them. Also, Jesus was an astute observer of life.

While he would often seek solitude, he did not lock himself away in a private world of his own. He became a keen student of life and human character. Very little escaped his penetrating notice. The man we meet in the Gospels is one who knows the countryside of Galilee intimately, its flowers and trees, fields and orchards, the activities of the people in work and worship, in their social, spiritual, political and economic affairs. The things he teaches and the realistic tales he tells to illustrate his teaching, are proof of how much he has absorbed. Such a store of information could only have been the outcome of prolonged and acute observation. There had been nothing somnambulistic in his walks abroad. He had deemed it to be vital to his equipment that he should have firsthand knowledge of the ways of the world (5?).

Jesus' recognition and realization of himself as the messiah must have presented Jesus with great personal struggles; it was not easy for Jesus to own himself as the man his people awaited. Such a recognition was not an act of megalomania, for Jesus saw himself as servant.

Jesus came forth as the messiah to put "into operation a

programme which was the outcome of his prior messianic investigations. . . . His visualisation of the role of the Messiah was highly theatrical," and the messianic predictions had "acquired the form of a drama."

He played out the part like an actor with careful timing and appreciation of what every act called for. His calculated moves, his symbolic actions such as the forty days in the wilderness and the choice of twelve apostles, his staging of the triumphal entry into Jerusalem and the Last Supper, all testify to his dramatic consciousness, as do many of his gestures and declamations. Only one who possessed such a consciousness could have conceived, contrived, and carried out the Passover Plot so masterfully and so superbly. But the portrayal of the Messiah's tragedy, and the anticipation of the happy ending, was utter sincere. This was reality not make-believe.

For Jesus it was of the essence of his faith that God in his mysterious ways had made choice of him, a descendant of David, as the means of fulfilling those purposes which from age to age the Lord had inspired his messengers to proclaim. It was a knowledge which he could not communicate to anyone, could not even hint at before his call came. He could only prepare himself, and wait (61).

With the appearance of John the Baptist, Jesus' "trying years of waiting were over" (65). Elijah had appeared as the prophetic oracles had predicted. Jesus went to be baptized by John—to undergo his anointment—confident that he would undergo a great experience and receive the gift of the Spirit.

Never had Jesus witnessed such a scene or listened to such words. Truly here was a prophet who spoke with the voice of God, spoke in language that united with all he had thought and believed! He stepped into the chill stream, and the hairy hand of John was upon him, sending him down, down into the depths. Jesus prayed. Slowly he rose up out of the water; and then he had the experience. Tradition says that he heard a Voice from heaven, and that the Spirit of God descended upon him like a dove, or in the likeness of a dove, and entered into him, thus signifying that he was the Messiah (68).

Jesus: The Messianic Schemer

With a faithfulness to unalterable divine decrees, Jesus began his ministry in Galilee. His messiahship however had to be kept secret, for its acknowledgement would have been disastrous. Since the messiah was the legitimate king, the Romans would have pounced upon him with the charge of sedition. So in the beginning, Jesus gave the impression of being a "harmless religious enthusiast" (74). In his call to repentance, his teachings, and his miracles, Jesus was "walking on a knife-edge" (75). He had to guard against any overenthusiasm by his followers and prevent his ministry from being cut short like that of John. So Jesus spoke of himself as the Son of man, a term which gave him external anonymity, since it was a term whose messianic connotations were understood only by the communities of the saints which posed no threat to him. Jesus had thus to secure for himself safety and freedom of movement. The inner circle of the disciples, who were patriotic and possessed by a simple faith, was physically strong and personally loyal. They made up a useful bodyguard and possessed boats which Jesus could use to avoid the multitudes or to flee from hostile sentiments.

The multitudes who were attracted to Jesus, primarily because of his miraculous cures, presented a problem to Jesus.

The essential problem which Jesus had to overcome was the difficulty created by the crowds which everywhere surrounded him and besought his help, and made it hard for him to extend quickly enough the areas in which he could hope to deliver his message personally. What with teaching and healing, and people struggling frantically to reach him, to touch even the sacred fringe of his robe as he passed, by the end of most days he was utterly exhausted. At one time by the lake to gain freedom to speak he used a boat moored off-shore as his pulpit. He even crossed to the other side for a brief respite. But the people ran round the coast to meet him as he landed, or followed in other boats. He could not get away (78).

To overcome this problem and to make the most of the valuable time available, Jesus sent out his twelve disciples on a preaching mission. But the disciples, who only reported success in demon subjection, and Jesus experienced this first phase of his career as a failure. He knew from prophecy that his message would not be received, but he still hoped for a miracle. His preaching had fallen on deaf eyes, and Jesus was moved and hurt by his failure. His feelings expressed themselves in some bitter and scathing words.

At the same time, some aspects of Jesus' preaching and some of his actions antagonized the Pharisees who devoted their days to attempts to produce a faithful people. These opponents set out, not to have Jesus killed, but put out of operation, silenced so that his influence would be checked.

The execution of John the Baptist triggered the second phase of Jesus' ministry—a phase in which he secretly taught his disciples his true identity. At Caesarea Philippi, Peter made it known to Jesus that his true identity had been revealed to his disciples. Jesus then began to teach his disciples of his forthcoming suffering in terms of the Old Testament oracles, almost like a testimony book, which spoke of the rejection, suffering, and execution of the messiah. Such oracles Jesus had extracted from the scriptures, interpreted them, and integrated them so that in one figure were woven together what have originally been distinct messianic personalities—the prophet like Moses, the suffering just one, the son of David, and the apocalyptic Son of man. "With the help of the Oracles Jesus had deduced that he was required to suffer ignominiously at the hands of the rulers at Jerusalem." The reaction of his disciples to his disclosures, however, made it plain to Jesus that "he could not take them fully into his confidence" (91). The disciples could participate in but they could not share in the knowledge about the greatest plot of all.

Jesus had now to prepare for the most difficult and dangerous part of his present mission, which demanded the utmost caution, and the most careful organisation and timing. He could not look to his disciples to assist him directly in the arrangements for his coming ordeal. He could not even trust them not to work against him if he told them too much; and they might easily ruin everything which he had to contrive. They were devoted to him, and loyal in their own way, but of limited intelligence, simple Galileans for the most part, who would not be at all at home in the sophisticated atmosphere of Jerusalem. What Jesus had need of now for the furtherance of his designs were dependable friends in Judea (92).

For Jesus' activity in Jerusalem and what transpired during the passion week, the Gospel of John provides the clues. Only the Fourth Gospel tells us of Nicodemus, Lazarus of Bethany, and the unnamed, beloved Judaean disciple. The Fourth Gospel is correct when it suggests a three-month ministry in Jerusalem extending from the Feast of Tabernacles (October) until the Feast of Dedication (January) with a period of withdrawal followed by the events of the final week.

Jerusalem at the time was caught up in a struggle between Pilate and the chief priests. The latter were openly friendly to Pilate while at the same time scheming to get him discredited so that the Emperor Tiberius would recall him. The priests had to make every effort to prevent any anti-Roman outbursts, for this would have played into Pilate's hands. The priests were distraught over Pilate's actions, for he had laid impious hands on the sacred treasury of the temple to build a water conduit to Jerusalem. By coming to Jerusalem, Jesus was adding a further complication to the top-level struggle already in progress.

Jesus' plans had to be well laid and executed to perfection, for he was now in critical Judea where a false move could have wrecked everything. In his preaching in the temple, Jesus was attaining two immediate objectives: "He was proclaiming his message where it would have the maximum effect, in the centre of Jewish worship, and he was bringing himself prominently to the attention both of rulers and people" (102). He taught not in the streets but in the temple where he could avoid undue risk, and he had available the family and home of Lazarus into which he could withdraw, rest, not be taken easily by surprise, and plan methodically his great final undertaking. For his confidants, Jesus chose two close Judaean disciples, Lazarus and the young unnamed priest—the disciple whom Jesus loved—whom Schonfield calls John. The latter was most important, for he had contact with secret disciples and the Sanhedrin and could be used in carrying messages and keeping Jesus informed of the plans and actions of the Council. In working out his plans, Jesus had his eye on one other man—Judas Iscariot.

By the time Jesus left Jerusalem in January his business there was very nearly finished and the stage set for the drama to be enacted at the Passover some three months later. There was every reason why he should choose this festival in particular as the season of his revelation and of his suffering. Its symbolism and associations were altogether appropriate and in keeping with the prophecies (104). . . .
Thus it was settled that at the coming Passover Jesus would reveal himself publicly to Israel as the Messiah. His hour, so long awaited, would have come (105).

Jesus withdrew from Jerusalem following the Feast of Dedication and crossed into Transjordan. His withdrawal was temporarily interrupted by news that Lazarus was seriously ill. Jesus returned to Bethany, and although what happened there can no longer be accurately ascertained, it gave rise to the report that Jesus had performed a major miracle. The Sanhedrin—the Council—heard this report and suspected that Jesus was now making his move to lead an uprising. In a specially convened session, the Sanhedrin reached the decision that Jesus must now be liquidated. Friends on the Council, among whom was Nicodemus, speedily provided an intelligence report to Jesus informing him of the results of the meeting. Jesus quickly withdrew again, ultimately making his way to Galilee where he would stay until he returned to Jerusalem for Passover accompanied by a substantial body of Galileans.

Jesus proclaimed publicly his messiahship upon his triumphal entry—a well-laid plan carried out through the aid of Lazarus, who arranged for the ass upon which Jesus could ride as the predicted king. "Jesus came to Jerusalem as a king in the most open manner" (114). He was acclaimed by the crowd as Son of David. Jesus' well laid plans had assured that the Sanhedrin could not intervene. Accompanied by his Galilean and some Judaean supporters, Jesus' popularity meant that the Sanhedrin would be treated as Roman lackeys if they took action. At the same time, the Sanhedrin could not ignore the matter; otherwise they were open to the charge of aiding and abetting treason and would thus incur Rome's disfavor. "This Jesus, in his mad folly, had placed them between the devil and the deep blue sea" (116).

With Jesus' triumphant entry into Jerusalem, "the die was cast, and now there could be no turning back. Jesus had boldly and publicly committed himself in the way he had planned. . . . By so doing he had made himself guilty of treason against Caesar. . . . The action of Jesus had been intentional and deliberate, and he was fully aware that there could be only one outcome, his arrest and execution" (114).

The events which preceded the crucifixion were all played according to the plan masterminded by Jesus and executed with special help unknown to his twelve disciples. Jesus' anointment in Bethany was carried out by private arrangement with Mary, sister of Lazarus, in order to trigger Judas' betrayal as well as to point toward Jesus' death.

Judas knew that Jesus expected to be betrayed. He had been saying so again and again, and once more now he had spoken about his death. We may believe, however, that not until this moment had Judas thought of himself as the betrayer. It was the worth of the ointment and Jesus talking about his burial which put it into his head. Suddenly like an inspiration it came to him that money was to be made by doing what Jesus plainly wanted. It seemed as if in a subtle way Jesus was telling him this, inviting him to profit by doing his will. The tempter came in the guise of his Master (129).

Judas went to the Council to lay plans for the betrayal. Both he and the Council were unknowing participants in the greatest drama of Jesus' ministry. "The Council might imagine they were exercising their own free will in determining to destroy Jesus, and Judas Iscariot might believe the same in betraying him; but in fact the comprehensive engineer of the Passover Plot was Jesus himself. Their responses were governed by his ability to assess their reactions when he applied appropriate stimuli. Thus it was that the Scriptures would be fulfilled" (130-31).

The Last Supper was observed in the Jerusalem home of the beloved disciple who was the eye-witness source behind the Fourth Gospel. Arrangements were made and executed, all without the knowledge of the Twelve. There were fourteen at the supper that night, Jesus, the Twelve, and the beloved disciple.

Jesus' trial was based on his political pretensions, not on theological grounds. As always, Jesus' actions and especially his silence while on trial were to fulfill the prophetic oracles—"he was dumb like a sheep before his shearers" (Isaiah 53:7).

Just as he had always planned ahead so Jesus had calculated about his death and resurrection.

The plans of Jesus were laid with remarkable care for timing. He had singled out a particular Passover as the season when he would suffer, and had taken every precaution to ensure that he would not be arrested beforehand. During the first half of Passion Week, keeping himself in the public eye by conducting his activities in the Temple, he had aggravated the ecclesiastical authorities to the pitch that they were determined to destroy him as soon as it should be feasible without risk of a tumult; but he was careful not to help them by staying in the city after dark. Not until Wednesday evening did Jesus apply the pressure that decided Judas to go to the Council with an offer to betray him, and by his secret arrangements he saw to it that the arrest would not take place until Thursday evening after he had partaken of the Last Supper in Jerusalem with his disciples. All this suggests that he intended that his crucifixion should be on Friday, which would be the eve of the Sabbath. Calculating that it would require some hours on Friday morning for the Council to obtain his condemnation by Pilate, which could not be withheld as the charge was treason against the emperor, and knowing that in accordance with custom he would not be left on the cross over the Sabbath, but would be taken down well before sunset when the Sabbath commenced, Jesus could roughly reckon that he would experience crucifixion for not much more than three or four hours, whereas normally the agonies of the crucified lasted for as many days (153-54).

Jesus was convinced that he must suffer but not die on the cross, since the messiah would survive his terrible ordeal. Thus he laid plans to insure that this was the case. One cannot follow the Gospel accounts on what happened here, since their authors worked with such scanty material and were influenced by various legends and misunderstood stories, some from the writings of Josephus. For the success of the rescue from the cross, Jesus had to have a drug administered to him to create the impression of death, and he had to arrange for a speedy delivery of his body to his secret disciples. At the signal words, "I am thirsty," Jesus was passed the drug and lapsed quickly into unconsciousness. Swiftly, Joseph of Arimathea, a secret disciple, carried out the prearranged plans and asked Pilate for the body. Pilate, checking with the centurion in charge and thinking that death had occurred, turned over what he thought was the corpse of Jesus.

As Schonfield reconstructs the subsequent events, Jesus was taken to the tomb of Joseph, an act witnessed by the women. In the course of the night, he was brought out of the tomb by the persons involved in the scheme. For a time, he regained consciousness and commissioned one of the secret followers to carry a message to his disciples. Jesus died later that night from his wounds, especially the unplanned soldier's spearthrust in his side. Instead of returning the body to the original tomb where the burial clothes had been left, his body was "quickly yet reverently interred" elsewhere (165). The women coming to the garden discovered the empty tomb and saw a man, probably the same person who had passed the drugged drink to Jesus at the time of the crucifixion. John the priest and Peter came to the tomb, saw the burial clothes, and John was convinced of the resurrection. Although John had participated in part of the plot, Jesus had dealt singly and individually with his Judaean followers who were in a position to aid his plans, and had not brought everyone in on the whole plot. John thus knew nothing of the crucifixion phase of the plot. Mary Magdalene encountered the man in the garden who tried to pass along the final message of Jesus, but was mistaken for Jesus. The man who appeared to the two on the road to Emmaus and to the disciples in Galilee was the same man who appeared in all the resurrection stories. He was anxious to deliver to the disciples the message which Jesus had given him as he lay dying. His message was that the messiah had risen in accordance with the scriptures. "Finally he was able to discharge his obligation" (172).

In proclaiming the resurrection, there was no deliberate untruth perpetuated by the disciples. On the basis of the evidence, they had reached the inescapable conclusion. Jesus too had acted in faith to fulfil the scriptures.

Neither had there been any fraud on the part of Jesus himself. He had schemed in faith for his physical recovery, and what he expected had been frustrated by circumstances quite beyond his control. Yet when he sank into sleep his faith was unimpaired, and by an extraordinary series of contributory events, partly resulting from his own planning, it proved to have been justified. In a manner he had not forseen resurrection had come to him. And surely this was for the best, since there would have been no future for a Messiah who returned temporarily to this troubled world possibly crippled in mind and body.

By his planning beyond the cross and the tomb, by his implicit confidence in the coming of the Kingdom of God over which he was deputed to reign, Jesus had won through to victory. The messianic programme was saved from the grave of all dead hopes to become a guiding light and inspiration to men. Wherever mankind strives to bring in the rule of justice, righteousness and peace, there the deathless presence of Jesus the Messiah is with them. Wherever a people of God is found labouring in the cause of human brotherhood, love and compassion, there the King of the Jews is enthroned. No other will ever come to be what he was and do what he did. The special conditions which produced him at a peculiar and pregnant moment in history are never likely to occur again. But doubtless there will be other moments having their own strange features, and other men through whom the vision will speak at an appointed time. Meanwhile we have not exhausted the potentialities of the vision of Jesus (173-74).

11. JESUS: THE FOUNDER
OF A SECRET
SOCIETY

All this history is merely plausible, and plausibility is not proof. Things probably happened thus, though they may have happened otherwise. History, however, is by definition the search for the *most probable* explanations of preserved phenomena. When several explanations are possible, the historian must always choose the most probable one. But the truth is that improbable things sometimes happen. Therefore truth is necessarily stranger than history. —Morton Smith, *The Secret Gospel* (p. 148)

Quite early in the history of the church, secret and closed groups sprung up within Christianity claiming to possess a superior knowledge (gnosis) and a truer understanding of Christianity than that available to the church at large. These gnostic groups had many similarities to the mystery religions which were widespread in the Greco-Roman world at the time of the church's earliest days. Persons were especially initiated into the mystery community. Initiation rituals generally involved purifications of various types, instruction in the secrets and mysteries of the group, and various rites. Generally a myth about the founder or the god concerned with the group formed an important element in their belief system. Initiation and community rituals generally involved some form of union with the deity and promised the worshiper personal salvation and beatitude. Members were generally sworn to secrecy about the community's beliefs and practices.

The Dead Sea Scrolls community, which will be discussed in the next chapter, was in a way a mystery community. It possessed its special beliefs, unique interpretation of Old Testament scriptures, and ritual practices. Initiates were taught the beliefs and secrets of the community and advanced into full membership by stages. Members were sworn to secrecy not to divulge the innermost beliefs upon penalty of death.

The existence of gnostics in early Christianity is evidenced by Paul's refutation of some of their beliefs. The Johannine epistles polemicize against Christians with gnostic characteristics among which were a denial of the full humanity of Jesus. Numerous church fathers combated heretical teachers and movements in early Christianity which claimed to possess a secret, esoteric form of Christianity traced back to an origin in the life and teachings of Jesus or to special revelations granted by the risen Christ.

In the 1940s, a number of manuscripts belonging to a gnostic form of Christianity were discovered at Nag Hammadi in Egypt. The community to which these belonged may go back in time to the beginning of the second century A.D. Some of these documents were gospels in form. The most famous of these is the so-called Gospel of Thomas which contains approximately 112 sayings attributed to Jesus. Many of these sayings are similar and some identical to sayings of Jesus contained in the canonical Gospels. Others are quite different and present a gnostic interpretation of Jesus stressing salvation through knowledge. The opening lines of the Gospel of Thomas read: "These are the secret words which Jesus the Living spoke and which Didymus Judas Thomas wrote. And He said: He who will find the interpretation of these words will not taste death." This introduction stresses the idea of secret sayings communicated by Jesus, that is, sayings which were not for the whole of the church but for the special few. The sayings are traced back to the disciple Thomas and thus claim an apostolic origin. Possession of a proper understanding of the sayings carried with it the promise of salvation over death.

Throughout church history, groups have claimed that Jesus taught in two different forms, one openly for the multitudes and one in esoteric and secret fashion for the special elect. In modern times, the Rosicrucians, whose movement dates from the seventeenth century, are a secret brotherhood whose philosophy is partially based on secret teachings traced back to Jesus.

The theory that Jesus was the founder of a closed secret society has been recently proposed by Morton Smith in his popular work *The Secret Gospel: The Discovery and Interpretation of the Secret Gospel According to Mark* and his scholarly volume *Clement of Alexandria and a Secret Gospel of Mark*. Smith's theory is based on a passage from a secret gospel of Mark which he discovered in 1958 in the library of the Mar Saba monastery. The monastery, founded in the fifth century, is located in the mountainous desert region about twelve miles southeast of Jerusalem. Mar Saba is, in addition to St. Katherine in the Sinai, one of the great desert monasteries of the Orthodox Church.

Smith discovered a copy of a letter of Clement of Alexandria while photographing manuscripts in the Mar Saba library. The letter had been copied into the back of an edition of the letters of St. Ignatius of Antioch published in Amsterdam in 1646. The material in the letter was previously unknown, although Smith has shown, with reasonable probability, that the seventy-two line fragment is a copy of an authentic letter written between A.D. 175 and 200. Clement was an important leader in the Alexandrian church where he headed the Catechetical School until he was forced out of Egypt during the persecution of the church by the Roman emperor Septimius Severus about A.D. 202.

The heading of the document states that it is from the letters of Clement and was addressed to someone named Theodore. The letter commends Theodore for opposing the Carpocratians, a gnostic sect during the second century. Carpocrates worked in Alexandria sometime during the first half of the second century. According to the church father Irenaeus, Carpocrates "believed that Jesus was the son of Joseph and was brought up in Judaism, realized the inadequacy of the Jewish law, turned to higher truths, and so received a supernatural power by which he was enabled to rise above the angels who had created this world, purging himself of his worldly passions as he went, and ascend to the supreme god" (*The Secret Gospel,* 134). He seems to have believed that a similar contempt for the human law would allow men to experience a similar possession of power. They would then dominate the angelic powers and utilize these powers in the performance of miracles. He seems also to have taught that one must commit all possible sins in order to satisfy the spiritual rulers of this world and thus be freed for the heavenly world. Thus Carpocrates advocated a libertine approach to life, arguing that man was saved by faith alone. Reincarnation of the soul was apparently also taught by him. Carpocrates and his followers appealed to secret teachings of Jesus contained in their sectarian writings. Smith sums up the main evidence about the Carpocratians: "From Irenaeus' arguments against them it appears that they had considerable fame as miracle workers, denied the resurrection of the body, and practiced (or were accused of) extreme libertinism, especially in sexual relations." Their basic emphasis seemed to have stressed "gift of the spirit, ascent to God, freedom from the law, and magical powers" (135).

In the letter, Clement opposed the Carpocratian teaching and spoke of the sect's abandonment of the way of the commandments for a life of carnal and bodily sins. Clement points out that they pride themselves in knowledge but denies that they possess the truth.

The letter then proceeds to discuss the claims of the Carpocratians "about the divinely inspired Gospel according to Mark." Clement discusses the origin of Mark's Gospel by saying that Mark wrote an account of the Lord's doing while Peter was staying in Rome. However, Mark did not write down everything but omitted many of the secret things. After Peter's death, according to the letter, Mark came to Alexandria bringing along his own and Peter's notes. In Alexandria, "he composed a more spiritual Gospel for the use of those who were being perfected." This was done by supplementing his former work in such a way as to aid in the progress toward gnosis. In spite of producing this spiritual gospel, Mark still did not divulge some of the secret things nor write down the hierophantic teachings of the Lord—that is, the teachings dealing with the secret mysteries. Mark's spiritual gospel, according to the letter, was preserved and guarded in Alexandria where it was read only to those who were being initiated into the great mysteries. Carpocrates secured a copy of this secret gospel by deceiving an elder in the Alexandrian church. He then, according to this letter, perverted the secret gospel with his own admixture of doctrine and shameless lies.

Clement then seeks to inform Theodore, who had written to him, about the content of this secret gospel over against the falsified version of the Carpocratians. He quotes a passage from this secret Gospel saying that it occurs after what is now Mark 10:34. The passage from the *Secret Gospel* is as follows:

And they come into Bethany, and a certain woman, whose brother had died, was there. And, coming, she prostrated herself before Jesus and says to him: "Son of David, have mercy on me." But the disciples rebuked her. And Jesus, being angered, went off with her into the garden where the tomb was, and straightway a great cry was heard from the tomb. And going near Jesus rolled away the stone from the door of the tomb. And straightway, going in where the youth was, he stretched forth his hand and raised him, seizing his hand. But the youth, looking upon him, loved him and began to beseech him that he might be with him. And going out of the tomb they came into the house of the youth, for he was rich. And after six days Jesus told him what to do and in the evening the youth comes to him, wearing a linen cloth over [his] naked [body]. And he remained with him that night, for Jesus taught him the mystery of the kingdom of God. And thence, arising, he returned to the other side of the Jordan (16-17).

After translating the text, Smith spent several years comparing the vocabulary and style of the entire letter with the known writings of Clement and comparing the quote from the *Secret Gospel of Mark* with the canonical Mark. In addition, other scholars were consulted on the date of the letter and its possible authenticity as well as the relationship of the Markan text to our Gospel of Mark. Some of Smith's conclusions were (1) that the story of the resurrection of the youth lies behind John's account of the resurrection of Lazarus, which romanticized and legendized the earlier material; (2) that the latter halves of the Gospels of Mark and John run parallel if the secret text is inserted into our present form of Mark; (3) that John and Mark may have been dependent in these parallel sections on an early Aramaic tradition; (4) that the youth in the story in the secret gospel is the same as the youth in the story of Mark 10:17-22; (5) that the secret text must be understood in relationship to a baptismal initiation; (6) and that the text represents an authentic early tradition which points toward an interpretation of Jesus as the founder of a secret society.

Smith proceeded to see if the evidence drawn from the New Testament and material contemporary with the early church allow for such an interpretation and understanding of Jesus. In the account of the secret gospel, Jesus is said to have taught the youth the mystery of the kingdom of God. Smith points to the fact that Mark 4:11-12 has Jesus say to his disciples: "To you has been given the secret of the kingdom of God, but for those outside everything is in parables, so that they may indeed see but not perceive, and may indeed hear but not understand; lest they should turn again, and be forgiven." This passage distinguishes between Jesus' public preaching in parables and his revelation of the secret of the kingdom to his intimate group of disciples. Smith, in noting parallels to the secret gospel tradition elsewhere in Mark, refers to the story of Jesus' planned movement into Jerusalem and his communal meal alone with his intimate circle (Mark 14:12-26) after which there follows the story of the events in Gethsemane (Mark 14:27-52). In this latter material, Jesus placed three of his disciples as guards. In the story of the arrest, reference is made to the fact that a "young man followed him, with nothing but a linen cloth about his body; and they seized him, but he left the linen cloth and ran away naked." Smith argues that if one reads Mark 14:51-52 in light of the secret gospel text, then Jesus was here inducting the young man into the secret society. "The business in hand was a baptism; the youth wore the required costume. The time—night—agrees with the story in the secret gospel; the place—beside a stream in a lonely garden—is suitable. The preceding secrecy has obvious prudential explanations." Thus in reading Mark and the secret gospel passage, Smith could conclude: "Jesus had a 'mystery of the kingdom of God,' a baptismal rite, which he administered to some, at least, of his disciples. It was nocturnal, secret, and Mark thought it required six days' preparation" (81).

In attempting to ascertain more explictly what the secret of the kingdom really was, Smith notes that secret cults and mystery groups who gave their mysteries to the new members at the time of initiation were widespread at the time of Jesus. By comparing John the Baptist with Jesus, Smith feels that one can ascertain Jesus' special relationship to the kingdom. What could and did Jesus offer his disciples and followers that John could not? John was a prophet preaching repentance and warning that the end was near at hand. He also proclaimed that his hearers could prepare for the coming judgment by undergoing a baptism for the remission of sins. This baptism was the unique factor that made John more than a prophet and distinguished his movement from all others. John not only announced the kingdom, he purified men for entrance into the coming kingdom. With Jesus, the kingdom was present. On the basis of his analysis of Mark and the secret gospel, Smith concludes that Jesus introduced a baptismal rite in which persons were inducted into the kingdom. Smith points to John 3:22 and suggests that the Aramaic of John 4:2 may have read—Jesus himself baptized no one except his disciples—to support the idea of Jesus' baptismal rite. Smith notes that Jesus himself was baptized and that the early church appears on the scene as a baptizing community. All of which supports the argument that Jesus baptized into the kingdom just as the early Christians baptized into the church. Thus Smith concludes: Jesus "could admit his followers to the kingdom of God, and he could do it in some special way, so that they were not there merely by anticipation, nor by virtue of belief and obedience, nor by some other figure of speech, but were really, actually, in" (94). "Jesus probably admitted his chosen followers to the kingdom by some sort of baptism. *This was the mystery of the kingdom—the mystery rite by which the kingdom was entered*" (96).

Smith argues that if one compares baptism as practiced by John the Baptist and baptism as practiced and understood by Paul, then one can determine how Jesus understood baptism. Smith assumes, unlike many scholars, that the theology of Paul is based directly on the theology of Jesus; so Paul could in no way be considered the creator of Christianity. Since only a few years separate John from Paul and since Paul, even though he was a creative thinker, was dependent upon the tradition passed along to him, such a comparison could allow one to determine the elements which came from Jesus.

The Baptist stood on one side of Jesus; on the other stood Paul. Jesus might be defined as the middle term between them—and a short middle term, at that. According to all reports, his ministry began soon after his baptism and lasted, at most, about three years. Paul's conversion, according to his own account in Galatians, must have occurred within four or five years of the Crucifixion, perhaps less. So not more than eight years, and probably less, separated Paul from the Baptist. Why not, then, compare the Baptist with Paul, determine the differences, and try to see how many of these could be traced back to Jesus? (74).

For Paul (see Romans 6:3-9; I Corinthians 12:12-13; Galatians 3:26-29; Colossians 2:9-3:4), according to Smith, the following are characteristic of his practice of baptism: "1. Paul's baptism was first of all a ritual for union with Jesus. . . . 2. The union in Paul's baptism was affected by the spirit. . . . 3. The closest parallels to Paul's baptism are found in magical material. . . . 4. Paul's baptism was connected with ascent into the heavens. . . . 5. Finally, Paul's baptism freed the recipient from the law" (101). Do these elements go back to Jesus?

Smith argues that since Jesus introduced the communion ritual in which union with Christ was achieved through eating his body and drinking his blood, it is entirely possible that Jesus introduced also the ritual baptism of union with himself. Since the Spirit is so closely associated with Jesus in the Gospels, for example, it descends upon him at his baptism, it seems probable that the work of the Spirit in baptism goes back to Jesus. Since the marvelous and miraculous power of Jesus in the Gospels—his exorcisms, cures, etc.—show his magical power, so the element of magical ritual probably goes back to him as well. The idea of ascent into heaven—the kingdom of God par excellence— probably also goes back to Jesus. The experience of the heavenly world, shared in by Jesus and his disciples, is probably most clearly reflected in the transfiguration story. Smith claims that the idea of the experience of translation to the heavenly world was not unknown at the time. Even Paul claims to have been carried into the third heaven (II Corinthians 12:2). Statements of Jesus about knowing the truth which could set one free and that the law and prophets were until John but from then on the kingdom of God is proclaimed suggest that Jesus too conceived of entrance into the kingdom as freedom from the law. Smith summarizes his arguments as follows:

Thus from the differences between Paul's baptism and that of the Baptist, and from the scattered indications in the canonical Gospels and the secret Gospel of Mark, we can put together a picture of Jesus' baptism, "the mystery of the kingdom of God." It was a water baptism administered by Jesus to chosen disciples, singly and by night. The costume, for the disciple, was a linen cloth worn over the naked body. This cloth was probably removed for the baptism proper, the immersion in water, which was now reduced to a preparatory purification. After that, by unknown ceremonies, the disciple was possessed by Jesus' spirit and so united with Jesus. One with him, he participated by hallucination in Jesus' ascent into the heavens, he entered the kingdom of God, and was thereby set free from the laws ordained for and in the lower world. Freedom from the law may have resulted in completion of the spiritual union by physical union [homosexual practices]. This certainly occurred in many forms of gnostic Christianity; how early it began there is no telling (113-14).

The theory of Jesus as the founder of a secret society, a society oriented toward admission to the kingdom and union with Jesus, suggests a number of elements in the life of Jesus. Jesus' followers must have been divided into various circles already during his lifetime. Smith suggests three circles: an inner circle to whom he had given the secret and whom he had baptized, one or more outer circles such as his less intimate followers, his family, and acquaintances to whom the secret was not revealed, and the circle of those outside, that is those hostile and indifferent to Jesus.

Jesus' teaching to these groups would have been quite different. If one examines the New Testament, Jesus' teaching on the law, for example, seems to reflect contradictory statements. On the one hand, he proclaims a freedom from the law (Luke 16:16; Matthew 11:12-13; Mark 2:22; Luke 5:36; Mark 2:28; Matthew 11:18-19; Mark 2:15-16; Matthew 11:29-30; John 1:17-18; Luke 10:22; John 8:31-32), but on the other hand, Jesus preached that the law is still binding (Matthew 5:17-20 and elsewhere). Smith explains this phenomenon in the following way: "the legalistic material represents Jesus' teaching for 'those outside.' For them he held that the law was still binding and he interpreted it as did the other legal teachers of his time; about one point he would have a more lenient opinion, about another, a stricter one—such variation appears in the rulings of almost all ancient rabbis. But he himself was free of the law, and so were those who had been baptized with his spirit. The contradictions of the present Gospels probably result from a gradual seepage of secret material into texts originally meant for outsiders . . . it was probably from Jesus' secret teaching and practice that Paul derived, through the intermediation of Jesus' immediate followers, his notion that

209

baptism freed the baptized from the requirements of the law"
(112-13).

The resurrection visions "are best understandable as
consequences of Jesus' baptismal practice, reflections of the
visions he suggested to the young men he initiated" (116).
Spirit possession and ecstatic experience, characteristic of
early Christianity, go back to the individual possession
experienced in Jesus' baptism. Jesus seems to have had a
special attraction to and hold over schizophrenic types—
"persons whose suppressed impulses had broken through
their rational control and expressed themselves in violent and
destructive actions explained as the work of 'demons'";
"women who had been cured of evil spirits (Luke 8:2)"; and
disciples whose willingness totally to abandon ordinary life to
follow Jesus reveals an instability in character (116-17).
Jesus' society as a group freed from the law explains the fact
that Jesus was a "figure notorious for his libertine teaching
and practice. He broke the Sabbath, he neglected the purity
rules, he refused to fast, made friends with publicans and
sinners, and was known as 'a gluttonous man and a
winebibber.' He not only taught his disciples that the law had
come to an end with the Baptist, and that the least in the
kingdom was greater than the Baptist, but he also administered a baptism of his own—'the mystery of the kingdom of
God'—by which he enabled some of his disciples, united with
himself, to enter the kingdom and to enjoy his own freedom
from the law" (130).

The divisions within the early and developing church can
thus be traced back to Jesus himself.

Therefore, in our picture of pre-Pauline Christianity,
alongside the legalistic interpretation of the religion we must
set the libertine. The legalistic interpretation went back to
the (mainly Pharisaic?) converts of the Jerusalem church,
and appealed to the tradition of Jesus' exoteric teaching. The
libertine interpretation went back to Jesus himself and
preserved and developed elements of his esoteric teaching. It
was dominant in the Jerusalem church in the earliest days,
but it lost its hold as the small group of Jesus' original,

initiated disciples was outnumbered by the new converts under the leadership of Jesus' brother, James, and it went underground when Peter, the leader of the original disciples, was driven out of the city by the persecution under Herod Agrippa I. This libertine tradition, its strength, its diffusion, its unanimity, and its evident age, is explicable only by our understanding of Jesus' teaching about the mystery of the kingdom. This is strong evidence that the understanding is correct (131).

Thus, the secret gnostic sects—like the Carpocratians—were the true heirs of Jesus' secret teachings—although they infused these teachings were diverse materials drawn from other sources—and were the true continuation of Jesus' secret society.

12. JESUS: THE QUMRAN ESSENE

> If . . . we look at Jesus in the perspective supplied by the
> scrolls, we can trace a new continuity and, at last, get some
> sense of the drama that culminated in Christianity. We can
> see how the movement represented by the Essenes stood up
> for perhaps two centuries to the coercion of the Greeks and
> the Romans, and how it resisted not merely the methods of
> Rome but also the Roman ideals. We can guess how, about a
> half century before its refuge was burned together with the
> Temple of the Jewish God, this movement had inspired a
> leader who was to transcend both Judaism and Essenism,
> and whose followers would found a church that was to
> outlive the Roman Empire and ultimately be identified with
> Rome herself.—Edmund Wilson, *The Scrolls from the Dead
> Sea* (p. 97)

In late 1947 and early 1948, the scholarly world became
acquainted with the story of the discovery of the now famous
Dead Sea (or Qumran) Scrolls. Sometime earlier, probably in
the spring of 1947, a young Arab bedouin of the Ta'amireh
tribe, Muhammad the Wolf, had accidentally discovered
seven ancient scrolls in a cave near where the Wadi Qumran
flows into the Dead Sea. It was several months before the
true antiquity and nature of the scrolls were determined.
When their true character became known, the scrolls were
declared by W. F. Albright to be the "greatest manuscript
discovery of modern times" which could "revolutionize our
approach to the beginnings of Christiantiy."

Since 1947, ten other caves in the Qumran area and a
dozen or so caves elsewhere in the near vicinity have yielded
manuscripts or manuscript fragments. Most of these scrolls
have been dated to a period extending from the fourth
century B.C. to the second century A.D. In addition, ar-
chaeologists have explored, often trying unsuccessfully to
beat the bedouin to finds, and excavated dozens of caves and
ruins along the western bank of the Dead Sea.

Jesus: The Qumran Essene

Our concern here is with only those scrolls from the Qumran area. The hundreds of manuscripts, almost all in very fragmentary form, have not yet been fully published. However, it is possible to give a general description of the Qumran materials by dividing them into four categories. Some of the manuscripts are copies of Old Testament biblical books. Fragments of every Old Testament book, except for Esther, have been found. Some of these provide scholars with copies of parts of the Old Testament a thousand years older than the texts from which our Old Testament translations are made. A second group of manuscripts are Old Testament texts with running commentary. Passages are quoted and an exegesis and interpretation are given relating the text to events and factors later than the text. Sometimes these commentaries do not follow the order of a particular book but are collections of texts from various books accompanied by exegetical interpretation. A third group of manuscripts are copies of books which did not make it into the Old Testament canon but which have been known in various translations from ancient times. A fourth class of manuscripts are writings unique to the community and previously unknown. These texts present the fullest expression of the beliefs of those who produced the documents.

The quantity of documentary material recovered from the Qumran caves is enormous. What is also historically intriguing is the fact that several ancient writers made references to scrolls being found in the area in antiquity—as early as the fourth and as late as the ninth century of the present era.

Ruins located in the vicinity of the caves were excavated in the early fifties. These ruins seemed to have been the center for a rather large community. Dining halls, kitchens, storage rooms, pantries, and a kiln were unearthed. In addition, the complex was supplied by an aquaduct which brought water into a network of large cisterns and smaller "baths." A cemetery in the area contains over a thousand graves and the skeletal remains of men, women, and children have been found in those graves, all with individual burials, which have been opened. The ruins of the community do not seem to reflect any living quarters in the buildings themselves. Apparently those who used the building complex lived elsewhere, perhaps some in the caves and in tents in the vicinity. No manuscript remains in any form were found in the ruins of the buildings although some writing paraphernalia—ink wells and perhaps writing desks—were recovered.

On the basis of the archaeological evidence and through attempts to date the scrolls, the majority of scholars now assign the existence of the community and the writing of the scrolls, which are related to the community, to a period roughly from the middle of the second century B.C. to the time of the first Jewish revolt which began in A.D. 66 and lasted until A.D. 73. Dating of the scrolls, however, is still a highly controversial issue. Some scholars assume that the scrolls and the ruins were at most only accidentally related; others date the scrolls either earlier or later, some consider them medieval in origin, if not fraudulent. The existence of the community and the scrolls at the time of Jesus' life, in spite of continuing controversy, is apparently a safe assumption.

From the scrolls we can know something of the community, its origin, beliefs, character, and history. The community was organized and led into the desert by a person called the Teacher of Righteousness. This teacher provided the community with many of its beliefs and its method of interpreting scripture in light of later events and especially in light of the community's particular history and beliefs. The Teacher of Righteousness was persecuted and perhaps put to death by a character called the Wicked Priest.

The community called itself by numerous designations— the many, the elect, the sons of light, the new covenant. Its members were composed of priests, levites, laymen, and possibly proselytes. Entrance into the community was made through several stages apparently extending over two or three years. Initiation into the community was a special affair. Members were sworn to secrecy about the important beliefs and actions of the community. Rules by which the community was governed were drawn up and display a strict loyalty to the law and rather severe penalties for infractions of the law of Moses and the special rules of the community.

The community believed itself to be the chosen people living in the end of days. Even the Jews outside the community were considered apostate. The community followed a calendar different from that used in the Jerusalem temple. The community, at least according to one document, was living in anticipation of the coming of a great prophet and two messiahs—one from the priestly house of Aaron and the other a political messiah from the house of David. The priestly messiah was to take precedence over the political messiah. The community celebrated a ritual meal of bread and wine interpreted in light of the great banquet to be eaten with the coming messiah(s). Ritual purification baths were part of the ordinary routine. The community was ruled over by persons who held administrative and/or teaching functions. There also seems to have been a special council of twelve or fifteen members. Some of the documents suggest that there was community ownership of property. Reading and study of the scriptures played an important role in the community's life.

The community believed that mankind was divided into two groups—the children of light (or the good spirit) and the children of darkness (or the evil spirit). Before the final consummation of God's purpose, there was to be a forty-year war between the two groups in which the elect would triumph.

After the discovery and study of the scrolls, many scholars began to compare the beliefs and the community with a Jewish sect known as the Essenes who are mentioned and described by the Jewish writers Josephus and Philo and the Roman historian Pliny. The persons who wrote the texts never refer to themselves as Essenes. Nonetheless, most scholars identify the two.

The parallels and similarities between the life and faith of the Qumran community and the early church immediately led to comparisons and in some cases to identification of the two. The church was compared to the community itself and Jesus to the Teacher of Righteousness. In 1950, the imminent French scholar A. Dupont-Sommer wrote:

Everything in the Jewish New Covenant heralds and prepares the way for the Christian New Covenant. The Galilean Master, as He is presented to us in the writings of the New Testament, appears in many respects as an astonishing reincarnation of the Master of Justice [Teacher of Righteousness]. Like the latter He preached pentitence, poverty, humility, love of one's neighbor, chastity. Like him, He prescribed the observance of the Law of Moses, the whole Law, but the Law finished and perfected, thanks to His own revelations. Like him He was the Elect and the Messiah of God, the Messiah redeemer of the world. Like him, He was the object of the hostility of the priests, the party of the Sadducees. Like him He was condemned and put to death. Like him He pronounced judgment on Jerusalem, which was taken and destroyed by the Romans for having put Him to death. Like him, at the end of time, He will be the supreme judge. Like him He founded a Church whose adherents fervently awaited His glorious return. In the Christian Church, just as in the Essene Church, the essential rite is the sacred meal, whose ministers are the priests. Here and there at the head of each community there is the overseer, the "bishop." And the ideal of both churches is essentially that of unity, communion in love—even going so far as the sharing of common property.

All these similarities—and here I only touch upon the subject—together, constitute a very impressive whole. The question at once arises, to which of the two sects, the Jewish or the Christian, does the priority belong? Which of the two was able to influence the other? The reply leaves no room for doubt. The Master of Justice died about 65-63 B.C.; Jesus the Nazarene died about A.D. 30. In every case in which the resemblance compels or invites us to think of a borrowing, this was on the part of Christianity. But on the other hand, the appearance of faith in Jesus—the foundation of the New Church—can scarcely be explained without the real historic activity of a new Prophet, a new Messiah, who rekindled the flame and concentrated on himself the adoration of men (*The Dead Sea Scrolls,* 99-100).

216

Jesus: The Qumran Essene

Some scholars initially argued that the texts clearly identified the Teacher of Righteousness with the messiah, spoke of his death by crucifixion, and proclaimed his return at the end of history. These judgments have not held up against further study, thus they have been either abandoned or considerably modified.

Are the life and teachings of Jesus to be understood against the background of the Qumran community? Many scholars would answer with an emphatic affirmative. Two books which received wide circulation were published early in the 1950s claiming that the Qumran community contributed significantly to the origin of Christianity. The first of these was by the internationally renowned critic Edmund Wilson. His work on the scrolls was originally published in the *New Yorker* magazine (May, 1955). Wilson's article brought the issue of the scrolls to the attention of a wide audience. Wilson accused Christian scholars of deliberately boycotting the scrolls because of fear of what they would find there. He spoke of a "certain nervousness, a reluctance to take hold of the subject and to place it in historical perspective" which characterized those who "have taken Christian orders or been trained in the rabbinical tradition" and were thus "inhibited in dealing with such questions . . . by their various religious commitments" (*The Scrolls from the Dead Sea,* 98). Wilson assigned a great significance to the scrolls for the possible light they would shed on Christianity as the following quote illustrates:

The spirit of the Essene brotherhood, even before its expulsion from its sunken base, had already thus made itself free to range through the whole ancient world, touching souls with that Gospel of purity and light to which the brotherhood had consecrated itself, and teaching the contempt of those eagles which they had noted—with evident astonishment—that the army of their enemy worshipped. The monastery, this structure of stone that endures, between the bitter waters and precipitous cliffs, with its oven and its inkwells, its mill and its cesspool, its constellation of sacred fonts and the unadorned graves of its dead, is perhaps, more than Bethlehem or Nazareth, the cradle of Christianity (97-98).

The second volume published on the scrolls arguing for a close connection between Qumran and Christianity was *The Meaning of the Dead Sea Scrolls* by A. Powell Davies. Davies' book does not make the type of claims asserted by Wilson. It was written from the perspective of a liberal theologian who could argue "that God can work through natural events in a gradual social evolution just as well as in some other way. Indeed, this is the way that he does work. A religion is not one whit the less because it has no supernatural origin, no miracles and not too much uniqueness. What we need is not the victory of one religion over other religions but the recognition of the noble and the good in all religions" (131). For Davies, the scrolls seemed to represent one more element in the scholarly recognition that Christianity probably didn't originate in the way it is commonly explained.

When theological scholars say, as they have recently been saying, that the discovery of the Scrolls has brought them no information that obliges them to revise their view of Christian beginning—or at least not extensively—it can be *for them* the truth. But they should go on to tell the laity in what sense it is the truth. What they mean, if they would express it more informatively, is *that they have known for a long time that the traditional view of Christian origins is not supported by history so much as theology.* Unlike the layman, they are familiar with New Testament historical problems to which it has never been possible to find historical solutions. Dogmatic solutions are another matter. But what the layman thinks he is dealing with in trying to grasp the meaning of the Scrolls is not theology but history, not dogma but fact.

Theological scholars have long been aware, for instance, of the impossibility of knowing, historically, where Jesus was born, or when, or by what means the portrait of him in the first three Gospels (the Synoptics) can be reconciled with the quite different portrait of him in the Gospel of John. This is only the beginning of the matter. Theological scholars know (again as the layman usually does not) something of the extensive debt of Christianity to Pagan religion during the first centuries of its development in the Mediterranean area.

Theological scholars have known for some time that there were important resemblances between Essenic organization and that of the early Christian churches and have had reason to suspect that the two may have been organically connected (84).

The Lost Years of Jesus by C. F. Potter, published in 1958, sought to associate closely not only the early church and the Essene movement but also Jesus and the Teacher of Righteousness. The title to his book implies an association of Jesus with the Qumran community prior to his public appearance.

Hundreds of . . . evidences of the Essene origin of the ideas, beliefs, and teachings of Jesus, John the Baptist, John the Disciple, Paul, and the other New Testament writers have been noted by scholars working on the Scrolls. . . .
And now that the proven Mother of Christianity is known to have been the prior community of the New Covenant commonly called the Essenes, the momentous question challenging the conscience of all Christendom is whether the child will have the grace, courage, and honesty to acknowledge and honor its own mother! (13)

Potter, like Wilson and Davies, accused scholars of not leveling with the church about the true nature of the Dead Sea Scrolls and the similarity between many of their teachings and those of early Christianity.

To date, the theologians have had time enough to tell their communicants the epochal significance of the finding of the Essene library, but their utterances have been—especially in America—singularly hesitant, reluctant, and incomplete. Some distort the meaning of the Scrolls for their own purposes. Others are waiting a generation or two before making up their minds! (13)

Potter assigned great significance to the fact that the Qumran community predated Christianity. Since this was the case, then similarity in thought, theology, and expression would point to dependence of Christianity upon the scrolls and not vice versa.

A century or more before the Christian New Testament was written, the Qumran Essenes were familiar with the ideas, proverbs, prayers, beatitudes, blessings, and even the beautiful sentences in Jesus' Sermon on the Mount, which he was quoting from Essene Scrolls, as he and his audience knew, though we may not. Even the preaching of the Gospel, the Good News, or, as the now current theological phrase has it, the "kerygma" of Kingdom Come, was evidently out of Qumran by John the Baptist, as well as the baptism wherewith he baptized Jesus "to fulfill all righteousness," a key Essenian phrase. And the very name of the Christian Bible, the New Testament, came from those monks of Qumran, who never called themselves Essenes, but the "Sons of Zadok" (King David's high priest), or, significantly, the Community of the New Covenant. And "New Covenant" was a better word to translate the Aramaic word which Christianity later translated as "New Testament" (12-13).

Those books of the Old Testament—Isaiah, Deuteronomy, and Psalms—which were most popular at Qumran are also the books most popular in the early church, assuming that New Testament quotations are an indication of popularity. For Potter, the book of Enoch which was quoted directly in the New Testament (Jude 14) was a link associating the early church with Qumran. Fragments of Enoch were found among the scrolls and Potter concludes that the similarities in ideas and vocabulary between passages in Enoch, and other apocryphal books, point to this literature as the missing link between the Old Testament and early Christianity. "Old Enoch is on his way back home now, after long exile, and should soon take his rightful place back in our Bible. For, if the Qumran community was the mother of Christianity, Enoch was the father" (101).

If a number of copies of Enoch were in the Qumran community library, and if Jesus spent part of the so-called "silent years" as a member, or associate member, or even only as a resident student, that might explain why he and his disciples were so well acquainted with the Enochan literature that we find not merely the same ideas and doctrines in the New Testament, but even the same phrases and sentences (52).

Jesus: The Qumran Essene

In their view of the last days and the coming of the messiah, Potter notices many similarities between Christianity and the Qumran community.

In a very real sense, since the word Christian means Messianist (the Greek word Christos being the exact equivalent of the Hebrew word Messiah, meaning the anointed one), and since the Essenes were very much concerned with the coming of Judgment Day and the Messiah, they were Messianists; and, to use the Greek form of the word, they were Christians before Jesus Christ was born. The fact that later generations of the followers of Jesus filled the words "Christ" and "Christian" and "Christianity" with complicated theological meanings, adding more and more doctrines for several centuries, until being a "Christian" meant believing a complex system of dogmas that the Jewish Jesus never heard of, does not alter the fact that when his disciples were first called Christians at Antioch in Syria, they were Christians much like the Essenes were, or any pious Jew who was waiting in earnest expectation of the Messiah (129).

Jesus must be understood as having contact of some sort with the Qumran Essene community prior to his public ministry. It was during this contact that the content of Jesus' preaching was developed. "Indeed, the opinion that Jesus either lived for several years in the Qumran Community which produced the Scrolls or at least visited it often is gaining ground among unprejudiced students" (139). Thus the scrolls provide the clue for understanding Jesus and his origin.

Now the scientists, in the light of the Qumran discoveries, can get much closer to that remarkable young man who emerged from "the wilderness" to give to the world his synthesis of the wisdom, faith and hopes of several cultures he had studied in the remarkable community and its wonderful library by the shore of the Salty Sea (83).

What the laymen suspected when the scrolls were first published—that they challenged the uniqueness of Jesus— and what scholars generally refused to admit may be correct.

What the laymen suspect regarding the cave finds is true. The dogmas and doctrines, the theological twists and turns, the tampering with texts to corroborate newly invented creedal statements, all these additions of later centuries to the simple ethical humanitarian faith of Jesus the Teacher of Righteousness are revealed by these older Scroll manuscripts to have been like the tawdry tinsel and bright-colored finery with which ignorant peasants adorn the statues of their gods.

For Jesus the Galilean, baptized by John the Baptist into the great fellowship of the pacifistic, socialistic, cooperative Essenes of the New Covenant, later evidently carried out in its principles into the wide world, improving those principles in some respects, but preaching them best by living up to them to the limit, even to death on the Roman cross (155).

13. JESUS: THE SEXUAL BEING

> To speak of Jesus as being truly human is also to speak of
> him as a sexual being. Whatever ways he may have chosen to
> express or to re-channel his sexuality (and about this we
> know nothing), it is clear that when his sinlessness is
> mentioned we do not, or should not, take this to imply
> a-sexuality. Alas, however, much Christian thinking has
> done just this; in consequence we have the anaemic, lifeless,
> almost effeminate Christ of the Victorian stained-glass
> windows and of some popular portraits. Had Jesus been
> married, the exercise of sexuality within that relationship
> would not have constituted sin; were he not of the marrying
> kind, his homosexual tendency would not have constituted
> sin. To think otherwise is to denigrate God's creation, to
> succumb to a Manichean view of nature, and to deny the
> goodness of the sexuality with which God has endowed his
> human (and other) creatures.—Norman Pittenger, *Christol-
> ogy Reconsidered* (p. 61)

A dominant concern behind the quest of the historical
Jesus has been a desire to rediscover him as a human being.
This desire to understand Jesus as truly human has raised
the question of Jesus' sexuality. If Jesus was a man like every
other man, did he undergo normal sexual development, pass
through puberty, and experience sexual drive and desires? If
so, how did Jesus react to and channel these sexual drives
and passions?

Some recent study of Jesus, perhaps influenced by the
so-called "sexual revolution" which has brought the matter of
sex into open discussion, has argued that no serious search
for the real Jesus can avoid dealing with the question of
Jesus' sexuality.

The question of Jesus' sexuality is of course not an issue
which the church has never discussed. At the same time, the
matter has never been a dominant concern of church
theology and has been discussed primarily within the context
of theories expounding sexual ethics for Christians, and
particularly for Christian clerics.

The New Testament is silent on the question of Jesus' sexuality. It contains no reference or discussion of the matter although several sayings of Jesus are related to the question of man's sexuality.

The writers of the New Testament and the early church fathers combated any theory that suggested Jesus was not fully human. Quite early, some Christians expounded the belief that Jesus was not fully human, that he was totally divine and only appeared to be human. He was more like an angel who masqueraded as a man but without undergoing hunger, thirst, suffering, or death. This theory that Jesus was not human was called "Docetism" from a Greek word meaning "to appear." The letters of I and II John denounced and proclaimed as unorthodox any belief that denied the humanity of Jesus. "Many deceivers have gone out into the world, men who will not acknowledge the coming of Jesus Christ in the flesh; such a one is the deceiver and the antichrist" (II John 7). "By this you know the Spirit of God: every spirit that confesses that Jesus Christ has come in the flesh is of God" (I John 4:2). At the same time, the church proclaimed that Jesus had undergone the gamut of human temptations: "We have not a high priest who is unable to sympathize with our weakness, but one who in every respect has been tempted as we are, yet without sinning" (Hebrews 4:15). Nonetheless, in discussing the humanity and temptations of Jesus, the New Testament does not so much as allude to the question of his sexuality.

Quite early, in the mainstream of the Christian tradition, theologians argued that Jesus' life was one of complete celibacy, that Jesus took a disparaging attitude toward sexuality in general, and that these two attitudes should be characteristic of Christians and especially of the priesthood. Several sayings of Jesus contained in the Gospels were used to support such theories. These are the sayings most frequently used in expounding such a view:

You have heard that it was said, "You shall not commit adultery." But I say to you that every one who looks at a woman lustfully has already committed adultery with her (Matthew 5:27-28).

If any one comes to me and does not hate his own father and mother and wife and children and brothers and sisters, yea, and even his own life, he cannot be my disciple (Luke 14:26).

There are eunuchs who have been so from birth, and there are eunuchs who have been made eunuchs by men, and there are eunuchs who have made themselves eunuchs for the sake of the kingdom of heaven. He who is able to receive this, let him receive it (Matthew 19:12).

Jesus said to the Sadducees, "The sons of this age marry and are given in marriage; but those who are accounted worthy to attain to that age and to the resurrection from the dead neither marry nor are given in marriage, for they cannot die any more, because they are equal to angels and are sons of God, being sons of the resurrection" (Luke 20:34-36).

Exegesis of these passages combined with theological speculation led to the theory that virginity, celibacy, and sexual abstinence were superior to married life and that in marriage sex should be engaged in only with the object of procreation. Sexual drives thus came to be understood as sinful. The epitome of this argument was reached with Saint Augustine who argued that sinful nature was transmitted through sex, and since Jesus was sinless and born of a virgin he possessed no sexual drives or passions. Jesus was fully human but being born in a manner that bypassed sexual activity, Jesus possessed no real sexuality.

This theory of sexual ethics which stressed the superiority of virginity and celibacy was challenged at the time of the Protestant Reformation. Such a challenge opened the way for the discussion of Jesus' sexuality although the topic does not seem to have occupied much concern among the reformers. Luther, for example, suggested in one of his discussions that Jesus probably had sexual relations with Mary Magdalene and perhaps other women (*Tabletalk,* number 1472). The comment by Luther however was recorded without any reference to the context of his statement or to exactly what he meant or implied by such a statement. Since Luther no where else in his writings takes up this theme, one should not take the statement as representative of his interpretation of Jesus. Luther was prone to make rather earthy off-the-cuff comments which often didn't represent his sober thought on a subject. At any rate, the statement does suggest that he had given some thought to the question of Jesus' sexuality.

Some of the early Mormon theologians like Orson Hyde and Brigham Young, according to a secondary source in the case of the latter, not only argued that Jesus was a man of normal sexual impulses but also that he was a polygamist having been married to Mary Magdalene as well as to Mary and Martha, the sisters of Lazarus. The marriage feast in Cana of Galilee at which Jesus turned the water into wine (John 2:1-11) was understood by some of the early Mormons as one of Jesus' own weddings.

Until quite recently, few modern interpreters of Jesus had given consideration to the question of his sexuality. It has occasionally been hinted at as, for example, in the following quote from John Erskine:

It has been suggested . . . that during these eighteen silent years he was moved by the hopes and ambitions proper to manhood—love, marriage, parenthood—and that in equal measure he suffered disappointment or bereavement. There is no basis in fact for these theories . . . yet just because man's normal emotional life is near to us all, it does not seem improbable that he did fall in love and have some experience of parenthood. Here I try to choose my words carefully, not to start unworthy thoughts or to seem to invent for the Saviour any acquaintance with cheap romance. But reading his words carefully as I have done all my life, I long ago had the impression that he understood women very well indeed, with the special understanding of a man who has been hurt by one of them. In the development of his character there was, I am inclined to believe, over against the blessed influence of Mary, another influence far less happy. I think he early met someone who charmed but who was unworthy, someone he idealized, and by whom he was cruelly disillusioned. . . .

Though we have no specific details about his early manhood, yet the accounts of the public ministry contain facts which may throw light on the unrecorded years. The Gospels indicate that Jesus had an extraordinary fondness for children, and a special understanding of the relation between father and son. . . . Whether, as some people would like to believe, he ever married and had a son is an irrelevant question. What is pertinent is his capacity for love and his genius for parenthood. The father of the Prodigal Son is not a portrait of Joseph, but the record of human yearning for a child. Whether these emotions in Jesus ever attached themselves to particular objects, the story does not say, but his character renders it for me utterly impossible that his youth and manhood could have been unmoved by warm, human emotions. . . . If he really took our nature upon him and was human, then he had our equipment of sex. . . . I interpret the history of the unknown years as a period, not of indecision, but of a wrestling with the human loves which might have held him back from a love universal and divine. Perhaps the conflict was never entirely ended until the hours on Calvary (*The Human Life of Jesus*, 27-28).

Poets and novelists have, on occasion, dealt with the questions of Jesus' sexuality and his confrontation with sexual temptations. In his poem, *Judas,* Ronald Duncan depicts an imaginary encounter between Jesus and a prostitute:

> Remembering the brothel we'd passed outside the city
> Where an old whore had lifted her skirts in the doorway
> And challenged Jesus to prove He was a man
> And how He had surprised us by going up to the woman
> And had drawn the sore from her lips, the years
> from her eyes
> and,—it was this that shocked Peter—
> How He had then kissed her, and pulled her hair
> in a tease as she repeated her challenge
> Not realising that He had proved much more.

Two novelists—D. H. Lawrence and Nikos Kazantzakis —have made the issue of Jesus' sexuality a central theme of two of their works. In his short story, *The Man Who Died,* Lawrence depicted the true meaning of Jesus' resurrection, with some punning with holy phraseology, as his awakening and surrendering to sexual desire which he had

227

previously suppressed and denied. In *The Last Temptation of Christ,* Kazantzakis portrays Jesus as tempted constantly through his life by sexual passion, especially with regard to Mary Magdalene. Kazantzakis' Jesus is depicted as a man locked in a fight between spiritual vocation and carnal love who in the end repudiated domestic love for vocational service. Although in Kazantzakis' work Jesus does not give in to sexual desire, he is portrayed as one who was fully sexual, tempted as all men.

During the 1960s, the sexual revolution and human sexuality were topics of widespread discussion. Simultaneously, a renewed interest in the sexuality of Jesus developed. This discussion of the sexuality of Jesus was not simply a reflex to the social trend with its general interest in sexuality. It was also reflective of a genuine desire to recover a more human figure behind the Christ of faith and the reconstructed pictures of the historical Jesus. Professor Tom Driver expressed the issues in the following manner:

Exegesis might go on forever proving that sex is not necessarily sin. Ethics might echo the tune. But if The Man for Men was conceived to be without sexuality—was never, unlike the saints, even tempted by sex—then all would labor in vain who strove to prove that the Christian God looks favorably upon the sexual life of humanity. Hunger Jesus knew, and thirst. Death He endured. Pride, sloth, envy, desire for power, idolatry—all came close to Him and were overcome in favor of the virtues of which they are the perversions. But where do we find Jesus taking our sexuality upon Him? Human love, yes. Love extended liberally even to those who, in a sexual way, have "loved much." But never, so far as we are told, a man stirred in himself by that desire which for the rest of us is part of our created nature.

To put it bluntly, a sexless Jesus can hardly be conceived to be fully human. As long as Jesus is somehow above masculinity or femininity, the drift toward a Docetic Christ is inevitable. I do not know why this has not been more often observed. Lacking such a pervasively human element, the humanity of Christ tends to become a mere affirmation, a matter of pure dogma. Jesus is then man in principle but not in fact. If to this is added the belief that He was conceived in the womb of a virgin, His separation from our sexuality

228

becomes complete. "Veiled in flesh," He is not flesh. He has the appearance of humanity but not its limiting substance, however much might be said in the abstract about "finitude." It is an inherent part of my finitude, and yours, that our lives are shaped in many decisive ways by our sexual histories ("Sexuality and Jesus," 239). . . . The traditional view of the Gospel's silence about sexuality in Jesus himself must be abandoned and a new interpretation put on the facts. . . . If we take it that the Gospels do not intend to present a Docetic Christ, if this may be true even of the Fourth Gospel, which in any case speaks most about Jesus' love for particular individuals, then the absence of all comment in them about Jesus' sexuality cannot be taken to imply that he had no sexual feelings. That would land us back into the traditional view, according to which the Christ redeems us *from* sexuality, it being the part of our nature He did not share. If the Christian, who is a member of the Body of Christ, is to grow up into a psychologically healthy and morally right sexual life, then the God-Man cannot be totally apart from the sexual realm ("Sexuality and Jesus," 243).

Those who place some emphasis on the sexuality of Jesus generally take one of four alternatives in offering suggestions as to how Jesus dealt with his sexual drives. One alternative suggests that Jesus was a fully sexual being with normal sexual passions but who controlled these so that they were never given overt expression. This alternative would be the most widely accepted current view. A second alternative would be to argue that Jesus gave expression to his sexuality in heterosexual relations outside marriage. *Jesus Christ Superstar* certainly raises this issue with regard to Jesus and Mary Magdalene but leaves the matter as an open question. In this regard, Timothy Rice who wrote the lyrics for *Superstar* has denied that the work intends to make any theological statement about Jesus beyond "seeing Jesus as a man, so He can be better understood by today's young people, who'd rather listen to rock than go to church. . . . It merely tells the old story in new terms. In no respects does it clash with fundamental Christian teachings. No intelligent churchman would take *Superstar* as anything more than an entertainment. It's ridiculous to give it theological importance it doesn't deserve. The only importance is its commercial success" ("'Superstar' Gospel Is Shekels," 12). Nonetheless, any discussion which aims at "seeing Jesus as a man" involves a theological perspective. In the opera, it is only Mary Magdalene who treats Jesus with total respect, and she is shown caressing and kissing him, but a bit bewildered by not knowing how to love him. All to the consternation of Judas. At the same time, Jesus is made to say that Mary was the only one who tried to give him what he needed here and now. Jesus is certainly not pictured as either sexless or homosexual. Neither is he depicted beyond sexuality.

A third alternative is the suggestion that Jesus' sexuality was basically homosexual rather than heterosexual in orientation. (See the discussion of Morton Smith's presentation in chapter eleven.) Without discussing whether Jesus even gave overt expression to his sexuality, Canon Hugh Montefiore, vicar of Great St. Mary's in Cambridge, England, has offered the suggestion that Jesus was homosexually inclined.

My concern to show Christ's complete identification with mankind . . . raises for me a question about our Lord's celibacy. I raise it with reference to those thirty "Hidden Years" at Nazareth, when it seems that as yet he did not know either his vocation to be Messiah or his status as Son of God. Why did he not marry? After all he was fully a man. Of course there is no evidence, and we can only speculate, and speculation must be done with reverence. But having raised the question we must look it in the face—why did he not marry? Could the answer be that Jesus was not by nature the marrying sort? I want to make it crystal clear that when I suggest this possible answer, no question of Jesus being less than perfect was or is involved or implied. It is of course important not to confuse temptation with sin. Jesus was tempted as we all are in every possible way; yet without sin (*For God's Sake,* 182).

In elaboration of this proposal, Montefiore has stated, in an effort to be "serious and relevant," the following: "Women were his friends, but it is men he is said to have loved. The homosexual explanation is one we cannot ignore" (*Newsweek*, August 7, 1967, 83).

A fourth possibility is the suggestion that Jesus gave expression to his sexuality in marriage. This view has been most fully developed by William E. Phipps in his two books *Was Jesus Married?* and *The Sexuality of Jesus*. Phipps concludes that "Jesus most probably was married to a Galilean woman in the second decade of life" (*Was Jesus Married?* 70). How does he arrive at such a conclusion?

First of all, Phipps begins with an affirmation of Jesus' true humanity which involved sexuality.

Along with all orthodox Christians I believe that Jesus was fully human and, endorsing the sciences of man, I think that sexual desire is intrinsic to human nature. I do not agree with Luther that this desire is so irrepressible among the heterosexually oriented that all must gratify it by coitus. However this means of gratification, in the context of marriage, has been the ordinary way in which most humans throughout history have attempted to deal with the basic psychological as well as physical need. The question that concerns me is whether there are sufficient grounds in the sources pertaining to the life and times of Jesus to substantiate the common assumption that he followed a different pattern of sexual behavior from that of most other humans (13).

Secondly, Phipps argues that in light of the sexual attitudes in Judaism at the time of Jesus, it is highly unlikely that Jesus did not marry. Ancient Judaism highly valued married life and disdained celibacy; it should be assumed that as a first-century Jew, Jesus shared these views.

In the Old Testament licit gratification of sexual passion was encouraged and marriage was a religious duty that every man took seriously. Further, there was virtually no moral contamination associated with marital intercourse and there are no instances of life-long voluntary celibacy in the entire Old Testament history (26). . . .

Celibacy was rejected both in theory and in practice by the Hebrews. Hirschel Revel is not indulging in overstatement when he asserts: "The voluntary renunciation of marriage is a conception utterly foreign to Judaism." It is not found in the Old Testament, the Apocrypha, the Pseudepigrapha, the Qumran scrolls, the Mishnah, or in the Talmud. The traditions that may have influenced Jesus are virtually all contained in these sources. But the Hebrews were much more positive toward sexuality than the mere avoidance of celibacy. They valued sex, in the context of marriage, for procreation, companionship, and recreation. The many-splendored purposes of connubial love were extolled and the extremes of undisciplined license and sexual deprivation were abhorred (33).

As a good Jew, Jesus and his father Joseph would have accepted the responsibility and blessing attendant upon Jesus' marriage.

The Jewish imperative regarding parental duties, accompanied by New Testament information about Jesus' early family relations, gives weighty evidence that Joseph betrothed his children even as he himself had been betrothed. In his time a Jewish father's obligation to a son was clearly defined: "He must circumcise him, redeem him, teach him Torah, teach him a trade, and find a wife for him" [*Talmud, Kiddushin* 29a]. What evidence is there that Joseph fulfilled these five duties? (47).

Phipps argues that Joseph fulfilled these duties because he was a just man who lived by the law. The fulfillment of the first four duties are referred to or can be deduced from the New Testament. The lack of any evidence concerning the fifth can be explained because "the duty of becoming betrothed shortly after puberty was as axiomatic in ancient Judaism as celibacy was in St. Benedict's monastry. Consequently, there is no mention of celibacy in Benedict's *Rule* nor do the Gospels allude to [Jesus'] marriage" (48).

Thirdly, Phipps denies that any of the sayings of Jesus which have traditionally been used to support an ascetic view of sex and a celibate Jesus can be used to disprove the theory that Jesus married.

The alleged evidence in the Gospels for Jesus' celibacy has been weighed and found wanting. The traditional "proof-texts" for his perpetual virginity, which have been ripped from their contexts by ascetically oriented interpreters, not only do not hint that he never married but can more properly be used to show that he endorsed permanent marriage as being of penultimate value. His use of the bridegroom metaphor [Mark 2:19a] proves no more than that he had a life-affirming general outlook and a positive view of weddings. His teaching about sexual desire [Matt 5:27-28] means that the libido should not be adulterated by adulterous schemes. The hyperbolic saying about "hating" one's wife and family [Luke 14:26] means that in cases of irreconcilable conflict domestic allegiance should be subordinated to commitment to God's cause. The eunuch saying [Matthew 19:12], if authentic, pertains to Jesus' sanctioning fidelity to a wayward spouse in hope of eventual mutual reconciliation. His response to the Sadducees [Luke 20:34-36] displays that the resurrected life will surpass but will not negate earthly love between spouses. Thus the five passages from the Gospels that are most frequently relied upon for justifying vows of celibacy and that at first glance may appear to condone or encourage such vows are legitimately open to quite different and even opposing interpretations (98).

Fourthly, Phipps argues that "the Hellenistic sexual asceticism that infiltrated Gentile Christianity in the post-apostolic era has been responsible for the dogma that Jesus was perpetually virginal" (187).

Sexual asceticism can be traced throughout the course of our civilization. It was advocated by a number of Greek philosophers; it waxed in the Roman and medieval eras; and it has continued with diminishing vigor in modern history. Many important philosophers, in their life-styles and teachings, have denigrated the libidinous. They have assumed that devotion to the life of the immaterial intellect should result in antipathy toward satisfying sensual desires.

The influence of Plato has been especially heavy in this regard. He believed that lovers of wisdom should strive to become disincarnate psyches (*The Sexuality of Jesus*, 91). . . .

Through the discipline of crushing tender passions it was thought that the divine immortal soul could best be emancipated from its carnal dungeon. In medieval Catholicism moral dualism was the main, though not the exclusive, theoretical basis for the practice of celibacy. Those theologians in church history who have advocated sexual asceticism have often unwittingly held a doctrine of man closer to Athens than to Jerusalem. The self-mortification they have defended stems more from the dialogues of Plato than from the writings of the Bible (93-94).

14. JESUS: THE CREATION OF THE EARLY CHURCH

> The worshippers of the sacred mushroom saw in the fungus a microcosm of nature; it rose from the womb or volva, flourished, and within hours had died again, to be renewed in the continuing cycle of creation. Thus the "Jesus," born of a virgin womb, lifted high on a cross as a sign to men, killed and raised again to eternal life, became a personified enactment of the life cycle of the sacred mushroom, and to the Christian today, persuaded of the historicity of the myth, serves as the supreme example of God's creative and redemptive activity in the world.—John M. Allegro, *The End of a Road* (p. 91)

In the course of modern study of the historical Jesus, several scholars have taken a position which may be called radical skepticism. That is, they have denied the existence of a historical Jesus. Doubting Jesus' historicity, they have viewed him as the product of the faith and imagination of the early church.

Bruno Bauer, for example, argued that the life of Jesus was the creation of the writer of the gospel of Mark. The life of Jesus was produced from elements drawn from Stoic Philosophy and Roman and Alexandrian culture of the second century combined with the influence and personality of the Roman philosopher Seneca.

The Englishman John M. Robertson traced the picture of Jesus back to mythological elements drawn from Judaism and pagan sources. Others have seen astral myths as the ultimate source of the portrait of Jesus.

Albert Kalthoff saw in the figure of Jesus the reflection of and the embodiment of a social movement among the lower classes of the Roman Empire.

The American, William Benjamin Smith, has argued for the idea that the historical Jesus was created out of mythological elements and concepts.

Just after the turn of the century, the most vocal of the scholars denying the historicity of Jesus was the German Arthur Drews. For Drews, the historical Jesus was a creation of the church produced primarily by the historicizing of Old Testament texts.

An historical Jesus, as the Gospels portray him, and as he lives in the minds of the liberal theologians of today, never existed at all; so that he never founded the insignificant and diminutive community of the Messiah at Jerusalem. It will be necessary to concede that the Christ-faith arose quite independently of any historical personality known to us; that indeed Jesus was in this sense a product of the religious "social soul" and was made by Paul, with the required amount of reinterpretation and reconstruction, the chief interest of those communities founded by him. The "historical" Jesus is not earlier but later than Paul; and as such he has always existed merely as an idea, as a pious fiction in the minds of members of the community. The New Testament with its four Gospels is not previous to the Church, but the latter is antecedent to them; and the Gospels are the derivatives, consequently forming a support for the propaganda of the church, and being without any claim to historical significance (*The Christ Myth*, 286). . . .

More or less all the features of the picture of the historical Jesus, at any rate all those of any important religious significance, bear a purely mythical character, and no opening exists for seeking an historical figure behind the Christ myth. It is not the imagined historical Jesus but, if any one, Paul who is that "great personality" that called Christianity into life as a new religion, and by the speculative range of his intellect and the depth of his moral experience gave it the strength for its journey, the strength which bestowed upon it victory over the other competing religions. Without Jesus the rise of Christianity can be quite well understood, without Paul not so (19).

When one studies the Gospels critically, according to Drews, not a single passage can be shown to be historical. "The fact is that there is *nothing, absolutely nothing,* either in the actions or words of Jesus, that has not a mythical character or cannot be traced back to parallel passages in the Old Testament or the Talmud, and is therefore under suspicion of being derived from them" (*The Historicity of Jesus,* 290).

If one asks who the creative personality was who lies behind the historical Jesus other than Paul, Drews would answer: "In the long run the contents of the gospels may be traced to the prophet Isaiah, whose 'predictions,' sayings, penitential appeals, and promises reappear in the Gospels, in the form of a narrative. *Hence Isaiah, not Jesus, would be the powerful personality to whom Christianity would owe its existence.*" "It is more probable that *Jesus and Isaiah are one and the same person* than that the Jesus of liberal theology brought Christianity into existence" (*The Historicity of Jesus,* 296).

Drews saw behind the Christian Jesus not only special mythological elements and the influence of Old Testament references but also a certain idea of the deity.

At the base of all the deeper religions lies the idea of a suffering god, sacrificing himself for humanity, and obtaining spiritual healing for man by his death and his subsequent resurrection. In the pagan religions this idea is conceived naturalistically: the death of the sun, the annual dying of nature, the happy revival of its forces in spring, and the victorious conquering of the power of winter by the new sun—this is the realistic background of the tragic myth of Osiris, Attis, Adonis, Tammuz, Dionysos, Balder, and similar deities. The great advance of Christianity beyond these nature-religions is that it spiritualised this idea by applying it to the man Jesus Christ, blended the many saviour-gods in the idea of the one god-man, and gave it the most plausible form by connecting it with an historical reality (*The Historicity of Jesus,* 305-6).

Behind Drews' arguments against the historicity of Jesus lies his philosophical argument that a purely historical understanding of Jesus does not meet the philosophical needs nor satisfy the religious consciousness of modern man. In a way, he was combating the historical Jesus as reconstructed by liberal theology as much as he was denying the historicity of Jesus. "To bind up religion with history, as modern theologians do, and to represent an *historical religion* as the need of modern man, is no proof of insight, but of a determination to persuade oneself to recognise the Christian religion alone" (*The Historicity of Jesus,* 308).

Religion is a life that emanates from the depths of one's innermost self, an outgrowth of the mind and of freedom. All religious progress consists in making faith more intimate, in transferring the centre of gravity from the objective to the subjective world, by a confident surrender to the God within us. The belief in an historical instrument of salvation is *a purely external appreciation of objective facts.* To seek to base the religious life on it is not to regard the essence of religion, but to make it for ever dependent on a stage of mental development that has long passed in the inner life (x-xi).

In more recent times, many of the ideas of Drews have been restated by the Frenchman P. L. Couchoud who saw the life of the historical Jesus as a mythical fabrication primarily constructed on the basis of Old Testament texts. Like Drews he pointed to the close similarity between Psalms 22 and the depiction of the crucifixion and death of Jesus and argued that the latter were constructed on the basis of the former.

The most recent and extensive attempt to see Jesus as the creation of the church is the work by John M. Allegro, *The Sacred Mushroom and the Cross: A Study of the Nature and Origins of Christianity Within the Fertility Cults of the Ancient Near East.* His ideas have been given a more popular expression in his book *The End of a Road.*

Allegro argues that all Near Eastern religions had their origin in man's questioning about how life originated and how man could ensure his own survival. Man saw himself dependent on the powers and forces of nature and at the same time frustrated by these powers and forces. The same forces that produced his food and provided his sustenance could also parch his crops, destroy his animals, and challenge man himself. Religion was born out of this sense of dependence and frustration.

Man saw that his basic needs centered in the quest for fertility of flock, field, and family. If man were to overcome the needs of life, he must establish communication with the source of fertility and maintain a proper relationship with it. The ultimate powers of fertility were understood by ancient man in terms of human and animal reproduction. The heavenly power was thus conceived as the male whose semen in the form of rain fertilized and fructified the female, the earth. Man's religious rituals were intent on creating, stimulating, and producing this fertilizing sexual union. The deity or forces of nature were not only the source of the life-creating semen but were also the source of knowledge. However much man learned and advanced, he always found some impenetrable mystery which he could not grasp. Man therefore hoped in religion not only to induce the gods to produce fertility and to gain union with the gods but also to grasp and/or experience divine illumination and glimpse the beauty and glory of the divine world. With the gradual evolution of religion, the focus tended to shift away from the cruder desires to control the weather and all forms of fertility and became more concerned with the acquisition of wisdom and knowledge, especially about the future.

In order to understand the essence of religion for ancient man, one must do so through the writings man has left behind. This means, for Allegro, that philology, the science of words is of overriding importance. "The written word is a symbol of thought; behind it lies an attitude of mind, an emotion, a reasoned hypothesis, to which the reader can to some extent penetrate" (*The Sacred Mushroom*, 3). Of special importance is the etymology, the root meaning of words. In language, religious terminology is least susceptible to change. Therefore if the original root meaning of a word can be established, then this meaning can frequently be traced through history in the appearance of this word or the root form.

The first ancient religion for which there exists a written

literature is that of ancient Sumer from the fourth millennium B.C. The Sumerian cuneiform in which these texts are written is seen by Allegro as the bridge, or the common factor, to all the Near Eastern Indo-European and Semitic civilizations. In other words, lying behind the two linguistic families is Sumerian. Thus, on the basis of Sumerian religious terms, one can penetrate to the root-meanings of later religious terminology, related deities, plants, heroes, and so forth and trace the continuity of religious understanding.

In the language and culture of the world's most ancient civilization, Sumerian, it is now possible to find a bridge between the Indo-European and Semitic worlds. The first writing known is found on tablets from the Mesopotamian basin, dating some five thousand years ago, and consisting of crude pictures drawn with a stylus on to soft clay. Later the recognizable pictures became stylized into ideograms made up of nail- or wedge-shape impressions, so-called cuneiform signs, each representing syllables of consonants and vowels. These syllables made up "word-bricks" which resisted phonetic change within the language, and could be joined together to make connected phrases and sentences. To such word-bricks we can now trace Indo-European and Semitic verbal roots, and so begin to decipher for the first time the names of gods, heroes, plants and animals appearing in cultic mythologies. We can also now start penetrating to the root-meanings of many religious and secular terms whose original significance has been obscure (18).

Lying behind the names of the gods in Sumerian, Greek, and Hebrew is the idea of the god as the source of fertility.

If we are to make any enlightened guess at "primitive" man's ideas about god and the universe it would have to be on the reasonable assumption that they would be simple, and directly related to the world of his experience. He may have given the god numerous epithets describing his various functions and manifestations but there is no reason to doubt that the reality behind the names was envisaged as one, all-powerful deity, a life-giver, supreme creator. The etymological examination of the chief god-names that is now possible supports this view, pointing to a common theme of life-giving, fecundity. Thus the principal gods of the Greeks and Hebrews, Zeus and Yahweh (Jehovah), have names derived from Sumerian meaning "juice of fecundity," spermatozoa, "seed of life." The phrase is composed of two syllables, IA *(ya,* dialectally *za),* "juice," literally "strong water," and U, perhaps the most important phoneme in the whole of Near Eastern religion. It is found in the texts represented by a number of different cuneiform signs, but at the root of them all is the idea of "fertility." Thus one U means "copulate" or "mount," and "create"; another "rainstorm," as source of the heavenly sperm; another "vegetation," as the offspring of the god, whilst another U is the name of the storm-god himself. So, far from evincing a multiplicity of gods and conflicting theological notions, our earliest records lead us back to a single idea, even a single letter, "U." Behind Judaism and Christianity, and indeed all the Near Eastern fertility religions and their more sophisticated developments, there lies this single phoneme "U" (20).

Since vegetation was the product of the god's union with earth, plants were assumed to be embodiments of the divine life of the god. Certain plants, however, came to be understood as truer and more complete embodiments than others. Plants endowed with the power to kill or heal, in other words, drug plants, were of special concern, and there grew up in culture a technical knowledge concerning their nature and usage. Likewise there developed a study of man's and individual persons' physiology and psychological make-up in relation to the use of these drug plants often utilizing astrological considerations. From the beginning then religion and drug arts were inseparable. The earliest mystery cults with their secrecy were developed around the collection and transmission of the knowledge of the healing arts and drugs.

Of special importance to ancient man was the mushroom, *Amanita muscaria,* with its characteristic red-and-white spotted cap and powerful hallucinatory poison. The mushroom has always been a mysterious plant. It grows without seed, makes a rapid appearance, grows swiftly, and disappears quickly. According to Allegro, every aspect of the mushroom's existence was fraught with sexual allusions. In its earliest growth, the mushroom button appears like an egg.

As the plant grows it assumes a phallic shape, and finally in its full form it appears as a phallus supporting the female groin. Since mushrooms grow shortly after the rain—that is after the divine fertilization—it was assumed that the mushroom was divinely created and a special embodiment of the divine semen. The mushroom was a "son of god" and a replica of the fertility god himself. When eaten it gave man the experience of union with the heavenly world, a trip to the celestial sphere.

Allegro finds numerous references to the sacred mushroom and the fertility deity throughout the Bible. "Mushroom stories abounded in the Old Testament" (42). We have already seen how he traces the names of the Greek god Zeus and the Hebrew god Yahweh back to a common Sumerian origin. In both testaments, many of the stories and sayings are to be seen as cryptograms and word-plays behind which are references to the fertility god and the mushroom cult. In other words, the biblical traditions are coded to provide the reader with references to fertility and the mushroom cult in what otherwise appear to be ordinary stories. Allegro argues that one must distinguish three levels of understanding which are involved in New Testament texts. There is, first of all, the plain meaning of the Greek text, the story or saying itself. But this is the outer husk with probably little historical reality at this level except for the social and historical background it reflects. Secondly, there is the Semitic level. At this level, when the materials are put back into their Semitic form are word plays, puns, and words with several levels of meaning. Thirdly, there is the level which expresses the basic concepts of the mushroom cult. "Here is the real stuff of the mystery—fertility philosophy." This is the real message being conveyed.

Here, then, was the literary device to spread occult knowledge to the faithful. To tell the story of a rabbi called Jesus, and invest him with the power and names of the magic drug. To have him live before the terrible events that had disrupted their lives, to preach a love between men, extending even to the hated Romans. Thus, reading such a tale, should it fall into Roman hands, even their mortal enemies might be deceived and not probe farther into the activities of the cells of the mystery cults within their territories (xiv).

The Old Testament as well preserved the fertility-mushroom code in its narratives and terminology. For example, the stories of David contain numerous veiled references to the fertility and mushroom cult. David's name means "lover" or "beloved." Allegro's translation of II Sam. 23:1 seeks to demonstrate how the passage teems with sexual references. "The oracle of David, son of Jesse; the oracle of the erect phallus (RSV: the man who was raised on high), the semen-smeared (RSV: anointed) of the God of Jacob, the Na'im (heavenly canopy, RSV: sweet) of the stretched penis (RSV: psalmist) of Israel" (II Sam. 23:1) (141). Even the family name of David, "son of Jesse," reflects an old Sumerian term BAR/USh-SA, "erect penis" (141).

The story of the exodus from Egypt has a mushroom name and epithet as the main ingredients of the story. "The story itself hinges on the play between the name of the fungus as *Mezar,* 'erect, stretched,' and *Masōr,* 'Egypt,' to set the place of the myth; and upon the common Semitic name of the mushroom *Pitrā',* and the root *p-t-r* which gave 'first-born,' 'release,' and 'unleavened bread'" (143-44). In light of such interest in sexual symbolism, Allegro suggests that it is no wonder that cultic prostitution—of both males and females—played such an important function in the cultic life of ancient Israel.

Behind much of the Old Testament, Allegro assumes, there may lie historical reality. There may have been a real David and so forth whose names and titles became the bearer of the secrets of the mushroom cult. But the New Testament is different.

A quite different situation obtains, however, with regard to the New Testament characters. Here, for reasons already stated and which by now should be apparent . . . , we are dealing with a cryptic document. This is a different kind of mythology, based not on pious aggrandizement by later admirers, as has been so often assumed in the past, but a deliberate attempt to mislead the reader. There is every reason why there should *not* have been a real Jesus of Nazareth, at least not one connected with the sect of Christians, nor a real John the Baptist, Peter, John, James, and so on. To have named them, located their homes and families, would have brought disaster upon their associates in a cult which had earned the hatred of the authorities (150).

In the growth of the mushroom, the normal process of fertilization seemed to the ancients to have been bypassed. The god had simply spoken his creative word which was carried to the earth as if by an angelic messenger of the god and the result was the mysterious embodiment of the god. The mushroom was the man child of the god.

Every aspect of the mushroom's existence was fraught with sexual allusions, and in its phallic form the ancients saw a replica of the fertility god himself. It was the "son of God," its drug was a purer form of the God's own spermatozoa than that discoverable in any other form of living matter. It was, in fact, God himself, manifest on earth. To the mystic it was the divinely given means of entering heaven; God had come down in the flesh to show the way to himself, by himself (xv).

Here lies the true background of the story of the virgin birth. "Jesus" was born without earthly father; like the mushroom, he came into existence through the direct creative act of the god.

In the phallic mushroom, the "man-child" born of the "virgin" womb, we have the reality behind the Christ figure of the New Testament story. In a sense he is representative also of the initiates of the cult, "Christians," or "smeared with semen," as the name means. By imitating the mushroom, as well as by eating it and sucking its juice, or "blood," the Christian was taking unto himself the panoply of his god, as the priests in the sanctuary also anointed themselves with the god's spermatozoa found in the juices and resins of special plants and trees. As the priests "served" the god in the temple, the symbolic womb of divine creation, so the

244

Christians and their cultic associates worshipped their god and mystically involved themselves in the creative process. In the language of the mystery cults they sought to be "born again," when, purged afresh of past sin, they could apprehend the god in a drug-induced ecstasy (61).

John the Baptist is also a veiled reference to the mushroom cult. The name John comes from the Sumerian word GAN-NU meaning "red dye," and red was the color of *Amanita muscaria*. The designation Baptist goes back in origin to the Sumerian word TAB-BA-R/LI which means mushroom. His camel's hair clothing points to the two humps of the camel which in turn points to the mushroom volva's two halves. "The name and title of 'John the Baptist' in the New Testament story then, means no more than the 'red-topped mushroom'" (122). The word for camel contains a pun on the Hebrew word, *kirkarah,* and the Greek word for mandrake, *Kirkaia,* both going back to the Sumerian root KUR-KUR, a name for the Holy Plant. The reference to locusts, *gōbāy,* is a play on the word *gab'a,* "mushroom," and both go back to a Sumerian original GUG meaning "pod." The entire story of John's death by beheading must be seen as built around various names from the mushroom. The reference to the platter (*tablā'*) on which his head lay denotes the mushroom TAB-BA-LI. The name Herodias as well as the name Herod serve as vehicles for punning on the names of the mushroom. Herod—which means "heron" which is in Latin *ardeola*—was a term which would reflect the Semitic word *'ardīlā',* "mushroom." Similarily, the name of Rhoda who opened the door to Peter after his release from prison (Acts 12:13).

The opening lines of the Lord's Prayer—"Our father which art in Heaven"—is the Greek version of an Aramaic phrase which was derived by word-play from the Sumerian. "Our father" was originally "Abba, pater," a combination of Aramaic and Greek, but is actually a play on the Sumerian AB-BA-TAB-BA-RI-GI, a mushroom title. "'Our father who art in heaven,' then, is a cryptic way of expressing the name of the Saviour-god, the sacred mushroom'" (162).

Throughout the New Testament, Allegro discovers where the writers have gone to the trouble of concealing by ingenious literary devices secret names of the mushroom. A prime example of this is his decipherment of Mark 3:17 which refers to "James the son of Zebedee and John the brother of James, whom he [Jesus] surnamed Boanerges, that is, sons of thunder." Allegro claims that "sons of thunder" was a well-known name for the mushroom fungus "found elsewhere in Semitic texts, and supported by the old Greek name *keraunion*, 'thunder-fungus,' after *keraunos*, 'thunder.' The reference is to the belief that mushrooms were born of thunder, the voice of the god in the storm, since it was noticed that they appeared in the ground after rainstorms" (101-2). Allegro argues that Boanerges cannot under any explanation mean sons of thunder in Aramaic. The title goes back to a Sumerian term—GEShPU-AN-UR—meaning "'mighty man (holding up) the arch of heaven,' a fanciful image of the stem supporting the canopy of the mushroom, seen in cosmographical terms" (101). The conclusion drawn from such an explanation is: "If, for instance, 'Boanerges' is correctly to be explained as a name of the sacred fungus, and the impossible 'translation' appended in the text, 'Sons of Thunder,' is equally relevant to the mushroom, then the validity of the whole New Testament story is immediately underminded" (192-93).

The name Peter is a play on the Semitic word *pitra'* meaning "mushroom" and his surname Bar-jonah goes back to an original BAR-IA-U-NA, a fungus-name cognate with Paeonia, the Holy Plant. The name Barnabas is derived from two words meaning "skin" and "giraffe" or "red-with-white-spots"; thus Barnabas is a veiled reference to the red, white-spotted skin of the *Amanita muscaria*.

The crucifixion is understood in terms of mushroom mythology. "The idea of crucifixion in mushroom mythology was already established before the New Testament myth-makers portrayed their mushroom hero Jesus dying by this method. The fungus itself was probably known as 'The Little Cross'" (106). The cross was a symbol of copulation with the upright phallic symbol holding up the woman's crotch. So the reference to "Christ crucified" is a reference to the "semen-anointed, erected mushroom." And to take up one's cross was a "euphemism for sexual copulation" (105).

Thus the early church was a drug-sex cult whose members in their ritual consumed the body of the Christ—the mushroom—and in their ecstasy experienced union with the divine. The opposition to the early church on the part of the Romans was directed against the drug cult whose secrets its members sought to preserve in the cryptic message of the New Testament. Later Christian generations, the orthodox, lost or suppressed the clue to the true interpretation of the New Testament and thus ascribed historicity to what had originally been merely the means to transmit and protect the secrets of the sex-drug initiates.

If it now transpires that Christianity was only a latter-day manifestation of a religious movement that had been in existence for thousands of years, and in that particular mystery-cult form for centuries before the turn of the era, then the necessity for a founder-figure fades away, and the problems that have so long beset the exegete become far more urgent. The improbable nature of the tale, quite apart from the "miracle" stories, the extraordinarily liberal attitude of the central figure towards the Jewish "quislings" of the time, his friendly disposition toward the most hated enemies of his people, his equivocation about paying taxes to the Roman government, the howling of Jewish citizens for the blood of one of their own people at the hands of the occupying power, features of the Gospel story which have never rung true, now can be understood for what they have always been: parts of a deliberate attempt to mislead the authorities into whose hands it was known the New Testament documents would fall. The New Testament was a "hoax," but nevertheless a deadly serious and extremely dangerous attempt to transmit to the scattered faithful secrets which the Christians dare not permit to fall into unauthorized hands but to whose preservation they were irrevocably committed by sacred oaths (193-94).

The created Jesus of the early sex-drug cult called Christians, who was one of the symbolic carriers of the mushroom mysteries, came however to be looked upon as a historical figure. In the presentations of the Christians, the secrets of the New Testament were lost.

The ruse failed. Christians, hated and despised, were hauled forth and slain in their thousands. The cult well nigh perished. What eventually took its place was a travesty of the real thing, a mockery of the power that could raise men to heaven and give them the glimpse of God for which they gladly died. The story of the rabbi crucified at the instigation of the Jews became a historical peg upon which the new cult's authority was founded. What began as a hoax, became a trap even to those who believed themselves to be the spiritual heirs of the mystery religion and took to themselves the name of "Christian." Above all they forgot, or purged from the cult and their memories, the one supreme secret on which their whole religious and ecstatic experience depended: the names and identity of the source of the drug, the key to heaven—the sacred mushroom (xiv).

BIBLIOGRAPHY

CHAPTER ONE

Anderson, Charles C. *Critical Quests of Jesus*. Grand Rapids: Wm. B. Eerdmans, 1969.

Anderson, Hugh. *Jesus*. Englewood Cliffs, N. J.: Prentice-Hall, 1967.

Braaten, Carl E., and Roy A. Harrisville, eds. *The Historical Jesus and the Kerygmatic Christ: Essays on the New Quest of the Historical Jesus*. Nashville: Abingdon Press, 1964.

Bruce, F. F. *Jesus and Christian Origins Outside the New Testament*. Grand Rapids: Wm. B. Eerdmans, 1974.

Case, S. J. *Jesus Through the Centuries*. Chicago: University of Chicago Press, 1932.

Finegan, Jack. *Hidden Records of the Life of Jesus*. Philadelphia: Pilgrim Press, 1969.

Goguel, Maurice. *Jesus and the Origins of Christianity*. Volume 1: *Prolegomena to the Life of Jesus*. Trans. by Olive Wyon. New York: The Macmillan Company, 1933.

Grant, Robert M. *The Earliest Lives of Jesus*. New York: Harper & Brothers, 1961.

Harnack, Adolf. *What is Christianity?* Trans. by Thomas Bailey Saunders. New York: G. P. Putnam's Sons, 1901.

Keck, Leander. *A Future for the Historical Jesus*. Nashville: Abingdon Press, 1971.

Klausner, Joseph. *Jesus of Nazareth: His Life, Times, and Teaching*. Trans. by Herbert Danby. New York: The Macmillan Company, 1929.

McArthur, Harvey K. *The Quest Through the Centuries: The Search for the Historical Jesus*. Philadelphia: Fortress Press, 1966.

————. *In Search of the Historical Jesus*. New York: Charles Scribner's Sons, 1969.

Renan, Ernest. *Life of Jesus*. Trans. by Charles Edwin Wilbour. New York: Carleton, 1867.

Schweitzer, Albert. *The Quest of the Historical Jesus*. Trans. by W. Montgomery. London: A. & C. Black, 1910.

CHAPTER TWO

Smith, David. *The Days of His Flesh: The Earthly Life of Our Lord and Saviour Jesus Christ*. London: Hodder & Stoughton, 1905.

Stauffer, Ethelbert. *Jesus and His Story*. Trans. by Richard and Clara Winston. New York: Knopf, 1960.

CHAPTER THREE

Schweitzer, Albert. *The Mystery of the Kingdom of God*. Trans. by Walter Lowrie. New York: Dodd, Mead & Company, 1914.

————. *The Quest of the Historical Jesus: A Critical Study of its Progress from Reimarus to Wrede*. Trans. by W. Montgomery. London: A. & C. Black, 1910; New York: The Macmillan Company, 1950, reissued with a new introduction by James M. Robinson, 1968. The second, enlarged German edition was published under the title *Geschichte der Leben-Jesu-Forschung* (Tübingen: J. C. B. Mohr, 1913).

Weiss, Johannes. *Jesus' Proclamation of the Kingdom of God*. Trans. and ed. by Richard H. Hiers and David L. Holland. Philadelphia: Fortress Press, 1971.

Wrede, William, *The Messianic Secret*. Trans. by J. O. G. Greig Cambridge: J. Clark, 1971.

CHAPTER FOUR

Barton, Bruce. *The Man Nobody Knows*. Indianapolis: The Bobbs-Merrill Company, 1925.

Enslin, Morton. *The Prophet From Nazareth*. New York: McGraw-Hill, 1961.

Bibliography

Matthews, Shailer. *Jesus on Social Institutions.* New York: The Macmillan Company, 1928.

CHAPTER FIVE

Ben-Chorin, Schalom. *Bruder Jesus: Der Nazarener in jüdischer Sicht.* Munich: P. List, 1967.

Buber, Martin. *Two Types of Faith.* Trans. by Norman P. Goldhawk. London: Routledge & Kegan Paul, Ltd., 1951.

Cohn, Haim. *The Trial and Death of Jesus.* New York: Harper, 1971.

Flusser, David. *Jesus.* Trans. by Ronald Walls. New York: Herder & Herder, 1959.

Klausner, Joseph. *Jesus of Nazareth: His Life, Times, and Teaching.* Trans. by Herbert Danby. New York: The Macmillan Company, 1925.

Lapide, Pinchas E. "Jesus in Israeli Literature," *Journal of Theology for Southern Africa,* V (Dec., 1973): 47-56.

Polish, David. *The Eternal Dissent.* New York: Abelard-Schuman, 1961.

Vermes, Geza. *Jesus the Jew: A Historian's Reading of the Gospels.* New York: The Macmillan Company, 1973.

CHAPTER SIX

Bornkamm, Günter. *Jesus of Nazareth.* Trans. by Irene and Fraser McLuskey with James M. Robinson. New York: Harper & Brothers, 1960.

Bultmann, Rudolf. "Is Jesus Risen as Goethe?" in Werner Harenberg, ed., Der Spiegel *on the New Testament.* Trans. by James H. Burtness. New York: The Macmillan Company, 1970, pp. 226-39.

————. *Jesus and the Word.* Trans. by Louise Pettibone Smith and Erminie Huntress Lantero. New York: Charles Scribner's Sons, 1934.

————. *Jesus Christ and Mythology.* New York: Scribner's, 1958.

————. "New Testament and Mythology," in Hans Werner Bartsch, ed., *Kerygma and Myth: A Theological Debate.* Trans. by Reginald H. Fuller. London: S. P. C. K., 1957, pp. 1-44.

————. "A Reply to the Theses of J. Schniewind," *Kerygma and Myth,* pp. 102-23.

————. "The Primitive Christian Kerygma and the Historical

Jesus," in *The Historical Jesus and the Kerygmatic Christ,* pp. 15-42.

————. "The Significance of the Historical Jesus for the Theology of Paul," *Faith and Understanding,* vol. 1. Trans. by Louise Pettibone Smith. New York: Harper, 1969, pp. 220-46.

Fuchs, Ernst. *Studies on the Historical Jesus.* Trans. by Andrew Scobie. London: SCM Press, 1964.

Jaspers, Karl, and Bultmann, Rudolf. *Myth and Christianity: An Inquiry into the Possibility of Religion Without Myth.* New York: Noonday Press, 1958.

Kähler, Martin. *The So-Called Historical Jesus and the Historic, Biblical Christ.* Trans. and ed. by Carl E. Braaten. Philadelphia: Fortress Press, 1964.

Käsemann, Ernst. "The Problem of the Historical Jesus," *Essays on New Testament Themes.* Trans. by W. J. Montague. London: SCM Press, 1964, pp. 15-47.

Robinson, James M. *A New Quest of the Historical Jesus.* London: SCM Press, 1959.

CHAPTER SEVEN

Bowman, John W., *The Intention of Jesus.* Philadelphia: Westminster Press, 1943.

————. "The Life and Teaching of Jesus," in *Peake's Commentary on the Bible.* Ed. by Matthew Black and H. H. Rowley. London: Thomas Nelson and Sons, 1962, pp. 733-47.

————. *Which Jesus?* Philadelphia: Westminster Press, 1970.

Dodd, C. H., *The Apostolic Preaching and its Development.* London: Hodder & Stoughton, 1936.

————. *The Founder of Christianity.* New York: The Macmillan Company, 1970.

Hoskyns, Edwyn, and Davey, Francis Noel. *The Riddle of the New Testament.* London: Faber and Faber, 1931.

Manson, T. W. "The Life of Jesus: Some Tendencies in Present-day Research," in *The Background of the New Testament and its Eschatology.* Ed. by W. D. Davies and D. Daube. London: Cambridge University Press, 1954, pp. 211-21.

————. *The Servant-Messiah: A Study of the Public Ministry of Jesus.* London: Cambridge University Press, 1953.

————. *The Teaching of Jesus: Studies in its Form and Content.* London: Cambridge University Press, 1931.

Taylor, Vincent. *The Formation of the Gospel Tradition.* London: Macmillan and Company, 1933.

Bibliography

CHAPTER EIGHT

Brandon, S.G.F. *Jesus and the Zealots: A Study of the Political Factor in Primitive Christianity.* Manchester: The University Press, 1967.

Carmichael, Joel. *The Death of Jesus.* New York: Macmillan, 1962.

Eisler, Robert. *The Messiah Jesus and John the Baptist (According to Flavius Josephus' recently discovered 'Capture of Jerusalem' and other Jewish and Christian Sources).* English edition by A. H. Krappe. New York: Dial Press, 1931.

Kautsky, Karl. *Foundations of Christianity.* New York: International Publishers, 1925.

Reimarus, H. S. "Concerning the Intention of Jesus and His Teaching," in *Reimarus: Fragments.* Ed. by C. H. Talbert and trans. by Ralph S. Fraser. Philadelphia: Fortress Press, 1970.

Wellhausen, Julius. *Einleitung in die drei ersten Evangelien.* Berlin: Georg Reimer, 1905.

CHAPTER NINE

Cleage, Albert. *The Black Messiah.* New York: Sheed & Ward, 1968.

Cone, James H. *Black Theology and Black Power.* New York: The Seabury Press, 1969.

———. *A Black Theology of Liberation.* Philadelphia: Lippincott, 1970.

Johnson, Joseph A., Jr. "Jesus: The Liberator," *Andover Newton Quarterly* 10 (Sept., 1969–Mar., 1970) 85-96.

Roberts, J. Deotis. *A Black Political Theology.* Philadelphia: Westminster Press, 1974.

———. *Liberation and Reconciliation: A Black Theology.* Philadelphia: Westminster Press, 1971.

Wilmore, Gayraud S. *Black Religion and Black Radicalism.* Garden City, N. Y.: Doubleday, 1972.

CHAPTER TEN

Schonfield, Hugh J. *The Passover Plot.* London: Hutchinson & Co. Ltd., 1965.

CHAPTER ELEVEN

Smith, Morton. *Clement of Alexandria and a Secret Gospel of Mark.* Cambridge: Harvard University Press, 1973.

————. *The Secret Gospel: The Discovery and Interpretation of the Secret Gospel According to Mark.* New York: Harper, 1973.

CHAPTER TWELVE

Davies, A. Powell. *The Meaning of the Dead Sea Scrolls.* New York: Signet Key Books, 1956.
Dupont-Sommer, A. *The Dead Sea Scrolls: A Preliminary Survey.* Trans. by E. Margaret Rowley. Oxford: B. Blackwell, 1952.
Potter, C. F. *The Lost Years of Jesus.* New York: Fawcett Publications, 1958.
Wilson, Edmund. *The Scrolls from the Dead Sea.* New York: Oxford University Press, 1955.

CHAPTER THIRTEEN

Driver, Tom. "Sexuality and Jesus," *Union Seminary Quarterly Review,* 20 (Nov., 1964–May 1965): 235-46.
Eichelbaum, Stanley. "'Superstar' Gospel is Shekels," *Sunday Scene, San Francisco Sunday Examiner and Chronicle,* July 15, 1973, p. 12.
Erskine, John. *The Human Life of Jesus.* New York: William Morrow and Company, 1945.
Montefiore, Hugh. *For God's Sake.* Philadelphia: Fortress Press, 1969.
Phipps, William E. *Recovering Biblical Sensuousness.* Philadelphia: Westminster Press, 1975.
————. *The Sexuality of Jesus: Theological and Literary Perspectives.* New York: Harper, 1973.
————. *Was Jesus Married? The Distortion of Sexuality in the Christian Tradition.* New York: Harper, 1970.
Pittenger, Norman. *Christology Reconsidered.* London: SCM Press, 1960.

CHAPTER FOURTEEN

Allegro, John M. *The End of a Road.* New York: Dial Press, 1971.
————. *The Sacred Mushroom and the Cross: A Study of the Nature and Origin of Christianity Within the Fertility Cults of the Ancient Near East.* London: Hodder & Stoughton, 1970.
Drews, Arthur. *The Christ Myth.* Trans. by C. Delisle Burns. Chicago: Open Court Publishing Company, 1911.

Bibliography

————. *The Witnesses to the Historicity of Jesus.* Trans. by Joseph McCabe. Chicago: Open Court Publishing Company, 1912.

Kalthoff, Albert. *The Rise of Christianity.* Trans. by Joseph McCabe. London: Watts & Co., 1907.

Robertson, John M. *Christianity and Mythology,* 2nd. ed. London: Watts & Co., 1910.

Smith, William Benjamin. *Ecce Deus, Studies of Primitive Christianity.* London: Watts & Co., 1912.

publishers who gave us permission to include the materials in this volume:

Ida Klaus for "The Emerging Relationship," an address given at the University of Chicago, February 5, 1965.

The School of Labor and Industrial Relations, Michigan State University, for "Employee Organizations in Public Employment."

Labor Education and Research Service, Ohio State University for Robert Repas, "Collective Bargaining Problems in Federal Employment," in Eugene C. Hagburg (ed.), *Problems Confronting Union Organizations in Public Employment* (Columbus: Ohio State University, Labor Education and Research Service, College of Commerce and Administration, April 1, 1966), pp. 1–5 and 17–20.

Cornell University for Joseph Krislov, "The Independent Public Employee Association: Characteristics and Functions," *Industrial and Labor Relations Review*, XV (July 1962), 510–520.

Charles T. Schmidt, Jr., for "Representation of Classroom Teachers," *Monthly Labor Review*, 91 (July 1968), 27–36.

Douglas Weiford and Wayne Burggraaff for "The Future for Public Employee Unions," *Public Management*, XLV (May 1963), 102–107.

The New York Times Company for A. H. Raskin, "City Workers Get Right to Organize in Union of Choice," *The New York Times*, April 1, 1958.

Cornell University for Wilson R. Hart, "The Impasse in Labor Relations in the Federal Civil Service," *Industrial and Labor Relations Review*, XIX (January 1966), 175–189.

Eli Rock for "The Process and Procedures of the Long-Standing Relationship," an address given at the University of Chicago, February 5, 1965.

Social Science Research Bureau of Michigan State University for Charles T. Schmidt, Jr., "Collective Negotiations: An Overview" and "Negotiating the Local Agreement," in Charles T. Schmidt, Jr., Hyman Parker, and Bob Repas, *A Guide to Collective Negotiations in Education* (East Lansing: Michigan State University, Social Science Research Bureau, 1967), pp. 1–16, 56–60.

Commerce Clearing House, Inc. for David G. Shenton, "Compulsory Arbitration in the Public Service," *Labor Law Journal,* XVII (March 1966), 138–147.

Marc Somerhausen for "The Right to Strike in the Public Service," *Free Labour World,* CLXXVI (February 1965), 3–8.

Cornell University for Jean T. McKelvey, "The Role of State Agencies in Public Employee Labor Relations," *Industrial and Labor Relations Review,* XX (January 1967), 182–197.

CONTENTS

ix

COLLECTIVE BARGAINING IN THE PUBLIC SERVICE

I

INTRODUCTION

Collective bargaining in public employment is
developing in the fastest growing sector of the
economy. The number of public employees has
expanded greatly in the postwar years, especially
in state and local governmental units. In the
first selection, Dr. Daniel H. Kruger traces the
growth of public employment for the years
1946–1966. His analysis of growth patterns by
functions helps to explain why government services are expanding.

In the second selection, Ida Klaus discusses the
nature of the emerging relationship in collective bargaining between public employers and
employee organizations representing public employees.

Trends in Public Employment, 1946–1966

DANIEL H. KRUGER

Government has become one of the nation's largest employers.
Public employment has expanded significantly as a result of
population growth, war and national defense, urbanization, increased technology, and public demand for more and better

Written for this volume. The author is Professor of Industrial Relations,
School of Labor and Industrial Relations, Michigan State University.

services. Our concern here is with the growth, between 1946
and 1966, in the number of civilian public employees—those
paid officials and civilian employees in over 91,000 governmental
units, including the national government, 50 states, the District
of Columbia, 3,043 counties, 18,000 municipalities, 17,142 townships, 34,678 school districts, and 18,323 special districts.

Public employment rose from 5.6 million civilian employees
in 1946 to 11.5 million in 1966, a 100 percent increase. By comparison, nonfarm employment increased 47 percent during the
same period, from 46.9 million to 68.9 million. Governments in
1946 accounted for about 13 percent of all nonfarm employees
and 17 percent in 1966. Thus, 1 out of every 6 employees in
1966 was a public employee.

Since 1946, there has been a significant shift in the distribution of employees among the three levels of government—federal, state, and local. In 1945, half of all government employees
were in the federal service. Following World War II, the proportion declined from two-fifths of the total in 1946 to one-
third in 1950. In 1966, the federal government employed about
25 percent of all public employees. State governments accounted
for 13 percent of all public employees in 1946 and 19 percent
in 1966. The largest increase in public employment has been in
local governmental units. In 1946, local governments employed
nearly half (46 percent) of all public employees and in 1966,
nearly three-fifths (56 percent) of the total.

In this section we shall briefly review the functions in which
public employees were employed during this twenty-year period.
Such an analysis of employment by functions will help to explain the significant growth of employment in the public sector
of the economy.

Employment in the Federal Government

From a peak of 3.5 million employees in 1945, the number of
federal civilian employees declined to 2.7 million in 1946. A
year later the federal government employed 2 million persons.
The cold war, Vietnam, international commitments, and rockets
and space explorations have all contributed to increased federal

employment since 1947. In 1956, there were 2.4 million federal employees; ten years later, there were 2.6 million.

National defense and post office operations—both constitutional functions—employ the largest number of federal civilian employees. Together these two functions accounted for 70 percent of all federal employment in 1946 and approximately 66 percent in 1966. In 1946, the defense activities employed 1.4 million persons and in 1966, about 1 million. Put another way, defense activities accounted for 53 percent of all federal civilian employment in 1946 and for about 40 percent in 1966.

Employment in post office operations rose from 454,000 in 1946 to 626,000 in 1966, a gain of nearly 40 percent. The postal service accounts for nearly one-fourth of all federal employees in 1966 as compared with 17 percent in 1946.

All other functions of the federal government, including health, welfare, conservation, and natural resources, employed 826,000 persons in 1946 and 885,000 in 1966. During these years, the number of civilian employees in these functions increased only 7 percent In 1946, these functions accounted for 30 percent of the total federal employment and in 1966, 34 percent.

Employment in State Governments

From 1946 to 1966, the number of employees in state governments increased from 804,000 to 2,211,000, an increase of 175 percent. Since 1946, state governments have consistently accounted for roughly one-fourth of all nonfederal public employment.

The largest single user of state employees is education, especially institutions of higher education. State educational activities employed 233,000 persons in 1946 and 866,000 in 1966, an increase of 270 percent. In 1946, one-fourth of all state employees were in education, as compared with two-fifths in 1966. In 1966, 804,000 state employees were employed in institutions of higher education. Of this number, 253,000 were instructional personnel. Similar data are not available for 1946, but in 1961, of the 477,000 persons employed in state institutions of higher education, 148,000 were instructional personnel.

Employment in other state functions increased 135 percent,

Full-time and Part-time Employment in Select Functions
of State Governments, 1946–1966[1]
(in Thousands)

Function	1946[2]		1966[3]	
	Number	*Percent*[4]	*Number*	*Percent*[4]
Total	804	100.0	2,211	100.0
Education	233	25.2	866	39.2
All noneducational functions	572	74.8	1,344	60.8
Highway	141	17.5	292	13.2
Hospitals	119	14.8	382	17.3
General control[5]	58	7.3	119	5.4
Natural resources	45	5.6	130	5.9
Public welfare	28	3.5	70	3.2
Health	22	2.7	41	1.9
All other functions	158	19.6	309	14.0

[1] The data are not exactly comparable, but do give a general picture of the distribution of employment in state governments.
[2] As of July 1946.
[3] As of October 1966.
[4] Due to rounding, totals may not add to 100.
[5] Includes tax enforcement, financial and general administration, legislative bodies, courts, central staff agencies, and chief executives.

SOURCE. *State Distribution of Public Employment,* 1946 and 1966 (Washington, D.C.: Bureau of the Census).

from 572,000 in 1946 to 1,344,000 in 1966 (see table). Highways and state hospitals are other large users of manpower. Together they accounted for about one-third of total state employment in both 1946 and 1966.

State highway departments employed 141,000 persons in 1946 and 292,000 in 1966, a gain of 107 percent. The number of employees in state hospitals in the same period increased from 119,000 to 382,000, or 220 percent.

In 1946, these three functions—education, health and highway—employed 58 percent of all state employees. By 1966, the "big three" accounted for 70 percent of the total.

The growth in employment in these functions is the result of the dramatic social, economic, and technological changes occurring in American society. Growing student enrollments in state-supported institutions of higher learning account for the significant increases in educational employment. The emphasis on highway safety and improvements, the inauguration of the interstate highway system, and the expansion of suburbs explain, in part, the increases in the number of employees in state highway departments. One explanation for the impressive growth in hospital employment is that more extensive and intensive health and medical services are being provided. In 1966, about 1 out of every 6 state employees was employed in hospitals, as compared with 1 out of every 7 in 1946.

In 1966, the remaining 30 percent of state public employees were performing other services and general control functions. (The latter category included only 5 percent of the state employees.)

Local Government Employment

Employment in local governments increased from 2.8 million in 1946 to 6.4 million in 1966, a gain of 125 percent. Schools are the largest users of manpower in local governments. In addition to classroom teachers, the educational employment category includes administrators, principals, consultants, office and maintenance personnel, dietitians and their staffs, nurses, and bus drivers. There were 1.2 million employees in local public institutions in 1946 and 3.5 million in 1966, a gain of almost 200 percent. In 1946, over two-fifths (44 percent) of all local government employees were employed in educational institutions but by 1966, the proportion had risen to 55 percent.

Employment in such noneducational functions as police and fire protection, highways, health and hospitals, and natural resources increased from 1.5 million in 1946 to 3.5 million in 1966, or 133 percent. In 1946, these nonschool functions accounted for 55 percent of all local public employment. With the significant growth in educational employment since 1946, the proportion of nonschool employment declined to 45 percent of the total in 1966.

The second table in this chapter shows the distribution of employment by functions in local governments for 1952 and 1966. (Data are not available by functions prior to 1952.) The

Employment in Select Functions of Local Governments, 1952–1966
(in Thousands as of October)

Function	1952		1966	
	Number	Percent[1]	Number	Percent[1]
Total	3,418	100.0	6,407	100.0
Education	1,537	45.0	3,538	55.2
Noneducational functions	1,881	55.0	2,869	44.8
Highways	269	7.9	297	4.6
Health and hospitals	222	6.5	438	6.8
Police protection	217	6.4	369	5.8
Fire protection	174	5.1	246	3.8
Natural resources	37	1.0	33	.5
General control	NA	—	418	6.5
Water supply	92	2.7	109	1.7
Other local utilities	135	4.0	144	2.2
Public welfare	56	1.6	120	1.9
Sanitation	106	3.1	173	2.7
All other functions	572	17.0	523	8.2

[1] Due to rounding, totals may not add to 100.

SOURCE: *State Distribution of Public Employment*, 1952 and 1966 (Washington, D.C.: Bureau of the Census).

major noneducational functions were police and fire protection, health and hospitals, highways and streets, and museums, libraries, recreation parks, zoos, etc. Taken together, police and fire protection accounted for about one-tenth of all local public employment. From 1952 to 1966, employment in these functions increased about 60 percent, from 391,000 to 615,000. Population increases, growth of suburbs, and shorter work weeks help to explain this growth.

Another rapidly growing area of public employment is health protection and hospital care. About one-fifth of the nation's 7,100 hospitals are operated by local governments (cities and counties). Between 1952 and 1966, employment in these functions increased almost 100 percent, from 222,000 to 438,000. This growth reflects, for the most part, more extensive use of hospital facilities.

Employment in the city and county road departments increased approximately 10 percent between 1952 and 1966, from 269,000 to 297,000. As a rule, these departments plan new streets and roads and maintain existing ones; new construction is generally done by private contractors.

Together these three functions—police and fire protection, health and hospitals, and highways and streets—accounted for almost half of all noneducational employees in local governments. In 1966, about 7 percent of all local public employees were engaged in general control functions, whereas 93 percent were providing a variety of services to the residents of local governmental units.

In summary, population growth alone does not account for all the increases in public employment in the last twenty years. At the federal level, the defense program has become the largest user of manpower, a position held by the post office department prior to World War II. To maintain the peace requires not only adequate military strength but also a large number of civilian personnel possessing a wide variety of skills. The growing complexity of the national government has also led to significant increases in federal employment.

The increase in school enrollments in all levels of public education is not solely the result of population growth. More persons are attending the nation's schools. In addition, school systems are providing more extensive educational and noneducational services. These factors have created a demand for additional personnel to man the nation's public educational system.

Another factor contributing to the growth in government employment is the population movement from the rural areas to urban centers and from urban centers to the suburban areas of the large metropolitan cities. In 1960, about 70 percent of the population lived in urban areas, as compared with nearly three-fifths in 1930. With a larger proportion of the population living in urban centers, the demand for government services has increased. Population growth and mobility have exerted both a quantitative and a qualitative impact on government employment. Citizens are demanding more and better public services.

As for the future, the pressures for continued growth in public employment are already present. The public concern for rebuilding the large cities, minimizing air pollution, cleaning up the nation's rivers and streams, and establishing and expanding antipoverty services to include the lower classes, as well as the growing need for special services for the increasing number of aged persons—will affect the demands for additional personnel in government employment. Moreover, international tensions do not appear to be slackening and this pressure will affect employment in defense activities. Employment involved with the exploration of outer space will undoubtedly continue to expand. Lastly, public employment will continue to increase, reflecting the fact that Americans view their government as the servant of the people—an entity that they control in accordance with their own needs and purposes.

The Emerging Relationship

IDA KLAUS

The field of public employment is today's New Frontier in the realm of labor-management relations. *Business Week* has characterized the tremendous potential of this field as the real "growth stock" of the trade-union movement.

The field has indeed assumed great importance to the men who lead labor in the United States (witness the fact that George Meany himself intervened in a strike of the New York City welfare workers). To those who manage the governmental enterprise at all levels, the field of employee relations has become a challenge of first order of priority—a problem of the highest urgency. This is particularly true in the field of public education, where the subject of employee relations has, at times, taken second place only to the problems of integration. The subject has also

Address given before the Conference on Public Employment and Collective Bargaining, University of Chicago, February 5, 1965. Printed by permission of the author.

Ida Klaus is Director of Staff Relations, Board of Education of the City of New York.

commanded the attention of civic leaders, of university studies and programs, and naturally, of candidates for the Ph.D.

As recently as 1955, when I first began to explore the field for the New York City government, I saw employee relations as the wave of the future. At that time, the subject of labor relations in public employment could not have meant less to more people, both in and out of government. Public employment was simply a strange and different world into which few men of research or labor traveled.

It was a world in which employees at all levels were excluded from the protection of our national and state labor relations laws. It was a world closed off from our expressly declared national policy of collective bargaining through freely chosen representatives.

Why the public sector was excluded from the sheltering arm of our labor policy is not clear. The United States Supreme Court and a New York court have ventured the following explanations: (1) Public employees were so well taken care of by the governmental parent they served that they did not need to band together to achieve better working conditions. (2) Collective bargaining was not shown to be as necessary in public employment as it was in private industrial life.

These explanations no longer hold true. The past few years have brought great changes at a rapidly accelerating pace. Louder and more persistent employee demands, increased employee organization and better employee leadership, public awakening and governmental enlightenment, social contagion, and perhaps even political expediency have all played their wholesome part in fostering and shaping new relationships.

Progress in the field has been marked by two separate phases. The first and very important phase has been that of making fundamental policy and providing machinery for the enforcement of this policy—that is, officially declaring what the rights of public employees are and how those rights will be enjoyed. Practically speaking, this first phase is one in which government has made collective bargaining possible for its employees by guaranteeing them freedom of organization and by allowing them to participate, through their duly chosen representatives, in the formulation of the terms and conditions of their employment. In this phase, government, although making policy as to its own employees, is acting in an essentially public role, much as it would for private employees.

In the second phase, government has assumed the direct role of employer; it has applied its newly declared policy to itself by attempting to establish and maintain what is, in essence, a collective bargaining relationship between itself and its own employees.

The first phase, that of basic policy-making, has found its best examples in the New York City Executive Order of the Mayor (1958), in the federal Executive Order 10988 of President Kennedy (1962), and in the Wisconsin Employment Relations Law as amended in 1962. Each of these documents is, in its own way, a *Magna Charta* for public employees. In each, public employees are guaranteed the right to organize for their mutual aid and protection, to participate in various ways through representatives of their own choosing in the formulation of the terms and conditions of their employment, and to present grievances and have them resolved fairly. In each, they are also given some measure of assurance against early unilateral governmental action when differences cannot be composed.

The New York City program was the first thoroughgoing code of labor relations for municipal employees anywhere in the United States. Its history and background and its form and structure parallel very much the National Labor Relations Act of 1935.

The mayor's order came about as a response to the demonstrated needs of both the city and its employees and their organizations. In 1958, there was as much need for eliminating chaos, conflict, and strife in the city's relations with its own employees as there was for the elimination of the causes of strikes and industrial unrest in private industry in 1935. The answer in 1958 in New York City was the enunciation of a mayoral policy for city employees expressly designed, as A. H. Raskin states, *"to further and promote in so far as possible the practice and procedures of collective bargaining prevailing in private labor relations."* The order sought to give meaning to that policy by adopting the majority rule of exclusive recognition; by prescribing procedures for unit determination and certification; and by providing machinery for resolving a bargaining impasse.

Since its enactments, the order has been given vital meaning. New York City employees are now enjoying collective bargaining of a very advanced and mature nature. Through the pragmatic process of day-to-day efforts, government and numerous certified organizations have hammered out means for allowing the collective bargaining process to operate with surprising effectiveness within the peculiar character of the governmental employing enterprise.

But the really big breakthrough out of the vacuum came with the federal program of 1962. In technique and in form, the federal order has followed and built upon the Mayor's Executive Order 49—with a number of important differences. The orders are alike in that both represent executive policy-making in this field, rather than legislative or administrative action. Both declare the basic policy of freedom of association for participation by their employees in the terms and conditions of their employment. Both recognize that such policy advances the purposes of government as it enhances the interests of employees. Both set out basic types of representative status (the federal order much more explicitly) and the ground rules for achieving this status. Both permit extraordinary recourse for the resolution of grievance disputes.

The differences between the federal order and the New York City order reflect basic differences between the two areas in the kind and extent of employee organization prevailing at the time each program was adopted. In New York City, although many organizations attempted to speak for the same types of employees (clerical, administrative, welfare, hospital, sanitation), some of these organizations had a substantial membership. To the latter organizations, the only answer was exclusive recognition for the majority in an appropriate unit—otherwise, the program would have been worth nothing to them. In the federal government, the different stages and strengths of organization were very marked. If only exclusive recognition were to be given, very few organizations would have been able to enjoy any advantage under the order. In other words, federal employees, generally speaking, were not ready for exclusive recognition based on majority representation in an appropriate unit. Hence, the federal order devised different types of recognition status based on the extent of representation. These grades of recognition are perhaps the most ingenious aspect of the federal program; they honor the status quo yet offer great inducement for expansion and change—especially exclusive recognition for a majority representative.

The federal order, by its terms, also eliminates problems that arose under the New York City program and that had to be resolved administratively. Here the federal order profited from the city's experience. It spells out definite standards. For example:

1. It contains a clear definition of the term "labor organization."
2. It imposes restrictive qualifications for recognition—that is, no strike policy, no subversive commitment, no discrimination, no domination by corrupt influences.
3. It deals with conflict of interest—by those representing management yet seeking participation in employee activities.
4. It spells out the areas that are closed to bargaining—namely, those of governmental policy and so-called management prerogative. (The absence of such express limitations can cause considerable frustration in establishing a bargaining relationship.)
5. It calls for written agreements. (This device for memorializing the fruits of collective bargaining is actually an aid to the bargaining process. It should be used in government as it is in private industry. Its usefulness in dealing with teachers in New York City has been fully demonstrated.)
6. It provides a code of fair practices for government agencies and for labor organizations.

The federal order, however, has made two important omissions.

First, it does not provide for a central administrative body to enforce and apply the policies and procedures of the order. Instead, it leaves compliance to the voluntary discretion of the agency head. Labor organizations have found this to be a nearly fatal defect.

Second, it makes no specific provision for dealing with an impasse in negotiations. Here, the agency head has the last word. In New York, an arsenal of weapons—and most recently, ad hoc "advisory arbitration," mediation and fact-finding—have been made available. Labor Secretary Willard Wirtz withstood pressures from federal employee organizations for compulsory arbitration. He urged them to preserve the collective bargaining process by providing, in their own agreements, techniques for breaking bargaining logjams.

How much *practical* value the federal order has had for employees, for labor organizations, and for government agencies is still difficult to determine. Considerable advantages have been enjoyed under it in such well-organized areas as postal service. Little or no progress has been noted among other groups. Last year's report (1964) of the American Bar Association summarizes the effect of the order with the observation that it "has provided for improved employee-management relations" and that "continued progress is being made". The report notes that the prognosis for the future is "good." One wonders whether the absence of a central enforcement agency has held back the advance on a broad front into the second phase of actual established collective bargaining relationships. But there is, in any event, some question as to whether the eventual federal pattern of labor relations can be expected to assume the same shape as that of local governments.

The third example of policy-making is the Wisconsin law as amended in 1962. Unlike the New York and federal orders, the Wisconsin law does not embody an express majority rule of exclusive representation and does not fully endorse the practices and procedures of collective bargaining. Yet it represents the most advanced and solid technique for policy-making and enforcement in this field, for it uses the device of a statute to declare basic rights and to have them enforced through an established expert state agency—that is, the Wisconsin Employment Relations Board. With some modifications, the Wisconsin law may well serve as a model for other areas.

A completely separate and independent area from which new policy and new relationships have been emerging is that of public education. Here again, New York City has taken the lead —a distinction some might find dubious. But this policy was shaped in response to a seriously mounting drive by employees for a substantial voice in the determination of salaries and working conditions. After long delays by its predecessor, a newly appointed New York City school board progressed at an almost breathless pace from policy declaration, to resolution of the question of representation, to the establishment of what is probably the most sophisticated and advanced collective bargaining relationship anywhere in the public service.

Generally, the greatest progress, and at the fastest pace, will, I think, be made in the field of education—in part, because of the growing stress upon the significance of education in our society and with it, the awareness of the importance of the teacher. Whether the orientation will be toward trade-unionism or toward so-called professionalism does not seem to matter at the moment. Whether emanating from the House of Labor or the Halls of Academe, the basic objectives, and perhaps even the vital tactics, of both movements are not that different.

Now, what of the emerging relationship? Establishment of a bargaining relationship—whether in education or elsewhere in government—will place a serious strain on fundamental concepts, practices, and attitudes. Considerable accommodation will have to be made to the changed process of decision-making. As the shapes are already forming in my crystal ball, I would say that the principal problems of accommodation for the near and not-too-distant future for New Yorkers, and for governmental employers elsewhere will be mainly in the following areas.

The Principle of Sovereign Prerogative. This principle holds that those charged with the duty and responsibility of administering a particular governmental function may and must exercise that function themselves, and in the public interest. Welfare, health, law enforcement, fire fighting, education—are all governmental functions entrusted to appointed or elected officials who perform them in behalf of organized government and society. In the context of the collective bargaining relationship, the practical issue will be how much of an area can or will government open up to the joint decision-making process of collective bargaining? May or should any of the policy aspects of government management not directly involving working conditions be determined through collective bargaining? Employee organizations will push toward the opening up of these areas to joint decision-making as labor has done in private industry. Government will want to stand on prerogative.

The Board of Education in New York faced up to the conflict by instituting a system of periodic consultation and communication (but not bargaining) with the teacher's union on matters of educational and professional policy of common concern, which initially resulted in some benefit for both sides. The problem is one of containment.

Appropriations and the Budget-Making Process. Government divisions and agencies may spend only the money allocated to them through general governmental budget-making authority. Will unions insist that collective bargaining enter the agency and city budget-making authority so as to assure adequate funds to satisfy demands rather than restrict demands to funds already appropriated? Will this mean that bargaining will take place in advance of budget-making with the agency for presentation to the municipality and with the municipality for presentation to state officials?

The New York Board of Education has experimented in this area in three ways: The first year, they bargained before knowing how much money would be appropriated to them. The second year, they bargained after submitting a budget and after the extent of their appropriation became known. This year they bargained in advance of submitting a budget request, with a view to arriving at a mutually satisfactory estimate of the cost of improved salaries and working conditions. Each technique revealed new difficulties in accommodating the collective bargaining process to governmental structure and operations.

The Merit System. The cardinal principle of the civil service is that appointment and promotion shall be based on merit and fitness. Will organized groups use their strength to force government to abandon the civil service concept of appointment and promotion on the basis of merit and fitness determined by competitive examination? Will unions try to storm this sometimes solid fortress against the predatory political spoils system

(a) by demanding to participate through collective bargaining in the formulation of the standards for determining what is merit and fitness for a particular job? (b) by introducing seniority as a factor in appointment and promotion? (c) by insisting on union membership as a condition of hire or continued employment (as in Philadelphia)? Some unions have promoted the view that collective bargaining in these fields will help to build and preserve a true merit system.

Existing Personnel Policies and Practices. Government at all levels has evolved, by unilateral action over the years, personnel policies and practices designed to accord fair and equal treatment to its employees. Salary plans and classification systems—often conscientiously and scientifically formulated—have been the principal features of personnel policies and practices.

It is precisely these significant aspects of the employment relationship that government unions will wish to open up to the joint decision-making technique of the collective bargaining process. The problem will not be one of policy alone. More urgently, it will be a practical challenge of how to fit collective bargaining into the administrative structure of these policies and practices.

In New York City, the challenge was met quite early. The city's Board of Estimate had adopted, for most civil service titles, an elaborate system of salary review and position classification known as the Career and Salary Plan. In practice, the plan was executed jointly by the Personnel Director and the Budget Director, and their recommendations were put into effect by the Board of Estimate. With the advent of the city's labor policy, the certified organizations made a strong appeal for participation through collective bargaining in the administration of the Career and Salary Plan. A practical accommodation was devised and salary increases were negotiated and obtained within the framework of the Career and Salary Plan. Some believe that collective bargaining has in fact displaced the purposes and procedures of the plan.

The Strike. Universal policy is against all strikes by public employees. This derives from the basic notion that a strike against government is a strike against organized authority and cannot be sanctioned—regardless of the particular function involved. Is this attitude realistic? How can it be maintained where strong unions are militantly seeking to obtain concessions by all forms of pressure? If this fundamental policy is to be honored, more will be required than blind faith in compliance with law.

Government will have to be as diligent in its search for techniques to prevent serious disputes with its own employees as it has been in its efforts in critical areas of private employment. Where does the deterrent power lie?

1. In fact-finding, as in Wisconsin?
2. In a Labor Peace Agency, as has been recommended by the Feinsinger panel for the four public groups in Milwaukee?
3. In a special mediation panel comparable to the Atomic Energy Panel or the Missile Sites Panel?
4. In continuing mediation efforts by the presence of a third party to advise and consult during the course of the year on difficult issues?
5. In a joint committee to function outside regular procedures, as in the Human Relations Committee in steel? (A committee established jointly by the steel industry and the United Steelworkers Union.)

We cannot afford to rely on the expediency of the moment as the sound guide for the future.

So much for the stresses and strains for government. And, for their part, what responsibilities are the employee organizations prepared to assume in the interest of the employees they represent and in consideration of the public and the public purpose?

In the last analysis, the essential character of the emerging relationship will be determined by the legislatures, the courts, and the community. Will they be willing to accept collective bargaining and its profound economic, social, legal, and political consequences?

NOTE

1. See, for example, James J. Healy (ed.), *Creative Collective Bargaining* (Englewood Cliffs, N.J.: Prentice-Hall, 1965).

II

THE PUBLIC EMPLOYEE
ORGANIZATIONS

Beginning with a brief review of the expanding membership figures of the principal employee organizations active in public employment, this section offers both a broad understanding of some of the major organizations involved and a critical assessment of their functions, similarities, and future prospects.

The first item is a listing of employee organizations that are engaged in collective bargaining in the public sector. In addition to national unions affiliated with the AFL-CIO, the local education associations of the National Education Association are becoming increasingly involved in collective bargaining on behalf of teachers, state nurses associations are involved in bargaining on behalf of professional nurses in public hospitals.

Next, Robert Repas offers a historical picture and classification of the employee organizations active within the federal government and gives major emphasis to postal unions and associations and the blue-collar AFL-CIO Metal Trades Department affiliates. Repas notes the relative lack of success of effective organization of white-collar workers in federal employment and compares this failure with similar trends in the private section of the economy.

Adding a significant dimension to the total picture of public employee organizations is the study of state, independent, and unaffiliated public employee associations by Professor Joseph Krislov. Krislov's pioneering work shows that these organizations are assuming functions that are normally ascribed to unions. He notes that they will play an important role in the development of public employment bargaining as they fight for survival.

Dr. Charles T. Schmidt, Jr., presents two case studies in the selection of Bargaining Representatives for Michigan Teacher Groups and by so doing vividly illustrates the similarities and differences in tactics, organizations, goals, and preparation of the two rival teacher organizations; the MFT and the MEA.

Finally, Douglas Weiford and Wayne Burggraaff, two keenly observant public officials, point out that organization and bargaining in public employment will require extensive changes in both the outlook and the practice of public personnel administration. Furthermore, they note that management opposition to this changing environment can lead only to conflict and defeat. The only reasonable course of action suggested for the public official is recognition that public employee organizations are "here to stay," that they will have an increasing impact upon public administration decision-making, and that public officials must be prepared to meet and react effectively to changing demands and new circumstances.

Employee Organizations in Public Employment

A growing number of employee organizations are involved in collective bargaining in public employment. These organizations can be classified as follows:

1. Affiliates of the AFL-CIO that bargain for federal employees (postal workers, machinists in government shipyards, and office workers).

From Employee Organizations in Public Employment, a table compiled by the School of Labor and Industrial Relations, Michigan State University. Printed by permission of Michigan State University.

2. Independent unions (not affiliated with the AFL-CIO) that bargain for federal employees, such as the National Postal Union.

3. Affiliates of the AFL-CIO that bargain for state and local government employees, such as the American Federation of State, County and Municipal Employees.

4. Affiliates of the AFL-CIO that bargain for particular groups of local government employees, such as the American Federation of Teachers and International Association of Fire Fighters.

5. Independent organizations that have become the spokesmen for certain groups of workers in both state and local governmental units. State employee associations are also becoming more involved. [See, for example, Joseph Krislov's article

Membership in Representative Employee Organizations
in Public Employment

Employee organization				
Postal Unions	*1943*	*1960*	*1962*	*1965*
AFL-CIO				
National Association of Letter Carriers	64,500	138,000	150,144	167,913
National Association of Post Office Mail Handlers, Watchmen and Messengers	1,500	4,000	14,000	29,000
National Association of Special Delivery Messengers	1,000	2,000	1,500	1,500
National Federation of Post Office Motor Vehicle Employees	—	5,000	5,000	6,200
United Federation of Postal Clerks	45,000	135,000	145,000	139,000
Independent				
National Postal Union	—	32,000	43,000	62,000
National Rural Letter Carriers' Association	28,066	38,321	39,852	42,300
National Alliance of Postal Employees	10,047	18,000	25,000	26,000
National Association of Postal Supervisors	9,400	19,250	26,000	28,000

Employee organization				
Postal Unions	*1943*	*1960*	*1962*	*1965*
National Association of Post Office and General Services Maintenance Employees	—	7,400	8,000	8,424
National League of Postmasters of the United States	18,000	12,984	14,000	14,500
Other Federal Employees' Unions				
American Federation of Government Employees, AFL-CIO	33,500	70,322	106,042	138,642
National Federation of Federal Employees, (Ind.)	75,000	53,000	49,500	—
State and Municipal Employees' Unions and Associations				
American Federation of State, County and Municipal Employees, AFL-CIO	50,000	210,000	220,000	234,839
American Federation of Teachers, AFL-CIO	35,000	56,156	70,821	100,000
International Association of Fire Fighters, AFL-CIO	38,200	95,000	109,035	115,358

SOURCES: 1943: Florence Peterson, *Handbook of Labor Unions* (Washington, D.C.: American Council of Public Affairs, 1944).
1960, 1962, 1965: *Directory of National and International Labor Unions of the United States* (U.S. Dept. of Labor Bulletins No. 1320, No. 1395 and No. 1493).

beginning on p. 29.] Local units of the National Fraternal Order of Police bargain for policemen in several cities. In addition, local independent police officers' associations represent their members in negotiations with cities in several large municipalities.

6. Professional associations that bargain for certain groups of government employees. (For example, the state nurses' associations, affiliated with the American Nurses Association, bargain for registered nurses employed in publicly owned hospitals and public health departments, and local education associations, affiliates of the state and of the National Education Association, bargain for public school teachers employed by local school boards.

The table accompanying this article lists representative employee organizations involved in collective bargaining for public employees. This listing does not include all employee organizations. As noted above, the state nurses' associations in a few states bargain for groups of registered nurses in publicly owned hospitals. Data were not available for the number of members of the National Education Association covered by collective bargaining agreements in 1968. The craft unions of the AFL-CIO that represent federal employees in shipyards and naval bases also are not included.

The same table also presents membership data for these organizations. Some of the organizations have very small memberships. The National Association of Special Delivery Messengers had 1,500 members in 1965, whereas in the same year, the American Federation of State, County and Municipal Employees had almost a quarter of a million members. There are no estimates of the number of public employees covered by labor agreements throughout the United States. In some public jurisdictions, formal agreements are replaced by memorandums of understanding between the employee organization and the public employer, but for all practical purposes the memorandum is synonymous with a labor agreement.

Collective Bargaining Problems in Federal Employment

ROBERT REPAS

The Federal Employment Picture

When the Civil Service Act was first passed in 1883, only 130,000 civilians were employed by the federal government.[1] Although employment at this level has expanded rapidly over the years,

Reprinted from "Collective Bargaining Problems in Federal Employment," *Problems Confronting Union Organizations in Public Employment,* ed.

it still represents only about 25% of total *public* employment in this country. In fact, federal employment in 1965 was about 400,000 below the 1944 World War II all-time high figure of 2,900,000.[2]

Public Employment—1965

2,500,000	Federal government employees
1,700,000	State government employees
5,200,000	Local government employees
	(includes public school teachers)
9,400,000	Total Public Employees

Federal employees in turn are usually broken down on the basis of the method used to determine their wage payments: the white collar employees have their own classification system with wage scales set by congressional legislation; postal employees have a separate classification system, with their wages also set by congressional action; federal blue collar workers usually have their pay scales determined by surveying prevailing wages in the vicinity.

Classification of Unions

Historically, three major classifications of unions have existed in federal employment: (1) unions organizing solely in the post office, (2) unions composed primarily of employees in private employment but also organizing blue collar workers in federal employment, (3) unions restricting their membership to federal employees except those employed by the post office.

POSTAL UNIONS

The earliest postal union dates back to 1863 when the letter carriers in New York City organized.[3] Today there are about a dozen unions in the postal field with the United Federation of

Eugene C. Hagburg (Columbus: Ohio State University, Labor Education and Research Service, College of Commerce and Administration, April 1, 1966), pp. 1–5 and 17–20, by permission of the author, editor, and publisher.

Robert Repas is Professor of Industrial Relations in the School of Labor and Industrial Relations, Michigan State University.

Postal Clerks and the National Association of Letter Carriers being the two largest. Seven of these unions have attained exclusive recognition on the national level under Executive Order 10988.[4] An important merger discussion is currently taking place between the two major organizations in the clerk craft, with the possibility that several other unions will follow suit.

METAL TRADES AFFILIATES

Blue collar unions currently affiliated with the AFL-CIO Metal Trades Department have a long history of organization in federal employment. Trade union activity by early craft unions dates back to the 1830's in the navy yards.[5] The normal pattern for metal trades affiliates is to organize on a local council basis. These unions presently have the bulk of their membership in the Department of Defense.

The most important of the metal trades affiliates is the International Association of Machinists which, in 1904, set up District 44 with a separate staff to work solely in the area of federal employment.[6]

FEDERAL EMPLOYEE UNIONS

Historically, certain unions have restricted their membership solely to federal employment—excluding postal employees. The first of these was the National Federation of Federal Employees which was established in 1917 primarily as a result of support received from the AFL.[7] It organized both blue collar and white collar employees in federal employment providing these workers also belonged to their appropriate craft union.

In 1931, the AFL, at the instigation of craft unions having members in federal employment, went on record opposing the report of the U.S. Personnel Classification Board because it had recommended the extension of the classification principle to all federal employees including the skilled crafts. The NFFE which strongly favored the classification principle for federal white collar employees left the AFL in protest over the fact that they were not consulted concerning AFL position on this issue. An underlying issue in this dispute was the industrial versus craft argument.[8]

Part of the NFFE membership remained behind and in 1932

was chartered as the American Federation of Government Employees. Partially as a result of its isolation, the NFFE has dwindled in size. In addition, it has been unable to make up its mind whether it is an association or a union. It has opposed the concept of collective bargaining and challenged the constitutionality of Executive Order 10988.[9] The National Federation of Federal Employees presently is the exclusive representative of only 8,828 federal employees while the AFGE represents almost 120,000 and is the largest union in federal employment.[10]

Growth of New Unions

A new development under the Executive Order has been the certification as unions of what were only associations in the past. Two such former associations which have so qualified presently represent over 20,000 employees.[11] One of them, the National Association of Internal Revenue Employees, has its membership confined to one agency, the Internal Revenue Service. But the other, the National Association of Government Employees has exclusive units in five agencies. Originating in New England it now has a unit in Virginia. Although initially white collar in composition, it has successfully invaded the wage board field. It will be interesting to see if this union can successfully challenge the established organizations in federal employment.

Extent of Unionization Under Executive Order 10988

The present extent of unionization in federal employment can be determined best by examining the matter in relation to the three basic categories of federal employees: classified, postal, and wage board.

The figures below show that about one third (815,946) of a total of 2.5 million federal employees are in bargaining units holding exclusive recognition. However, if postal employees are deducted from this total the percentage of workers in units with exclusive recognition drops to 16%.[13] Sizable gains have taken place the last two years in the wage board end. This is not surprising since these are the federal employees that are most

	Total Employment[12]	Membership in Unions with Exclusive Recognition		Employees Covered by Agreements	Per cent of Employees in Unions with Exclusive Recognition	
		1963	1965[12]	1965[12]	1963	1964
Classified	1,260,000	74,000	91,044	52,050	6%	7%
Wage Board	621,000	121,000	209,580	170,000	16%	33%
Postal	592,000	490,000	515,000	515,332	83%	87%
	2,473,000	685,000	815,946	738,072		

SOURCE: *Exclusive Recognition and Collective Bargaining Coverage Under Executive Order 10988*, AFL-CIO Education Department, December 15, 1964.

comparable to those organized in private industry—blue collar and craftsmen.

However, unionism among classified personnel who represent the largest segment of federal employment is still almost in its infancy. Here, too, the picture closely follows the pattern of private industry—just as it has been difficult to organize white collar workers in private employment, so, too, has this been the case in federal employment. Again, similar to private industry, no major union in federal employment has made a determined effort to organize this sector of the labor force.

NOTES

1. Sterling D. Spero, *Government as Employer* (New York: Remsen Press, 1948), p. 5.
2. National Industrial Conference Board, *The Economic Almanac, 1964* (New York: National Industrial Conference Board, 1964), p. 80.
3. Spero, *op. cit.*, p. 106.
4. Postal unions with exclusive recognition at the national level are: National Association of Letter Carriers (AFL-CIO), National Association of Special Delivery Messengers (AFL-CIO), United Federation of Postal Clerks (AFL-CIO), National Association of Post Office and General Services Maintenance Employees (Ind.), National Rural Letter Carriers' Association (Ind.), National Association of Post Office Mail Handlers, Watchmen, and Messengers (AFL-CIO).
5. Spero, *op. cit.*, p. 79.
6. *Ibid.*, p. 95.

7. *Ibid.*, p. 179.
8. *Ibid.*, pp. 188–190.
9. The case was filed June 15, 1964, in the U.S. District Court, District of Columbia; *Government Employment Relations Reporter, A-9, June 15, 1964.* It was subsequently dismissed on the grounds that proper recourse should be made to the President because he issued the Executive Order.
10. All figures in this section relating to the status of collective bargaining under Executive Order 10988, unless otherwise stated, are from a pamphlet, *Exclusive Recognition and Collective Bargaining Coverage Under Executive Order 10988*, December 15, 1964, which was produced by the AFL-CIO Education Department and is based on figures available from the U.S. Civil Service Commission concerning developments through June 30, 1965.
11. *Ibid.*, Table II.
12. *Ibid.*, p. 1.
13. *Ibid.*

The Independent Public Employee Association: Characteristics and Functions

JOSEPH KRISLOV

Administrative and legal opposition to the unionization of government employees has declined in the past decade. Several states and a number of cities have enacted legislation guaranteeing the right of employees to join unions; the federal government has also promulgated a new labor relations' program. Despite this more favorable organizational climate, the unionization of state employees will encounter opposition from independent public employee associations in a number of states. These associations have considerable membership, and in a few states have organized at least half of the full-time employees. Moreover, some of them have been in existence for more than twenty-five years, and two of them have been in existence for

Reprinted from *Industrial and Labor Relations Review*, XV (July 1962), 510–520, by permission of the publisher. Copyright © 1962 by Cornell University. All rights reserved.

Joseph Krislov is Professor of Economics at the University of Kentucky, Lexington, Kentucky.

fifty years. It would seem, therefore, that they warrant some recognition and analysis as employee organizations.

To obtain information for such an analysis, the author sent a brief questionnaire to thirty state-wide public employee associations.[1] Twenty-five associations in twenty-three states filled out and returned the questionnaire, and also supplied copies of their constitutions, and of any formal agreements, grievance procedure, and insurance programs. These materials and the completed questionnaire are the basis for this article. The twenty-five associations claimed a dues-paying membership of 355,000— 318,000 of whom were state employees and 37,000 local government employees (see table). The five non-responding associations probably had a membership of 37,000.[2] Hence, the thirty known associations probably had a total estimated dues-paying membership of 392,000.

Several conclusions emerge from an analysis of the information supplied by the associations. First, the associations have succeeded in organizing significant numbers of state employees, but have made little progress (with one exception) in organizing local government employees.[3] Second, the structure and government of these associations is not too different from those of unions, but the dues are generally lower. Third, some of the associations have probably developed into effective employee organizations; others seem to be so poorly financed as to preclude any effectiveness. Fourth, "membership recruitment" and "legislative representation" appear to be the major staff functions. If the association provides a group insurance program or handles grievances, a minor proportion of staff time is devoted to either or both of these activities. Fifth, considerable antipathy exists between associations and the organized labor movement, and it seems unlikely that the associations will seek affiliation with the organized labor movement.

Jurisdiction, Membership, and Extent of Organization

In seven of the twenty-five associations, both state and local government employees were eligible for membership; in the other eighteen, membership was limited to state employees only.

Almost all of the twenty-five associations permitted member-

*Membership, Annual Dues, Number of Active Chapters, and Year of
Organization of Independent Public Employee Associations.*[1]

Name of Association	Mem-bership	Annual Dues	Active Chapters	Year of Organization
California State Employees' Association	89,086	$12.00	145	1931
Colorado State Civil Service Employees' Association	5,152	12.00	31	1928
Connecticut State Employees' Association	11,374	8.58	159	1941
Hawaiian Government Employees' Association				
All members	9,342	27.00	5	1934
State	4,361			
Local	4,981			
Idaho State Employees' Association	1,226	12.00	7	1959
Illinois State Employees' Association	10,276	3.00	31	1921
Indiana State Employees' Association	2,000	3.00	19	1953—reorganized in 1957
Kansas Highway Employees' Council	[2]	[2]	[2]	1958
Michigan State Employees' Association	13,400	10.40	86	1950
Montana Public Employees' Association				
All members	3,500	1.00	[3]	1945
State	2,500			
Local	1,000			
Nevada State Employees' Association	690	12.00	8	1955

[1] All data as of July 1, 1961. Excludes associations in the following states with estimated memberships as follows: Alaska—400; Florida—600; Maine—6,000; Maryland—12,000; and Massachusetts—18,000.

[2] The Kansas Highway Employees' Council reported that it represented some 4,000 highway employees; its by-laws provide that "there shall be no dues collected." The membership was organized into seven sectional groups.

[3] The Montana Public Employees' Association reported that it had no chapter organization.

Membership, Annual Dues, Number of Active Chapters, and Year of Organization of Independent Public Employee Asscoiations.[1] (Cont'd)

Name of Association	Membership	Annual Dues	Active Chapters	Year of Organization
New Hampshire State Employees' Association	3,400	$ 7.80	4	1941
New Jersey Civil Service Association				
All members	20,000	[4]	[4]	1911
State	5,000			
Local	15,000			
Council of State Employees (New Jersey)	5,000	5.00	6	1948
Civil Service Employees' Association (New York)				
All members	96,000	10.40	200	1910
State	81,000			
Local	15,000			
North Carolina State Employees' Association	10,083	3.00	12	1946–1947
North Carolina State Highway and Prison Employees' Association	8,396	4.00	100	1947
Ohio Civil Service Employees' Association				
All members	15,440	7.50	56	1938
State	14,676			
Local	764			
Oregon State Employees' Association	11,128	10.80	85	1943
Rhode Island State Employees' Association	3,600	13.00	11	1945
South Carolina Employees' Association	6,200	1.00 to 3.00	[5]	1943

[4] The New Jersey Civil Service Association reported an annual per capita tax of $1.00 for affiliation with the state association. The association had twenty-two subordinate councils, organized primarily on county lines. A "typical" council had a $6.00 dues; $1 is paid to the state organization, the other $5.00 is retained by the subordinate council.

[5] If annual salary is less than $2,000, dues are $1.00 yearly; if annual salary is over $2,000 but less than $3,000, dues are $2.00 yearly; if annual salary is more

Name of Association	Mem-bership	Annual Dues	Active Chapters	Year of Organization
Texas Public Employees' Association	22,016	$ 5.00	75	1946
Utah State Public Employees' Association	2,563	12.00	6	1959
Vermont State Employees' Association	2,491	7.28	18	1944
Washington State Employees' Association	2,000	12.00	7	1956

than $3,000, dues are $3.00 yearly. Three active subordinate units were reported, one of which was organized in early 1961.

6 The Utah State Public Employees' Association reported that it had no chapter organization.

7 The Washington State Employees' Association reported that it had no chapter organization, but that it had seven district organizations.

ship of employees who would normally be considered "management" in private industry[4]—that is, elected officials; officers appointed directly by the governor, mayor, or legislature; and department heads. Of the seven associations which organized both state and local government employees, only two limited membership to civil service employees; three denied membership to elected officials and to those appointed directly by the governor or mayor; and two permitted all public officials of the state and political subdivisions to join (one association specifically included elected officials). Of the eighteen associations limiting membership to state employees only, eight permitted all state employees to join (three specifically included elected officials). One association excluded elected officials; four associations excluded elected officers and those appointed by the governor; one excluded elected officers and all members of the armed forces of the state; and one association excluded "heads of departments, heads of institutions, officers elected by the people, or the legislature and members of legislature." Of the three remaining associations, two limited their membership to specific departments; one admitted to membership only employees of the Highway Department and the other admitted to membership only employees of the Highway and Prison Department. And the third association admitted to membership only employees "covered by the State Personnel Act."

The two associations in New Jersey appear to be competitive organizations. The two in North Carolina, however, apparently cooperate and have agreed on a jurisdictional division, one association admitting to membership only highway and prison employees and the other organizing all other state employees. The constitution of the latter organization, however, clearly indicates that all state employees are eligible for membership.

Only five of the seven associations that included local government employees within their jurisdictions reported any local government membership. The combined local government membership constituted but 10 percent of the total membership of the responding associations, but the proportion for the five associations reporting such membership varied. About three-fourths of the membership of the New Jersey Civil Service Employees' Association are local government employees, as compared with a bare majority for the Hawaiian Government Employees' Association. In Montana, local government employees constituted about one-third of the membership of that association. And in New York and Ohio, local government employees constituted about 15 and 5 percent, respectively, of the membership of these two associations (see table).

In Hawaii, the association has organized more than half of the estimated number of full-time local government employees. The associations in each of the other four states have organized a much smaller proportion, certainly no more than 15 percent. And in one state, the association's membership is less than 1 percent.

The twenty-five responding associations reported a total dues-paying state employee membership of 318,000; it is believed that the membership of the non-responding associations is concentrated among state employees. Hence, it can be concluded that approximately 350,000 state employees are members of the thirty known associations. These 350,000 members probably constitute around 25 percent of the estimated full-time state employees (as of July 1961).

In each state the proportion of the estimated full-time state employees who were association members varied, but the associations in California and New York have succeeded in organizing more than 75 percent of the estimated number of full-time state employees. Associations in Connecticut, New Hampshire, North Carolina,[5] Oregon, and Vermont have probably succeeded in organizing more than half of the estimated full-time state employees in their respective states.

Structure, Government, and Dues

The typical structure of an association does not differ substantially from that of a union. Nineteen associations had a local organization, usually called a "chapter" (see table). A chapter was typically defined as "an autonomous organization of persons qualified for membership in the Association which holds an unrevoked charter"; generally, from seven to twenty-five members could petition for a charter. Two associations reported no local unit organizations, and one reported that it is now developing local unit organizations. The three remaining associations reported subordinate units which were organized on a broader base than the typical chapter; that is, as sectional groups, district organizations, and county units, respectively.

Of the nineteen associations with chapters, ten had subordinate units similar to the "intermediate body" of unions.[6] Nine associations had intermediate bodies organized on a geographic basis; one association had intermediate bodies organized into the following groups: education, highway, institutional, and departmental. The associations' constitutions suggest that these intermediate bodies may play a significant role in the administration and government of the associations.

The associations' constitutions frequently provide for considerable direct participation by the membership in policy making. The three associations which had no local unit organization held annual meetings of the membership. In addition, four other associations hold annual meetings of the membership. Seventeen associations held conventions, attended by delegates from the local unit organizations and, frequently, from the intermediate bodies as well. Fifteen of these seventeen associations hold annual conventions; two reported holding conventions every two years.

The associations' officers are usually elected at the convention, although four associations elect officers by a secret mail ballot.

In addition, one association elects its vice-president by a secret ballot; the vice-president then automatically succeeds to the presidency the following year. Officers are usually elected for a one-year period, but a few associations which hold annual meetings elect officers for a two-year period.

The governing body between conventions usually consists of officers and several additional board members, who are frequently representatives of the intermediate body. These additional board members are typically elected by their respective districts or geographic units; they usually have longer terms than the officers. The associations' constitutions suggest that these governing boards meet often and may, therefore, play a significant role in developing policy. By constitutional provisions, seven of these governing boards were required to meet monthly. Three or four meetings a year, however, seems to be more common.

More than half of the constitutions specify that the governing board may employ full-time employees. The constitution may also outline the duties, responsibilities, and authority of the major full-time employee (typically called executive secretary, executive director, or general manager).

Compared with unions, dues are low[7] (see table). The associations in Hawaii and Kansas are atypical; Hawaii had $27 annual dues, Kansas had no dues. In addition to Hawaii, seven other associations had annual dues of at least $12 a year; while three had annual dues of from $10 to $12 a year. Five reported dues of from $5 to $10, and eight reported dues of less than $5. Only eleven of the twenty-four associations reported having dues deducted, but the membership of these eleven associations accounted for almost 70 percent of the total association membership. Only one association reported any initiation fee, which was $1.

The constitutions of eleven associations did not indicate whether any division of the dues is made between the association headquarters and subordinate bodies (the three associations without any subordinate units are of course excluded). In the absence of any constitutional provision, it seems likely that subordinate units do not receive any share of the dues. Moreover, the constitutions of at least three associations suggest that subordinate units are authorized to establish their own dues. Ten associations definitely provided for the distribution of dues to the subordinate units, with eight allocating 75 percent or more of the dues to the association headquarters; the remaining proportion was allocated to the local unit organizations. One association, however, allocated a portion of the dues to the intermediate body.

Recognition, Grievances, and Legislative Activity

Only one association claimed "formal recognition," and supplied as evidence a statute guaranteeing the right of state employees to organize, and to present grievances. If the guarantee of the right to organize and to present grievances is the equivalent of formal recognition, then associations in other states could have made similar claims because they, too, have been accorded these rights by statute or by executive order.[8] Of course, formal recognition usually implies more than a statutory right to organize and to present grievances; it usually implies a "right" (sometimes an "exclusive right") to be consulted on all matters of interest to the organization's members. In the past decade, unions in government have become more vocal in their demands for formal recognition;[9] nevertheless, the responding associations evidently have been either uninterested in or unable to secure formal recognition.

All of the twenty-four other organizations, however, indicated that they were accorded "informal recognition." As specific examples of informal recognition, four associations reported that they selected the employee members of official state committees, such as management-labor councils and retirement boards; three reported that management officials "consulted" with them; and one reported that their officers were given time off for association business. Despite these evidences of informal recognition, the responses to the question, "Is your association consulted on all major personnel matters affecting your membership?", indicate some lack of consultation. Eleven associations reported that they were not consulted on all major matters; two replied with a qualified yes, and twelve, yes.

Associations were also asked to indicate if management discouraged or encouraged employees to join. Seven associations reported that employees were sometimes discouraged from joining; ten reported that employees were encouraged to join. When asked to describe management's specific acts, the associations typically reported that department heads either encouraged or discouraged participation. Two associations reported that certain employees (state police and employees in the offices of the secretary of state, attorney general, and governor, respectively) were forbidden to join.

Nine associations reported that they did not handle individual grievances; one reported handling grievances other than those involving discipline; and fifteen reported handling grievances.[10] Four of these fifteen associations reported handling four hundred or more grievances per year; four reported one hundred or more; and the remaining seven reported fewer than one hundred or failed to supply any specific figure. Six associations reported that a formal grievance procedure had been established by law or executive order, and supplied the statute or executive order establishing the procedure. The grievance procedure typically permitted four appeals after the immediate supervisor's decision, including a final appeal to the state personnel board or to the governor.[11] Three additional associations indicated that they had a formal written grievance procedure, but did not supply the document. One association reported that it had a grievance procedure in one department only; the remaining five reported no formal grievance procedure. These five associations reported handling grievances informally with supervisors and department heads.

Ten associations indicated that they had initiated and supported legal action in the courts for "individuals or groups" having grievances, but only three reported ten or more such suits in the past five years. Typically, these suits involved discipline, classification, or salary problems.

All associations reported some legislative activity, including drafting, sponsoring, and lobbying for the passage of legislation. Seventeen associations reported that they participated frequently with state administrative officials and legislative leaders in drafting "agreed bills"; four reported only occasional participation in drafting agreed bills; and four indicated no such participation. Although these replies suggest that associations have considerable influence on legislation, they seem inconsistent with the replies received on the extent of consultation. It seems unlikely that administrative officers who did not consult on all major personnel matters would permit employee representatives to participate so actively in drafting legislation. On the other hand, the associations' influence may be concentrated on legislative rather than administrative officers.

Other Association Activities, Staff, and Staff Activities

Associations were asked to report on four other activities: strikes, political activity, insurance programs, and communications with their membership.

Ten associations reported that they have a constitutional provision or convention resolution prohibiting strikes by their members. However, none of the fifteen associations which did not prohibit strikes reported authorizing a strike within the past decade. It would seem therefore that, even if an association does not have a written policy prohibiting strikes, it rarely, if ever, authorizes a strike.

Only one association replied affirmatively to the question: Does your association support candidates for state offices? That association's board of directors recommended candidates to the membership and then publicized the recommendation in the association's publication. Three other associations reported furnishing the membership with the voting records of political candidates. The remaining twenty-one associations indicated no political activity.

Eleven associations reported offering their membership the opportunity to participate in a group insurance program, typically life insurance. (At least one association provides a death benefit financed from membership dues.) In addition to life insurance, at least four associations also offer other programs, such as disability protection or a hospital, medical, and surgical program.[12] These insurance programs are usually underwritten by a life insurance company, and undoubtedly make available to members protection at a lower cost than would have been possible on an individual purchase. (Four associations volunteered the information that they administered a credit union; perhaps other associations perform this function.)

To communicate with members, twenty-three of the twenty-five associations issued a publication which was "mailed at regular intervals." Two reported a weekly publication; twelve reported a monthly publication; four, biweekly; four, quarterly; and one, yearly. Many associations also reported issuing weekly bulletins summarizing legislative developments when their respective state legislatures were in session.

In implementing these activities, associations are undoubtedly hampered by lack of staff. The relatively low dues' structure is of course reflected in the full-time staff that associations can employ. Only three associations reported more than ten professional staff members. Most associations reported from two to five staff members; three reported only part-time staff; two (including Kansas) reported no professional staff.

Seventeen associations were able to supply estimates of the percentage of time the professional staff devoted to various functions. Some of these seventeen associations had one or more employees who devoted fulltime to the insurance program; others did not. In reporting their estimates of staff activity, most associations reported the time devoted to the insurance program separately. For the others, the time devoted to other activities was recalculated (excluding the insurance program) to provide a basis for comparison. Since association membership is required before one can enroll in the insurance program, it can be argued that the "insurance activity" is also a "membership recruitment" activity.

For the six associations which did not handle grievances, membership recruitment and legislative representation combined usually accounted for more than 50 percent of the professional staff time. Membership recruitment constituted 50 percent or more of the staff time for two of the six associations; legislative representation constituted a high of 35 percent for two associations. Public relations, research, and administration completed the remaining proportions of staff time, with considerably more staff time devoted to public relations or administration than to research.

For the eleven associations which reported handling grievances, the proportion of staff time devoted to grievances is small. Seven of the associations reported less than 10 percent; two reported proportions as high as 25 and 30 percent, respectively. Seven associations reported 20 percent or more for membership recruitment; four reported more than 25 percent, with a high of 55 percent. The proportion of staff time for legislative representation was reported as low as 6 percent but as high as 60 percent, with 20 or 25 percent being typical. Combined, these three activities—grievances, membership recruitment, and legislative representation—typically accounted for more than 65 percent of staff time. Public relations, research, and administration accounted for the remaining proportions, with the same pattern as was indicated by the associations not handling grievances.

It can be concluded, therefore, that membership recruitment and legislative representation are the two major staff activities, with grievances (when they are handled), public relations, research, and administration constituting the remaining activities. Because the administration of the insurance program varied, it has not been possible to estimate the proportion of staff time devoted to it. For associations who actually participate in the program's administration, the staff time may be significant; for associations who do not participate in the administration, the staff time may be negligible.

Associations and the Organized Labor Movement

Associations were asked whether other employee organizations represented state employees and to estimate the membership of these organizations. The American Federation of State, County, and Municipal Employees, AFL-CIO (AFSCME) was mentioned by associations in sixteen states. Almost all of the associations claimed that their membership equalled or exceeded their estimate of AFSCME's membership. The Building Service Employees' International Union was reported as representing a few hundred state employees in each of two states, while the International Brotherhood of Teamsters was reported to represent an unknown number of state employees in a third state.

The Hawaiian Government Employees' Association reported that the United Public Workers, the American Federation of Teachers, and the Hawaiian Education Association also represented state and local employees within their state. Their estimated membership of these three organizations, combined with their own membership, suggest that almost all state and local employees in that state belong to an employee organization.

The affiliated unions regard associations as "company unions." [13] Whether they are or are not dominated by management cannot be satisfactorily investigated except by close contact with each association. Consequently, this study can supply only limited data which would be relevant to that issue. In response to the question, "Have there been any attempts by 'management' to guide or influence the policies or programs of your association?", four associations reported affirmatively. Their replies were as follows: one reported attempts to influence legislative policy; one reported attempts to influence their position on a constitutional amendment on Civil Service; a third reported that department heads had attempted to control policy; and a fourth reported that there were attempts at control but did not describe them. Moreover, as indicated previously, department heads were eligible for membership in almost all of the associations and encouraged employees to join in sixteen states. It would seem therefore that employees who would not be eligible for membership in employee organizations in private industry may play active roles in these associations. Whether this fact means that these employees control association policy and that associations are company unions remains open for further research.

Antipathy toward labor unions is, in turn, manifested by the associations. Six had constitutional provisions forbidding affiliation with any labor organization; a seventh association's constitution provided only that it "may affiliate with a self-governing body of state employee associations"; and an eighth association's constitution provided that any proposal to affiliate would require a two-thirds' affirmative vote by both the board of directors and the convention. Moreover, two associations indicated that a nucleus of state employees who had been members of a union had disaffiliated and were instrumental in establishing their respective associations. It would seem unlikely, therefore, that many associations will seek voluntarily to affiliate with the organized labor movement.

Summary

Obviously, this exploratory study, based primarily on the associations' responses, is not sufficient to establish definitive conclusions. Further investigations will be needed to evaluate the independence and effectiveness of associations. Studies which would determine the extent of "political" and "supervisory" influence, as contrasted with the influence of rank-and-file members, would be particularly valuable. An analysis of the occupations and job classifications of an association's officers, executive board members, and chapter leadership would be helpful; but even more revealing, would be an evaluation of an association's program and activities. Do the associations, as charged by the unions, tend to support policies which provide greater benefits for supervisory and higher paid employees? Do they, as charged by the unions, neglect the interests and needs of the lower paid employees? Does the supervisory influence, as charged by the unions, explain the associations' limited emphasis on grievances?

Coupled with a study of an association's program should be some evaluation of the organization's effectiveness. What influence (if any) has it had in improving the wages, hours, and working conditions? How have employees represented by an association fared as compared with federal employees, other state employees, local government employees, and industrial workers? Do associations which handle grievances accept the difficult as well as the simple problems? And after accepting the grievances, do they have the resources and the ability to resolve them in favor of the employee?

A case study of an association and a union of about equal size in a single state could be extremely significant. Among the questions for research are: (1) Who are the members of each group? (2) How many and why do employees join both organizations? (3) What is the extent of rank-and-file participation in each organization? (4) Who are the leaders of each organization? (5) How do the two organizations' programs and activities differ? (6) How do their methods differ? (7) Which organization is more influential in the legislature? (8) Why? (9) Which is more effective with the administration? (10) Why? (11) Do both organizations handle grievances? (12) Do they differ in the types of grievances handled? (13) Which organization receives the 'better press'? (14) Why? (15) To what extent does each organization participate in the broader social and economic problems of the state?

Finally, studies of associations must concern themselves with the future of this form of employee organization. Is it correct, as has been predicted here, that few associations will seek to affiliate with the organized labor movement? If the associations do not affiliate, will the organized labor movement launch a serious attempt to raid and absorb the associations? And if the organized labor movement does attempt to raid the associations, which of them will be absorbed and which will survive? Undoubtedly, the weaker, poorly financed associations will be inviting targets, but the information reported by the associations suggests that some of them may be able to resist the labor movement's organizational efforts. It would seem, therefore, that these associations will continue to be the spokesmen for significant numbers of state employees for some time.

NOTES

1. The names and addresses of most of the thirty associations are available in a listing supplied by the Assembly of Government Employees entitled *Directory—Independent Public Employee Associations.* The assembly, organized in 1955, is a loose federation of these associations. Copies of the listing may be obtained from the Colorado Civil Service Employees' Association, 1280 Sherman Street, Room 212, Denver 3, Col.

2. Based on estimates made by the Assembly of Government Employees, see *ibid.*

3. There are, of course, an unknown number of local employee associations. For a study of these groups in California, see California State Employees' Association, *Formal Systems of Representation for California Public Employees,* September 1960.

4. For a discussion of the status of supervisors in public employment, see New York City Department of Labor, *Organization and Recognition of Supervisors in Public Employment,* Serial L.R.5, August 1955. A report of a federal task force on labor relations recommended that "no unit should be established for purpose of exclusive recognition which includes" supervisory personnel; see *Report of the President's Task Force on Employee-*

Management Relations in the Federal Service: A Policy for Employee-Management Cooperation in the Federal Service, Nov. 30, 1961, p. 28.

5. The membership of both associations in that state were added to obtain this estimate.

6. Herbert Lahne, "The Intermediate Body in Collective Bargaining," *Industrial and Labor Relations Review,* Vol. 6, January 1953, pp. 163–179. See also, Ligouri Alphonsus O'Donnel, "An Inquiry into Union Structure: The Intermediate Body," *Dissertation Abstracts,* Vol. 22, September 1961, pp. 761–762.

7. Data on union dues are available in *Report for Fiscal Year 1960* (Washington, D.C.: U.S. Department of Labor, Bureau of Labor-Management Reports, 1960), p. 26.

8. See "Trends in Labor Legislation for Public Employees," *Monthly Labor Review,* Vol. 82, December 1960, pp. 1293–1294.

9. See my "The Union Quest for Recognition in Government Service," *Labor Law Journal,* Vol. 9, June 1958, pp. 421 ff., and Wilson R. Hart, *Collective Bargaining in the Federal Civil Service,* 1961, chaps. 8 and 9.

10. Academic students of labor relations in some of these states have informed the writer that the associations are not aggressive in handling grievances. One association informed the writer that "we do not urge grievances."

11. Almost all union contracts in private industry provide for the final disposition of grievances by an appeal to a neutral third party; some unions in government have been able to secure agreements which also provide for arbitration of grievances. See Jonas Silver, "Union Agreements with Municipalities," *Monthly Labor Review,* Vol. 56, June 1943, p. 1167, and Robert L. Stutz, *Collective Dealing by Units of Local Government in Connecticut* (Storrs: University of Connecticut Labor-Management Institute, Bulletin No. 8) May 1960, pp. 21, 23. Charles Killingsworth reported that the American Federation of State, County, and Municipal Employees had supplied him with a list of more than seventy cities which had agreements providing for arbitration of grievances by neutrals. See his "Grievance Adjudication in Public Employment," *American Arbitration Journal,* Vol. 13, No. 1 (1958), p. 9.

12. One association reported a health insurance program for retired members.

13. See, for example, Solomon Barkin, *The Decline of the Labor Movement and What Can Be Done about It,* 1961, p. 34.

Representation of Classroom Teachers: Two Case
Studies in the Selection of Bargaining
Representatives for Michigan
Teacher Groups

CHARLES T. SCHMIDT, JR.

With the enactment of Michigan's public employment collective bargaining legislation in July of 1965,[1] the stage was set for the contest to determine which organizations (if any) would represent classroom teachers, and how this representation would be apportioned among a variety of possible bargaining units.

Characteristics, positions, and strategies of the contesting organizations have been reasonably well determined, and the statewide results of bargaining unit determinations and representation drives have been examined and quantified in other research. But necessary and important as these statistics are to obtain a meaningful view of the total unit determination and representation activity, to judge the scope and relative success of each of the major organizations involved, they do not present the total nature of the dynamics of the representation drive by the employee organizations.

For this view, two case studies are presented involving specific teacher organizations and their attempts to gain representation.

Case Study—Detroit

Following World War II, Detroit's teachers found themselves in virtually the same position as were their counterparts after World War I, with average salaries lagging behind those in private industry. Unions were vigorously seeking and receiving higher wages for their members, consumer demands were high,

Reprinted from *Monthly Labor Review*, 91 (July 1968), 27–36, by permission of the publisher.

Charles T. Schmidt is Associate Professor of Industrial Relations at the University of Rhode Island.

and industrial profits soared. The growth in numbers of pupils without an equivalent increase in facilities found the school system woefully inadequate in size and often in quality. Suburban school systems drew off many city teachers, and the postwar shift of rural minority groups to urban ghettos was emphasized by the frequent requests of senior teachers to transfer out of the core, center-city schools.

When New York City's United Federation of Teachers began an active drive for exclusive representation, union officials in Detroit made a careful analysis of the process. Heartened by the success of the UFT drive in New York, the Detroit Federation of Teachers (DFT) decided to seek exclusive bargaining rights for Detroit teachers, and a campaign to this purpose was initiated early in 1963. This concept and effort were resisted by both the Detroit Board of Education and the Detroit Education Association (DEA), rival of the DFT.

Detroit at that time faced a financial crisis and scheduled an election to increase its property tax millage. The April 1963 millage campaign definitely influenced the timing and intensity of the exclusive representation campaign. According to Mary Ellen Riordan, DFT president, the Federation postponed its request for a representation election until after the April vote "because we wanted to place our full resources behind the millage campaign." [2]

THE MILLAGE CAMPAIGNS

Generally speaking, proposals to finance local schools have been received with much reluctance.[3]

Not until 1957 were the first signs of organized opposition seen in the Detroit area. The most active group was the Detroit Chamber of Commerce, which held the position that it would be better to raise funds through a bond issue than a millage request. The Chamber's campaign was mounted mainly in the last 10 days of the election, and successfully as the proposal was soundly defeated.[4]

Prior to the next proposal, submitted in 1959, the Board of Education began a program of community involvement in school affairs. A Citizens Advisory Committee on School Needs was formed, involving large numbers of citizens of varying economic and social backgrounds. Their comprehensive recommendations served as the foundation for the Board's financial proposals. At this time the Detroit community embarked upon the first half of a 10-year program when the voters—presented with a blueprint for a quality educational system—endorsed it by passing a 7.5 millage proposal and a $60 million bond issue for school construction and renovation. No major opposition developed in this election, and organized groups of parents, educators, and union and church members took strong positions in favor of increased financial support. The Detroit Chamber of Commerce did not take a public stand.

During the next 4 years, the Board of Education attempted to make as many of the recommended improvements as possible in curriculum development, personnel, integration, building construction, and other needs specified in the study.

But as the end of the first 5-year program drew near, the schools were confronted by a falling tax base, a recently approved city income tax, increased sales taxes, and rising operating costs. To renew existing millage would not be sufficient to maintain the type of program suggested by the Citizens' Report. The Board requested not only the continuation of the previous 7.5 mills, but an increase of 5.3 mills and a separate $90 million bond issue.

Almost immediately many groups publicly opposed both propositions. Some of the most vocal were homeowners' associations, originally formed to fight neighborhood racial integration, local groups of Negroes who were dissatisfied with the efforts to provide equal opportunities for education and housing, and small groups of retired people.[5] These groups, with the support of small neighborhood newspapers and newsletters in both the white and Negro communities, were successful in defeating both proposals.

At this point, the educational system was faced with financial disaster. The superintendent moved toward austerity by cutting services to extend existing and forthcoming funds: needed additional teachers were not hired, and special services were cut; classes for the first, fourth, and seventh grades were reduced to one-half days. One-third of the physical education staff was released and sent to other schools as resource teachers, in actuality as "permanent substitutes."

These moves brought the teachers up in arms, and the public as well. Community groups and newspaper, radio, and television editorials denounced the action. After 6 weeks of chaos, a court order restrained the Board from continuing its course, on the grounds that it was illegally withholding funds which were allocated until 1964. At midsemester the school system returned to its previous organization. In the meantime, however, a number of the staff had transferred to other systems, and teachers who would have been procured for the new semester had found jobs elsewhere.

The Board then requested special permission to propose another millage increase, but this time asked only that the 7.5-mill increase, which was about to expire, be continued for 10 years. While the public was truly aroused, by a glimpse of how an underfinanced educational system would affect its children, the Board reached out for total community support for the renewed millage campaign. Local parent groups were organized and campaigned hard for the proposal, with vigorous support from public media. Labor unions, real estate boards (fearing losses in property values), the NAACP, the Urban League, the Wayne County Democratic Association, the United Auto Workers, and the Detroit Chamber of Commerce actively supported the issue. The only distinguishable opposition was two groups of white homeowners, but fearing public wrath, they gave only token resistance. The millage proposal was passed, and the superintendent and staff made an earnest effort to meet its educational objectives under a very limited budget. Fortunately, the Board was able to offset some of its expenses with Federal funds.

RISING TEACHER DISSENSION

Detroit's financial crisis, however, led to overcrowded classes and to the reassignment of hundreds of teachers with little consideration for their areas of specialization, subsequent disruption of existing programs, and inconvenience to the individual teacher.

Widespread teacher dissension resulted, prompting the creation of an Assignment Review Committee to review cases of hardship and to recommend alleviation. Hundreds of requests were made for assignment reviews, and many more teachers were seriously affected, but did not request a review. The DFT promised action where violations of seniority rights, previous policy, or contract had occurred. Thus, teacher discontent reached a high level due to indiscriminate reassignment, half-day sessions, large class loads, and the failure to raise pay levels.

In the meantime, the drive for exclusive representation was somewhat muted because the school board had decided to campaign again for a November millage election for the extension of the present millage funds. Nevertheless, both teacher organizations, the DFT and the DEA, continued to be heard and to make recommendations to the Board.

DEMAND FOR REPRESENTATION

The success of the November millage election gave impetus to the DFT's drive for exclusive negotiation. A large segment of the teachers were in a militant mood; they were not going to subsidize education for parents who had shown themselves unwilling to pay the full bill by refusing to support the larger proposed millage increase in the April election. A march to the School Center Building demonstrated the urgency of their demand for a representation election.[6]

> More than 2,000 Detroit public school teachers staged a demonstration march to the Board of Education headquarters Tuesday in a show of strength to emphasize union demands for a collective bargaining election . . . Mrs. Riordan told the Board, "We march to enforce our petition which the Board has not answered . . . Teachers simply do not understand your delay . . ."[7]

As 1964 began, the Board maintained its position that the Hutchinson Act forbids exclusive recognition of one employee organization to bargain for all of the teachers. A strike to enforce its demand for an election was authorized by the DFT membership on February 27, 1964.[8]

The Board's problem of the legality of an election took a slight shift in the face of this threat, and the DEA supported the Board's position:

> The president of the Board of Education said Thursday night that

the strike vote by the Detroit Federation of Teachers will not change the Board's position on a bargaining agent for teachers. *Even if the board* did grant the right to hold an election, it still would not have the right to designate any single bargaining agent, said Leonard Kasle.

.   .   .

The executive secretary of the DEA which vies with the DFT for membership called the decision to strike "flying headlong into a dangerous precedent." Patrick Basile said the election results are not very indicative of the will of the majority and do not speak for the total teaching staff of the City of Detroit.[9]

While Kasle and Basile were citing legal restrictions and moral obligations, the tempo of militancy was increasing:

"I'm not a bit worried about State law," snapped Mrs. Geraldine O'Loan . . . , a teacher at Halley Elementary. "They give us all parental responsibility, the children, then take away our rights. We should have the right to vote for collective bargaining and if we can't have that I wouldn't hesitate to go on strike despite the law."

.   .   .

Wm. Meade . . . said, "Teachers have been forced to a strike vote; no one wanted it. . . . But it's long overdue and it's the only way we're going to get a hearing. I don't feel the law will hold up. And anyway teachers don't fit under its definition. We're not a threat to public security." [10]

In the meantime, the Detroit Board of Education showed its own muscle. In an obvious attempt to set an example, Superintendent Brownell invoked the Hutchinson Act against 21 school maintenance workers—members of the mechanical trades union—who had struck in defiance of an administrative directive to report to work on schedule. All 21 were fired.

However, within 10 days following the DFT strike vote, the Board of Education moved from this extreme position and agreed to discuss a plan for teacher representation. The plan was a variation of one in use by the Dearborn Board of Education and later incorporated into a number of State laws such as those in California and Minnesota. Its principal component was a delegate form of representation, whereby the percentage of the membership of the bargaining team for each teacher organization is based upon the number of members certified by each organization. Although strongly endorsed by the press and incorporated into the policy of the Detroit Board of Education, the plan was rejected by the DFT as a system which would lead to chaos. The only alternative, in the DFT's view, was a single and exclusive bargaining agent.

INFORMATIONAL PICKETING

Meanwhile, during the week of March 10, 1964, Detroit Federation members set up informational picket lines at seven schools from 7 A.M. until the start of classes, to emphasize their demands for an exclusive representation election. The DEA maintained its longstanding position that being a professional made it impossible for a teacher to engage in pressure tactics. Patrick Basile, executive secretary of the DEA, was quoted as saying:

> . . . Picketing is not a constructive measure but . . . the teacher representation plan presented by the board is not to our liking. We hope to make refinements in it, but this picketing is just an out-of-hand demonstration.[11]

Neither appeals to professionalism nor placation or paternalism by the Board, deterred the DFT membership. They were psychologically ready for a confrontation, legal or not, and they set the strike date for April 15, 1964.

> Members of the DFT voted Tuesday to strike the city's schools April 15. Whether the DFT orders its members out of their classrooms hinges on a proposal hammered out earlier Tuesday at a school board meeting. The Board proposed that a secret ballot be conducted April 8 at which Detroit's 10,000 classroom teachers would decide:
> I. To keep the situation as is with DFT and DEA submitting grievances separately.
> II. To adopt a board plan for a Teacher's Representation Committee.
> III. Or to have all teachers represented by a single organization.[12]

Part of the Detroit Board's position change—to allow the secret ballot poll—can be attributed to a March 1964 opinion by Michigan's Attorney General, Frank Kelley, that teacher strikes were illegal, but that school boards did have the power to accept the organization selected by a majority vote of teachers as the sole bargaining agent. Even so, the Board was hesitant and explained that the April 8, 1964, teacher poll would be strictly advisory and not necessarily a mandate. One week before the teacher poll some members of the Board of Education attempted to rescind the previous agreement to conduct the poll; only through the efforts of the Board's president was this proposal withdrawn.

The April poll results startled the Board of Education. Out of more than 9,000 Detroit teachers, 7,510 voted that they preferred to have one organization represent them; that is, they chose exclusive representation over the other alternatives on the ballot.

Subsequently, on April 11, just 4 days before the DFT's authorized strike action,

> The Detroit Board of Education agreed . . . to hold an election in which Detroit teachers will choose one organization to represent them in negotiations with the school board.
> Board president Leonard Kasle emphasized that the winning organization will work within the framework of the Teacher Representation Committee established by the Board March 4.[13]

By this time, the DEA was campaigning for exclusive representation rights but still deploring DFT tactics. The battle for teacher representation was on and continued until May 11, 1964, when 5,800 out of approximately 9,600 teachers voted the DFT as exclusive bargaining agent in the Board of Education-conducted election.

More recently, on April 19, 1967, in a representation election conducted by the Labor Mediation Board because of a DEA-initiated decertification petition, 6,400 teachers approved the DFT's continuing as sole negotiating agent.

Case Study—Grand Rapids

In 1954, two organizations of teachers in Grand Rapids claimed to speak for teachers: The Grand Rapids Teachers Association and the Grand Rapids Federation of Teachers, Local 256 of the American Federation of Teachers.[14]

The Grand Rapids Teachers Association, which in 1963 became the Grand Rapids Education Association (GREA) was affiliated with the Michigan Education Association (MEA) and the National Education Association (NEA). Membership in these organizations was voluntary and an individual might belong to any one, two, or all three. The Grand Rapids Federation of Teachers (GRFT) was affiliated with the Michigan Federation of Teachers (MFT) and the American Federation of Teachers (AFT), which is in turn affiliated with the American Federation of Labor–Congress of Industrial Organizations.

In addition, there was an active chapter of the Association of Childhood Education, the Grand Rapids Association of Childhood Education (GRACE), a Grand Rapids Elementary Principals Association (informal), a school men's club, and a school women's club. In addition, each of the secondary schools and some of the elementary ones had a "building council," which might to some extent be concerned with working conditions in the building. Primarily, however, the teachers looked to the GREA and GRFT to improve working conditions and salary, and to protect them in the event of some problem in their employment. However, both the "improvement" and "protection" activities of the organizations can at best be described as consultations with the Board of Education. Each year both the GREA and GRFT, along with other groups, made presentations regarding working conditions and salary before the Board of Education, when after the completion of the agenda at board meetings the board would allow "presentations from the floor." In addition, in the spring, a special board meeting would be held to hear presentations from employee groups on the subject of working conditions and salaries.

Otherwise, from time to time some special area of concern might be taken up with the superintendent and members of his staff. The conclusion of such a meeting was usually either the reassurance that the problem was being considered and dealt with, or the creation of a committee—of the superintendent's selection—to study and report on the issue.

An example of the nature of the consultations can be illustrated by the 1954 confrontation. That year the GREA took a hard line on salaries and for the first time employed a local attorney to represent it before the Board of Education. As the controversy developed, the GREA took the position, "$3,500 or else." Various actions were considered by the association to cover the "or else" category, and the chief one was the withholding of contracts. The Board of Education finally adopted a beginning salary of $3,400, and the president of the GREA publicly thanked the board for its action.

FEDERATION OF TEACHERS

In 1955 the GRFT had about 240 members. Its president had been instrumental in a successful campaign to have the Board establish a uniform policy giving credit in the salary schedule for military service. The Federation ranks were swelled with people who had joined in his support. However, the active membership (as opposed to those who simply paid dues) was somewhat less than 20, of whom no more than 5 were willing to participate beyond attendance at an occasional meeting.

In 1958, the GRFT had approximately 94 dues-paying members (the active membership remained about 5 or 6), but by 1960 the paid membership had fallen to 24. During that school year, a motion to deactivate the local was defeated by a vote of about 7 to 3.

In August 1960, the schedule for secondary schooldays was changed. When school resumed, teachers in all high schools found that they no longer had 50 to 60 minutes for lunch, but only 25 to 30 minutes. Neither the GRFT or the GREA took any strong position on this issue.

During the fall of 1960, representatives from the high schools and junior high schools created an organization called the "Secondary Teachers Association," with $5 dues to be used for attorney's fees to challenge the Board of Education. Between 325 and 350 teachers joined, including both GRFT and GREA members. This organization was led by a council chosen from the representatives from the schools.

In the spring of 1961 the Board of Education, uncertain of expected revenues, issued letters of intent instead of contracts. The letters expressed the Board's intent to continue a teacher's employment and asked that he sign and return a statement that he intended to return to employment the following fall.

The Secondary Teachers Association attempted to obtain an injunction to prohibit the superintendent and the school board from collecting these letters of intent, but the injunction was refused by the local circuit court. An attempt to obtain a temporary restraining order from the Michigan Supreme Court pending a hearing was denied.

Nevertheless, as a result of this activity, the attorney for the Secondary Teachers Association was able to convince the board that a clause should be added to the individual contracts issued by the board. The clause stated that changes in board policy which would change the working conditions of the certificated staff would not be affected during the period of contract without the approval of the teachers' group.

During school year 1961–62, the leaders of the Secondary Teachers Association had only a few meetings; no membership drive was carried on, and by late 1962 the organization ceased to function.[15] However, it was from this group of secondary teachers that the GRFT sought to draw its strength in the later unit determination and representation battles with the GREA.

The constitution of the GRFT specifically disavowed the strike as a weapon. The local constitution also denied membership to any supervisors. (These provisions were local and not necessarily characteristic of the other locals in the State nor of the State organization. Detroit, for example, did have principals in their early membership and the MFT did advocate the use of the strike.) The issue of the admission to membership of administrators was of particular concern to some of the long-standing members of the GRFT; both the previous and present superintendent had once been members of the GRFT, and both had also served as president of the GREA.

Membership in the GRFT from 1960 to 1964 is indicated by the following figures published by the Michigan Department of Labor:

Year	Members	Year	Members
1960–61	42	1963–64	175
1961–62	69	1964–65	172
1962–63	58	1965–66	141

For the year 1966–67 the only available figure is the GRFT president's estimate of 170 members.

EDUCATION ASSOCIATION

In 1954 the GREA membership had reached about 1,000, which represented almost all of the teachers in Grand Rapids.[16] The local dues at that time were $4. Most teachers were members locally, even though they might be members of other organizations as well. GREA membership from 1960 to 1966 was as follows:[17]

Year	Members	Year	Members
1960–61	1,108	1964–65	915
1961–62	1,193	1965–66	835
1962–63	1,256	1966–67	859
1963–64	1,008		

In 1960–61 the GREA was beginning a transition that would bring its practices into line with those that were developing across the country. For one, the question of employing staff instead of depending on the work of volunteers was beginning to be considered; the first movement in this direction occurred when the local president paid his wife to do some clerical chores. At that time the constitution of the organization provided that stipends be paid to the officers, but they had no expense account. In 1961–62 the association employed a secretary on a part-time basis during the school year.

In 1962–63 the GREA, in cooperation with the State organization, paid part of the salary of one of the State organization's field representatives to serve as a half-time executive secretary for the GREA. For this purpose the dues were raised. It also became apparent that the constitution needed revision to authorize the employment of a staff and to change the governing authority from general meetings to some more workable device. (General membership meetings usually had less than 20-percent attendance.) During the year an elected committee worked on a . revision of the constitution, which was to be a completely new document. Further, proposals by the salary chairman for the GREA (a former and future GRFT president) brought about the adoption of a policy of requesting a graduated salary schedule with increments expressed as ratios of the beginning salary. Finally, a campaign was mounted to amend the permissive State tenure law to make it mandatory.

The new constitution,[18] which was ratified in the spring of 1963, provided that the governing authority of the organization would be a representative assembly. It provided for a president-elect, president, and past-president rather than the 1-year presidency, and for the employment of an executive secretary.

The administration of the school district was most active in the creation of the new constitution and, through their delegate, major issues were raised and re-raised for discussion. Out of this debate came the compromise of the representative assembly.

The first representative assemblies were held in the fall of 1963, and efforts were commenced to wrest control of the organization from the "old guard." A proposal that the GREA secure office space outside the schools was finally rejected. Requests were made for a negotiated agreement, for dues checkoff, for exclusive recognition determined by membership, and for the assignment of committees by the association rather than by the superintendent. None of these requests were accepted, but a series of regular meetings was started between the representatives of the GREA, the superintendent, and some members of the Board of Education, where these requests and others on salaries and other economic items were discussed and debated through 1964. During this period the GRFT also presented a petition seeking recognition and the establishment of a negotiation procedure, with the representative group to be chosen by election.

Teachers started the 1965–66 school year without contracts pending important decisions by the Labor Mediation Board. Unfair labor practice charges had been filed by the GRFT, which asked, among other things, for the disestablishment of the GREA as a possible teacher representative because it was dominated and assisted by the employer. The GRFT had also filed a petition for a unit determination decision based on a 7-to-12 grade unit.

A new constitution was drafted in 1965 and reflected the results of an evaluation undertaken by the NEA of the GREA. It took into account the provisions of the Public Employment

Relations Act (PERA) amendments. The presidency was made a 1-year term with no president-elect or past-president positions.

THE REPRESENTATION FIGHT

Upon the passage of the PERA amendments, both the GREA and the GRFT were faced with some immediate problems.

The GREA found itself in the embarrassing position of having a president who was a principal (and viewed as a management representative) and having its offices located (rent free) in the school building where the principal was assigned. Throughout the State, the MEA found itself confronted with the dilemma of either (1) accepting the amendments and seeking to win the largest number of unit recognitions, while at the same time upsetting its traditional structure of encompassing the aims and interests of school administrators and school teachers, or (2) refusing to seek recognition for its locals in hopes of further amending the act to create a special set of rules. In the face of competition from the Federation of Teachers, the decision was made to seek recognition for MEA's local affiliates and to attempt to support them in the negotiation process. The GREA not only faced decisions as to how to conform to the requirements of the act but, more important, how to win recognition as the bargaining agent in the light of the feeling on the part of some of the teaching staff that it was substantially a "company union."

On its part, the GRFT faced the question of how best to create a situation in which it might win an election as the exclusive bargaining agent and provide for its own survival. The decisions which were made resulted in the overwhelming defeat of the GRFT. It is clear that the intent of the GRFT and the decisions reached were based upon a combination of real concern for teachers' interest and an opportunity for institutional growth.

The GRFT began with these assumptions: (1) We are best able to carry on the process of collective bargaining; (2) the GREA and its affiliates, by tradition and by intent, are not able to carry on effective collective bargaining; (3) therefore, it is important that we win recognition for at least part of the teachers in Grand Rapids; (4) in any event, the GREA and the employer must be made aware of the practices and attitudes that prevent the real representation of teachers' interests.

The local attorney employed to represent the GRFT had been a Democratic candidate for office in a Republican stronghold and a support of unions in a determinedly open shop town. Further, he was unfamiliar with policies of the State and National Federation of Teachers. These factors played an important role in shaping the decisions that were reached.

The GRFT first filed several charges of unfair labor practices, and then a petition for a unit determination on the basis of a division of the total staff into that segment which it was believed might be won in an election, the secondary division of grades 7 through 12.

CONTRADICTION IN POSITION

As the cases began to develop, a conviction grew that the GREA might in fact be disestablished. This posed a serious problem for the GRFT, in light of its petition seeking a 7-to-12 unit determination. As a result the GRFT's position in the unit determination case became one of wishing to postpone the hearing until the unfair labor charges were decided, and of refusing to stand on their 7-to-12 unit request for fear that if the GREA were disestablished they would have then renounced a large part of a unit they might have had by default. These actions had all been taken unilaterally by the GRFT and their attorney. The MFT, hoping to win several other districts, some in which their strength was in the elementary level, wanted no part in a 7-to-12 unit determination controversy and hence did not file briefs or give any substantial aid to the local.

Once having embarked on the two contradictory courses, the GRFT could do nothing but press on, rationalizing as they went. From the GRFT's point of view, the situation became more and more serious as the months went by as no decision was forthcoming on the unfair labor practice charges. The Labor Mediation Board's ultimate decision to determine the bargaining unit question without a prior decision on the unfair labor charge (specifically the question of disestablishment of the GREA) removed any credibility from the GRFT's stand in those hearings.

In the meantime the GREA had sought and received assistance from the MEA. Their strategy was to intervene in the unfair labor practices charge and to attempt to disqualify the relevance of GREA activities before the amendments were passed, and thus prevent the disestablishment of the GREA; to assert publicly a belief that the board of education was guilty of the alleged unfair labor practices, but that to press the issue would result only in frustrating the teachers' best interests; and finally, in the unit hearing, to try to prevent the separation of the teachers into more than one unit.

On these grounds, the GREA asked for an election to determine the exclusive bargaining agent. It accused the GRFT of placing organizational objectives over the interest of teachers. In the face of the two-pronged attack by the GRFT, the GREA defended itself by saying that it was ready, able, and willing to have the agent determined, and if the GREA were chosen, it would effectively represent and negotiate for the teachers. In the fall of 1965 the GREA had two tasks: to rid itself of administrators, and to petition for an election as the exclusive bargaining agent for all teachers (K-12) in the district.

The following is a synopsis of the charges, arguments, and findings that ensued at the unfair labor practice and unit determination hearings conducted by the labor mediation board.[19]

RESULTS OF THE HEARINGS

At the unfair labor practice hearing, the Federation charged that (1) evidence of activities prior to the effective date of the act should be considered to show violations of the act after its effective date; (2) the employer violated section 10A of the act by unilateral action changing the conditions of employment; and (3) the employer assisted and dominated the Grand Rapids Education Association so that an order should be issued to cause it to cease and desist; this domination should disqualify the GREA from participation in the election.

The Board of Education argued that (1) the events before the act should not apply; (2) domination and assistance were not exercised because while administrators were members they were so individually and not by direction of the employer, while assistance was given, it was offered to both organizations on an equal basis and therefore did not favor one; (3) the employer did not in fact encourage membership in the GREA to the exclusion of the GRFT; and (4) the employer did not in fact take unilateral action contrary to law, in that it consulted with the various employee groups and the action it took followed from earlier employee requests; there was no bargaining unit with whom to bargain the issue.

The Grand Rapids Education Association intervenor arguments were (1) membership by supervisory employees in a labor organization does not constitute support or domination of the labor organization, and (2) the alleged assistance and domination by reasons of free use of Board facilities was offered to the GRFT and used by the GRFT, albeit to a lesser degree, and therefore was not a reason to disqualify the GREA in the pending election.

The Michigan Labor Mediation Board found that the interference by supervisors, the holding of offices in organizations by supervisors, the presence of a supervisor at a labor organization meeting, and the participation by a supervisor in an association election were violations of sections 10A and 10B of the act; that the membership of supervisors in employee organizations was not a violation of section 10; that the use of school mails and the use of school office space were not violations of the act; that the adoption of the MEA Code of Ethics in the employer's personnel policy was a violation of sections 10A and 10B; and that employer censorship of association material was a violation of section 10A. The Board dismissed the charge of unilateral action by the board affecting working conditions, and ruled that the issues did not justify the disestablishment of the association.

At the unit determination hearing, the GREA and the Board of Education held that the appropriate unit should be K-12. The Federation took the position that the appropriate unit should be 7-12, but that the unit should not be established until after the decisions had been issued on the unfair labor practice charges, and that the unit determination decision should be reserved until after the above decision (when the Federation —if it won—would then support a K-12 determination). The

Michigan Labor Mediation Board found the appropriate unit to be K-12.

Since the issue of unit determination was heard before the rendering of the decision of the unfair charges hearing, the GRFT made no clear case for a unit other than K-12 and thus the precedent was established, in essence that the unit should be the largest appropriate for an employer.

In the election which followed the 18 months of delay after the original representation petition, the GREA received more votes than its membership.

The election results were decisive, and devastating to the GRFT. The teachers apparently felt that the GRFT and its attorney had prolonged the dispute for its own advantage against the interest of teachers.

		Votes in election held *November 9, 1966*
Approximate total eligible to vote		1,450
Total votes cast		1,352
GREA		1,151
GRFT		172
Neither		13
Challenged		16

Significance of the Case Studies

Although the MFT was successful in Detroit, this success was achieved before the legislative amendments were implemented and before the MEA had displayed its later militancy. At the time of the first Detroit election the MEA had to decide whether to oppose the DFT in the aggressive and militant manner that later became an acceptable and a standard alternative, but by doing so to face the potential loss of other upstate districts by prematurely revealing this possible policy shift. At this juncture, without firm evidence that its own legislative proposals would not be enacted, the risk was too great. Further, the historical evolution of the DEA and DFT organizations and leadership indicates that Detroit would have been a rather poor risk for the MEA at the time.

The contrast with the Grand Rapids organization is startlingly clear. The GREA was well-organized and financially secure. Historically, it had represented the majority of teachers in Grand Rapids even though the evidence of employer domination was substantiated. Further, and most important, when the issue of employer domination was raised, the local organization was not left to its own defense but received the support—albeit the control of its defense—from the State organization. This defense coincided with and supported the changed stance and policy of the MEA to effectively represent and bargain for the classroom teacher throughout the State, utilizing whatever means necessary to achieve this end. This message and evidence of support was not lost by other local teacher groups, nor was the State organization's assistance denied elsewhere.

Further, the MEA successfully capitalized on its national professional image to convince many boards and administrators throughout the State that it was a "safe" organization. The preponderance of first-year voluntary recognitions that were achieved testifies that the strategy was effective. It was not until later, when the nature of the position change of the MEA became evident through strike actions and hard bargaining, that the school boards or other employer representatives recognized the effect of their early, often uncontested recognitions. It was then obviously too late.

NOTES

1. Section 15 of the Public Employment Relations Act provides for collective bargaining between a public employer and the representatives of its employees. This representative must be chosen by a majority of the employees in an appropriate unit. He may be granted recognition voluntarily by the employer, or he may be elected by a majority of employees in a designated unit.

For a fuller treatment of the provisions of the act and the representation procedures of the Michigan Labor Mediation Board, see Hyman Parker, "The Michigan Public Employment Relations Act and Procedures Under the Act," in Charles T. Schmidt, Jr., *et al., A Guide to Collective Negotiations in Education* (East Lansing: Michigan State University, Social Science Research Bureau, 1967), pp. 20–27.

2. *The Detroit Free Press,* May 16, 1963.

3. Otis A. Crosby, "Taxes and Tensions—Battle of Ballots," *Public Relations Gold Mine Volume Six* (Washington: National School Public Relations Association, 1964), p. 43.

4. "Millage and Bond Election, April 1957" (unpublished history of the campaign on file at the Detroit Board of Education), p. 2.

5. *Ibid.*

6. *The Detroit Free Press*, February 15, 1964. 6,848 teachers had signed petitions supporting this demand for a representation election.

7. Roberta Mackey, *The Detroit Free Press*, December 11, 1963.

8. *The Detroit Free Press*, February 28, 1964. The strike vote was passed 2,109–387.

9. *Ibid.*

10. Roberta Mackey, *The Detroit Free Press*, February 28, 1964.

11. *The Detroit Free Press*, March 10, 1964.

12. *The Detroit Free Press*, March 25, 1964.

13. Roberta Mackey, *The Detroit Free Press*, April 11, 1964.

14. I am grateful to David England, former president of both the Grand Rapids Federation of Teachers and the Grand Rapids Education Association, for his assistance in reconstructing the early history and organizational dynamics of these two organizations.

15. The Secondary Teachers Association is the organization referenced in the unit determination dispute between the GREA and GRFT. See State of Michigan, Labor Mediation Board: Case Nos. R65 I 91 and R65 J 169: *Grand Rapids Board of Education* v. *Grand Rapids Education Association and Grand Rapids Federation of Teachers*, August 29, 1966, p. 7.

16. Dual membership in both the MFT and MEA was a common practice throughout the State.

17. From the MEA membership files, headquarters, East Lansing, Mich.

18. *Proposed Constitution,* Grand Rapids Education Association, Grand Rapids, Mich., April 1963.

19. The summary and much of the preceding discussion was taken from the following: (a) Partial transcript of the proceedings had and testimony taken in the hearing in *The Matter of the Grand Rapids Board of Education Hearing Before the State Labor Mediation Board*: Grand Rapids, Mich., March 22 and 23, 1966, (b) *Ibid.*: Case Nos. R65-I-91 and R65-J-169. (c) *Memorandum Brief on Behalf of GREA*: Re: Appropriate Unit Grand Rapids Teachers: May 31, 1966, Theodore Swift, Attorney. (d) *Brief of Grand Rapids Federation of Teachers*, Re: Case Numbers C65, L-37, Charges of Unfair Labor Practices, February 16, 1966, A. Robert Kleiner, Attorney, GRFT. (e) *Exceptions to Trial Examiner's Decision and Recommended Order and Brief in Support Thereof*, Re: Case Nos. C-65-L-37; July 13, 1966. A. Robert Kleiner, Attorney—GRFT. (f) *Brief of Grand Rapids Education Association*, Re: Case Nos. C65, L37; undated, Theodore Swift, Attorney, GREA. (g) *Exceptions to Decision and Recommended Order of Trial Examiner*, Re: Case Nos. C65, L37: July 15, 1966, J. Michael Warren, Attorney, GREA. (h) *Brief of the Grand Rapids Board of Education*, Re: Case Nos. C65, L37; February 15, 1966, Roger Anderson, Attorney, Board of Education. (i) *Written Exceptions to Trial Examiner's Decision and Recommended Order*, Re: Case Nos. C65, L37; July 13, 1966, Roger Anderson, Attorney, Board of Education. (j) *Trial Examiner's Decision and Recommended Order*, Re: Case Nos. C65, L37; June 14, 1966, Robert Pisarski, Chief Trial Examiner.

The Future for Public Employee Unions

DOUGLAS WEIFORD

AND WAYNE BURGGRAAFF

The hour was late, and the Eau Claire council members were tired. The business agent for Local 284 spoke sharply. "We are here to bargain in good faith, gentlemen, I ask you again: What is your counter proposal?" The reporters eyed their notes, waiting for the reply. No one spoke. The council president looked around at the other members as though wondering whether to call a recess to permit a few moments of private discussion. The silence was heavy, almost oppressive. No one knew exactly what to do.

In 1959 the Wisconsin legislature had enacted a public employee labor relations law which deliberately moved public employee negotiations closer to the methods and techniques used in private industry. The Eau Claire city council, faced with more questions than answers, groped to meet the requirements and implications of the law, conducted lengthy negotiating sessions with the three employee organizations, heard demands for a 25 per cent increase in police salaries, listened to arguments for drastic changes in the city's position-classification and pay plans, made offers and counteroffers, and wearily made final decisions.

But unlike earlier years, the task was not finished nor was it likely to be for several months. Dissatisfied with the council's final decision, the police "collective bargaining unit" rejected it and proceeded under the terms of the new law to request the Wisconsin Employment Relations Board to institute "fact finding" procedures.

Only one thing was really clear. The easy going "home rule" concept of conducting labor relations in Wisconsin was dead and was not likely to be restored. The new emphasis would center on

Reprinted from *Public Management*, XLV (May 1963), 102–107, by permission of the authors and publisher.

Douglas Weiford is City Manager of Eau Claire, Wisconsin. Wayne Burggraaff is Assistant to the City Manager of Des Moines, Iowa.

legally protected union activity, on collective bargaining, and on fact finding and mediation by the state. Where would this new road lead? What changes in long-established practice would have to be made? There were no immediate answers, only the certainty that the ways of the past had come to an end.

The Changing Pattern

The unfamiliar role in which the Eau Claire city council found itself was beginning to be reenacted throughout Wisconsin. In other states, too, the growing strength of organized labor was being felt. Actually, the trend toward unionization of government workers had been evident for many years. According to the *Municipal Year Book* only about 32 per cent of the cities over 10,000 population had one or more employee organizations in 1938. By 1950 this figure had risen to 66 per cent, and today it is estimated that about 80 per cent of all such cities have one or more employee organizations. More and more of these groups are affiliating with national labor organizations. In 1962, 68 per cent of the cities over 10,000 reported one or more employee groups affiliated with a national organization.

The trend has spread throughout the various levels of government. Today more than 1 million of the 9 million civilian persons employed by federal, state, and local governments belong to a labor organization, evidence aplenty that organized labor's recruitment and lobbying procedures are beginning to roll in high gear. In addition to favorable legislation recently gained by labor in some cities and states, the President in 1962 issued an executive order requiring all agencies of the federal government to recognize and negotiate with properly constituted labor organizations. The President's action is the first such policy statement ever made and will doubtless result in a substantial increase in union membership throughout the federal government.

The increased unionization of government employees is in direct contrast to the situation in private industry where the growth of unions among production workers has apparently been halted by automation and changing technology. In 1954 organized labor claimed 35.1 per cent of the total nonfarm work force; by 1960 this figure had dropped to 32.1 per cent.

If the labor movement is to maintain its effectiveness and recoup its membership losses it obviously must move in new directions. The announced plan of labor leaders is to turn to the unorganized groups: the industrial white collar employees and the hundreds of thousands who labor in various service occupations. Government workers comprise a substantial percentage of these nonunionized employees.

The changing pattern thus is clear. There has been and will continue to be a steady growth in the number of governmental employee unions and in the strength and influence brought to bear on government on all matters affecting public personnel. The public official must recognize the fact that organized labor, protected by law and armed with weapons of negotiating power, is emerging as a major force in the affairs of government.

.   .   .

Many Questions—Few Answers

The American labor movement in business and industry is based on the right of workers to form labor organizations and through them to bargain collectively with employers. Collective bargaining is intended to terminate in a binding mutual agreement on matters under negotiation and may proceed for many months before agreement is reached. When negotiations are unsuccessful management and labor frequently call in impartial persons for fact finding, mediation, or arbitration. If all attempts to reach agreement fail, labor may resort to the economic weapons of the strike, the boycott, or the picket line.

There are of course substantial differences between public and private employment, and these are nowhere so apparent as in labor relations. Where private workers may utilize the threat or actuality of strikes as their principal negotiating weapon, the use of economic weapons by public employees is considered repugnant. Indeed, no sensible person would argue that public employees have the inherent right to paralyze the government, to halt its processes, and to force it to its knees.

Nor is collective bargaining as practiced in industry transplantable to government. Negotiations in government may not continue indefinitely. The budget must be adopted and the tax rate fixed, and failure to reach agreement cannot stay these inexorable deadlines. At some specific point of time the legislative body must act, and labor relations and all else must bow to these higher demands for final and unilateral legislative decision.

Even the simple question of "Who should negotiate?" constitutes a complex problem. By contrast, negotiations in private industry are generally more simple and direct than in government. Private management and union negotiating teams often have authority to make final decisions, and once made, management implements them. In government only the city council can make final decisions on policy matters. Councils, however, are not ordinarily a closely knit group in the manner of a board of directors. Given the setting of the open meeting with its political atmosphere and with reporters and other outsiders present, can effective bargaining between a city council and labor unions take place at all?

On the other hand, assume that the council forms a committee or assigns the city manager to meet with the unions and negotiate. Since representatives of the council cannot make binding agreements, how can negotiations in the give-and-take spirit of industry be brought to the affairs of government? It has been argued that a council can establish, in advance of bargaining, how far it is willing to go in reaching an agreement, and that the council's representative can then work within these guidelines at the bargaining table. Such arguments tend to be naïve, for it is extremely unlikely that a politically diversified legislative body could come to such a decision and then keep quiet about it. Labor leaders will know as much about such "guidelines" as the council's representative even before bargaining begins.

But if the prior establishment of guidelines is suspect, the alternative is equally poor. What happens if the finance committee or city manager after endless hours of argument and debate agrees to a union demand and the council, aloof and detached from the earthy process of battle, decides that the agreement should not be honored? In such cases does bargaining start anew between labor and the entire council?

Or take the case where the preliminary negotiations collapse. After all, nothing is lost by the unions in failing to reach agreement at this stage. Labor knows full well that only the council can make final decisions and that a direct confrontation is not only desirable but sometimes essential. So once again the legislative body is cast in the unlikely role of negotiator, its members trying to keep a collective eye on the attendant publicity, the next election, and the tax rate all at the same time. The simple question of how negotiations should be conducted remains unanswered because no one really knows.

And then there are other important points to consider. In seeking official recognition unions attempt to gain exclusive rights to bargain for certain classes of employees. Is such exclusive recognition appropriate to the public service? Many would claim that this practice is undemocratic and constitutes a denial to non-union members of the right to petition the legislative body for redress of grievances. If it were resolved that exclusive recognition is permissible, would the related but more far-reaching concept of the union shop also be appropriate in governmental agencies?

It was stated earlier that economic weapons should be barred, but in lieu thereof can satisfactory settlement procedures be devised which are specifically tailored to the nature of government? In such a procedure how should "deadlock" be defined? Does a bona fide deadlock automatically exist whenever a council does not give a union what it wants? If fact finding and mediation are suitable elements of settlement machinery in government, is the same true of arbitration? Can a city council ever lawfully delegate decision-making power on legislative matters to "impartial" arbitrators? If, as in Wisconsin, advisory third party referees are provided to help resolve deadlocks, how can unions be prevented from using such machinery to the point of abuse?

There is as yet no general agreement on such questions. Indeed, their meaning and significance are little understood in public circles, and the conclusion is evident that public officials are ill-equipped to cope with well organized union forces.

Impact

If basic terminology is little understood in public circles, the forthcoming impact of strong employee unions on established governmental procedures is hardly understood at all.

The financial impact is obvious. The cities that have not kept pace with advancing wages, changing working conditions, and modern personnel management will find aggressive union activity reflecting heavily on the municipal treasury. Perhaps equally important is the fact that various institutional procedures are certain to be challenged. Chief among these are the civil service system and the integrated pay plan. Indeed, the historic civil service system may be headed for a life and death struggle on the battlefield of collective bargaining.

Merit systems of pay increases will come under bitter attack and, because they are based principally on hard-to-defend subjective standards, will often be replaced with across-the-board increases in each collective bargaining unit. The standard types of classification and pay plans will face frequent union onslaughts; annual attacks may be anticipated on pay ranges and classifications for various positions. Individual job holders on union advice can be expected to refuse work assignments unless the duties are set forth specifically in written job specifications. Joint management-union evaluation of job classifications will become common.

The diversified nature of municipal work encourages separate union organizations. Where a number of such unions exist they will be in competition with each other as well as with management. Each will struggle to better its position with the result that the traditional concept of "equal pay for equal work" on a government-wide basis and the maintenance of an over-all system of values in the classification plan will be increasingly difficult to maintain.

Aggressive unions may win concessions which are not awarded to nonorganized employees, resulting in problems of morale and the organization of additional bargaining units. Seniority rather than performance will be stressed as the principal criterion for promotion to nonsupervisory positions. Disciplinary problems will be carefully watched by unions, and members will be defended by union attorneys. Union membership will be considered by the individual worker in certain classes of position as more significant and more protective than civil service status.

Local governing bodies will be required to spend considerable portions of each year both in direct negotiations and in time-consuming preliminary preparations. Staff personnel from the division head to the chief executive will likewise spend much time in labor relations work. Struggles during negotiating sessions will become emotional at times, requiring formal procedures to minimize personal involvements on both sides of the bargaining table. As individuals, city councilmen can expect to receive pressures from unions both prior to and during negotiations. If all else fails, it should be anticipated that unions will bring political pressures including direct appeals to the public for sympathy and support. When agreements are finally reached they will increasingly be placed in contract form to be signed by both management and labor.

.   .   .

The Road Ahead

The road ahead is not apt to provide smooth traveling. In the sense that public employee unions are essentially political organizations there will be interjected into the daily routine of the public official substantial and sometimes startling changes. The growth of strong unions will surely facilitate the erosion of some personnel practices dear to the heart of the purist. Among many governmental officials there will be head shaking, murmurings of disaster, spirited discussion, and occasionally violent argument. But those who elect to oppose the rising tide will likely achieve little more than conflict, frustration, and finally defeat.

In the midst of such dire portents we return again to our basic conclusion: that no defensible reason exists for denying to public employees the right of self-organization. Having reached this conclusion all else described above must inevitably follow. The formation of employee organizations flows from deep seated human needs. They will continue to be formed and will grow stronger. The public official should recognize this and prepare himself for what lies ahead.

III

THE LEGAL FRAMEWORK

The evolving law of public employment collective bargaining can be classified into the following five categories:

1. *Nonexistent.* In states or political subdivisions that have not enacted legislation providing for collective bargaining activities.

2. *Restrictive.* In states or political subdivisions that have enacted legislation that severely restricts or prohibits collective bargaining activities.

3. *Permissive.* In states or political subdivisions that permit a form of collective representation and bargaining but generally fail to establish procedures, guidelines, and administrative agencies to implement the intent of the legislation.

4. *Mandatory.* In states or political subdivisions that have enacted legislation providing collective bargaining along with the necessary administrative regulations and mechanism to implement effectively the collective bargaining process. With minor variations, these laws closely parallel the intent and procedures of federal legislation dealing with collective bargaining in the private sector.

5. *Executive Orders.* A variation of enabling legislation whereby the chief executive of a political entity has formulated and issued an executive administrative order requiring that public agencies under his direct administrative

control follow specified policy and procedural regulations to implement the collective bargaining process. These orders have generally been "hybrids" that combine aspects of both the permissive and mandatory types of legislation.

Attention is called to the bibliography for examples of comparisons of the content of many of the different state laws. Because of the rapid change in and amendments to state legislation, much of the material is already obsolete. The most accurate and up-to-date sources for state legislative developments in collective bargaining are found in the major specialized labor relations reporting services; e.g., Bureau of National Affairs, Commerce Clearing House, and Prentice-Hall.

The selections in this section include Michigan's Public Employment Relations Act, an excellent example of the mandatory type of legislation; "Executive Order 10988: Employee-Management Cooperation in the Federal Service," which provided a philosophical and procedural basis for the subsequent enactment of state legislation (especially regulations generally permissive in character); and finally, an article in *The New York Times* by A. H. Raskin, describing an early attempt by New York City, through an executive order, to institutionalize the collective bargaining relationship with its employees.

§ *AN EARLY ADJUSTMENT BY A MAJOR CITY*

City Workers Get Right To Organize in Union of Choice

A. H. RASKIN

A "Little Wagner Act" granting city employees many of the same bargaining rights as workers in private industry was signed

Reprinted from *The New York Times*, April 1, 1958, by permission of the publisher. © 1958 by The New York Times Company.

A. H. Raskin is the Assistant Editor of the editorial page of *The New York Times*.

March 31, 1958, by Mayor Wagner. The new labor code took the form of an executive order guaranteeing Civil Service workers the right to join unions of their own choosing. Organizations designated by a majority of the employees in their bargaining units are to receive exclusive recognition in negotiations on wages and other grievances. The signing came after months of behind-the-scenes conflict at City Hall over the political and budgetary consequences of the proposed order.

Increased Pressure Seen

Some of the Mayor's aides took the view that strengthening Civil Service unions would lead to increased pressure for higher wages and other rises in operating costs. Others contended that the establishment of orderly machinery for the presentation of labor problems would bring stability to municipal agencies and promote higher efficiency. Observers felt that the Mayor's decision to act now was influenced by a desire to conciliate major union groups on the eve of the publication of the executive budget for the fiscal year beginning July 1, 1959.

It is no secret that the budget, to be submitted to the Board of Estimate, calls for no across-the-board pay raise for the city's 200,000 employees. The only cheer for them in the Mayor's message will be that provided by mandatory raises for certain workers under automatic pay schedules.

The bargaining order will apply initially to nearly 100,000 workers in departments directly responsible to the Mayor. However, the Borough Presidents' offices and other municipal agencies will be invited to adopt identical procedures.

Firemen will be covered by the code, but the uniformed police force will be outside "pending further study and possible public hearings on the special problems in this area." Most firemen already belong to the Uniformed Firemen's Association, an affiliate of the merged labor federation. Unionization of policemen has been a subject of political controversy for many years. Also exempt from the Wagner program will be employees of the Board of Education and the Transit Authority, which establish their own labor policies under state law.

The plan's principal sponsor is Labor Commissioner Harold

A. Felix, whose office will ascertain the appropriate bargaining units, conduct representation elections, and intervene in disputes that are not settled directly by unions and agency heads.

The executive order was drafted by Miss Ida Klaus, counsel to the Labor Department and former solicitor of the National Labor Relations Board. The order extends into the Civil Service field key features of the original Wagner Act of 1935, which labor hailed then as its "Magna Charta." The act was drawn up by the Mayor's father, the late Senator Robert F. Wagner, Sr.

Union Hails Step

The Mayor's signing of the new code was described as "a monumental forward step" by Jerry Wurf, regional director of the American Federation of State, County, and Municipal Employees. This union was threatening a strike of its 25,000 members in city departments during the last week of March, 1958. Mr. Wurf said his organization would move for recognition at once in a half-dozen agencies. He predicted that the union's membership would double by the end of 1958. Similar expressions of jubilation were expected from most other unions of municipal employees.

However, there was one conspicuous exception. Fred Q. Wendt, president of the Civil Service Forum, an independent organization with members in many departments, called the new order a "Wagner Slave Labor Act." He accused the Mayor of reneging on a pledge he had made before the November elections to hold a public hearing before he issued the order. Mr. Wendt said the sole effect of the code would be to "put caviar on the table of money-hungry union leaders."

The Mayor expressed confidence that his program would lead to "more harmonious, mature, and responsible relations between the city and its employees." He added that it would also provide a vehicle for testing the worth of "new and untried concepts and principles" before they were embodied in permanent legislation.

The order rules out any form of compulsory union membership for employees unwilling to join. Its provisions for exclusive bargaining rights for majority unions are tailored to by-pass some of the headaches the Transit Authority has encountered in its extension of sole recognition to Michael J. Quill's Transport Workers' Union on the city-owned subways.

Minority Rights Explained

The authority's refusal to give any hearing to so-called splinter unions was a pivotal point in the pre-Christmas walkout of subway motormen and members of other craft groups. Under the Wagner plan, minority unions will retain the right to present to city officials the views and requests of their members. Bargaining on all issues, including the adjustment of grievances, will be restricted to the majority spokesman.

No fixed procedure was set up for the peaceful settlement of disputes that could not be resolved through direct negotiations. Commissioner Felix was vested with authority to "take such steps as he may deem expedient to effect an expeditious adjustment."

§ *THE FEDERAL GOVERNMENT APPROACH*

Executive Order #10988: Employee-Management Cooperation in the Federal Service

WHEREAS participation of employees in the formulation and implementation of personnel policies affecting them contributes to effective conduct of public business; and

WHEREAS the efficient administration of the Government and the well-being of employees require that orderly and constructive relationships be maintained between employee organizations and management officials; and

Order issued from the White House, January 17, 1962, by President John F. Kennedy.

WHEREAS subject to law and the paramount requirements of the public service, employee-management relations within the Federal service should be improved by providing employees an opportunity for greater participation in the formulation and implementation of policies and procedures affecting the conditions of their employment; and

WHEREAS effective employee-management cooperation in the public service requires a clear statement of the respective rights and obligations of employee organizations and agency management:

NOW, THEREFORE, by virtue of the authority vested in me by the Constitution of the United States, by section 1753 of the Revised Statutes (5 U.S.C. 631), and as President of the United States, I hereby direct that the following policies shall govern officers and agencies of the executive branch of the Government in all dealings with Federal employees and organizations representing such employees.

Section 1. (a) Employees of the Federal Government shall have, and shall be protected in the exercise of, the right, freely and without fear of penalty or reprisal, to form, join and assist any employee organization or to refrain from any such activity. Except as hereinafter expressly provided, the freedom of such employees to assist any employee organization shall be recognized as extending to participation in the management of the organization and acting for the organization in the capacity of an organization representative, including presentation of its views to officials of the executive branch, the Congress or other appropriate authority. The head of each executive department and agency (hereinafter referred to as "agency") shall take such action, consistent with law, as may be required in order to assure that employees in the agency are apprised of the rights described in this section, and that no interference, restraint, coercion or discrimination is practiced within such agency to encourage or discourage membership in any employee organization.

(b) The rights described in this section do not extend to participation in the management of an employee organization, or acting as a representative of any such organization, where such participation or activity would result in a conflict of interest or otherwise be incompatible with law or with the official duties of an employee.

Section 2. When used in this order, the term "employee organization" means any lawful association, labor organization, federation, council, or brotherhood having as a primary purpose the improvement of working conditions among Federal employees, or any craft, trade or industrial union whose membership includes both Federal employees and employees of private organizations; but such term shall not include any organization (1) which asserts the right to strike against the government of the United States or any agency thereof, or to assist or participate in any such strike, or which imposes a duty or obligation to conduct, assist or participate in any such strike, or (2) which advocates the overthrow of the constitutional form of Government in the United States, or (3) which discriminates with regard to the terms or conditions of membership because of race, color, creed or national origin.

Section 3. (a) Agencies shall accord informal, formal or exclusive recognition to employee organizations which requests such recognition in conformity with the requirements specified in sections 4, 5 and 6 of this order, except that no recognition shall be accorded to any employee organization which the head of the agency considers to be so subject to corrupt influences or influences opposed to basic democratic principles that recognition would be inconsistent with the objectives of this order.

(b) Recognition of an employee organization shall continue so long as such organization satisfies the criteria of this order applicable to such recognition; but nothing in this section shall require any agency to determine whether an organization should become or continue to be recognized as exclusive representative of the employees in any unit within 12 months after a prior determination of exclusive status with respect to such unit has been made pursuant to the provisions of this order.

(c) Recognition, in whatever form accorded, shall not
(1) preclude any employee, regardless of employee organization membership, from bringing matters of per-

sonal concern to the attention of appropriate officials in accordance with applicable law, rule, regulation, or established agency policy, or from choosing his own representative in a grievance or appellate action; or

(2) preclude or restrict consultations and dealings between an agency and any veterans organization with respect to matters of particular interest to employees with veterans preference; or

(3) preclude an agency from consulting or dealing with any religious, social, fraternal or other lawful association, not qualified as an employee organization, with respect to matters or policies which involve individual members of the association or are of particular applicability to it or its members, when such consultations or dealings are duly limited so as not to assume the character of formal consultation on matters of general employee-management policy or to extend to areas where recognition of the interests of one employee group may result in discrimination against or injury to the interests of other employees.

Section 4. (a) An agency shall accord an employee organization, which does not qualify for exclusive or formal recognition, informal recognition as representative of its member employees without regard to whether any other employee organization has been accorded formal or exclusive recognition as representative of some or all employees in any unit.

(b) When an employee organization has been informally recognized, it shall, to the extent consistent with the efficient and/or orderly conduct of the public business, be permitted to present to appropriate officials its views on matters of concern to its members. The agency need not, however, consult with an employee organization so recognized in the formulation of personnel or other policies with respect to such matters.

Section 5. (a) An agency shall accord an employee organization formal recognition as the representative of its members in a unit as defined by the agency when (1) no other employee organization is qualified for exclusive recognition as representative of employees in the unit, (2) it is determined by the agency that the employee organization has a substantial and stable membership of no less than 10 per centum of the employees in the unit, and (3) the employee organization has submitted to the agency a roster of its officers and representatives, a copy of its constitution and by-laws, and a statement of objectives. When, in the opinion of the head of an agency, an employee organization has a sufficient number of local organizations or a sufficient total membership within such agency, such organization may be accorded formal recognition at the national level, but such recognition shall not preclude the agency from dealing at the national level with any other employee organization on matters affecting its members.

(b) When an employee organization has been formally recognized, the agency, through appropriate officials, shall consult with such organization from time to time in the formulation and implementation of personnel policies and practices, and matters affecting working conditions that are of concern to its members. Any such organization shall be entitled from time to time to raise such matters for discussion with appropriate officials and at all times to present its views thereon in writing. In no case, however, shall an agency be required to consult with an employee organization which has been formally recognized with respect to any matter which, if the employee organization were one entitled to exclusive recognition, would not be included within the obligation to meet and confer, as described in section 6(b) of this order.

Section 6. (a) An agency shall recognize an employee organization as the exclusive representative of the employees in an appropriate unit when such organization is eligible for formal recognition pursuant to section 5 of this order, and has been designated or selected by a majority of the employees of such unit as the representative of such employees in such unit. Units may be established on any plant or installation, craft, functional or other basis which will ensure a clear and identifiable community of interest among the employees concerned, but no unit shall be established solely on the basis of the extent to which employees in the proposed unit have organized. Except where otherwise required by established practice, prior agreement, or special circumstances, no unit shall be established for purposes of exclusive recognition which includes (1) any managerial executive, (2) any employee engaged in Federal personnel work in other than a purely clerical capacity, (3) both supervisors who officially evaluate the performance of employees and the employees whom they supervise, or (4) both professional employees and nonprofessional employees unless a majority of such professional employees vote for inclusion in such unit.

(b) When an employee organization has been recognized as the exclusive representative of employees of an appropriate unit it shall be entitled to act for and to negotiate agreements covering all employees in the unit and shall be responsible for representing the interests of all such employees without discrimination and without regard to employee organization membership. Such employee organization shall be given the opportunity to be represented at discussions between management and employees or employee representatives concerning grievances, personnel policies and practices, or other matters affecting general working conditions of employees in the unit. The agency and such employee organization, through appropriate officials and representatives, shall meet at reasonable times and confer with respect to personnel policy and practices and matters affecting working conditions, so far as may be appropriate subject to law and policy requirements. This extends to the negotiation of an agreement, or any question arising thereunder, the determination of appropriate techniques, consistent with the terms and purposes of this order, to assist in such negotiation, and the execution of a written memorandum of agreement or understanding incorporating any agreement reached by the parties. In exercising authority to make rules and regulations relating to personnel policies and practices and working conditions, agencies shall have due regard for the obligation imposed by this section, but such obligation shall not be construed to extend to such areas of discretion and policy as the mission of an agency, its budget, its organization and the assignment of its personnel, or the technology of performing its work.

Section 7. Any basic or initial agreement entered into with an employee organization as the exclusive representative of employees in a unit must be approved by the head of the agency or any official designated by him. All agreements with such employee organizations shall also be subject to the following requirements, which shall be expressly stated in the initial or basic agreement and shall be applicable to all supplemental, implementing, subsidiary or informal agreements between the agency and the organization:

(1) In the administration of all matters covered by the agreement officials and employees are governed by the provisions of any existing or future laws and regulations, including policies set forth in the Federal Personnel Manual and agency regulations, which may be applicable, and the agreement shall at all times be applied subject to such laws, regulations and policies;

(2) Management officials of the agency retain the right, in accordance with applicable laws and regulations, (a) to direct employees of the agency, (b) to hire, promote, transfer, assign, and retain employees in positions within the agency, and to suspend, demote, discharge, or take other disciplinary action against employees, (c) to relieve employees from duties because of lack of work or for other legitimate reasons, (d) to maintain the efficiency of the Government operations entrusted to them, (e) to determine the methods, means and personnel by which such operations are to be conducted; and (f) to take whatever actions may be necessary to carry out the mission of the agency in situations of emergency.

Section 8. (a) Agreements entered into or negotiated in accordance with this order with an employee organization which is the exclusive representative of employees in an appropriate unit may contain provisions, applicable only to employees in the unit, concerning procedures for consideration of grievances. Such procedures (1) shall conform to standards issued by the Civil Service Commission, and (2) may not in any manner diminish or impair any rights which would otherwise be available to any employee in the absence of an agreement providing for such procedures.

(b) Procedures established by an agreement which are otherwise in conformity with this section may include provisions for the arbitration of grievances. Such arbitration (1) shall be advisory in nature with any decisions or recommendations subject to the approval of the agency head; (2) shall extend only to the interpretation or application of agreements or agency policy and not to changes in or proposed changes in agreements or agency policy; and (3) shall be invoked only with the approval of the individual employee or employees concerned.

Section 9. Solicitation of memberships, dues, or other internal employee organization business shall be conducted during the non-duty hours of the employees concerned. Officially requested or approved consultations and meetings between management officials and representatives of recognized employee organizations shall, whenever practicable, be conducted on official time, but any agency may require that negotiations with an employee organization which has been accorded exclusive recognition be conducted during the non-duty hours of the employee organization representatives involved in such negotiations.

Section 10. No later than July 1, 1962, the head of each agency shall issue appropriate policies, rules and regulations for the implementation of this order, including: A clear statement of the rights of its employees under the order; policies and procedures with respect to recognition of employee organizations; procedures for determining appropriate employee units; policies and practices regarding consultation with representatives of employee organizations, other organizations and individual employees; and policies with respect to the use of agency facilities by employee organizations. Insofar as may be practicable and appropriate, agencies shall consult with representatives of employee organizations in the formulation of these policies, rules and regulations.

Section 11. Each agency shall be responsible for determining in accordance with this order whether a unit is appropriate for purposes of exclusive recognition and, by an election or other appropriate means, whether an employee organization represents a majority of the employees in such a unit so as to be entitled to such recognition. Upon the request of any agency, or of any employee organization which is seeking exclusive recognition and which qualifies for or has been accorded formal recognition, the Secretary of Labor, subject to such necessary rules as he may prescribe, shall nominate from the National Panel of Arbitrators maintained by the Federal Mediation and Conciliation Service one or more qualified arbitrators who will be available for employment by the agency concerned for either or both of the following purposes, as may be required: (1) to investigate the facts and issue an advisory decision as to the appropriateness of a unit for purposes of exclusive recognition and as to related issues submitted for consideration; (2) to conduct or supervise an election or otherwise determine by such means as may be appropriate, and on an advisory basis, whether an employee organization represents the majority of the employees in a unit. Consonant with law, the Secretary of Labor shall render such assistance as may be appropriate in connection with advisory decisions or determinations under this section, but the necessary costs of such assistance shall be paid by the agency to which it relates. In the event questions as to the appropriateness of a unit or the majority status of an employee organization shall arise in the Department of Labor, the duties described in this section which would otherwise be the responsibility of the Secretary of Labor shall be performed by the Civil Service Commission.

Section 12. The Civil Service Commission shall establish and maintain a program to assist in carrying out the objectives of this order. The Commission shall develop a program for the guidance of agencies in employee-management relations in the Federal service; provide technical advice to the agencies on employee-management programs; assist in the development of programs for training agency personnel in the principles and procedures of consultation, negotiation and the settlement of disputes in the Federal service, and for the training of management officials in the discharge of their employee-management relations responsibilities in the public interest; provide for continuous study and review of the Federal employee-management relations program and, from time to time, make recommendations to the President for its improvement.

Section 13. (a) The Civil Service Commission and the Department of Labor shall jointly prepare (1) proposed standards of conduct for employee organizations and (2) a proposed code of fair labor practices in employee-management relations in the Federal service appropriate to assist in securing the uniform and effective implementation of the policies, rights and responsibilities described in this order.

(b) There is hereby established the President's Temporary Committee on the Implementation of the Federal Employee-Management Relations Program. The Committee shall consist of the Secretary of Labor, who shall be chairman of the Committee, the Secretary of Defense, the Postmaster General, and the Chairman of the Civil Service Commission. In addition to such other matters relating to the implementation of this order as may be referred to it by the President, the Committee shall advise the President with respect to any problems arising out of completion of agreements pursuant to sections 6 and 7, and shall receive the proposed standards of conduct for employee organizations and proposed code of fair labor practices in the Federal service, as described in this section, and report thereon to the President with such recommendations or amendments as it may deem appropriate. Consonant with law, the departments and agencies represented on the Committee shall, as may be necessary for the effectuation of this section, furnish assistance to the Committee in accordance with section 214 of the Act of May 3, 1945, 59 Stat. 134 (31 U.S.C. 691). Unless otherwise directed by the President, the Committee shall cease to exist 30 days after the date on which it submits its report to the President pursuant to this section.

Section 14. The head of each agency, in accordance with the provisions of this order and regulations prescribed by the Civil Service Commission, shall extend to all employees in the competitive civil service rights identical in adverse action cases to those provided preference eligibles under section 14 of the Veterans' Preference Act of 1944, as amended. Each employee in the competitive service shall have the right to appeal to the Civil Service Commission from an adverse decision of the administrative officer so acting, such appeal to be processed in an identical manner to that provided for appeals under section 14 of the Veterans' Preference Act. Any recommendation by the Civil Service Commission submitted to the head of an agency on the basis of an appeal by an employee in the competitive service shall be complied with by the head of the agency. This section shall become effective as to all adverse actions commenced by issuance of a notification of proposed action on or after July 1, 1962.

Section 15. Nothing in this order shall be construed to annul or modify, or to preclude the renewal or continuation of, any lawful agreement heretofore entered into between any agency and any representative of its employees. Nor shall this order preclude any agency from continuing to consult or deal with any representative of its employees or other organization prior to the time that the status and representation rights of such representative or organization are determined in conformity with this order.

Section 16. This order (except section 14) shall not apply to the Federal Bureau of Investigation, the Central Intelligence Agency, or any other agency, or to any office, bureau or entity within an agency, primarily performing intelligence, investigative, or security functions if the head of the agency determines that the provisions of this order cannot be applied in a manner consistent with national security requirements and considerations. When he deems it necessary in the national interest, and subject to such conditions as he may prescribe, the head of any agency may suspend any provision of this order (except section 14) with respect to any agency installation or activity which is located outside of the United States.

John F. Kennedy

The White House
January 17, 1962

Public Employment Relations Act

Act 336 of the Public Acts of 1947 as amended.

An act to prohibit strikes by certain public employees; to provide review from disciplinary action with respect thereto; to provide for the mediation of grievances and the holding of elections; to declare and protect the rights and privileges of public employees; and to prescribe means of enforcement and penalties for the violation of the provisions of this act.

The People of the State of Michigan enact:

17.455(1) STRIKE DEFINED.

Sec. 1. As used in this act the word "strike" shall mean the concerted failure to report for duty, the wilful absence from one's position, the stoppage of work, or the abstinence in whole or in part from the full, faithful and proper performance of the duties of employment, for the purpose of inducing, influencing or coercing a change in the conditions, or compensation, or the rights, privileges or obligations of employment. Nothing contained in this act shall be construed to limit, impair or affect the right of any public employee to the expression or communication of a view, grievance, complaint or opinion on any matter related to the conditions or compensation of public employment or their betterment, so long as the same is not designed to and does not interfere with the full, faithful and proper performance of the duties of employment.

17.455(2) STRIKES BY PUBLIC EMPLOYEES PROHIBITED.

Sec. 2. No person holding a position by appointment or employment in the government of the state of Michigan, or in the government of any 1 or more of the political subdivisions thereof, or in the public school service, or in any public or special district, or in the service of any authority, commission, or board, or in any other branch of the public service, hereinafter called a "public employee," shall strike.

17.455(3)   AUTHORIZING STRIKE, ETC., UNLAWFUL.

Sec. 3.   No person exercising any authority, supervision or direction over any public employee shall have the power to authorize, approve or consent to a strike by public employees, and such person shall not authorize, approve or consent to such strike, nor shall any such person discharge or cause any public employee to be discharged or separated from his or her employment because of participation in the submission of a grievance in accordance with the provisions of section 7.

17.455(4)   APPOINTMENT, ETC., TERMINATED.

Sec. 4.   (Repealed by Public Acts 1965 No. 379).

17.455(4a)   STATE EMPLOYEES.

Sec. 4a.   The provisions of this act as to state employees within the jurisdiction of the civil service commission shall be deemed to apply in so far as the power exists in the legislature to control employment by the state or the emoluments thereof.

17.455(5)   REAPPOINTMENT, ETC., CONDITIONS.

Sec. 5.   (Repealed by Public Acts 1965 No. 379).

17.455(6)   WHEN DEEMED ON STRIKE.

Sec. 6.   Notwithstanding the provisions of any other law, any person holding such a position who, by concerted action with others, and without the lawful approval of his superior, wilfully absents himself from his position, or abstains in whole or in part from the full, faithful and proper performance of his duties for the purpose of inducing, influencing or coercing a change in the conditions or compensation, or the rights, privileges or obligations of employment shall be deemed to be on strike but the person, upon request, shall be entitled to a determination as to whether he did violate the provisions of this act. The request shall be filed in writing, with the officer or body having power to remove or discipline such employee, within 10 days after regular compensation of such employee has ceased or other discipline has been imposed. In the event of such request the officer or body shall within 10 days commence a proceeding for the determination of whether the provisions of this act have been violated by the public employee, in accordance with the law and regulations appropriate to a proceeding to remove the public employee. The proceedings shall be undertaken without unnecessary delay. The decision of the proceeding shall be made within 10 days. If the employee involved is held to have violated this law and his employment terminated or other discipline imposed, he shall have the right of review to the circuit court having jurisdiction of the parties, within 30 days from such decision, for determination whether such decision is supported by competent, material and substantial evidence on the whole record.

17.455(7) MEDIATING GRIEVANCES.

Sec. 7. Upon the request of the collective bargaining representative defined in section 11, or if no representative has been designated or selected, upon the request of a majority of any given group of public employees evidenced by a petition signed by said majority and delivered to the labor mediation board, or upon request of any public employer of such employees, it shall be the duty of the labor mediation board to forthwith mediate the grievances set forth in said petition or notice, and for the purposes of mediating such grievances, the labor mediation board shall exercise the powers and authority conferred upon said board by sections 10 and 11 of Act No. 176 of the Public Acts of 1939.

[Sections 10 and 11 of Act No. 176 of the Public Acts of 1939 are Found Below:]

Sec. 10. After the board has received the above notice, or upon its own motion, in an existing, imminent or threatened labor dispute, the board may and, upon the direction of the governor, the board must take such steps as it may deem expedient to effect a voluntary, amicable and expeditious adjustment and settlement of the differences and issues between employer and employees which have precipitated or culminated in or threatened to precipitate or culminate in such labor dispute. To this end, it shall be the duty of the board:

   (a) To arrange for, hold, adjourn or reconvene a conference or conferences between the disputants and/or 1 or more of their representatives;

(b) To invite the disputants and/or their representatives to attend such conference and submit, either orally or in writing, the grievances of and differences between the disputants;

(c) To discuss such grievances and differences with the disputants or their representatives; and

(d) To assist in negotiating and drafting agreements for the adjustment or settlement of such grievances and differences and for the termination or avoidance, as the case may be, of the existing or threatened labor dispute.

In carrying out any of its work under this act, the board may designate 1 of its members or an officer of the board to act in its behalf and may delegate to such designee 1 or more of its duties hereunder and, for such purpose, such designee shall have all of the powers hereby conferred upon the board in connection with the discharge of the duty or duties so delegated.

Sec. 11. The board and each member thereof and each person designated thereby shall have power to hold public or private hearings at any place within the state, subpoena witnesses and compel their attendance, administer oaths, take testimony and receive evidence. Subpoenas may be issued only after the mediation of a dispute shall have been actually undertaken.

(a) In case of contumacy or refusal to obey a subpoena issued to any person, the circuit court of any county within the jurisdiction of which the inquiry is carried on, upon application by the board or commission, shall have jurisdiction to issue to such person an order requiring such person to appear before the board or commission, to produce evidence or to give testimony touching the matter in question. Failure to obey any such order may be punished by the court as a contempt thereof.

(b) Process and papers of the board or commission may be served either personally or by registered mail or by telegraph or by leaving a copy thereof at the principal office or place of business of the person to be served. Return by the individual serving the same setting forth the manner of such service, return post office receipt or telegraph receipt therefor, shall be proof of service of the same.[1]

17.455(8) MISDEMEANOR, PENALTY.

Sec. 8. (Repealed by Public Acts 1965 No. 379).

17.455(9) FORMING OR JOINING LABOR ORGANIZATIONS; COLLECTIVE BARGAINING.

Sec. 9. It shall be lawful for public employees to organize together or to form, join or assist in labor organizations, to engage in lawful concerted activities for the purpose of collective negotiation or bargaining or other mutual aid and protection, or to negotiate or bargain collectively with their public employers through representatives of their own free choice.

17.455(10) INTERFERENCE OR DISCRIMINATION BY EMPLOYER PROHIBITED.

Sec. 10.   It shall be unlawful for a public employer or an officer or agent of a public employer (a) to interfere with, restrain or coerce public employees in the exercise of their rights guaranteed in section 9; (b) to initiate, create, dominate, contribute to or interfere with the formation or administration of any labor organization: Provided, That a public employer shall not be prohibited from permitting employees to confer with it during working hours without loss of time or pay; (c) to discriminate in regard to hire, terms or other conditions of employment in order to encourage or discourage membership in a labor organization; (d) to discriminate against a public employee because he has given testimony or instituted proceedings under this act; or (e) to refuse to bargain collectively with the representatives of its public employees, subject to the provisions of section 11.

17.455(11) EXCLUSIVE BARGAINING REPRESENTATIVES; RIGHTS OF INDIVIDUAL EMPLOYEES.

Sec. 11.   Representatives designated or selected for purposes of collective bargaining by the majority of the public employees in a unit appropriate for such purposes, shall be the exclusive representatives of all the public employees in such unit for the purposes of collective bargaining in respect to rates of pay, wages, hours of employment or other conditions of employment, and shall be so recognized by the public employer: Provided, That any individual employee at any time may present grievances to his employer and have the grievances adjusted, without intervention of the bargaining representative, if the adjustment is not inconsistent with the terms of a collective bargaining contract or agreement then in effect, provided that the bargaining representative has been given oportunity to be present at such adjustment.

17.455(12) PETITION; INVESTIGATION; HEARING; ELECTION;
STIPULATION FOR CONSENT ELECTION; PROCEDURE.

Sec. 12. Whenever a petition shall have been filed, in accordance with such regulations as may be prescribed by the board:

(a) By a public employee or group of public employees, or an individual or labor organization acting in their behalf, alleging that 30% or more of the public employees within a unit claimed to be appropriate for such purpose wish to be represented for collective bargaining and that their public employer declines to recognize their representative as the representative defined in section 11, or assert that the individual or labor organization, which has been certified or is being currently recognized by their public employer as the bargaining representative, is no longer a representative as defined in section 11; or

(b) By a public employer or his representative alleging that 1 or more individuals or labor organizations have presented to him a claim to be recognized as the representative defined in section 11;

the board shall investigate the petition and, if it has reasonable cause to believe that a question of representation exists, shall provide an appropriate hearing after due notice. If the board finds upon the record of the hearing that such a question of representation exists, it shall direct an election by secret ballot and shall certify the results thereof. Nothing in this section shall be construed to prohibit the waiving of hearings by stipulation for the purpose of a consent election in conformity with the rules and regulations of the board.

17.455(13) BARGAINING UNIT;
STATUS OF FIRE FIGHTING PERSONNEL.

Sec. 13. The board shall decide in each case, in order to insure public employees the full benefit of their right to self-organization, to collective bargaining and otherwise to effectuate the policies of this act, the unit appropriate for the purposes of collective bargaining as provided in section 9e of Act No. 176 of the Public Acts of 1939: Provided That in any fire department, or any department in whole or part engaged in, or having the responsibility of, fire fighting, no person subordinate to a

fire commission, fire commissioner, safety director, or other similar administrative agency or administrator, shall be deemed to
be a supervisor.

[Section 9e of Act No. 176 of the Public Acts of 1939 is Found
Below:]

Sec. 9e. The board, after consultation with the parties, shall determine
such a bargaining unit as will best secure to the employees their right
of collective bargaining. The unit shall be either the employees of 1
employer employed in 1 plant or business enterprise within this state,
not holding executive or supervisory positions, or a craft unit, or a
plant unit, or a subdivision of any of the foregoing units: Provided,
however, That if the group of employees involved in the dispute has
been recognized by the employer or identified by certification, contract or past practice, as a unit for collective bargaining, the board
shall adopt such unit.[2]

17.455(14)   ELECTIONS; TIME FOR HOLDING;
   DETERMINING ELIGIBILITY; RUNOFF;
   EFFECT OF COLLECTIVE BARGAINING AGREEMENT;
   CONTRACT BAR.

Sec. 14. An election shall not be directed in any bargaining
unit or any subdivision within which, in the preceding 12-month
period, a valid election has been held. The board shall determine who is eligible to vote in the election and shall establish
rules governing the election. In an election involving more than
2 choices, where none of the choices on the ballot receives a
majority vote, a runoff election shall be conducted between the
2 choices receiving the 2 largest numbers of valid votes cast in
the election. No election shall be directed in any bargaining unit
or subdivision thereof where there is in force and effect a valid
collective bargaining agreement which was not prematurely extended and which is of fixed duration: Provided, however, no
collective bargaining agreement shall bar an election upon the
petition of persons not parties thereto where more than 3 years
have elapsed since the agreement's execution or last timely renewal, whichever was later.

17.455(15)   COLLECTIVE BARGAINING DUTY OF EMPLOYER;
   WHAT CONSTITUTES BARGAINING.

Sec. 15. A public employer shall bargain collectively with the
representatives of its employees as defined in section 11 and is

authorized to make and enter into collective bargaining agreements with such representatives. For the purposes of this section, to bargain collectively is the performance of the mutual obligation of the employer and the representative of the employees to meet at reasonable times and confer in good faith with respect to wages, hours, and other terms and conditions of employment, or the negotiation of an agreement, or any question arising thereunder, and the execution of a written contract, ordinance or resolution incorporating any agreement reached if requested by either party, but such obligation does not compel either party to agree to a proposal or require the making of a concession.

17.455(16) UNFAIR LABOR PRACTICES; REMEDIES AND PROCEDURE.

Sec. 16. Violations of the provisions of section 10 shall be deemed to be unfair labor practices remediable by the labor mediation board in the following manner:

(a) Whenever it is charged that any person has engaged in or is engaging in any such unfair labor practice, the board, or any agent designated by the board for such purposes, may issue and cause to be served upon the person a complaint stating the charges in that respect, and containing a notice of hearing before the board or a member thereof, or before a designated agent, at a place therein fixed, not less than 5 days after the serving of the complaint. No complaint shall issue based upon any unfair labor practice occurring more than 6 months prior to the filing of the charge with the board and the service of a copy thereof upon the person against whom the charge is made, unless the person aggrieved thereby was prevented from filing the charge by reason of service in the armed forces, in which event the 6-month period shall be computed from the day of his discharge. Any complaint may be amended by the member or agent conducting the hearing or the board, at any time prior to the issuance of an order based thereon. The person upon whom the complaint is served may file an answer to the original or amended complaint and appear in person or otherwise and give testimony at the place and time fixed in the complaint. In the discretion of the member or agent conducting the hearing or the board, any other member may be allowed to intervene in the proceeding and to present testimony. Any proceeding shall be conducted in accordance with the provisions of section 5 of Act No. 197 of the Public Acts of 1952, as amended, being section 24.105 of the Compiled Laws of 1948.

(b) The testimony taken by the member, agent or the board shall be reduced to writing and filed with the board. Thereafter the board upon notice may take further testimony or hear argument. If upon the preponderance of the testimony taken the board is of the opinion that any person named in the complaint has engaged in or is engaging in the unfair labor practice, then it shall state its findings of fact and shall issue and cause to be served on the person an order requiring him to cease and desist from the unfair labor practice, and to take such affirmative action including reinstatement of employees with or without back pay, as will effectuate the policies of this act. The order may further require the person to make reports from time to time showing the extent to which he has complied with the order. If upon the preponderance of the testimony taken the board is not of the opinion that the person named in the complaint has engaged in or is engaging in the unfair labor practice, then the board shall state its findings of fact and shall issue an order dismissing the complaint. No order of the board shall require the reinstatement of any individual as an employee who has been suspended or discharged, or the payment to him of any back pay, if the individual was suspended or discharged for cause. If the evidence is presented before a member of the board, or before examiners thereof, the member, or examiners shall issue and cause to be served on the parties to the proceeding a proposed report, together with a recommended order, which shall be filed with the board, and if no exceptions are filed within 20 days after service thereof upon the parties, or within such further period as the board may authorize, the recommended order shall become the order of the board and become effective as prescribed in the order.

(c) Until the record in a case has been filed in a court, the board at any time, upon reasonable notice and in such manner as it deems proper, may modify or set aside, in whole or in part, any finding or order made or issued by it.

(d) The board may petition the court of appeals for the enforcement of the order and for appropriate temporary relief or restraining order, and shall file in the court the record in the proceedings. Upon the filing of the petition, the court shall cause notice thereof to be served upon the person, and thereupon shall have jurisdiction of the proceeding and shall grant such temporary or permanent relief or restraining order as it deems just and proper, enforcing, modifying, enforcing as so modified, or setting aside in whole or in part the order of the board. No objection that has not been urged before the board, its member or agent, shall be considered by the court, unless the failure or neglect to urge the objection is excused because of extraordinary circumstances. The findings of the board with respect to questions of fact if supported by competent, material and substantial evidence on the record considered as a whole shall be conclusive. If either party applies to the court for leave to present additional evidence and shows to the satisfaction of the court that the additional evidence is material and that there were reasonable grounds for the failure to present it in the hearing before the board, its member or agent, the court may order the additional evidence to be taken before the board, its member or agent, and to be made a part of the record. The board may modify its findings as to the facts, or make new findings, by reason of additional evidence so taken and filed, and it shall file the modifying or new findings, which findings with respect to questions of fact if supported by competent, material and substantial evidence on the record considered as a whole shall be conclusive, and shall file its recommendations, if any, for the modification or setting aside of its original order. Upon the filing of the record with it the jurisdiction of the court shall be exclusive and its judgment and decree shall be final, except that the same shall be subject to review by the supreme court in accordance with the general court rules.

(e)   Any person aggrieved by a final order of the board granting or denying in whole or in part the relief sought may obtain a review of such order in the court of appeals by filing in the court a complaint praying that the order of the board be modified or set aside, with copy of the complaint filed on the board, and thereupon the aggrieved party shall file in the court the record in the proceeding, certified by the board. Upon the filing of the complaint, the court shall proceed in the same manner as in the case of an application by the board under subsection (d), and shall grant to the board such temporary relief or restraining order as it deems just and proper, enforcing, modifying, enforcing as so modified, or setting aside in whole or in part the order of the board. The findings of the board with respect to questions of fact if supported by competent, material and substantial evidence on the record considered as a whole shall be conclusive.

(f)   The commencement of proceedings under subsections (d) or (e) shall not, unless specifically ordered by the court, operate as a stay of the board's order.

(g)   Complaints filed under this act shall be heard expeditiously by the court to which presented, and for good cause shown shall take precedence over all other civil matters except earlier matters of the same character.

(h)   The board shall have power, upon issuance of a complaint as provided in subsection (a) charging that any person has engaged in or is engaging in an unfair labor practice, to petition any circuit court within any circuit where the unfair labor practice in question is alleged to have occurred or where such person resides or exercises or may exercise its governmental authority, for appropriate temporary relief or restraining order, in accordance with the general court rules, and the court shall have jurisdiction to grant to the board such temporary relief or restraining order as it deems just and proper.

(i)   For the purpose of all hearings and investigations, which in the opinion of the board are necessary and proper for the exercise of the powers vested in it under this section, the provisions of section 11 of Act No. 176 of the Public Acts of 1939, being section 423.11 of the Compiled Laws of 1948, shall be applicable, except that subpoenas may issue as provided in section 11 without regard to whether mediation shall have been undertaken.

(j)   The labor relations and mediation functions of this act shall be separately administered by the board.

NOTES

1. Sections 10 and 11, Michigan Labor Mediation Act, Act 336 of the Public Acts of 1947.

2. Section 9e, Michigan Labor Mediation Act, Act 336 of the Public Acts of 1947.

IV

THE STUDY COMMITTEE REPORTS

As a result of the turmoil, confusion, and uncertainty with regard to bargaining activities in
the public sector over the past four or five years
(1963–1968), there has been continuous assessment of collective bargaining relationships, administrative practices, and laws, as well as intensive study proposals recommending specific
legal and administrative guidelines. These study
reports and commission findings are direct descendants of similar activities that have been in
vogue in the private sector for some time, but
because they are being advanced at an early
stage in the development of the collective bargaining in the public sector, they are certain to
have a profound impact on the collective bargaining process and relationships between the
parties.

The four most important and well-publicized
reports are:

1. New York State Governor's Committee on
   Public Employee Relations, *Final Report,*
   March 31, 1966. This is a report by a study
   committee of distinguished labor relations experts that was given the task of assessing the
   failure of New York State's Condin-Wadlin
   Act and proposing the substance and justification for new, appropriate legislation.
2. Labor-Management Institute of the American

Arbitration Association, *Memorandum of Agreement,* New York City, March 31, 1966. This is a report of the American Arbitration Association's Labor-Management Institute Panel, which was given the task of assessing New York City's labor-management policies, as declared and practiced under Mayor Wagner's executive order, and of suggesting substantive changes in practice and policy.

3. *Report and Recommendations, Governor's Advisory Commission on Labor-Management Policy for Public Employees,* Urbana, Illinois, March, 1967. A study and report issued by a select governor's committee charged with the responsibility of developing a proposal for legislation in Illinois (where none existed). The recommendations of this committee were to be based not only on the limited experience to that time in Illinois, but, more importantly, on the experience in other states.

4. Advisory Committee on Public Employee Relations, *Report to Governor George Romney,* Lansing, Michigan, February 15, 1967. This report was also compiled by a governor's panel of labor relations experts that was charged with the task of assessing the impact of new "public employee" legislation in Michigan after the legislation had been in effect approximately one year. If necessary, the panel was also to propose amendments to the new legislation.

The New York City and Michigan reports are included in this section.

Report to Governor George Romney by the Advisory Committee on Public Employee Relations

Our assignment is specified in the Governor's "charge" of July 29, 1966 (Appendix A). It is to recommend any changes which we believe are needed in existing Michigan law or its administration in order "best to fulfill the 'basic objectives,' (a) of establishing a sound framework for public employee self-organization and collective bargaining (negotiation), and (b) of protecting the general public against interruptions or impairment of essential governmental services." Michigan's public policy, relevant to these "objectives," is now expressed primarily in the Michigan Public Employment Relations Act of 1965.

We made an Interim Report to the Governor on August 23, 1966, relating to the (then) prospective "Labor Day" public school situation (Appendix B). We have met with various interest groups, or their representatives, as well as other persons, and held a public hearing in Lansing on December 22, 1966 (see Appendix C). We have also conferred with a number of "neutral" persons who have been (or now are) engaged in making studies of unionism and collective bargaining in public employment.

We have encountered widely differing views on the questions with which we are concerned (summarized in Appendix D). Some think the Public Employment Relations Act is generally sound in approach and properly administered. Others contend that the Act is misconceived and that there is really no place for collective bargaining in public employment. Some do not question the propriety of an attempt to extend "rights of unionization" to public employees, but believe the "no-strike" policy embodied in the Act should be strengthened. Another view, however, is that the "right to strike" should be recognized except, perhaps, in the case of police and firefighters. Some persons accept the basic approach embodied in the Act but urge amendments dealing with specific substantive or procedural matters. Others believe that our experience to date under the Act has been too limited to provide a basis for definitive judgments concerning its merits but, on the whole, indicates that there are no serious problems. Those holding this view, as well as some other persons, suggest that any changes in the law be deferred.

Experience under the Act

The Act generated a prompt response by employee organizations. Those already established primarily to represent public employees increased their organizing activities. Certain other employee organizations vigorously turned their attention toward public employees. As a result, several hundred bargaining relationships have been created by formal State Labor Mediation Board (SLMB) certification or by voluntary recognition in public schools, institutions of higher education, municipalities, county agencies, road commissions, and miscellaneous other employing agencies. In addition there has been a formalization of many pre-existing situations in which units of public employees had previously engaged in bargaining with their employers.

In the vast majority of cases collective bargaining has resulted in the consummation of agreements without interruptions of public service. Some bargaining situations, however, have produced impasses, especially in the public school area, and there have been strikes, threats of strike, concerted refusals (by teachers) to tender employment contracts, and threats of mass resignations.

In late August, 1966, there was the possibility that a number of schools would not open as scheduled after Labor Day because of unsettled collective bargaining disputes. We brought this fact to the Governor's attention in our Interim Report of August 23, 1966. The Governor requested that certain school district and employee organization representatives meet with him in Lansing on September 1. The result of this meeting was a pledge of the parties involved, and the SLMB, to engage in immediate, accelerated, intensive mediation and fact finding. This pledge was met, and a number of settlements were reached over the Labor Day weekend, or shortly thereafter. Most of the "crisis" situations were resolved to the great credit of all concerned.

On the whole, as a matter of statistical generality, the initial period of experience under the Act has produced relatively few interruptions of public service. But there have been some. There have also been some problems in the disposition of "representation" issues under the Act, some delays in the resolution of these and "unfair labor practice" issues, and some difficulties of administration. A more detailed recital of the main areas of experience under the Act is summarized in Appendix E.

Summary of Committee's Views

Our views, more fully outlined later in this Report, may be summarized as follows:

(1) The basic premises and policy of the Michigan Public Employment Relations Act in granting "rights of unionization" to public employees seem to us to be sound and should be continued. These include the right to join unions or other types of organizations for purposes of collective bargaining free of employer restraint, the principle of exclusive representation, and the right to engage in collective bargaining with respect to terms and conditions of employment.

We believe, however, that there are important differences between employment in the private and public sectors which make appropriate a continuing appraisal of the procedures and substantive aspects of public sector collective bargaining. The objective should be to insure that the collective bargaining process in this area will be responsive to the distinctive environment in which it takes place. Students of collective bargaining as practiced in the private sector have noted its flexibility and adaptibility, and have urged even greater movement in this direction. We think that in the long run the prospect for successful collective bargaining in the public sector may well depend upon the ability and willingness of those concerned to be at least equally flexible and inventive in dealing constructively with those problems which are unique to governmental service.

(2) A major specific problem in the public sector is whether collective bargaining can be effective in the absence of the right to strike. Rephrased, the question is whether dispute settlement processes and procedures can be developed which will make the strike (or the threat of strike) an unnecessary element in the bargaining process. To say as some do that there cannot be effective collective bargaining without the right to strike is to suggest the conclusion either that such right should be recognized or that public policy does not provide for effective collective bargaining in the public sector.

Our view is that we have not yet reached the point where this "ultimate issue" has to be or can realistically be decided. We think the emphasis, for the present, should be on the development of effective collective bargaining and dispute settlement procedures, short of compulsory arbitration, along with a continuance of the existing "no-strike" policy, subject to one exception. We urge adoption, experimentally, of a system of compulsory third-party binding dispute determination in the case of police and firefighters.

(3) We have considered the wide range of detailed substantive and procedural changes in the present Act which have been suggested. We have also considered the argument that any changes at this time would be premature. We believe some statutory changes are of sufficient immediate importance to make early action urgent. In part, this view is predicated on our belief that strike threats are likely to increase during the ensuing year. The changes we think should now be made are outlined below. Our judgment concerning other possible changes

is not necessarily that they lack merit, but that consideration of them should be deferred pending more extensive experience under the law. (See Appendix F.)

(4) State employers and employees subject to the jurisdiction of the Michigan Civil Service Commission, and the state universities, are, or may be, constitutionally exempt from coverage under the Public Employment Relations Act. We do not advocate any change in constitutional status of these agencies, and we express no opinion on the question whether the universities may constitutionally be subjected to the Act, an issue now in litigation. It is our belief, however, that every constitutionally exempt state agency should nevertheless, on its own motion and as a matter of its own internal "legislation," adopt and apply, with respect to its employees, the basic principles concerning rights of unionization embodied in the Act (without, however, necessarily deciding to have recourse to the SLMB procedures for resolving disputes concerning representation and other matters). We think that neither the Civil Service System employers (or Commission) nor the universities are sufficiently distinguishable from other public employers in terms of their relationships with their employees, or otherwise, to justify a refusal by any of them to accept and apply the policies adopted by the legislature with respect to public employers generally.

(5) The legislature and the Governor should give sympathetic consideration to budgetary requests made by the SLMB in view of the additional heavy work load imposed upon the Board by the Michigan Public Employment Relations Act.

(6) We think, finally, that the matter of public employee unionism, and the operation of the Act, should be made the subject of continuing examination by a commission of "public" members, with suitable budgetary support. This commission should be established by statute with appointment by the Governor.

In the remainder of this Report we indicate more specifically those changes in the law which we believe should be made at this time, without, however, attempting to reduce our suggestions to detailed, statutory language.

Dispute Settlement Procedures

We think the primary objectives of the law should be to maximize the opportunities for equitable settlement of employee relations disputes in the public sector while rejecting, at this juncture, both resort to the strike and (except in the case of police and firefighters) compulsory third party determination of unresolved new contract issues. We believe the SLMB has functioned admirably, on the whole, with skillful leadership and staff work, in dealing with the massive problems introduced by the Act. However, the Board has been handicapped by lack of adequate resources. We therefore recommend that the legislature and the Governor give sympathetic consideration to any request the Board may make for increased budgetary support.

There should be a revision of the provisions of the Act relating to dispute settlement procedures (mediation, fact finding, etc.). Use of the statutory procedures should be mandatory upon the parties if they fail to establish their own procedures for resolving new contract disputes without interruptions of public service. There should be no ambiguity concerning what the statutory procedures are or concerning the authority of the SLMB. To implement these principles, we suggest that the statute should be amended as follows:

(1) It should be provided that all specified procedures for the settlement of disputes concerning new contracts, or modifications of contracts (notification, collective bargaining, mediation, fact finding) should be instituted and concluded, insofar as practicable, at appropriate times in the context of the operations of the particular public employer. Since budget-making and other pertinent operational facts vary from agency to agency, it seems unwise to attempt to spell out in the statute a specific, universal schedule of procedures. Instead, the SLMB should be authorized and directed to promulgate, by rule after hearing, the time limits within which the applicable statutory procedures shall be instituted and completed, by categories of public employers. This may mean that some public employers and employee organizations who have short term collective bargaining agreements will be required to begin negotiations on their next contract at an early point during the term of the existing contract. But we think this may well be a salutary development of the collective bargaining process in the public sector.

(2) The statutory dispute settlement procedures should be specified as (a) appropriate advance notice to the other party and to the SLMB, (b) collective bargaining, (c) mediation by or under the auspices of the SLMB, and (d) fact finding and non-binding recommendations, except that with respect to police and firefighters, recommendations shall be binding.

(3) Statutory mediation and fact finding should be redesigned. The

SLMB should be expressly authorized to institute the processes of mediation and fact finding at any time, but in any event at such times as will enable the statutory procedures to take place during the period within which all statutory procedures are required to be completed.

The "fact finding" function (which should include the making of recommendations) should be carried out through the instrumentality of a Public Employment Relations Panel, the members of which should be appointed by the Governor to serve for terms of two years. There should be twelve members of the Panel, one of whom should be designated as Chairman. The members of the Panel should be persons of recognized stature, competence, and fairness. The Governor should be authorized to enlarge the membership of the Panel, ad hoc, to the extent necessary. The Panel, for its initial two years of operation, should be attached to the executive offices of the Governor. Members of the Panel should serve as needed and be reimbursed for their expenses and compensated on a per diem basis. An Executive Secretary should be provided to assist in coordinating the operations of the Panel.

Upon the certification of the SLMB of an unsettled dispute to the Panel, the Chairman (or, in his absence, a Vice-Chairman designated by him) should assign the matter to one or more members of the Panel to carry out the functions of the Panel. In every such case the Panel member or members so designated (hereinafter called "the Case Panel") should be authorized to conduct hearings upon notice to the parties, to attempt mediation, to make private and tentative recommendations to the parties, and should be required, if the dispute remains unsettled within some stipulated time thereafter, to make formal public recommendations.

It should be provided that each party shall notify the Case Panel, within a stipulated period after public recommendations have been made, whether or not the party accepts the recommendation made concerning each issue in dispute, and, if not, the basis for its objection. It should further be provided that, if, after a period to be specified in the recommendations, the dispute remains unsettled, the Case Panel should conduct a summary "show cause" public hearing for the purpose of inquiring why agreement has not been reached; and that, if the dispute remains unsettled thereafter for a stipulated period of time, the Case Panel should report to the Governor all the relevant facts with an assessment of responsibility for the failure to reach agreement.

Several reasons support the establishment of the suggested Panel procedure, as distinguished from retaining the fact-finding function in the SLMB or its designees, or providing for the appointment of fact finders on a case-by-case basis by the Governor. The designation of a Panel by the Governor would enhance the prestige and increase the effectiveness of the fact finders. Advance designation of the members of the Panel, to serve for a stipulated period of time, would accomplish the desirable objective of reducing involvement and pressures upon the Governor in particular disputes. Moreover, it could reasonably be expected that establishment of the Panel would help assure the availability of competent persons to serve the fact-finding function, build up a body of experience which would be useful in view of the comparatively uncommon aspects of public employee relations, and tend toward some consistency of approach.

(4) In the case of police and firefighters all the procedures specified in (3) above should be applicable, except that the Case Panel's recommendations, with such modifications as it deems desirable after the "show cause" hearing, should be made binding. This procedure is suggested as one to be undertaken, as a matter of public policy, on an experimental basis, for a three-year period. We believe it would be in the public interest to experiment with compulsory determination in this limited area in order the better, ultimately, to be able to assess its virtues and deficiencies as a method of dispute settlement in the public sector. (We assume that a determination of any issue by the Case Panel would be subject to judicial review of any claim that the determination would require action to be taken by the employer which, by virtue of some legal restriction, it is unable to take.)

The "Strike" Issue

The question has been raised whether the basic "no-strike" policy expressed in the present law should be revised so as to recognize the right to strike either generally (i.e., without any specific prohibition) or at least in non-critical situations. On this issue there appear to be (or to be developing) highly polarized positions between public employers and most organizations representing public employees. The former insist that the "no-strike" prohibition represents sound public policy, and that it must be applied uniformly and be supported by adequate sanctions. The organizations, for the most part, disagree, although we find a general consensus among them that police officers and firemen should not strike. "Neutral" opinion is divided, although predominantly, so far as our inquiries indicate, accepting the view that for a variety of reasons the strike is inappropriate in public employment. However, there appears to be wide disagreement on the kinds of sanctions which should or can, with effectiveness, be used.

We think the ultimate disposition of the strike issue is far from clear. Experience in the United States and in other countries over the next several years will clarify the underlying considerations and increase the experience necessary for sound evaluation.

We think, however, that existing Michigan policy with respect to the strike issue—which is reflective of state and federal policy generally—should be continued, at least pending further experience. Consistently therewith, certain changes should be made in the law which, on the one hand, will fairly and appropriately implement that policy, and, on the other hand, will clarify it in the important matter of the distinction between group or concerted action and individual employee action.

The legislature, in enacting the amendments of 1965, continued to make strikes by public employees illegal. Controversy exists as to whether it intended to restrict available sanctions to discipline or discharge action taken by the employer. We think in any event that there should, in addition, be available in appropriate circumstances the remedy of the injunction. We reject, however, the views, variously expressed, that criminal penalties should be applied; that strikers should automatically forfeit all job rights and be denied the opportunity for re-employment; that injunctions should always be sought and, whenever sought, should always be issued, regardless of circumstances, upon a finding that a strike has occurred or is threatened; that an injunction, once issued, should be supported by a fixed scale of fines for violation of the court's order, which may not be "forgiven"; and that other sanctions, such as loss of representation rights, should be used. In our opinion these provisions could be unduly punitive, or impractical, or damaging to the collective bargaining process.

We think that, where strikes are undertaken *before* the required statutory bargaining and other dispute settlement procedures are fully exhausted (and, in the case of police and firefighters, at any time), injunctive relief should be mandatory when requested. In all other cases, the courts should be authorized to exercise their traditional right to make the injunctive remedy available if warranted in terms of the total equities in the particular case (including, of course, as a primary consideration, the impact of a strike on the public) and should retain their traditional right to adapt sanctions imposed for violation of injunctions to the particular situation.

The court, under this approach, would be expected to inquire into all the circumstances pertinent in the case, including any claim made by the defendants that the employer has failed to meet some statutory obligation. This approach assumes that not all strikes will be enjoined, or at least enjoined forthwith, but by the same token it seems to us to be inconceivable that a strike which involved serious damage to the public interest will not be enjoined. It has been argued that the circuit courts should be removed from responsibility in the area of injunctive relief since they are subject to varying "political" pressures and are too close to the scene of the dispute. To the contrary, we believe the very facts that courts are in the locale of the dispute, bear a direct and immediate responsibility for total law enforcement, and are part of the "political" process in the broadest sense, mean that the responsibility for administering the statutory no-strike policy should rest with them whenever this legal remedy is sought.

We propose then, specifically, with respect to the strike issue, that the statute be amended in the following manner:

(1) The definition of "strike" (Section 1 of the Act) should be changed in two respects. *First,* language therein which seems to make it illegal for an individual employee to withhold his services should be deleted. Individual employee action, where not part of concerted action, should be left to the normal employer-employee processes. *Second,* language should be added which will make it clear that the strike prohibition includes, in addition to concerted action by employees, action taken by a labor organization in calling, instigating, or assisting a strike, or failing to take appropriate action to end a strike.

(2) A provision should be added specifically authorizing the circuit courts to enjoin strikes in violation of the statute in a suit brought by the public employer (in addition to continuing the jurisdiction of the courts in suits instituted by the SLMB). The granting of injunctive relief should be made *mandatory,* upon determination that a strike has occurred or is threatened, where it occurs or is threatened before

all applicable statutory procedures for resolving the issues in dispute have been completed (including both "representation" and "dispute settlement" procedures), and, in any event, in the case of police and firefighters. The granting of injunctive relief in *other* contexts (e.g., where statutory procedures have been exhausted) should be stated to be available in accordance with traditional "equity" principles. The courts should be expressly authorized to take into account any claim made by the defendants that the public employer is in violation of some obligation imposed by the Public Employment Relations Act; to investigate such claim to the extent the court deems this to be desirable; and to condition the issuance of an injunction on evidence of compliance with the law by the public employer or to issue a cross-decree against the employer directing compliance.

Other Substantive Changes or Clarifications in the Law

Among the various proposals which have been made for other kinds of substantive changes in or clarifications of the existing law, we think some are of sufficient importance to justify immediate attention. Accordingly, we recommend the following changes:

(1) Public employers and unions should be expressly authorized to include in their collective bargaining agreements "union security" provisions of any type authorized, in the case of private employers, by the National Labor Relations Act, including "agency shop" provisions, subject to the condition that membership in the union should be open to every employee in the bargaining unit on a non-discriminatory basis.

We believe there is no substantial basis for differentiating between private and public employers in the application of this policy. The kind of union security provision permissible would not include the "closed shop" or the traditional "union shop" under which full union membership, with all attendant obligations, may be compelled as a condition of employment. In substance, the only permissible kind of union security provision would be one which conditions employment on payment or tender to the union of an amount equivalent to union dues.

(2) Public employers and unions should be expressly authorized to agree to settle by arbitration any dispute as to the terms of a new contract or concerning the interpretation or application of an existing contract.

(3) There should be added provisions imposing certain obligations

upon public employees and unions, in addition to the obligation to refrain from strike action. These should include the kinds of conduct specified in Sections 9f, 17, and 17a of the Michigan Labor Mediation Act. In addition, the refusal of a union to bargain in good faith should be an unfair labor practice. Under the Labor Mediation Act this is an obligation imposed upon private employee unions, but it is not an unfair labor practice. (At some point *both* statutes should be given a general overhauling to eliminate unjustifiable inconsistencies and ambiguities, and to restructure enforcement and other provisions.)

(4) The "collective bargaining duty" (Section 15) should be revised to include the obligation to comply with the dispute settlement procedures stipulated by statute and by implementing SLMB rule and to include a requirement that the parties shall be obligated to include, as a mandatory subject of bargaining, procedures for settling "grievance" disputes (i.e., disputes concerning the interpretation or application of an existing collective bargaining agreement). Further, it should be stated to be public policy to encourage the parties to agree upon arbitration as the method to be used in settling unresolved grievances.

(5) In the "representation" area the following changes should be made:

(i) A provision should be added which would make a collective bargaining agreement of reasonable duration, entered into between a public employer and a union which, at the time, represents a majority of employees, mutually agreed by the parties to constitute an appropriate unit, a "bar" against a challenge to the representative status of the union for the duration of the agreement, unless such challenge is made either during the course of negotiations leading to the agreement or within 30 days thereafter. The purpose of this provision would be to introduce a desirable element of stability into a collective bargaining relationship which has developed in a proper manner. The statute should further provide that the SLMB may, by rule or on a case by case basis, promulgate additional "contract bar" regulations.

(ii) A provision should be added dealing specifically with the status of supervisory employees. The general principle should be that supervisory employees should have the "rights of unionization" given nonsupervisory employees, except that they should be barred from being represented by a labor organization which represents, or is affiliated with any organization which represents, or might lawfully at any time seek to represent, non-supervisory employees of the employer. Because of the variance among kinds of public employers, and their supervisory structuring, the statute should not include a definition of "supervisory employee," but should empower the SLMB to promulgate, by rule, after notice and hearing, or on a case-by-case basis, such definition or definitions as it may deem appropriate.

This Public Employment Relations Act (Section 13) must by its terms be read together with Section 9e of the Labor Mediation Act, and hence seems to require supervisory employees to be excluded from any bargaining unit of non-supervisory employees. The LMA excludes supervisors from its definition of "employee" [Section 2(e)], with the result that in the private sector supervisory employees of employers subject to the LMA do not have "rights of unionization." This, likewise, is the policy of the federal law under the National Labor Relations Act. But under the PERA supervisory employees appear to have "rights of unionization." We think this policy is sound, even though inconsistent with the policy applicable in the private sector, provided only that supervisory employees, if they elect to exercise such rights, do so through an organization entirely independent of any organization representing non-supervisory employees. In our judgment, this qualification is appropriate in order to insure that supervisors will continue to exercise their responsibilities as representatives of "management" in dealing with non-supervisory employees.

(iii) A provision should be added prohibiting the representation of police officers (including combined firemen and police officers) by any labor organization which represents or is affiliated with any labor organization which represents or might lawfully at any time seek to represent, public employees other than policemen (or combined policemen and firemen). This kind of mandatory separation of police officer organizations from organizations representing other types of public employees seems to us to be necessary, in the public interest, to insure that persons charged with law enforcement responsibility will not become involved in "conflict of interest" or divided loyalty situations.

(6) There should be a requirement that a copy of every public sector collective bargaining agreement be filed with the SLMB.

Civil Service Employees and Employers: State Universities

A question of substantial importance relates to those public employers and their employees who are (or who may be judicially determined to be) exempt from the application of the Public Employment Relations Act. It is reasonably clear that those employers and employees who are within the jurisdiction of the Michigan Civil Service Commission are in this category by virtue of the constitutional provision which establishes the Commission and defines its powers. Litigation is currently pending involving the claim that state universities and their employees are likewise not subject to the Act in view of the constitutional status of these universities. However, it should be noted that most universities have voluntarily complied with the Act, or have determined that, irrespective of the constitutional issue, they should accept and apply the principles and procedures of the Act, or have promulgated and applied the basic principles of the Act while joining in litigation of the constitutional issue.

We recognize that important considerations, involving far more than employee relations, have led to the granting of constitutional autonomy to the Civil Service Commission and to the universities. We do not advocate any change in this constitutional status. Nevertheless, we believe there is no valid policy reason for any constitutionally autonomous agency to refuse to accept the same principles of employee relations that are prescribed by law for all other public employers in the state.

At present, the Civil Service Commission permits the employees under its jurisdiction to join the labor organizations if they wish; an employee may be represented by a labor organization, if he chooses, in the processing of a grievance; and employee organizations may from time to time present their views to employing agencies and to the Commission. However, the principle of exclusive representation of a unit of employees is not recognized, and there is no collective bargaining (in the usual meaning of the term) over wages, hours, and conditions of employment. The Commission retains complete unilateral authority over the terms of employment, except that it delegates limited decision-making power to the employing agencies in some matters—with instructions to these agencies not to engage in collective bargaining on these matters.

The members of the Civil Service Commission and top staff express the view that certain essential principles, such as the merit system of employment, could not survive the advent of collective bargaining. While we respect the sincerity of this view, we cannot agree with it. For several years the Federal government has been operating under the terms of an Executive Order which adopts the principles of exclusive representation and collective bargaining for most federal employees, including those subject to the civil service system. Some states with civil service systems but without the constitutional autonomy that the Michigan Civil Service Commission enjoys have decided upon a policy similar to that of the Public Employment Relations Act for civil service as well as other employees. Some municipalities, such as Philadelphia, have had civil service and collective bargaining systems co-existing for many years. Experience may demonstrate a need for some adaptations and limitations of collective bargaining in this area, but we think the necessary adjustments can be made.

In our judgment the arguments against permitting exclusive representation and collective bargaining to employees under the jurisdiction of the Michigan Civil Service Commission and the universities have no greater validity than corresponding arguments at one time made with respect to other public employees. In the private sector parallel arguments were weighed and rejected many years ago when national and state labor policies were being shaped. Today in Michigan the overwhelming majority of all employees, public and private, are guaranteed the right to have a voice in determining their conditions of employment through collective bargaining, if they so desire. The denial of this right to a minority of public employees, in the absence of any circumstances sharply distinguishing their situation from that of the majority, is a course which we believe cannot be validly defended. In our judgment there are no "sharply distinguishing" circumstances.

Some of the concern about applying the policy of the Public Employment Relations Act to the universities grows out of a belief that a grant of collective bargaining rights to non-academic employees will almost certainly be followed by the unionization of the academic staff. This strikes us as a most unlikely prospect in institutions where the academic staff, in accordance with widely accepted traditions of the academic community, have substantial control of their working relationships. In such universities, the most crucial judgments concerning an academician—recruitment, retention, dismissal, the granting of tenure, promotion, curricular content, and academic freedom—are made primarily by his professional peers. The institutions of faculty government also give the academician a strong voice in a broad range of other decisions within the university. At the same time we recognize that, in institutions where these conditions do not exist and faculty participation in important decision-making is not effective, there may be a tendency for members of the academic staff to turn to "unionization."

We therefore believe that the Michigan Civil Service Commission, and any universities which have not already done so, should adopt policies in relation to their employees granting "rights of unionization," including the principles of exclusive recognition and collective bargaining, comparable to those required of employers who are subject to the Public Employment Relations Act. If the pending constitutional issue is resolved against the position taken by some of the universities, they will, of course, be required to comply with the Act. If they win on this issue, they will continue to have the authority (as, quite clearly, does the Civil Service Commission) to adopt whatever policies in the area of employee relations and unionism which they deem to be appropriate. We believe that these policies, irrespective of the constitutional status of the Civil Service Commission and the universities, should include the grant of "rights of unionization," including the principles of exclusive recognition and collective bargaining, comparable to those required of employers who are subject to the PERA. However, we think it would not be inconsistent with this principle for a constitutionally exempt agency or institution to establish its own procedures for the implementation of these rights independent of the SLMB. For example, questions of bargaining unit determination or of compliance with a good-faith bargaining directive could appropriately be resolved by use of private arbitration or by some other agency jointly established by the employer and an organization or organizations of employees.

Concluding Observations

In many respects our most important recommendation is for the establishment of a continuing Commission on Public Employee Relations. As we have previously indicated, we have received many suggestions for changes in the existing statutes, and we have independently thought of others. Except as any of these are covered by specific recommendations made in this Report, we believe judgment on them should be deferred pending the accumulation of further experience. A more fundamental point is that collective bargaining, like all human institutions, is imperfect, and both the policies and procedures of the Public Employment Relations Act should be subject to continuing analysis and examination with the objective of finding even better methods of providing for employee participation in the determination of their terms and conditions of employment within the framework of the American system of representative government.

We recommend that this Commission be established by statute with appointment by the Governor, and that its members should include persons who are experts on industrial relations, preferably with knowledge also of labor relations in the public sector. The Commission should be provided with sufficient funds to support staff studies and analyses of public employee relations in Michigan and elsewhere. The Commission should make reports and recommendations to the Governor and the Legislature.

Finally, we wish to express our appreciation to all who have cooperated in giving us valuable information and the benefit of their views. We also express our gratitude for the able assistance of our Staff Counsel, David G. Heilbrun.

> GABRIEL N. ALEXANDER
> EDWARD L. CUSHMAN
> RONALD W. HAUGHTON
> CHARLES C. KILLINGSWORTH
> RUSSELL A. SMITH, *Chairman*

February 15, 1967

APPENDIX A

July 29, 1966

Dear Mr.——:

In 1965, Michigan amended its statutes relating to public employees by adopting provisions granting those employees the right to join unions or other organizations for the purpose of collective negotiations free from interference or infringement by public employers. The amendment further requires public employers to engage in collective negotiations. This legislation, broadly applicable to all categories of public employees and public employers, except for any constitutional limitations, was an important, progressive step and placed Michigan among the states which recognized that public employees have legitimate mutual concerns and interests which entitle them to associate together for the purpose of negotiating with their employers on these matters. At the same time, our legislation reflected the policy generally accepted throughout the nation, by forbidding strikes by public employees.

There have, nevertheless, been strikes despite this prohibition and there are reports that other strikes may occur. Moreover, there have been claims that some public employers are not meeting their full obligations under this legislation and, on the other hand, that in some instances organizations representing public employees seek through negotiation to achieve improper encroachments upon the responsibilities of public employers.

There are also questions whether statutory provisions, and procedures thereunder, are adequate for dealing with these and related problems. These are matters of vital concern to the citizens of Michigan and, therefore to me, as Governor.

To assist me in fulfilling the responsibilities of my office, I am requesting that you serve on the Governor's Advisory Committee on Public Employee Relations and I charge you with the following responsibilities:

1. The Committee shall determine what changes, if any, are needed to the existing law, or the Constitution in order best to fulfill the basic objectives (a) of establishing a sound framework for public employee self-organization and collective bargaining (negotiation), and (b) of protecting the general public against interruptions or impairment of essential governmental services.

2. In connection therewith, the Committee shall familiarize itself with the experiences of public employers and employee organizations and individuals under existing law. The Committee is not charged with any responsibility for mediation or dispute settlement in any given situation. If, however, the Committee determines that new policies or procedures not requiring statutory changes are desirable, I hope that it will recommend them to me in an interim report or reports.

Your acceptance of responsibility on this Committee is of vital interest to the people of the State of Michigan. You may be sure that all of the governmental departments concerned with labor negotiations will be instructed to render the fullest cooperation to this Committee.

Sincerely,

GEORGE ROMNEY

APPENDIX B: STATE OF MICHIGAN GOVERNOR'S ADVISORY COMMITTEE ON PUBLIC EMPLOYEE RELATIONS

Interim Report to the Governor

1. CURRENT PUBLIC SCHOOL SITUATION

In your "charge" to us you directed that we familiarize ourselves with the current collective bargaining situation and make interim reports from time to time if we should consider it advisable to recommend procedures which might usefully be undertaken, without requiring statutory changes, to help resolve collective bargaining disputes in public employment. This initial report is made pursuant to this directive.

We have attempted, as our first step in gaining some knowledge concerning experience under existing law, to appraise the status of collective bargaining in the public school sector with respect to teacher groups. Our information, obtained from various sources including representatives of the parties, indicates approximately the following as to recognized or certified bargaining units:

Bargaining representative	Contracts signed	Unsettled
MEA affiliates	218	270
MFT affiliates	18	3 (including Detroit)

In view of the brief period in which the present law has been in effect, the complexity of the bargaining issues, and the inexperience of the parties with collective bargaining, it is a noteworthy accomplishment that so many agreements have been reached.

An exact appraisal of the current collective bargaining situation is made difficult by the fact, as we are informed, that neither MEA nor MFT has authority to direct or control the negotiations or actions of the local teacher groups. Similarly each school board is an autonomous body. Because of this local autonomy and the large number of bargaining units involved (in the case of the MEA groups) there is in some instances a lack of liaison between parent and local groups. These facts also make it difficult for any person or agency, including the State Labor Mediation Board, to keep fully and currently informed on the collective bargaining picture, statewide.

The State Labor Mediation Board nevertheless is diligently attempting to keep abreast of the situation and is undertaking, within the limits of its resources, to use mediation and fact-finding procedures to help resolve disputes. We are advised by the Chairman of the Board that there is no instance, currently, where the Board's help has been sought but has not been made available, or where the dispute appears to the Board to be critical and the Board has not intervened.

It is impossible to determine, from the information we have received, how many of the currently unsettled collective bargaining situations should be placed in the "critical" category, despite the best efforts of the Board, in the sense that there is a likely prospect that, for lack of a settlement, the involved teacher group will refuse to report for duty when the school is scheduled to open. Opinions among knowledgeable persons differ on this. We think on the whole that there is some basis for genuine optimism, but, on the other hand, that there may well be as many as 15 situations which could be "critical."

2. THE LEGALITY OF STRIKE ACTION

The observer may well note with some surprise the fact of strike action by public employee groups in the past, and the prospect of further strike action or of failure to report for duty in the future, despite the clear statement in Act 336 that "no person [holding his position as a public employee] shall strike" (Section 2). The general intent of the law seems clear. Yet the fact is that legal questions have been raised about the scope of the "no-strike" ban as it presently exists and with respect to the remedies available under the law if there is a prohibited strike. For example, it is claimed that the strike prohibition does not apply if the public employer is in violation of its duty to bargain in good faith. Moreover, a distinction is drawn between a refusal by teachers to *enter into* contracts at the beginning of the school year and a concerted refusal to work at some point after contracts have been signed. Finally, some public employee groups have been counselled that, as the law now stands, the only remedy provided for a violation of the no-strike provision is disciplinary action by the public employer, and, accordingly, that injunctive relief through court action is not available.

We have not attempted, up to this point, to make any judgment on the merits of these various claims. Moreover, they are issues that can only finally be resolved by the courts. It does seem to us to be perfectly clear, however, that the basic policy of the existing law is that public employees shall not strike. We think this point can and should be emphasized.

3. SUGGESTED PROCEDURES

The prospect that as many as 15 school districts may not be able to open on schedule because of unsettled collective bargaining disputes seems to us to be of sufficient public concern that certain procedures should be undertaken, beyond and apart from those now being employed. Accordingly, we recommend the following course of action:

1. The Chairman of the State Labor Mediation Board should be requested to submit to you on Monday, August 29, 1966, a list of all school districts in which there are unsettled collective bargaining disputes. His statement should indicate to the extent possible the status of each such dispute (the nature, generally, of the dispute, whether mediation or "fact-finding" are proceeding, and his best judgment concerning whether the dispute will be settled by Labor Day and, if unsettled, whether the involved teacher group will or will not report for duty on the date set for opening the school).

2. On Wednesday, August 31, you should request local public employer and employee organization representatives from *each* such school district involved in an unsettled dispute which presents the serious prospect of a non-opening of schools on schedule to attend, with representatives of their affiliated state bodies, a meeting with you in Lansing on September 1 for the purpose of providing concrete informa-

tion concerning the status of the dispute, including the question whether, if the dispute is not settled, the teacher group will refuse to report for duty on the scheduled day for school opening, and for the purpose of considering how to proceed toward settlements without interruption of school opening.

3. In all districts where there is substantial doubt that schools will open as scheduled, we suggest that you urge upon the parties on September 1 the following:

A. That each school board and the organization representing its teachers enter into a special interim agreement not later than Saturday, September 3, which will provide, in substance, as follows:

(1) The teachers and the school board shall enter into interim contracts of employment for a period of 60 days beginning September 6, 1966, under terms and conditions which prevailed at the close of the last school year except as otherwise agreed upon;

(2) These agreements, both between the school board and the organization and between the school board and individual teachers, shall be wholly without prejudice to the claims of right or obligation which might be advanced by any party as of the date of the interim agreements under applicable law;

(3) During such 60-day period teachers will perform their duties without interruption in consequence of any outstanding, unsettled collective bargaining issue;

(4) Any agreement reached by the parties during such 60-day period, or thereafter, relating to terms and conditions of employment shall be retroactive to September 6, 1966, as to any additional benefits agreed upon, except as otherwise agreed by the parties;

(5) The interim agreements shall not become effective, if prior to the date scheduled for the opening of schools in the particular school district, the parties shall have resolved all unsettled collective bargaining issues or shall have agreed upon a method for resolving such issues which does not involve a suspension or interruption of school operations.

B. That the 60-day period of such interim agreements be utilized as follows:

(1) Until September 21, intensive mediation efforts shall be conducted under the auspices of the SLMB;

(2) If any of these disputes remain unsettled on September 21, the Governor will immediately appoint a Special Commission for each such dispute to investigate the matters in dispute and to submit recommendations for settlement to the parties and to the Governor, such report to be submitted not later than October 21. Such Special Commission will operate in lieu of the fact-

finding or other procedures provided under existing laws for use in disputes in public employment.

Respectfully submitted,

GABRIEL N. ALEXANDER
EDWARD L. CUSHMAN
RONALD W. HAUGHTON
CHARLES C. KILLINGSWORTH
RUSSELL A. SMITH, *Chairman*

August 23, 1966

APPENDIX C

The Committee held meetings with representatives of certain organizations and with various persons. These included the following, substantially in the chronological order in which the meetings occurred.

Chairman, Members, and Staff, State Labor Mediation Board
Michigan Federation of Teachers
Michigan Association of School Boards
Michigan Education Association
American Federation of State, County and Municipal Employees (AFL-CIO)
Detroit Federation of Teachers
Michigan State Employees Association
Michigan Civil Service Commission
Michigan Road Commissions Association
Michigan State Association of Supervisors
Personnel Director, City of Ann Arbor
Detroit Building Trades Council
Michigan Federation of Teamsters
Michigan Municipal League
Director, Bureau of Labor Relations, City of Detroit
Michigan State AFL-CIO
Administration, the University of Michigan
Administration, Michigan Technological University
"Fact-Finders"
Practicing Attorneys

On December 22, 1966, the Committee held a Public Hearing in the Court of Appeals Courtroom, Prudden Building, Lansing. Thirty-six persons were in attendance and of this group 11 persons expressed their views.

APPENDIX D

Proposals by Public Employers

1. Keyed to Sections of the Act
    Section 1—Clarify by specifying that allegations or findings of public employer unfair labor practices shall not excuse strike action.
    Section 2—Revise language to emphasize that strikes are absolutely prohibited and illegal.
    Section 7—Specify that SLMB may mediate without request of any party.
2. General Substantive Matters
    (a) Include a statement of "management rights" appropriate to efficient public personnel administration and subordinate collective bargaining subject to these "rights."
    (b) Authorize union and/or agency shop agreements; per contra, prohibit them.
    (c) Continue exemption from Public Employee Relations Act of state employees.
    (d) Add union unfair labor practices prohibiting coercion, discrimination, and refusal to bargain collectively.
    (e) Create spectrum of judicial and administrative remedies against strikes including, individually or in combination, injunctions, strike damage recovery, fines levied on strikers and/or striking unions, union decertification, and discharge or discipline of strikers. (One municipal employer deemed strike prohibitions unrealistic in view of the public employer's ability to prepare itself for a strike. This position was coupled with opposition to compulsory arbitration.)
    (f) Encourage and implement judicial power to restrain

pseudo strikes involving mass resignation or illness.

(g) Further strengthen strike prohibition by expressing use of dispute settlement procedures in mandatory terms.

(h) Subordinate collective bargaining agreements to existing laws, ordinances, resolutions, rules, or regulations.

(i) Authorize use of binding arbitration for resolution of contract interpretation disputes.

(j) Do not provide for compulsory arbitration of collective bargaining (contract term) disputes.

(k) Develop criteria pertinent to public employment for determining appropriate units.

(l) Define "supervisors" and exclude them from units of nonsupervisory employees, or exclude them entirely from coverage under the Act.

(m) Allow professional employees self-determination elections.

(n) Regulate public employee unions in terms of qualifications of union leadership and structure, stability, and financial responsibility of the organization.

(o) Prohibit unions from establishing sanctions against public employers.

(p) Prohibit representation of police and public safety employees by unions with general public employee membership.

(q) Create statutory authority for "limited powers" of public employers to reach collective bargaining agreements on "contracting out" of function and compulsory arbitration.

3. General Procedural Matters

(a) Protect voluntarily-reached bargaining relationships from premature raiding by rival unions.

(b) Create physical and total functional separation of SLMB labor relations and mediation functions; or private sector and public sector functions.

(c) Require SLMB to issue multiple certifications when petitioning local union is affiliated regionally or nationally.

(d) Require notice to SLMB in contract renewal and modification situations.

(e) Prohibit SLMB from ordering the pre-election furnishing of employee names and addresses for union use.

(f) Prohibit SLMB from conducting mail ballot elections.

(g) Allow public employers to unilaterally raise negotiated salary levels to meet emergency personnel conditions.

Proposals by Labor Organizations Representing Public Employees

1. Keyed to Sections of the Act
   Section 2 —Repeal this section (except for police and firemen).
   Section 4a—Repeal this section.
   Section 6 —Repeal this section.
2. General Substantive Matters
   (a) Expressly allow public employee strikes except in cases of police and fire fighters.
   (b) Allow determination of bargaining units based on extent of organization.
   (c) Authorize union shop agreements.
   (d) Reject any proposal to restrict subjects for bargaining.
   (e) Define covered public employers to include state employees and University employees under provisions of amended Act.
   (f) Construe Public Employment Relations Act as inapplicable to state employees because of undesirable effect of industrial and trade union practices on merit civil service systems.
3. General Procedural Matters
   (a) Increase SLMB budget and facilities to achieve more expeditious case handling.
   (b) Create physical and total functional separation of SLMB labor relations and mediation functions.
   (c) Require SLMB to issue and revise case handling rules and regulations.
   (d) Create dispute settling procedure whereby issuance of "tentative" fact-finding report is followed by period of further bargaining.
4. Miscellaneous
   Recommend (by Governor's Advisory Committee) that any need for statutory changes cannot yet be discerned because of insufficient experience under the amended Act and, further, that the very creation of the Committee was premature.

Proposals by Other Individuals, Groups, or Interested Organizations

1. Keyed to Sections of the Act
   None
2. General Substantive Matters
   (a) Harmonize Tenure Act to provide that teachers may not claim exceptions from strike definition when failing to commence teaching duties with school opening.
   (b) Require participation of school boards in teacher bargaining.
   (c) Authorize use of binding arbitration for resolution of contract interpretation disputes.
   (d) Permit compulsory arbitration in collective bargaining (contract term) disputes.
   (e) Eliminate cross-referencing between private and public labor relations acts.
3. General Procedural Matters
   (a) Enlarge SLMB facilities and grant it investigating powers into the merit of charges filed.
   (b) Require bi-partisan membership in SLMB and lengthen terms of members.
   (c) Require notification of SLMB of contract re-openings and voluntary recognitions.
   (d) Make mandatory the seeking of court injunction by public officer.
   (e) Formulate fact-finding procedures allowing early, orderly determinations.
   (f) Specify that fact-finding function includes the authority to formulate and publicize recommendations.

APPENDIX E

Introduction

The Michigan legislature enacted the Public Employment Relations Act with the provision that it be given immediate effect upon approval by the Governor, which occurred July 23, 1965. This Act substantially amended and liberalized the "Hutchinson Act."

Enactment of PERA resulted in substantially increased organizational activity by unions seeking to represent public employees. By the summer of 1966 it was clear that the provisions of the new Act were being extensively utilized and there had been a series of highly publicized proceedings involving issues being adjudicated by the SLMB, several public employee strikes, and lawsuits arising out of public employee negotiations. The *en banc* decision of the Genesee County Circuit Judges on June 20, 1966, refusing to enjoin a threatened strike of school employees, dramatized the ramifications of the new Act. By this time the facilities of the SLMB were under heavy strain because of its drastically increased caseload without a counterpart increase in staff.

SLMB Activity

The Act created a whole new basis for the exercise of procedures before the SLMB in the areas of representation petitions, mediation requests, fact-finding procedures, and unfair labor practice cases. The rate of mediation cases filed for the first half of F/Y 1967 is nearly double that of all of F/Y 1966. Public employee representation cases filed were four times the number of all private cases in F/Y 1966. To a considerable extent this preponderance represented the "first rush" of filings under the new Act; however the first half of F/Y 1967 shows the number of representation petitions in public employee cases to be exceeding those involving private employers.

Similarly unfair labor practice cases in F/Y 1966 showed extensive use of the Act by parties involved in public employee collective bargaining. A total of 90 public employee-related charges were received by the Board during this reporting period (all these charges were by unions against public employers with one known exception in which the reverse was true) and this was three times the volume of cases of this type involving private employers. The ratio of filings is increasing even more for F/Y 1967 with the number of public employee-related unfair practice charges approaching four times the number involving private employers.

The early strain on SLMB facilities gave rise to a considerable backlog and an inability in some instances to handle representation and unfair labor practice cases expeditiously. This situation has improved somewhat, although it remains a serious problem.

Types of Employers Involved

The Act has no express restriction as to coverage other than a section specifying that it is applicable to the state civil service only to the extent that the legislature has power in the constitutionally separated area. Accordingly, all public schools, counties, cities, villages, townships, road commissions, and special purpose public entities are subject to the Act. There appears to be no doubt as to the applicability of the Act to junior colleges. However, a question exists as to universities subject to Education Article (VIII) of the 1963 Constitution, notwithstanding an Attorney General's opinion of November 23, 1965, holding that the universities are subject to the Act. Several such universities have nevertheless elected to adopt and apply the provisions of the Act regardless of whether or not they are mandatory. On the other hand, certain other universities, including The University of Michigan, have contested the Act's applicability and this issue is being litigated. In early 1966 petitions were filed in regard to several groups of state civil service employees and these were dismissed by SLMB on grounds that the Act is not applicable to the state civil service.

Types of Labor Organizations Involved

In the field of public education, the Act was immediately invoked in a vigorous organizational contest between the two organizations representing professional teaching personnel. Locals of the Michigan Education Association and of the Michigan Federation of Teachers, affiliated with National Education Association and American Federation of Teachers (AFL-CIO), respectively, commenced efforts to secure formal bargaining recognition, often in rivalry with each other. Two significant factors existed in this regard. One was that the Michigan Education Association was historically established by years of informal recognition by numerous school districts throughout the state and the second was that the Detroit Federation of Teachers (Michigan Federation of Teachers' Detroit affiliate) had in 1964 achieved formal status as representative of all teachers of the Detroit school system. The result of intensified efforts by these organizations is that of the total number of school districts in the state, approximately 488 Michigan Education Association "locals" and approximately 21 Michigan Federation of Teachers "locals" currently have bargaining representative status.

In teachers' bargaining the parties typically recognize the provisions of the Tenure Act as controlling in regard to notice of continuation and review of disciplinary action. A sampling of teacher contracts shows that many of them are comprehensive and contain novel provisions peculiar to the educational function (e.g., joint study committees, special leave-of-absence provisions, intricate delineations of teacher rights and school board rights, and specification of transfer and promotion procedures).

In general public employment, the most active union is American Federation of State, County and Municipal Employees, which has historically functioned in the field. AFSCME presently has about 300 bargaining relationships in the public employee field in Michigan, many of which were formalized under the Act's provisions. Among the other unions that are active are the Building Service Employees, Building Trades, Teamsters, Fire Fighters, and Police Associations.

Strikes

During the period following the Act there have been approximately 23 public employee strikes or concerted withholdings of service. Most of these have been in public education. Highly publicized strikes involving Lansing city employees and the Detroit Department of Public Works were of brief duration.

Court Decisions

Aside from pending cases in which various universities of the state are contesting the Act's jurisdiction, cases dealing with injunction requests in the face of actual or imminent strikes have been the principal judicial activity. Approximately six injunction requests have been presented to circuit judges; however, most of these were rendered moot by settlement between the parties while the issuance of an injunction was under consideration. Only in Oakland County did the Circuit Judge issue an unequivocal injunction against a public employee strike. This contrasted with the previously-noted Genesee County case in which the Court held that the use of the strike injunction is not authorized under the Act.

APPENDIX F

The following proposals (in addition to others listed in Appendix D) are among those matters which should be deferred at this time, and considered later, after more extensive experience.

Substantive Proposals

1. Constitutional amendments relative to state civil service and universities.
2. Repeal or amendment of the (teacher) Tenure Act.
3. Whether a prerequisite to execution of a public employee collective bargaining agreement should be the opportunity for all interested groups to appear and be heard (including other unions, taxpayers, consumers, adjacent public employers, etc.).
4. Whether fact-finding proceedings should be open and public and provide an opportunity for interested groups in addition to the immediate parties to appear and express views on the issues involved.
5. Statutory description of subjects appropriate for bargaining.
6. Statutory statement of "management rights," to be outside the area of bargaining.
7. More complete and specific statutory statement of criteria to be used for unit determinations.
8. "Self-determination" provisions for professional employees.
9. Any referendum on contract ratification should be held among all members of the bargaining unit whether or not they are members of the union which negotiated the contract.

Procedural Proposals

1. Creation of a separate agency for handling public employment cases.
2. Separation of SLMB into separate agencies, one for the han-

dling of mediation and another for representation and unfair labor practice handling.

3. Preliminary investigation of unfair labor practice charges and dismissal of non-meritorious ones prior to hearing.
4. Require promulgation of SLMB rules of practice and procedure.
5. Require deposit of all public employee agreements with SLMB.

APPENDIX G: SUPPLEMENT TO REPORT TO
GOVERNOR GEORGE ROMNEY

December 21, 1967

The Honorable George Romney
Governor
State of Michigan
Lansing, Michigan

Dear Governor Romney:

As requested in your letter of October 5, 1967, our Committee has met and reconsidered the matters covered in our report to you of February 15, 1967. You asked us to consider whether we "would make any further or different recommendations . . . in light of the experience we have had this fall." In connection with this assignment we have invited and received comments from representatives of various public employers and public employee organizations in the State.

It was our central thesis that acceptance of the principle of collective bargaining in the public sector without, however, according the right to strike, represents sound public policy at this juncture, although presenting some unique problems, and should be given a further opportunity to demonstrate its viability as a means of helping to determine wages and other conditions of employment. It was our view that the State acted wisely and progressively in adopting this policy by means of the Public Employment Relations Act of 1965 but that the statute should be amended in certain respects to correct serious deficiencies. We think experience during the last ten months supports these views. We believe the observations and the specific recommendations made in our February report remain sound, and should be implemented. Without intending to minimize the recommendations not further discussed herein we emphasize in this report certain matters which seem to us to be especially important in the light of recent experience.

1. *Continuance of serious collective bargaining problems*
You will recall that it was our judgment in February that serious difficulties lay ahead in bargaining between public employers and their employee representatives, and that the prospect was for increasing resort to strike action or withholdings of services. This proved to be an accurate forecast.

It is our present judgment that during the year ahead the difficulties will be even greater. This will be due in part to a generally anticipated acceleration in the rate of increase in living costs with resulting pressure for increases in wage and salary levels. Morever, public employees will be influenced in their wage demands by significant wage settlements in private industry and by the recent salary level determinations made by the Michigan Civil Service Commission. On the other hand, most public employers face severe revenue problems, and this will tend to induce strong resistance to wage adjustments of the magnitudes likely to be demanded. In this setting collective bargaining disputes will intensify and increase the importance of dispute settlement procedures.

2. *"Fact finding" procedures*
The underlying premise of our February recommendations concerning fact-finding was that the best hope for effectuating successful collective bargaining without strikes or lockouts lay in the development and acceptance of procedures which, while not imposing settlements on the parties, would maximize public pressure and thus provide a viable substitute for economic action. We recognized the need for resort to court action to stop strikes which do occur, but it was and remains our view that the primary emphasis of public policy with respect to public sector collective bargaining disputes should be one means for rendering strikes in public employment unnecessary, and unacceptable, even from the point of view of employees and their representatives.

"Fact finding" is instituted in many instances under the present law and procedures only on the eve of a crisis, and is more often intensified mediation rather than a process of orderly and rational consideration of facts bearing on the merits of disputed issues. In our judgment experience with this type of "fact finding" process has shown its inadequacies. We wish to repeat and emphasize the importance of our recommendations for restructuring fact finding procedures. We believe such procedures should be started and concluded before the eve of a crisis and in accordance with a time table appropriate to the facts relating to the particular public agency. We believe that the availability of an established roster of qualified fact finders would be better than ad hoc designations. We believe that our suggested "show cause" hearing, together with assessment of responsibility for lack of settlements, would help to maximize public pressure on the parties and thus would expedite settlements. We do not present our recommendations in this area as a panacea. But we believe that the number of crisis situations would be substantially reduced by the use of the procedures that we have recommended.

3. Injunctions against strikes

Experience since February has focused additional attention on the "strike issue." We note that a case is now pending before the Michigan Supreme Court which involves basic questions, both procedural and substantive, concerning the injunctive powers of the courts in public employee (and particularly teacher) strikes or withholdings of services. If the Court affirms judicial authority to enjoin such stoppages, we think the statute should nevertheless be amended to deal expressly with this matter in accordance with our recommendations in the interest of establishing proper guideposts for judicial action. If the Court holds there is no authority under existing law to enjoin such stoppages, the desirability of implementing our recommendations is even clearer, given a policy opposing the use of strike action (unless, of course, the decision should be placed on constitutional grounds which would make any attempt to legislate futile). The experience in the Holland litigation may, however, in any event, suggest the need for further consideration of legislative regulation of the use of the injunction, particularly with respect to procedural matters, such as the propriety of the use of *ex parte* injunctions.

4. *Commission on Public Employee Relations*

We wish again to emphasize the importance of our recommendation for the establishment of a continuing Commission on Public Employee Relations. We are even more firmly convinced than before that there are many policy questions of basic importance in this field that should be studied in depth, and that evolving experience in Michigan and elsewhere should be subjected to continuing analysis. For example, there should be a careful examination of the question whether there should be wholly separate administration of the private and public sector statutes.

Respectfully yours,
Advisory Committee on Public
Employee Relations

RUSSELL A. SMITH, *Chairman*
GABRIEL N. ALEXANDER
EDWARD L. CUSHMAN
RONALD W. HAUGHTON
CHARLES C. KILLINGSWORTH

RAS/al
cc: Lt. Gov. William G. Milliken

A Summary of Major Recommendations from a Report to the Honorable John V. Lindsay, Mayor of New York City, by the Labor-Management Institute of the American Arbitration Association, March 31, 1966

Introduction

The memorandum presented a bargaining time-table and provides, in advance, for mediation and, if necessary, fact-finding recommendations for a fair disposition of disputes. These procedures will permit consideration of disputes by impartial persons in an atmosphere free of strike deadline pressures.

One of the greatest merits of the document is that although it is the product of agreement between the City and the representatives of the employee organization it is to be embodied in a City law.

There are basically three reasons for New York City disorder in labor disputes:

1. An absence of carefully administered and supervised procedures for effectuation of the proclaimed policy of collective bargaining.
2. A lack of clear understanding on the matters appropriate for bargaining and of the limitations on the parties' power to conclude agreements.
3. An absence of definite procedures established in advance for dealing with deadlocks in bargaining.

The parties to this document agree:

1. Employees will be treated fairly.
2. The City will be able faithfully to discharge its obligations as employer, without interruption to the public services it furnishes.
3. The people of the City will be protected, as they have a legal and moral right to be, in their access to essential public services.

Right to Organize and Bargain

The City and certified employee organizations shall bargain and conclude final agreements on matters within the scope of collective bargaining on which the major or agency heads under his jurisdiction have authority to make final decisions, notwithstanding that such matters are governed by orders, rules, and regulations previously promulgated by the mayor or such agency heads.

The City and certified employee organizations shall bargain on matters within the scope of collective bargaining which require action by a body, agency, or official whose actions are either not subject to or are not fully subject to the mayor's jurisdiction or control, provided that the bargaining on such matters shall be directed to the question, whether or not to request such body, agency, or official to take such action.

A dispute panel may determine that such action should be taken and will make such a recommendation to the body, agency, or official.

The City shall continue to bargain with employee organizations representing career and salary plan employees, police, fire, sanitation, and correction workers.

The City may meet with any employee organization representing employees who are affected for the purpose of hearing their views and proposals on city-wide matters or pensions.

Collective Bargaining Procedures

Collective bargaining procedures shall be subject to the guidance of an agency that is independent of either party known as the (O.C.B.) Office of Collective Bargaining. It has the duty to make certain that each party complies with its obligations hereunder; to oversee adherence to the collective bargaining procedures set forth herein; to administer procedures for resolving deadlocked disputes; to perform the functions involved in the determination of bargaining units, the certification or decertification of bargaining agents and related matters; and to recommend changes or improvements in these procedures.

Twice a year the chairman and the board shall conduct meetings between representatives of the City responsible for labor relations and the Steering Committee of the M.L.C. for the purpose of discussing mutual problems and developing solutions for them.

The fees and expenses of mediators, arbitrators, or members of dispute panels and related expenses shall be borne equally by the parties to the particular dispute.

The Municipal Labor Committee (M.L.C.) shall consist of representatives of qualified organizations of city employees. The existing labor committee of the Tri-Partite Panel shall serve as a temporary steering committee of the M.L.C. and shall draft rules governing membership eligibility, organization, and voting procedures of the M.L.C. and the method of designating M.L.C. members on the board of the O.C.B.

A newly certified employee organization may present a bargaining notice for the terms of a collective bargaining agreement.

Dispute Settlement

The chairman of the O.C.B. may designate a mediator to assist the parties in an agreement if such action warrants it.

Upon request of a dispute panel by both parties or upon the recommendation of the chairman, the chairman shall designate and establish a dispute panel if a majority of the board feels that collective bargaining has been exhausted.

The dispute panel may mediate, hold hearings, call witnesses by invitation or subpoena, request or subpoena data, and take whatever action it considers necessary to settle the dispute.

Collective Bargaining Agreements

Bargaining agreements shall in all cases contain provisions for grievance procedures in steps terminating with impartial arbitration of unresolved grievances. Impartial arbitration shall be final and binding to the extent permitted by law.

An employee organization does not have the right to strike, slow down, conduct work stoppages or mass absenteeism during the term of a collective bargaining agreement, and a provision to that effect shall be inserted in each collective bargaining agreement.

If an employee organization fails to accept the recommendations of a dispute panel within 30 days after such recommendations have been made, the Mayor shall have the right, upon 90 days' notice to terminate the applicability to such employee organization of any or all of the impasse and impartial arbitration procedures set forth herein.

Right to Strike

The memorandum of agreement, by specific terms, bars the right to strike during the life of a contract, during negotiations for a new contract, during Dispute Panel proceedings, and for 30 days after recommendations are made by such a panel.

V

COLLECTIVE BARGAINING EXPERIENCE
IN THE PUBLIC SECTOR

The wide range of recent and past experience in public employment bargaining is just beginning to be reported. However, in an anthology of this size, only a selected cross section of some of the early reported results can be presented.

The three articles in this section must be considered only as preliminary observations of bargaining relationships that, with the possible exception of Eli Rock's Philadelphia report, have not yet matured. However, we suggest that they are reasonably representative of the early bargaining developments in three distinct public arenas: the federal government, a large municipality, and public education in a state. Wilson Hart has examined bargaining relations in a number of federal agencies and has found that acceptance of the intent of Executive Order 10988, equal partnership in the determination of employee-agency relations, has not occurred. Eli Rock adds a further dimension by detailing the Philadelphia experience—a successful bargaining relationship considerably more advanced than that existing in most municipalities but one that still remains subject to change and experimentation. Finally, Dr. Charles T. Schmidt, Jr., discusses a rather classic model of collective bargaining and suggests that the first year's experience in bargaining between teacher organizations and school boards in Michigan closely parallels this model.

§ *FEDERAL GOVERNMENT*

The Impasse in Labor Relations in the Federal Civil Service

WILSON R. HART

> This, then, seems the likely future course of collective bargaining if it is to preserve its meaningfulness: . . . that there will be a converging and coordination of public and private decision making in the whole area of labor relations. There will be, in short, more reliance in collective bargaining on the principles of government, *more use in government of the resources and procedures of collective bargaining,* and more coordination of the two processes. (Italics added.)
>
> W. WILLARD WIRTZ,
> *Labor and the Public Interest*

In January 1962, the President of the United States made it clear, even to those most reluctant to believe, that the government itself had decided to lead the way from old style collective bargaining to what Secretary of Labor W. Willard Wirtz has described as "constructive bargaining, or, perhaps even better, creative bargaining." [1] At the recommendation of the then Secretary of Labor, Arthur Goldberg, President Kennedy signed Executive Order 10988, the very title of which committed his administration to a program of "Employee-Management Coopera-

Reprinted from *Industrial and Labor Relations Review*, XIX (January 1966), 175–189, by permission of the publisher. Copyright © 1966 by Cornell University. All rights reserved.

Wilson R. Hart is with the United Nations Technical Assistance Board, Kathmandu, Nepal.

tion in the Federal Civil Service." [2] By proclaiming in the very first sentence of his order that participation of employees, through representatives of their own choosing (i.e., through their unions), in the formulation and implementation of decisions which affect them "contributes to the effective conduct of the public business," the President appeared to be giving his own warm and potent endorsement to voluntary unionization of the federal civil service. The administration, which under two uncommonly able and eloquent Secretaries of Labor had been striving vigorously for "industrial democracy" in private industry, seemed determined to practice what it preached in its dealings with its own work force of two and one-half million employees.

Executive Order 10988 was initially greeted with unrestrained applause by spokesmen for both government management and employees. Today, however, much of the bloom is off the rose. Those who praised the new program most effusively in 1962 are now damning it with faint praise or in some cases—notably on the union side—criticizing it severely. For example, a leading management spokesman, Civil Service Commission Chairman John W. Macy, Jr., who had served as Secretary Goldberg's deputy on the Task Force which drafted the Order, hailed the new program at the time of its launching as our "biggest step forward in 50 years," as a "monument to all incorrigible optimists," as a "demonstration that we have not lost our capacity to achieve timely and fundamental reform," and as the end of the line for the "papa-knows-best attitude in any level of management." [3] Two years later, however, in a report to President Johnson, Mr. Macy expressed his feelings in a strikingly different, less sanguine vein: "The task of setting up new relationships between Federal managers and employee organizations has not been easy. There have been difficulties and some complaints." [4]

Impasse between Labor and Commission Approaches

Management's disenchantment has been mild, however, compared with that of leaders of government employees. Although union complaints take many forms, they tend to boil down to a single world: "impasse." Addressing an AFL-CIO national convention, President George Meany charged that "Certain departments of the Government do not agree wholeheartedly with the President's intent in promulgating an Order to give Federal employees representation rights." The convention responded by passing a resolution calling for a revision of Executive Order 10988 "to authorize binding arbitration to resolve negotiation impasses." [5]

Use of the word "impasse" to describe the type of ineffectual bargaining which sometimes occurs in negotiations between agency representatives and the unions selected by employees as their exclusive representatives under the "Employee-Management Cooperation" program is, however, misleading. Because all federal employee unions have renounced the right to strike—nudged in some instances, perhaps, by a statute which makes it a criminal offense to assert the right to strike against the government[6]—management representatives at the bargaining table are subject to no compulsion to make concessions or compromises leading to meaningful agreements, comparable to the threat of a crippling strike, which hangs over the heads of their counterparts in industry in comparable circumstances. Moreover, in negotiations under Executive Order 10988, refusal to bargain in good faith is not an unfair labor practice for which a guilty party can be haled before the National Labor Relations Board or any comparable body empowered to issue effective "cease-and-desist" orders. Therefore, a large proportion of the so-called "impasses" which frustrate and outrage government-employee union leaders are not impasses at all, in the technical sense in which the word is ordinarily used in industrial and labor relations. They are, instead, refusals to bargain in good faith.

In a larger, less technical sense, however, there is an impasse which is the root cause of the apparent failure of Executive Order 10988 to achieve its noble objectives. It is not a "bargaining impasse," but an impasse between two conflicting basic approaches to employee-management relations in the Federal government. (Presumably the same conflict exists, with or without significant minor variations, in other public jurisdictions.) The first, which for purposes of convenience shall be called the "Commission approach," because a large proportion of its leading proponents are present or past officials of the Civil Service Commission, is the approach which prevailed in the government before 1962. The second, which shall be called the "Labor approach," because it derives much of its support from present and former officials of the Labor Department (conspicuously including those who helped Secretary Goldberg draft Executive Order 10988) and from labor union leaders, is the approach advocated in the report of Secretary Goldberg's Task Force[7] and in the Order itself.

Basic Philosophies Underlying the Two Approaches

The Labor approach is based upon the proposition that collective bargaining is a form of democracy; that as such it is inherently good; and that the management of even the best-run establishment, public or private, stands to profit from the cooperation of strong, independent, responsible employee organizations. This concept is succinctly articulated in Secretary Wirtz's statement: "Collective bargaining is industrial democracy. We have to make it work." [8]

The Commission approach is based upon the proposition that the art of public personnel management has been so refined and developed that there is neither need nor justification for strong unions in any public agency where this art is skillfully practiced by the personnel managers. Conversely, the only good purposes that unions are capable of serving, as former Commission Executive Director Warren B. Irons has said, are the negative functions of "calling attention to management mistakes" and "keeping management honest." [9] Civil Service Commission inspection reports frequently equate the absence of active unions with enlightened management. A recent report stated, for example, "The lack of employee organization suggests good relations between supervisors and employees." In contrast, management which encourages or even permits strong, active unions to develop is presumed to be weak and derelict.

The ultimate in employee-management cooperation under the Labor approach is found in an agency such as the Tennessee Valley Authority, where strong and active unions not only exist but are welcomed and encouraged. They are acknowledged as partners of management in every phase of decision making which affects employees and also collaborate in personnel operations.

According to Harry Case, former TVA personnel director, unions make "a vital contribution to job training, safety, employee education and many other fields which might have been reserved to management prerogatives." He attributes this collaboration, in which TVA management takes great pride, to "democratic administration" which assumes "that employees will react responsibly to an attitude of trust on the part of management." [10]

Under the Commission approach, the ideal federal agency is one in which personnel management is conducted so skillfully that nobody feels disposed to join and pay dues to a union, much less to give time and energy unsparingly to the demanding and thankless job of organizing and running one. The objective of the Commission approach was ably articulated by a defense official in the Eisenhower administration, who told his department's personnel directors,

Our job is to sharpen our personnel practices to such a razor's edge that we will kill the incentive for unionization. There is no need for unions if we apply the enlightened principles that unions advocate.

The Labor approach is based primarily upon a positive value judgment that unions generally have earned, and deserve to keep, a position of honorable equality with business management and the other main elements of the American political economy. Secondarily it is based upon the proposition that unions of government employees should, insofar as feasible, be accorded the same privileges enjoyed by unions subject to the Taft-Hartley Act, excluding only those privileges denied by law (e. g., the no-strike law) or by contervailing public policy (e. g., the merit system and equal employment opportunity policies).

The Commission approach, on the other hand, approximates the traditional attitude of doctrinaire management in both government and industry—it is management's job (or right) to manage; the "owners" of the enterprise, whether they be stockholders or taxpayers, will reap bigger dividends if management is given a free hand, unencumbered by any "outside interference." Specifically, management manages best in those establishments where employees wisely elect, or can be persuaded, to remain unorganized. Where the establishment in question is the government, this doctrine can be either modified to convey the idea that management can best serve the public interest if unhampered by employee organizations or expanded to hold that any union which impinges upon the government managers' freedom of action is damaging the public interest and thereby performing an antisocial or subversive function.

Until this larger impasse between the two contending philosophic approaches to governmental labor relations is resolved, there is little chance of mitigating the smaller "bargaining impasses" about which government unions chronically complain. It is, in effect, an "impasse upon impasses." The differences between the Labor and Commission approaches are much more intense and fundamental than those which normally characterize struggle-for-power in-fighting between proud, vigorous agencies competing for ascendancy in the bureaucratic jungle. To appreciate how deeply they run, let us compare the methods which the two approaches employ, the principles which each applies, the sources from which they draw support and guidance, and the contrasting positions which they take upon some of the controversial questions which have arisen in the implementation of Executive Order 10988.

Different Routes to Policy Decisions

The methods of the Labor approach are typified by the quasi-legislative techniques of Secretary Goldberg's Task Force and by the quasi-judicial techniques of the arbitration proceedings which have been conducted under Section 11 of the Order. The Task Force held hearings, similar to the hearings of congressional committees. They were open to the public and were recorded and reported *verbatim*. The witnesses were numerous and represented a cross section of public opinion. The transcripts of the hearings and the records of the Task Force were retained and made accessible to scholars and other interested citizens. After its fact gathering was completed, the Task Force published a report similar to that which a congressional committee makes after it has held hearings on a bill. The Task Force report was given widest possible distribution. Public reaction— mostly favorable—was given ample opportunity to make itself felt before the final "legislative act" (the Executive Order) was signed by the President. The arbitration hearings follow similarly free and open procedures. The arbitrator is a disinterested third person, jointly selected by the contending parties. All interested parties are offered ample opportunity to submit briefs, to review and rebut each other's arguments, and to appear jointly in open hearing to testify and cross-examine one another before the arbitrator. The arbitrator renders a written opinion which normally includes a comprehensive analysis of the issues, an explanation of his *ratio decidendi,* and such *dicta* as he considers pertinent.

The methods of the Commission approach adhere to the "doctrine of completed staff work" developed in the military and widely used in semiautocratic corporate bodies where decision making is centralized. Rule making is done by faceless technicians, *in camera.* Public hearings are not held. If any record of the deliberations preliminary to the rule making is kept, it is considered privileged and not made public. No explanation of the rationale of the rulemakers need be offered. As a matter of practice, the rulemaker may solicit "concurrences" from interested parties, including selected union officials, to bolster the record and to give him "life insurance" in the event his rule should prove unpopular with higher officials. Whom he asks to concur and what action he takes on non-concurrences are matters which lie within his discretion; they are not matters for public scrutiny or debate. The rule-making authority of the Commission derives from Section 12 of Executive Order 10988, which stipulates that the Commission shall "provide technical advice *to the agencies* on employee-management relations." (Italics added.)

Rules are formulated, therefore, in response to questions, real or hypothetical, *from agencies,* and published and distributed as official Commission directives to all agencies. Although they are customarily labelled as "guidance and advice," they tend to be transformed quickly into binding directives of universal application through the alchemy of the unwritten but widely respected "doctrine of uniformity." How this process works is revealed in the Commission's earliest "Guidelines," which unveiled the still-controversial "60 Percent Rule." (Under the rule, a representation election won by a union is automatically invalidated if those who vote number less than 60 percent of those eligible.) In its transmittal letter, the Commission asserted that the attached material, which included the 60 percent rule, was for "guidance to agencies"; that it merely constituted "the best advice the Commission can offer"; and asserted it to be the "clear intention of the new program that consultations and negotiations with employee groups be largely on a decentralized basis so that understandings reached will be adapted to the needs and interests of particular groups and employees and individual establishments." Yet the rule itself, as set forth in the attachment to this blandly reassuring letter, tolerated no such eclectic permissiveness. On the contrary, it ended with the blunt injunction, ". . . a consistent rule should be applied by all agency heads on this point." [11]

Many of the questions from agency management, moreover, are couched in such terms as "are we required . . . ?" or "may we refuse . . . ?" When the answers to such questions are "agencies *may* refuse . . . ," they likewise tend to become transformed by the "doctrine of uniformity" into rules of universal mandatory application which read instead "agencies *must* refuse. . . ."

Another effective method for implanting Commission doctrine upon the federal service has been the public expression of allegedly private opinions by prominent officials. Illustrative of this technique is a speech made by Civil Service Commission Executive Director Irons during which, in what he characterized as "a personal aside," he said that he considered it "incongruous" for any government employee in a "management" position to belong to an employee organization.[12] (His definition of "management" was broad enough to include a sizeable percentage of all government employees.) In response to vehement union demands that Irons' "personal aside" be repudiated, Commission Chairman Macy wrote a letter to union (NFFE) President Nathan Wolkomir in which, largely by means of a series of rhetorical questions, he supported Irons. Technically, the speech and the letter are nothing more than the expressions of personal opinions by two American citizens who happen to be employed by their government. Neither could be justly accused of presuming to "repeal" either an act of Congress (the Lloyd-LaFollette Act,[13] which guarantees the right of union membership, without qualification, to *all* employees) or a directive of the President (Executive Order

10988, which encourages federal employee organization). Yet the pregnant passages of both the speech and the letter were headlined in the Washington press and given wide circulation throughout the government. It must be presumed that the average government employee, not noted for his rugged independence or rebellious spirit, read them as though an authoritative voice of the administration was saying to him, "If you hold a management job, or if you want to get one, don't belong to a union."

The reference or source material drawn upon to interpret the order in instances where the Labor approach is used is markedly different from that preferred by the Commission partisans. The Labor people, whether they be government professionals or freelance arbitrators, rely primarily upon the body of federal labor law, including the National Labor Relations Act and the common law derived from court and NLRB decisions and arbitrators' opinions. This reliance upon labor law, based, as it is, upon wisdom gained from practical experience with labor relations in the private sector, is anathema to most Commission people. Washington attorney David Barr has written that most federal personnel administrators are totally unfamiliar with labor law and, therefore, "strongly suspect the motives of those who would impose upon them a set of principles which had been formulated without their participation." They feel, he adds, that "the intrusion of 'established' doctrine would necessarily lessen their scope of power." To complete the circle, they argue, according to Barr, that

the Federal service is distinctly different from the private sector. . . .
The "public service" concept offers the attractive implication that greater resistance to "outside" interference in the affairs of management is justified than in the private sector.[14]

The Commission experts draw upon two principal sources: (1) the speeches, writings, and unpublished experiences and opinions of those who have achieved positions of prominence in the field of public personnel administration; and (2) the esoteric knowledge of those who were allegedly privy to "inside" information concerning what the members of the Task Force actually intended by the various things which their report and the Order either said or left unsaid. *"Don't* publish or perish" is better advice in the civil service than the obverse maxim so highly cherished in the academic community. Consequently, there is little commercially published material, other than textbooks, available in the field of public personnel administration, and that which does exist tends to skirt gingerly controversial topics. This shortage is not a serious handicap, however, since authorities are never cited in civil service regulations. Instead, important canons of doctrine are commonly introduced by such naked phrases as "It may be viewed as undesirable to . . ." or "It is not good practice to . . . ," which might be branded as egregious pontification by legal scholars in other fields, but which are standard practice in civil service administrative law. For example, after acknowledging that the Order neither authorizes nor prohibits the exclusive recognition of a single union on an agencywide basis, the Commission regulations neatly overcome that omission by saying, "In general, exclusive recognition at the national level should be avoided unless the agency believes it is not feasible to carry on meaningful negotiations on a smaller unit basis." [15] Since no agency or union is likely to admit that meaningful negotiation at the local level is ever totally infeasible, this "guide" has the practical effect of superimposing an important restrictive amendment upon the Order.

The Commission has explained that its guidelines are not based exclusively upon the Executive Order, supplementary directives, and Task Force documents, which are available to all interested parties, saying, "We have also consulted with those who participated with the Task Force in its discussions." [16] Since most of the Labor experts who were instrumental in shaping the Task Force decisions have left the scene, while many of their Commission aides have stayed behind, this source of wisdom is probably of greater value to the Commission people than to their Labor counterparts. The advantage is of limited value, however, because the Task Force went to such extraordinary lengths to explain its decisions and to make its records public. What its members said they said lucidly, and they left little unsaid.

Opposing Solutions to Practical Problems

The divergent attitudes and philosophies of the two approaches reveal themselves most sharply in the contrasting responses they give to specific issues which have arisen in the practice of "employee-management cooperation" under the Order. For example, those agencies which prefer the Labor approach generally strive to avoid disputation with unions over what constitutes a bargaining unit. They are disposed to follow the politician's maxim, "Give the people what they want" to the considerable extent that it is possible to do so without contravening the few mandatory restrictions imposed by the Order. Where two or more units are in contention over a bargaining-unit issue, agencies following the Labor approach seek to base their decisions upon the wishes of the employees involved. They have no unyielding attachment to units of a particular size. They are willing to approve small or large units, including nationwide units, if these reflect the preference of a majority of the employees with a "clear and identifiable community of interest." Assistant Postmaster General Richard J. Murphy, an influential alternate member of the Task Force and the top personnel official of a department which has approved over 23,000 bargaining units, including eight which are nationwide in scope, states, without perceptible apology or regret, that as a result of his Department's indulgent approach, "innumerable benefits in the form of improved working conditions, improved morale, and increased status for employee organizations have been achieved that otherwise would not have occurred. . . ." [17]

From the Commission viewpoint, this permissive approach to bargaining-unit disputes betrays a tendency toward weakness and appeasement which is inconsistent with "strong" management. Agencies which adopt the Commission view prefer to make a unilateral determination concerning what constitutes an appropriate bargaining unit, to state this determination clearly and forthrightly in a departmental regulation, and then to "hold the line" resolutely in the event of challenge by a union. Understandably, most of the Section 11 arbitration cases have occurred in agencies where the Commission approach has been followed. (In the preponderant majority of these Section 11 arbitration cases the arbitrators have not only handed down decisions favorable to the union involved but have contributed further to the chagrin of the Commission-oriented officials by basing their rulings upon NLRB precedents, notably the craft-severance doctrine of the *American Potash* case.[18] In the only case involving a union petition for recognition at the national level, however, *National Association of Internal Revenue Employees* vs. *Internal Revenue Service*,[19] the arbitrator decided in favor of the IRS, relying heavily in his opinion upon the Commission "guidance" that "exclusive recognition at the national level should be avoided. . . .")

The so-called "neutrality doctrine" further illustrates the difference between the two approaches. The word "neutral" does not appear anywhere in either the Order or the Task Force report. On the contrary, the report indicated sympathy with testimony that "the absence of a positive policy of support for employee-management relations" gave rise to "hostile and obstructionist attitudes" on the part of agency management. It endorsed "most emphatically the President's view that the public interest calls for a strengthening of employee-management relations within the Federal Government." [20] It did recognize the right of individual employees to refrain from union activity and prohibited interference with that right. It did not, however, prescribe neutrality, which goes far beyond proscribing interference, compulsion, or domination. The "neutrality doctrine" was articulated officially for the first time in the Commission's "Guidelines." [21] It has been reiterated so frequently that it is commonly believed, even by many Labor people, that it was laid down in the Order and that even a management endorsement of "employee-management cooperation" would violate management's duty to be neutral.

Adherents of the "neutrality doctrine" hold that the duty to protect the employee's right to join or refrain from joining a union imposes an absolute duty upon management to remain strictly neutral, eschewing any word or deed which might conceivably influence the employee's decision. This doctrine has become a tenet of the Commission approach. Proponents of the Labor approach do not reject the idea of neutrality entirely, but they do impose limitations upon it and apply it selectively, not absolutely. They would, for example, advocate a posture of neutrality on management's part where two or more unions are competing for recognition status. On the other hand, they would have no reluctance to endorse, officially and enthusiastically, the fundamental policy which the Order enunciated and which is its most important innovation: "Participation of employees in the formulation and implementation of personnel policies affecting them contributes to the effective conduct of the public business."

That policy statement was repeated over and over again in the Task Force report and in documents signed by the President of the United States. Yet today one may search in vain for any repetition or endorsement of that policy statement in the implementing directives of the preponderant majority of federal departments and agencies which follow the Commission approach. For agency management to go on record as endorsing employee participation (i.e., union participation) in management decision making would, *arguendo,* be a flagrant violation of the "neutrality doctrine." It contains the shocking implication that management should inform its employees that if they take full advantage of their privileges of selecting an exclusive representative and pressing that representative to negotiate creative, constructive agreements, they will be performing a useful *service to management!* Protagonists of the Labor approach contend, on the contrary, that this is exactly what should be done, and that to refuse to do it is a contravention of the Order itself.

A third example of how the two approaches differ in practical situations is found in their respective responses to the Order's "management prerogatives" clauses. These are Section 6(b), which lists certain "areas of discretion and policy" to which "the *obligation* to meet, confer, and try to negotiate agreements with unions granted exclusive recognition shall not be construed to extend," and Section 7, which lists certain other areas in which management officials "retain the *right*" to perform their assigned functions "in accordance with applicable laws and regulations." Prior to the publication of the Commission's "Guidelines," it was generally agreed that the wording of both sections expresses a clear intent that agencies should freely exercise their own discretion in each individual case whether to invoke their privilege of declining to negotiate on matters falling within the scope of either section or to waive that privilege. Of course, if the doctrine of uniformity is applied to this question, it must result, under the lowest-common-denominator concept, in taking this latitude for independent judgment away from the departments and agencies. Instead, *all* of them must be required to refuse to negotiate on any matter which the Order permits *any* of them to declare off limits. If mandatory uniformity is not imposed, hard-line agencies are liable to be whipsawed by union leadership in the event other agencies elect to follow more liberal practices. That the Task Force was opposed to the imposition of compulsory uniformity, however, seems clear from Chairman Goldberg's statement:

We are not proposing the establishment of uniform government-wide practices. The great variations among the many agencies of the government require that each be enabled to devise its own particular practices, in cooperation with its own employees.[22]

Nevertheless, the "doctrine of uniformity" was invoked when the Commission asserted categorically in its published "Guidelines" that the Order "clearly outlines the prerogatives which agency officials *must retain* in order to fulfill their management responsibilities for efficient Government operations." [23] Secretary Goldberg's permissive diversity, accordingly, has been largely replaced by the Commission's mandatory uniformity.

From the Commission viewpoint, then, these two sections of the Order set up an absolute bar. Agency management is prohibited from negotiating on any matter which can be identified as falling within the provisions of either section. Moreover, by declaring that as a matter of policy no union should be granted exclusive recognition at the national level, even where it can prove that it has been selected by a majority of the employees of an entire agency, the Commission has further substantially reduced the area of negotiability. It has made any decision which must be made or approved by management above the unit or installation level non-negotiable.

From the Labor viewpoint, the Order merely gives management, at whatever level negotiations are being conducted, the privilege of electing, freely and unilaterally, whether to negotiate on any of the specified subjects. Further, the Labor people would recommend that as a matter of policy, management should voluntarily waive its immunity in the majority of cases. Their rationale is that if management's objective is to exploit to the fullest its employees' capacity to "contribute to the effective conduct of the public business," it makes no more sense to restrict the scope of employee-management cooperation by arbitrarily declaring certain topics "out of bounds" than it would to place comparable restrictions on the scope of the employee suggestion program. This Labor contention has received support from Civil Service Commissioner L. J. Andolsek:

Many managers persist in protecting management 'prerogatives.' . . . Since these organizations represent employees, it is reasonable to assume that they reflect employee views. . . . If their representatives serve to bring a correctable condition to management's attention, it is in management's best interest. . . .[24]

The Commission approach restricts employee-management negotiations to those relatively few and minor personnel matters lying completely within the limited discretionary powers of low-level management. They might include, for example, scheduling leave and overtime; managing restaurant, recreation, and welfare facilities; allotting parking spaces; enforcing safety rules; and drafting and executing grievance procedures. Under the Labor approach, negotiation of procedures for union participation in promotion decisions (e.g., union membership on promotion panels), in locality wage surveys upon which government wage schedules are based, in formulation and execution of rules governing reductions in force and transfers of functions and jobs from agency to agency or area to area, and in all other comparable management decisions which have a vital and proximate effect upon working conditions are also considered fitting and proper. Some would maintain that such management decisions as whether to introduce automation, whether to "contract out" functions which have been performed "in house," and whether, in defense activities, to assign military personnel to "civilian" jobs are also typical matters affecting working conditions and, therefore, negotiable issues. Commission approach advocates would protest vehemently that such palpable interference with management's decision-making powers would usurp or undermine management's inviolable authority to manage. Managers who condescended to negotiate with unions on such sacrosanct subjects would certainly be guilty, in Warren Irons' words, of "taking the word 'cooperation' so literally that they have tended to bargain away their ability to manage effectively." [25]

The final controversial issue deserving attention concerns conflicts of interest. Most unions active in the federal service consider anyone who works for the government as eligible for membership. This is not only true of the AFGE and the NFFE (Franklin D. Roosevelt once belonged to the NFFE; in recent times, the heads of the Veterans' Administration and of the Civil Service Commission have belonged to the AFGE); it is also true of other unions such as the Letter Carriers and the Machinists. In the absence of regulatory safeguards, therefore, it would be theoretically possible, as Secretary Goldberg pointed out, for an employee to be "placed in the position of bargaining with himself." That hypothetical situation is such a palpable absurdity from every viewpoint that it is unlikely ever to occur in real life. Even the remote possibility can be easily eliminated, as Representative Morrison has done in his proposed "Employee-Management Cooperation Act of 1965," [26] by promulgation of a simple rule directing that no employee "be placed in a position where he is bargaining with himself."

Such a precaution will satisfy the Labor people, but it is grossly inadequate from the Commission viewpoint. The latter position is based upon the proposition, commonly propounded in government personnel directives before 1962, that unions are private organizations, formed to advance selfish private interests which can, and often do, conflict with the public interest. A government employee who joins and supports a union is, according to the Commission rationale, trying to "serve two masters." His loyalty to management is necessarily suspect. If he persists in his union activity, it is incumbent upon any strong, alert management to bar his advancement to supervisory positions. The contrary Labor position is bluntly but ably articulated in the Morrison Bill:

There can be no real conflict between the leaders of our Government agencies and the leaders of the employee organizations that qualify for recognition. . . . Difference of opinion can only exist over means; never over ends. The ultimate interest of both must inevitably be the same: to make the United States Government the best, the most efficient, and the most honorable in the world. [27]

The Choices of the Future

From the Commission approach, which prevailed without serious challenge throughout most of the government from 1883 to 1962, Executive Order 10988 was the work of "outsiders"— who, though brilliant in their own specialized fields of endeavor, "didn't understand the problem" in the federal service. They were gifted but misguided amateurs. Fortunately, however, none of them stayed behind, after executing the remarkable *tour de force* which gave birth to the executive order, to nurture their prodigious brainchild to maturity. That job was turned over to "professionals," who had never been persuaded to abandon the Commission approach by the precocious interlopers. They naturally considered it their duty to implement the Order so as to reduce the new program to a reasonably accurate facsimile of the *status quo ante*. They have accomplished their objective unobtrusively, but no less successfully than the Task Force did theirs.

It would be premature, however, to conclude at this juncture that the Commission protagonists have routed their opponents. The present situation is analogous to a schoolboy's baseball game at the end of the first half of the first inning. One side is far ahead on points, but the other side has not been to bat yet. Until recently the unions paid scant attention to the nibbling away of the imposing structure which the Order had erected and placed at their disposal. They were too occupied with representation contests, arbitration cases, contract negotiations, and membership drives. In all of these undertakings they were chalking up noteworthy advances. The Bureau of Labor Statistics reports, for example,

While union membership in private industry declined between 1960 and 1962, a significant increase was achieved in the Government service. Most of the increase was in the Federal service, reflecting both the continuation of a long term trend and, more significantly, the stimulation of a 1962 Executive Order. . . .[28]

The union membership drives were given potent boosts by such members of Congress as the late Senator Olin D. Johnston, who, far from finding anything "incongruous" in a government employee belonging to a union, frequently urged, "*All* government employees should belong to a union." As chairman of the Post Office and Civil Service Committee and a practicing politician often proclaimed "the best friend government employees have ever had," Senator Johnston made no bones about the motive for his counsel: "We in Congress who are their friends need the support of employee organizations to get employee programs and benefits approved, and the stronger the unions are, the easier it is for us to succeed." [29] After 1962 the unions reciprocated by retreating from their habitual hands-off, self-imposed "Hatch-Act" attitude toward involvement in politics. In the 1964 campaign they went to unprecedented lengths to "reward their friends and punish their enemies." Here too, they scored impressively. Most of their friends, including some Republicans, were elected.

By 1965 there was conclusive evidence that the Labor side was about to mount a counteroffensive to recover the ground it had lost to the Commission forces in the "legislative" area. The first big gun sounded when Representative Morrison, the dynamic vice-chairman of the House Post Office and Civil Service Committee and heir apparent to Senator Johnston as leader of the pro-civil service forces on Capitol Hill, introduced his "Federal Employee-Management Cooperation Act." [30] The Morrison Bill codifies Executive Order 10988, including its supplementary "Standards of Conduct" and "Code of Fair Labor Practices," but conspicuously omits—and thereby repeals—the "Commission amendments" appended to the Order by means of "guidelines," personal asides, and other methods.

It restates the fundamental policy: "Participation of employees, through employee organizations or other representatives of their own choosing, in decisions which affect them, contributes to the effective conduct of the public business." It disposes of the neutrality doctrine by providing that "strong, democratically run employee organizations voluntarily selected by a majority of the employees . . . are in the public interest and their development should be encouraged by lawful means." It encourages decentralization of management's decision-making authority as the best means to promote meaningful employee-management cooperation at the grass-roots level, but it also opens the door to negotiation of decisions reserved for departmental headquarters by removing the stigma from "nationwide exclusive recognition for national level bargaining." It states that "Government employees should, insofar as feasible and permissible under existing law . . . enjoy the same rights and privileges as persons . . . covered by the NLRA," and it designates "the established principles and guideposts" of the NLRB as the primary aids to navigation for those charged with implementing and interpreting the act. It specifies that refusals to bargain in good faith constitute unfair labor practices and provides effective remedies. It declares it desirable to encourage "capable, responsible people . . . to assume positions of leadership in employee organizations" and precludes further "conflicts of interest within management" by directing that "the partisan function of serving as the spokesman for management" will not be assigned, at any level of the government, to the same administrative official or body to whom the quasi-judicial functions of resolving disputes or complaints has been delegated.

President Kennedy's decision to establish the Goldberg Task Force is presumed to have been motivated by a desire to forestall the union-backed Rhodes Bill. The Morrison Bill does not contain the onerous provisions of the Rhodes Bill.[31] It does not "load the dice" in favor of unions by offering special privileges to union members. (On the contrary, it imposes upon unions with exclusive recognition the duty to represent all employees impartially, "without discrimination and without regard to employee organization membership.") It is free of the Rhodes Bill's punitive provisions imposing severe penalties upon administrators whose decisions unfavorable to unions are reversed upon appeal. It does, however, contain one substantive provision, the establishment of a "little NLRB," which the administration will probably find objectionable. If enough support builds up behind the Morrison Bill, the President might be persuaded to appoint a second task force to head off its enactment. Union leaders would undoubtedly do a little *pro forma* public grumbling if an accelerating legislative campaign were aborted in this manner, but they probably would "go along" with the President, provided he placed the task force in control of a chairman who, like Secretary Goldberg, was not committed to the Commission approach to employee-management relations.

If such a task force were appointed to review the progress and problems encountered in the implementation of Executive Order 10988 and to recommend to the President what action he should take to improve the program, two results could be predicted. First, the task force would find that the Civil Service Commission and the personnel directorates of the government departments and agencies have done such a superlative job of guiding and representing management that they should be assigned that function on a full-time basis, but they should be relieved of the quasi-legislative function of rule making and the quasi-judicial function of adjudicating disputes between unions and management. The evidence presented by the Labor witnesses would convince them that the present program is suffering an imbalance comparable to that which might be anticipated in the automobile industry if the NLRB's functions were transferred to the industrial relations director of the Ford Motor Company and Walter Reuther were told that he could appeal any unfavorable decision to Henry Ford. Second, it is predicted that the task force would make, in more precise form, the following general recommendations:

(1) Restate the "first principles" upon which the program is based. This restatement should leave no reasonable doubt in anyone's mind concerning the administration's position on the relative merits of employee-management cooperation vs. employee-management conflict; employee participation vs. employee exclusion from decision-making processes; and autocratic or oligarchic management practices vs. democratic management practices.

(2) Reshape the "doctrine of neutrality" to encourage positive management support of the objectives of the program without depriving the individual employee of his freedom of choice.

(3) Discard the "doctrine of uniformity" and encourage creative diversity and prudent, imaginative experimentation and innovation by the various agencies.

(4) Amend Section 3.2 of the Code of Fair Labor Practices so as to impose upon both agency management and upon unions the duty to negotiate in good faith, generally comparable to the obligation imposed upon private management and unions under Sections 8(a) (5) and 8(b) (3) of the Taft-Hartley Act.

(5) Add to the Order provision for third-party arbitration of representation disputes and complaints alleging violation of the Code of Fair Labor Practices, following procedures similar to those now used to settle bargaining unit disputes.

(6) Reject all proposals for the compulsory arbitration of bargaining impasses, recalling Secretary Wirtz's sound advice against "setting up procedures which will establish certainty in an area, the area of collective bargaining, part of the strength of which has always been that it does not provide a complete degree of certainty." [32]

It appears likely that the "impasse on impasses" will remain and perhaps grow more formidable unless or until it is removed, either by statute or by a comparable quasi-legislative order devised and recommended by an *ad hoc* body within the executive branch. Another alternative exists. In 1963 AFL-CIO President George Meany hinted darkly that unless the Commission-imposed rule against run-off elections in union representation contests were repealed, ". . . we may have to go back to the President himself." [33] In January 1964, Chairman Macy defended the ban, despite the endorsement of President Meany's complaints by Secretary Wirtz. Six months later the Commission not only replaced the ban with a run-off election rule similar to that laid down by the NLRB, but Chairman Macy told President Meany that he ". . . agreed that the present policy should be modified substantially *along the lines of your suggestion to the President.*" [34] The "impasse on impasses" could, therefore, be swept away if the President of the United States and the President of the AFL-CIO were to take a few minutes away from more pressing matters and "go to the well together."

NOTES

1. W. Willard Wirtz, *Labor and the Public Interest* (New York: Harper & Row, 1964), p. 57.

2. Executive Order 10988 (Jan. 17, 1962). For a full text of the Order, see *Industrial and Labor Relations Review,* Vol. 15, No. 4 (July 1962), pp. 548–553. For background and analysis of the Order, see Wilson R. Hart, "The U.S. Civil Service Learns to Live with Executive Order 10988: An Interim Appraisal," *Industrial and Labor Relations Review,* Vol. 17, No. 2 (January 1964), pp. 203–220.

3. See John W. Macy, Jr., "New Era in Employee-Management Relations,"

Civil Service Journal, January–March 1962, p. 2; and his "Partnership for Productivity in the Public Interest," an address at the American Federation of Government Employees banquet, Washington, D.C., Jan. 20, 1962.

4. Letter of Jan. 17, 1964 from J. W. Macy, Jr. to President Johnson, *Government Employee Relations Report,* No. 21, Feb. 3, 1964, p. C-1.

5. Report of AFL-CIO's Constitutional Convention, *Government Employee Relations Report,* No. 11, Nov. 26, 1963, p. A-2.

6. *United States Statutes at Large,* Vol. 69, p. 624.

7. *A Policy for Employee-Management Cooperation in the Federal Service* (Washington, D.C.: G.P.O., 1961).

8. Wirtz, *op. cit.,* p. 57.

9. Warren B. Irons, "State of the Art in Employee-Management Cooperation," an address to the Federal Bar Association Briefing Conference on Government Employee-Management Relations, Washington, D.C., April 8, 1965, *Government Employee Relations Report,* No. 83, April 12, 1965, p. D-1.

10. Harry Case, "Gordon R. Clapp: The Role of Faith, Purposes, and People in Administration," *Public Administration Review,* Vol. 24, No. 2 (June 1964), pp. 86–91.

11. U.S. Civil Service Commission, "E.O. 10988, A Sectional Analysis with Suggested Guidelines to Assist Agency Implementation of the Order," *Federal Personnel Manual,* Letter No. 700–1, April 24, 1962.

12. Irons, *op. cit.,* p. D-1.

13. *United States Statutes at Large,* Vol. 37, p. 555.

14. David Barr, "E.O. 10988: An Experiment in Employee-Management Cooperation in the Federal Service," *Georgetown Law Journal,* Vol. 52, Winter 1964, pp. 420–454.

15. *Federal Personnel Manual,* chap. 711, subchap. 7.

16. *Ibid.,* Letter No. 700–1.

17. Richard J. Murphy, address to the Federal Personnel Council of Southern California, Oct. 8, 1964, *Government Employee Relations Report,* No. 57, Oct. 12, 1964, pp. D-1–D-4.

18. *Decisions and Orders of the National Labor Relations Board,* Vol. 107, pp. 1418–1433.

19. Francis J. Robertson, "Decision on Appropriate Unit for Employees of Internal Revenue Service," *Government Employee Relations Report,* No. 83, April 12, 1965.

20. *A Policy for Employee-Management Cooperation in the Federal Service,* pp. 5–6.

21. *Federal Personnel Manual,* Letter No. 700–1.

22. Letter from Arthur Goldberg to President Kennedy transmitting the Task Force report, Nov. 30, 1963.

23. *Federal Personnel Manual,* Letter No. 700–1, p. 26.

24. L. J. Andolsek, "Stop, Look, and Listen," *Civil Service Journal,* Vol. 5, No. 1 (July–September 1964), pp. 2–5.

25. Irons, *op. cit.,* p. D-1.

26. H.R. 6883, 89th Cong., 1st sess., March 29, 1965.

27. *Ibid.*

28. H. James Neary, "American Trade Union Membership in 1962," *Monthly Labor Review,* Vol. 87, No. 5 (May 1964), pp. 501–507.

29. Wilson R. Hart, *Collective Bargaining in the Federal Civil Service* (New York: Harper & Row, 1961), p. 212.

30. H.R. 6883, 89th Cong., 1st sess., March 29, 1965. A companion bill, S. 2631, was introduced in the Senate by Senator Ralph Yarborough of Texas on October 12, 1965.

31. For a discussion of the Rhodes Bill, which was backed by most national unions in every session of Congress between 1949 and 1961, see Hart, *Collective Bargaining in the Federal Civil Service*, pp. 140–173.

32. W. Willard Wirtz, address to the AFL-CIO Metal Trades Department Convention, Nov. 11, 1963, *Government Employee Relations Report*, No. 10, Nov. 18, 1963, p. A-6.

33. George W. Meany, address to the AFL-CIO Constitutional Convention, *Government Employee Relations Report*, No. 11, Nov. 26, 1963, p. A-13.

34. Unpublished letter from J. W. Macy, Jr. to George Meany, July 1, 1964, italics added.

§ *A LOCAL GOVERNMENT EXPERIENCE—PHILADELPHIA*

The Process and Procedures of the Long-Standing Relationship

ELI ROCK

There are, of course, many examples of long-standing relationships in the public employee sector of collective bargaining, and they vary greatly. They exist at all levels of government, and I could not begin to speak as an expert on all of them, let alone even a small proportion. As we know, the record of written or published information regarding the details of individual relationships in the public service is sparse. This is particularly to be pitied because, lacking the basic legislative guideposts of the private sector and confronting a myriad of institutional obstacles, there is no doubt in this field a high premium on ingenuity and experimentation, on variations in local political patterns and personalities, and often on mere chance. Clearly,

Address given before the Conference on Public Employment and Collective Bargaining at the University of Chicago, February 5, 1965. Reprinted by permission of the author.

Eli Rock is a full-time arbitrator in Philadelphia.

much may have been developed here that we know little about and that could be of substantial value to those who are still feeling their way in the public sector—a category that must include virtually all of us.

I commend to you, as an indication of some of the variations that demonstrate themselves in even a single small state like Connecticut, the short survey study prepared on that subject in 1960 by Professor Robert L. Stutz, entitled *Collective Dealing by Units of Local Government in Connecticut* (Labor Management Institute, University of Connecticut).

My own remarks must therefore be recognized as representing only the knowledge based on a rather intensive experience in one city, Philadelphia, plus that based on some observations of a few other jurisdictions, some exchange of information with other individuals, and some reading of the available literature. I am certain that any number of persons would be qualified to rise from this audience to describe a separate set of reactions or observations, based on a separate set of experiences.

One other preliminary remark: My observations here will probably be somewhat more reflective of the type of relationship that tends in the direction of the nonlobbying pattern than of the lobbying pattern—a controversial set of terms, I recognize, and one where the lines of distinction are by no means always clear. I shall, however, also be making some observations that are reflective of both types of relationships, and it is not necessary to debate the merits of that particular question at this time.

The normal distribution of responsibilities related to the collective bargaining process in a governmental entity will spread over both the legislative and the executive or administrative branches, plus various subdivisions of the latter. Thus in a city like Philadelphia, the Mayor, the Managing Director (Philadelphia is that rarity, the Mayor-Manager combination form of government), the Civil Service Commission, the Personnel Director, the Finance Director, and the City Labor Relations Adviser all play important, basic roles in the annual negotiations. These officials, and in addition, departmental representatives, may be involved in the grievance-type problems between the annual negotiations. The legislative branch is primarily involved in the annual negotiations.

The circle of participants can be widened even beyond this, however, as for example, in some states where the state government may have authority in the determination of certain of the working conditions of local government employees, or at the level of federal government, where the complications may be substantially different. On the other hand, in a Board of Education where the authority is shared primarily by the Board and the administrator, these institutional obstacles may be substantially lessened.

Returning to the pattern in Philadelphia, the current procedures there have evolved over some twenty-five years or more, during which the employees have been unionized. Fire and police are in their separate unions, and the nonuniformed, larger remainder of the work force are represented solely by the American Federation of State, County and Municipal Employees. Prior to 1952, all three groups of employees exercised their functions, at least insofar as annual gains are concerned, through the time-honored straight political process. The passage of years has not changed the basic approach insofar as police and fire are concerned. Stripped of forms, primary reliance in their case is still on a final, prebudget conference with the Mayor, and ultimately on efforts with the City Council when it is passing upon the Mayor's proposed budget. Success under this type of approach has not always been marked in some of the more recent years.

With the nonuniformed employees, the evolution since 1952 has been toward a fundamentally different pattern. This aspect of our story has been told before, and I shall attempt here to describe it relatively briefly.

Philadelphia, as some may recall, had managed to achieve, between the days of its colonial distinction and the middle of the twentieth century, the reputation, easily, of one of the top three most politically corrupt cities in the nation. (Local pride alone inhibits me from claiming the number one spot.) Collective bargaining in the pre-Joe Clark era reflected, to a substantial extent, the highly political atmosphere of the city.

Having played a prominent role in the revolution of 1776, Philadelphia in 1952 participated in a second one—its own. A radically new and daring-at-the-time charter was enacted, and a literally dazzling reform administration was ushered in. The hunger for honesty in government gave product to a strong merit system and a Civil Service Commission unmatched in basic authority and responsibility.

The problem of labor relations presented itself at once. The state, county and municipal workers were strong even then, but their prior involvement with the up-to-then forever-in-office previous administration and the sincere difficulty that many of the good government people saw in attempting to reconcile collective bargaining with the new strong merit system and Civil Service Commission posed major obstacles. The decision of Mayor Joseph S. Clark, who was and is a liberal in outlook, was to attempt the reconciliation—but in a fashion that would be faithful both to the collective bargaining idea and the merit system.

Not surprisingly, this was regarded by many as an utopian ideal—both improper and impractical—and there were in fact some rather serious initial strains. Time and some, but not too many, difficult battles have, however, at least to the present, produced a stable and workable relationship, basically in the image originally visualized by the Clark administration.

The annual negotiations are conducted between a committee of top officers of the American Federation of State, County and Municipal Employees and a city team made up of the Managing Director, Personnel Director, Finance Director, and Labor Relations Adviser. In addition, in recent years a key member of the City Council has sat in. Prior to and during the course of the negotiations there are consultations back and forth between the city team and the Mayor, and occasionally with several additional members of the City Council, regarding the basic money items; similar discussions also occur between the Personnel Director and Labor Relations Adviser and the Civil Service Commission regarding the subject matter that may fall within the commission's jurisdiction. With the city's team thus aware of what will be generally acceptable on the city side, there is thus normally a strong likelihood that the terms of the agreement finally reached in the collective bargaining sessions with the union will be implemented as required. On frequent occasions also, and particularly where a difficult stalemate occurs, the Mayor may participate in the bargaining process. This, then, is the basic bargaining pattern prior to the implementation stage.

As soon as agreement has been reached at the negotiating level, this will be incorporated in an informal but not final document. Thereafter, steps are taken to implement the understanding through the Mayor's budget to the council and through proposed regulations by the Personnel Director to the Civil Service Commission. Together with city representatives, union representatives appear in the hearings before both bodies. At those hearings—and this is most important—both the city and the union people ask only for implementation of what was agreed upon in the negotiations—no more and no less.

Following the passage of the budget by the council and enactment of the regulations by the Civil Service Commission, the city and the union then incorporate the various results of their earlier bargaining into a written contract, signed by both sides. Although there have been difficulties at times, and occasional variations from the above procedures, basically this has been the pattern since 1952, and basically it has resulted in a peaceful resolution of issues during each year since then.

I believe there is little question that the merit system has remained essentially unaffected, at least insofar as the impact of the collective bargaining process on it has been concerned, and in fact, the union has, on at least some occasions, been a valuable ally to the sometimes-beleaguered good government people. (A recent battle concerning some proposed top exempt positions, although the union was not involved in this instance, demonstrates that our Civil Service Commission is still hardy and sound.)

On the union side, membership has gone from about 5,000 in 1952 to more than 12,000 in 1964, with total city employment having risen in a considerably lower proportion than that. The concrete gains achieved by the union for its membership, the prestige enjoyed by it at all levels of government as well as among the employees, its highly active and productive daily role at the grievance level, all leave little question that it has prospered greatly in this twelve-year relationship that I have described.

Many of the other examples of long-standing relationships in the United States have, of course, been equally successful. More often than not they may involve basic variations from the type of approach I have described in Philadelphia; and there is no question that there are a number of stable and successful relationships that place greater emphasis on the political or lobbying approach, in contrast with places where the shading has been in the direction of the nonlobbying technique.

Essentially—and this is a matter that I learned long ago in the private industry sector of bargaining, and I am still relearning it there daily—the ultimate ingredient of a stable collective bargaining relationship is attitude and quality of leadership on both sides. These are not assured by the mere age of the relationship, for attitudes and problems change, as do the leaders.

At the same time, the process and procedures and the structure that have been worked out over a period of time can play an important role in minimizing difficulties. Problems can arise where there need not be a problem, and anger and tension may stem from unnecessary misunderstanding; the established, successful procedure would presumably have recognized these and would have evolved techniques for avoiding them. Even for people who like to fight, a proper procedure can channel that instinct into a right time and place. New personalities will tend to take their cues, at least at the start, from an established procedure and structure, rather than to strike out completely on their own.

Although I have not hitherto referred to grievance procedure, much of these last observations refer to that, as well as to the process and procedure of the annual bargaining that I described for a place like Philadelphia. Obviously both areas are important, and the grievance procedure should grow in relative importance in an established, stable relationship, although the annual bargaining involves the larger sums and more dramatically highlights the basic relationship.

I have primarily dealt thus far with the matter of process and procedure as such, without examining its application in the specific areas of wages, hours, and working conditions. As those of you familiar with private industry bargaining know, the matter of proper subject matter for collective bargaining has often been a raging issue, but there is at least present, in the private area, basic legislation laying down certain rules. In the public sector, even where some legislation is beginning to appear, there are virtually no guideposts at all on this aspect, and the answers worked out often reflect the institutional obstacles of government. Even under the Kennedy Executive Order 10988, which is a revolutionary document that now provides for a system of recognition and bargaining at the federal level, the *sine qua non* of private industry bargaining—that is, wages and similar bread-and-butter issues—is not included among the subject matters of collective bargaining for most federal employees under the order, but rather is left to the lobbying arena.

For the typical long-standing relationship at other levels of government, however, the area of subject matter for bargaining is generally fairly broad and will include most of the bread-and-butter issues, plus more. Thus, where collective bargaining agreements exist, they may cover, in addition to wages, such items as hours, overtime, health and welfare benefits, holidays, vacations, reporting time, sick leave, and grievance procedure. In some instances, there will also be clauses on items like seniority, dues deduction, no-strike or lockout clauses, and special rights for union representatives. Where the exclusive bargaining agent concept has been accepted (and this of course is spreading), the contract may provide for definition of the bargaining unit and exclusive recognition.

There are, of course, a number of matters that may not be included and that would normally be encompassed by the private industry collective bargaining agreement. A principal example is the matter of pensions, but even here employee representatives on the Pension Boards, who have often been advanced as candidates of particular unions, can lead to at least a degree of bargaining participation in the decision-making process.

A major item of controversy in this respect has been the matter of classification problems, and a considerable number of the people on the Personnel or Civil Service Commission side of government feel that this particular aspect is not a proper subject for collective bargaining in the public service. Time does not permit treatment of the issue in depth, but I will at least say that a good many of the aspects of the classification problem, as well as of some of the other areas normally associated with the primary responsibility of the Personnel Departments and Civil Service Commissions, are often at least the subject of discussion between the union representatives and the Personnel Department people. Where, as in the case of the long-standing relationships, the habit and custom of bargaining have become well established, I would judge that the "discussion" on even these items is not far removed from the mutual-participation-in-problem-solving, or the give-and-take, that might normally be regarded as the hallmark of the collective bargaining idea. I would assume that this type of subject matter does not usually become incorporated in the collective bargaining agreement, at least where the merit system is well established; but in this whole field, where we know so little of the actualities, I would not bet that there are not numerous exceptions to this also.

The picture that I have attempted to paint is basically that, where a long-standing relationship has existed, the degree of employee participation in the decision-making process has tended to become extensive and meaningful. This is not to say that it is usually as meaningful as that of the unions in private industry bargaining, and the actuality is that it is not in most instances. On this one aspect at least, I may be able to speak with some authority, having had experience in both sectors.

On the other hand, in some respects it may be that the public organization will have areas of participation that are denied to the private union. One of the principal examples of this is in the teacher field, where the scope of "collective negotiation" may now, for various reasons, include some "professional" subject matter that would normally, in private industry, be regarded as part of the management area not subject to collective bargaining.

At the same time, there is little question that, in terms of effectiveness of bargaining power and in certain important areas of subject matter, the public union or organization is still substantially behind the private one. Two of the basic foundations of union strength in private industry, for example, are the union security clause and the arbitration of unresolved grievances. Although there are numerous individual examples of both of these techniques in various governmental entities, there can be no question that for the country and for public employment as a whole, these examples constitute a small fraction of the total.

On subjects such as these, as well as on many of the other subjects that I have earlier discussed, there will be an increasing need for ingenuity and originality in the efforts to seek accommodation between the opposing interests and positions of both sides. I believe, for example, that on the highly controversial subject of union security, the modified maintenance-of-membership clause adopted some years back in Philadelphia represents the type of imagination that a realistic appraisal of the growing strength and power of the public union movement in this country will require.

The details of this highly controversial clause in Philadelphia, which I will be happy to elaborate upon if time permits, no doubt will be regarded by some as too little, and by others as too much under a merit system form of government; but this clause, together with the numerous other techniques that can be found both in Philadelphia and in many other places around the country where the collective bargaining relationship is long standing and meaningful, illustrates, I believe, the type of imagination and the type of will-to-accommodate that, in my view, are essential in such a field as this, where basic legislative guideposts are lacking and where the institutional obstacles springing from the nature of government pose difficulties, or will pose them if they have not yet done so, that far transcend those confronting the average bargainers in private industry.

The difference between what now usually exists and what the public employee movement is or will be seeking can be summarized, I believe, as follows:

If the bargaining machinery in a particular instance, even under the structure in Philadelphia, only provides for a more sophisticated procedure for presenting requests or pressuring for requests, it is still not true bargaining or "negotiation" but only a particular or another form of lobbying. You may change the forms, but you do not thus change the real essence.

Bargaining or negotiation is a state of mind, reflected in a pattern of behavior, which is essentially that of *two relative equals, recognizing each other as such,* and participating jointly in the resolution of a problem. "Participation" as opposed to "presentation" are the two key words, and they describe the difference graphically.

§ *THE EDUCATION SCENE*

Collective Negotiations in Michigan Education: An Overview

CHARLES T. SCHMIDT, JR.

> If you have called a bad thing bad you have done no great matter; but if you have called a good thing good, you have accomplished much.
>
> —GOETHE

Collective bargaining, by definition, is an exercise in pragmatism. It requires an accommodation of potentially conflicting views of two parties who adapt the peculiarities of their own local social and financial environment to their employment relationship. The result is an agreement to which each has contributed and which each voluntarily agrees to support, but it may very well not completely satisfy either. Hence, we can make no implicit assumption that the views and recommendations expressed here are universally applicable. Rather, this section provides the necessary historical background, assumptions, definitions, procedures, attitudes, approaches, and tactics that newcomers to the process of collective bargaining in the area of education will need to understand the process itself. The focus here is more social-psychological and philosophic than economic.

Reprinted from "Collective Negotiations: An Overview" and "Negotiating the Local Agreement," in Charles T. Schmidt, Jr., Hyman Parker, and Bob Repas, *A Guide to Collective Negotiations in Education* (East Lansing: Michigan State University, Social Science Research Bureau, 1967), pp. 1–16 and 56–60, by permission of the publisher.

Charles T. Schmidt, Jr., is Associate Professor of Industrial Relations at the University of Rhode Island, Kingston, Rhode Island.

The material here is not based on a structured research design, although some of the material relies on evidence from research, past, present, and continuing. Rather, the information reflects my experience over the last ten years as a participant in the process of collective bargaining in private industry, as a student and teacher of employee-management relations and collective bargaining, and as the project director of an educational and research program in educational collective bargaining throughout the State of Michigan. Thus far, I have worked with more than 2,000 school administrators, board members, teachers and their association and federation officers, and non-teaching employee groups in Michigan.[1]

Whether or not the Michigan experience is typical or applicable elsewhere is obviously unknown. Nevertheless, collective bargaining, in almost the classical sense, was unbelievably successful in its first full year of implementation in public education in Michigan. Novices negotiated well over 400 complex collective agreements, and negotiations broke down in only about fifteen of these situations.[2] Whether this high degree of success can be sustained in the immediate future is certainly questionable. Continued success in collective negotiations will require certain changes in the roles and attitudes of the participants, and the next few years will be critical ones for the future of such negotiations in education. In my opinion the process can and will produce these desired accommodations if left unencumbered by legislative or administrative curbs. My position is that the collective bargaining process is a satisfactory and successful institution for the resolution of potential or actual employer-employee conflict in education.

The Collective Bargaining Process

To adequately understand the process of collective bargaining, one must first understand the nature, the roles, and the objectives of both the employee organization and the employer. In education, these groups include the teacher and non-teacher organizations and the board of education and the administrative staff.

The roles and objectives of the employee groups are fairly

easy to define, although there are obvious distinctions between some of the goals of the professional teachers and those of the non-teaching organizations. All employee groups, however, must be considered multi-dimensional in purpose; i.e., they are political, educational, economic, political action, and social institutions, and, for the teachers, they are professional organizations as well. It is only at substantial risk that any one of these purposes is thought to be superior to or independent of the others. Too many employers have been disillusioned to find, for example, that what they considered a straight-forward economic position taken by the employee organization was in reality a position based on internal political problems.

The goals, like the purposes, of all employee organizations engaged in collective bargaining are also multi-dimensional. These goals include at least the necessity (1) to survive as an organization and to grow, (2) to improve their members' wages, hours, and conditions of employment, (3) to control jobs for the membership of the organization (a goal already important to such professional groups as the American Medical Association, the American Bar Association, and others), and (4) to formulate and jointly administer with the management group a system for the adjudication of grievances and the resolution of disputes arising during the term of the collective agreement. In education there are the additional goals of promoting both the profession of teaching and the advancement of the individual teacher, and of providing a superior education for the nation's youth.

Quite obviously, since collective bargaining is not a one-sided process, we must also understand the goals of the employer. In public employment, and in education in particular, these goals are a question much more complex than a similar definition of goals in private industry. Even in private industry this definition is not precise now that the industrialist is asked to respond to ethical and moral questions and to consider the general public good and the social consequences of his actions. Nevertheless, the primary goal for the private employer still remains the economic survival and growth of the enterprise (profits).

This goal presents difficulties in public administration. The goal of profit is certainly not a consideration of a board of education or a city council. Rather, the fundamental purpose of the board of education is to provide the best possible education in the most efficient manner for the children within its jurisdiction. Yet the question of fiscal efficiency causes an inevitable conflict between school employee organizations and boards of education. Like their counterparts in private industry, the employee groups and the employer inevitably concentrate their bargaining on potentially conflicting views regarding the proper distribution of scarce resources (i.e., tax revenues).

In addition, major problems will develop between teachers and boards of education even when their goals are identical. For example, both teachers and boards of education have the common goal of providing a quality education for the children of their district. Although the definition and implementation of this goal should ideally be a decision shared by both parties, a conflict results if either party believes that such a definition or implementation is his own special prerogative. Other objectives of the public employer, such as serving as a positive influence on the community and being a good employer, are identical with those of the private employer except that, in practice, they may assume a higher priority and commitment.

Collective bargaining, then, is quite simply the process of accommodating the goals and objectives of both the employee and employer groups, writing down the results of these accommodations, and agreeing to accept these results for a specified period of time. Unfortunately, this simple explanation will not suffice, for not all (perhaps only a minority) of the citizenry accept or understand collective bargaining as a successful, social-psychological process for the institutional resolution of potential employer-employee conflict.

As a frame of reference for a further explanation of the process, I will draw extensively on the views expressed by Dr. Vernon Jensen of Cornell University in an article in the *Industrial and Labor Relations Review*. Dr. Jensen's article was written as an explanation and defense of collective bargaining in private industry, and it defines six basic postulates of meaningful collective bargaining. The comments following each of these postulates and their explanations assess the applicability of each postulate to collective bargaining in education. For simplicity, the discussion will be limited to teacher organization-school board relationships, but the discussion can easily be modified to apply to non-professional employee organizations in the school.

THE POSTULATES OF COLLECTIVE BARGAINING[3]

Postulate 1. A genuine interdependence exists between the parties . . . [and this] interdependence is more than pecuniary. It is also a reflection of ideological compatibility. Bargaining takes place within the . . . system and both parties are committed to the support of the system.

This postulate applies almost without exception. The schools can not exist without teachers, and teachers can not teach without schools. Even though mobility is sometimes high among young teachers, the majority of the faculty become permanent residents of the community and desire to continue, not terminate, their relationship with the school system. Given the long-term needs for additional teaching personnel, the retention of its staff is directly in the school board's interest. Finally, and probably most important to this postulate, education fosters the ideological compatibility between the teachers and the board of education to support, promote, and improve the educational system. Some educators, of course, believe that the system requires major structural changes; this consideration, however, leads to the second postulate:

Postulate 2. The parties, however, also have diverse or conflicting interests . . . One should not expect [an employee organization] leader to ignore his role as an advocate, and he should not be urged to be a statesman nor to be concerned primarily with the public interest.

Most can accept the major portion of this statement as it applies to education; only the last phrase may cause difficulties.

I have already discussed many of the diverse and conflicting interests that make it inevitable that the parties meet as adversaries on some issues. Because of his political role in the organization, the teachers' leader must be an advocate. However, the last phrase, "he should not be urged to be a statesman," is probably quite inappropriate if this were interpreted and applied to mean that the teachers' organization should not be concerned with the public interest—in this instance, the educational program of the district. Since we have already defined this specific interest as one of the paramount goals of the teacher organization, a better application of this part of the postulate should be made. Given the teachers' fundamental concern with the educational process, I suggest that (1) they cannot avoid a direct confrontation on some educational policies and issues, and (2) long-range educational objectives are not served by an automatic acquiescence to a school board's decisions or the taxpayers' resistance.

Postulate 3. [An employee group] is not a monolithic organization. At least three groups in it may be recognized: the hierarchy or paid staff, the dedicated or core group, and the rank and file. Each of these groups has separate needs. Other internal differences may be division between seniors and juniors, or between [specialized] and [unspecialized]. Each of these factors may have to be accommodated.

Management, too, in addition to having interests which in part are diverse from those of the [employee organization], is characterized by sub-groups, each of which has separate interests and needs.

Probably applying to a higher degree in education than in private employment, this postulate simply points out that the collective bargaining process is not a simple one-to-one accommodation. It involves an extremely complex network of coalitions based on power, personality, need, and interest. Representatives of both the employer and the employee must fully consider these factors.

Postulate 4. The parties to collective bargaining are not completely informed of the precise nature of the position of the other . . . Even when each of the chief negotiators understands the requirements of settlement, the internal bargaining in either the [employer] or the [employee group] may be critical. What may appear to be ritual is a necessary allowance of time to work out serious internal differences.

By and large, most of the negotiators in Michigan began as novices about two years ago. The ritual described in the postulate could not be observed at all during the first year's negotiations. An attempt at role playing by some of the more sophisticated bargainers occurred in the second year. Nevertheless, most of the parties would probably agree that their experiences have not been at all ritualistic thus far. Moreover, as long as the rivalry between the Michigan Education Association (MEA) and the Michigan Federation of Teachers (MFT) prevails and the associated necessity that both organizations be "creative" in their demands remains, a complete ritualistic approach to bargaining in education is precluded. Certain elements of ritual will inevitably develop, however, as the parties become more experienced in dealing with each other.

More significant, however, is the postulate's reference to the lack of knowledge of the precise nature of the other's position. Given the public nature of school finances, it is doubtful that the teacher organization lacks precise information about the total educational budget available or about the amount traditionally specified for salaries and for economic fringe benefits. The demands by the teacher groups (and others) for an increase in the share of the total educational budget is the area of indeterminacy most apparent. Thus, teacher organizations suggest that, since the total dollars are limited, expenditures for other educational services be curtailed in order to meet the teachers' salary demands. The teachers' bargaining representative generally does not know how far the board of education is willing to move or can move in this direction.

The board of education's knowledge of the precise nature of the teachers' position is also incomplete. It does not know what salary the teachers will actually accept. In the first two years of negotiations in Michigan, however, the state association circulated a proposed master agreement months in advance of negotiations, and thus gave the school boards considerably more information than they ordinarily would have expected to gain on their own initiative.

There was evidence in the first year (much less in the second) that some of the parties were not really bargaining, but were actually making their "true positions" known either at the first meeting or, in some instances, even before bargaining commenced. This approach was apparently successful at times, because of (1) an extremely mature, trustful relationship, (2) incredible naïveté, or (3) the weakness of one or both parties. The continued success of this approach can be achieved only in the first situation above, and then only when the trust is continued. This kind of relationship requires a delicate balance that is extremely difficult to maintain.

By and large, however, this postulate, like the others, is quite applicable.

Postulate 5. Both parties operate within certain internal and external restraints . . . Bylaws and policies, as well as the internal politics of the organizations, set limits for bargainers . . . The parties [also] must operate within the restrictions and limits imposed by society, whether in the form of laws, customs, economics, politics, or morals.

Both the teacher groups and boards of education are limited by internal policies and bylaws. In fact, the boards of education have many more limitations than management in private industry because of the public nature of their deliberations. The internal policies of the teacher groups also have a high degree of public visibility. One of the most serious problems that the teachers are presently facing is the development of policies and bylaws that will combine idealistic precepts of professionalism with the requirements for hard collective bargaining. In Michigan, in my opinion, the rapid internal accommodation of these two potentially conflicting policies has been most successful.

Although both parties engaged in educational collective bargaining are subject to external restraints and pressures that must be considered a part of the total bargaining environment, the board of education is the more seriously affected. Pressure by all citizens, even teachers, can be brought to bear on the school board member, and a response unknown in private industry is required. For not only can extreme pressure be applied on a board's collective bargaining policy and tactics, but, because he is a publicly elected official, the board member himself usually feels a responsibility to answer citizens' demands or criticisms.

It is quite apparent, therefore, that this postulate is extremely relevant as stated. The question, particularly with reference to the board of education, becomes: Can external restraints become so extreme and the maneuverability of one or both of the parties so restricted that the collective bargaining process becomes dysfunctional?

Postulate 6. It must be assumed that the parties, over time, find some balance of power . . . Power to paralyze is alien to the collective bargaining process.

In educational collective bargaining in Michigan, the balance of power has not yet materialized; yet it would be difficult to find many who, after two years, would deny that power is at least the backdrop to the collective relationship even if it is not the central theme.

Nevertheless, the latter point of this postulate is by far the more important. Newly acquired power by any group is potentially dangerous. The greatest responsibility held by the leaders of teacher organizations is using this power for the support, not the paralysis and eventual destruction, of collective bargaining.

SUBJECTS OF BARGAINING

No one issue in Michigan education has caused more debate than the issue of bargainable subjects. Unlike the administrative rules of the NLRB, the Michigan Labor Mediation Board has not yet developed guidelines defining mandatory and permissible subjects of bargaining in Michigan public employment. The division under federal law is based on the decision to allow strikes or lockouts (impasses) when mandatory issues are involved but to deny such action when permissive subjects are at issue. To illustrate: in private industry, there is nothing in the legislation or administrative procedures that prohibits the U.A.W., for example, from making the demand on General Motors that it wishes to bargain about policies that determine automobile styling (to use an extreme example of a permissible demand). Further, there is nothing to prevent G.M. from agreeing to such a demand. Alternatively, this type of demand would most probably be considered by the National Labor Relations Board as falling into the permissive category, and it would probably be construed as an unfair labor practice (bad faith bargaining) by the U.A.W. if such a demand were pushed to an impasse: a strike. Alternatively, if the demand were concerned with a pension plan, for example (a mandatory subject for bargaining), it could be bargained to an impasse and the union could strike with impunity.

Under Michigan law, this same type of rationale and procedure is impossible. In the first instance, the strike is illegal, and secondly, there are presently no unfair labor practices in the legislation that may be charged against the employee organization for bargaining in bad faith. We therefore have a situation where the entire burden for the definition of bargainable subjects falls on either the Michigan Labor Mediation Board (but only on its receipt of a charge by the employee group that the employer is bargaining in bad faith), or, alternatively, the State Courts (where the employer or perhaps a taxpayer might charge that a particular subject or subjects could not legally be bargained away by an elected body such as the local board of education). There is also the distinct possibility that the courts could require an employee organization to bargain in good faith since good faith is defined in the statute as a mutual obligation. In either instance, the decision is taken out of the control of the parties themselves.

Fortunately, in Michigan this kind of experience has not been great, and severe breakdowns in negotiations have not been evidenced, in large part, I believe, because both the Mediation Board and the Courts have not been called on to spell out in detail what the subjects of bargaining are or should be. This is a decision that should be left to the parties themselves to develop over the next five years or so, particularly in view of the recommendations by Mr. Weisenfeld. Furthermore, the parties must be given an opportunity to achieve the changes in roles, status, and attitudes that are so desperately needed in this new relationship. Any attempt at this time by any public body to define the scope of negotiable subjects cannot take into consideration the possible social, philosophical, role, attitudinal, technical, and financial changes that may take place within the next five years in education. Legislative action at this early stage would preclude adjustment to these changes.

Nevertheless, decisions and a recommendation attempting to define the scope of bargaining have been reported—one by a trial examiner of the Michigan Labor Mediation Board and one by a Michigan Circuit Judge. As might be expected at this early date in the implementation of the legislation, the Court decision and the recommended Board order are contradictory and offer little if any guidance to the parties.

Further, at this point, neither decision has had much, if any, impact even on the particular parties involved in the litigation.

The trial examiner's recommendation was not acted upon by the full Board, because the original charge was withdrawn by the charging party.[4] The Circuit Court's decision is currently on appeal to the Michigan Court of Appeals. A brief summary of the substance of these two polar positions follows.

In the North Dearborn Heights case, the Michigan Labor Mediation Board trial examiner's decision and recommended order said, in part:

The Union's proposals on working conditions included, but were not limited to, such items as requests for information that the Union may need during negotiations and/or enforcement of the contract, compensated release time for any teacher on any committee, agency, or other body established by the Employer, the right of the Union to have a regular staff member visit schools to investigate teacher problems, the right of the Union to appear on the School Board agenda, the right of the teachers to appeal discharge or demotions to the Board of Education, the right of the teachers to evaluate curriculum and class schedule, size of classes, selection of text books, materials, supplies, planning of facilities and special education, establishment of in-service training of teachers, procedures for the rating of effectiveness of teachers, the establishment of self-sustaining summer school programs for remedial purposes and severance pay.

The undersigned [trial examiner] considers all of the above terms and conditions of employment which are the proper subjects of collective bargaining. However, I wish to make it clear that I am not substituting my judgment for the judgments of the parties as to the desirability of approval, rejection, or modification by any of the parties of the Union's proposals, the parties may wish to take. I find that the Employer's action in refusing to discuss the terms and conditions of employment of teachers listed above because of the Employer's alleged belief that they were not terms and conditions of employment to be a violation of Section 10(a) and (e) of the Act.

In the Circuit Court decision, Judge James P. Churchill in the Circuit Court for the County of Lapeer on January 3, 1967, stated in part:

If, as asserted by plaintiff, a school board may surrender control of educational policies to teachers by contract, so too may a County Road Commission by contract surrender control of selection of road projects to its employees and so too may a City by contract surrender control of the area to be protected from fire to its firemen.

The Contract with which we are concerned goes full range. It, by its terms, requires participation in all . . . programs within certain categories without regard to cost or local need.

I am unable to find from the language of the statute, or otherwise, a legislative intent to make such a sweeping alteration in the structure of government. Rather it is my opinion that *the legislature intended to authorize collective bargaining with public employees with respect to working conditions within the framework of policies and projects selected, from time to time, by duly elected officials* (emphasis added). The contract provision is invalid.

Here we have a trial examiner who suggests that a very wide variety of issues can be mandatory subjects of bargaining and, later, a Circuit Court Judge (in a different case), who suggests that there is a very narrow range of bargainable issues, both mandatory and permissive.

Although following this kind of legal discussion is important, the immediate effect of either decision on the parties is negligible. Of far greater importance is a recognition of what subjects have actually been negotiated. A detailed analysis of the content of about 250 collective agreements in Michigan education is the subject of an ongoing research project of the School of Labor and Industrial Relations, Michigan State University. However, the results are not yet available. Nevertheless, the following subjects have been fairly typical of the issues bargained and included in many agreements.

Grievance procedure (including arbitration)	Teacher evaluation
Salaries	Discipline of teachers
Teaching hours and teaching loads	Salary schedules for the 1966–67 school year
Class size	Individual teacher contracts
Use of specialists	Teacher facilities
Non-teaching duties	Use of school facilities
Teacher employment and assignment	Sick leave
Transfers	Temporary leaves of absence
Vacancies and promotions	Extended leaves of absence
Summer school and night school	Sabbatical leave
	Student control and discipline

Protection of teachers	Retirement
Health insurance	Textbooks
Professional development and educational improvement	Dues deduction Duration

THE CONCEPT OF POWER IN PUBLIC BARGAINING

Given that legislation in the United States universally prohibits the use of the strike in public employment, whether collective bargaining in education or elsewhere in public employment can continue in the rather classical manner, emphasizing power that is available but ideally not exercised, is far from clear in June of 1967. I do not believe that the strike can be completely eliminated, by legislation or by other means. If, however, the threat of a strike (or simply the possibility of one), rather than the strike itself, becomes the major exercise of power, and if the use of the strike continues to be limited to less than four percent of the bargaining situations, as it was in Michigan education during 1965–66, it well may be that a balance can be struck. This balance would preserve the form and value of collective bargaining for the vast majority of bargaining relationships while at the same time would observe the intent, although not the exact letter, of the legislative prohibition of the strike. I believe that we cannot realistically expect any greater success, no matter what form of legislation is proposed.

It is interesting to note that, in Australia, where there has been no cultural experience with the concept of "voluntarism" in labor-management relations, long experience with compulsory arbitration, both private and public, has failed to eliminate the strike. The compulsory arbitration process in Australia has only reduced the length of the strike. Since public employment strikes in the United States, especially those involving professionals, have historically been short, even such extreme legislation as Australia's offers no complete solution to the strike. Nevertheless, if the use of power in educational collective bargaining is pushed to the extreme, we must experiment with other solutions, solutions that are broadly compatible with voluntary collective bargaining.

Allen Weisenfeld, Secretary of the New Jersey State Board of

Mediation, offered one such possible solution that is responsive in both its procedures and its philosophy to the problems of free collective bargaining in public employment. As a basic premise, Weisenfeld states that it "is possible to have meaningful collective bargaining without the right to strike only if the right is *voluntarily surrendered* (emphasis added). For this surrender, there must be a *quid pro quo*." [5]

The *quid pro quo* advanced by Weisenfeld includes the following:

Procedures designed to insure stability and peaceful labor relations in the public sector at the local level must be the joint product of public employer and organized employees. If organized public employees are to be persuaded that they are, in a sense, partners in a common effort with public managers on behalf of the commonweal, they must be given a sense of participation in matters that vitally concern them . . .

Desirable involvement of organized public employees in discussions of interest to them and public managers could be accomplished by establishing in communities a public counterpart of the Human Relations Committee in the basic steel industry. A continuing dialogue between responsible representatives of public employees and managers, absent deadlines, will lay bare problem areas. Such a dialogue, if accompanied by good will and conducted in good faith, will yield desirable results. First, it will reduce tensions and enhance respect for the problems each has to face and solve. Second, such solutions as are developed will be a joint product and success tends to feed upon itself. Finally, and by no means insignificant, is the fact that periodic bargaining will be conducted in an atmosphere of mutual respect rather than recrimination.

However, given the best of good will and good faith, differences of opinion during formal collective bargaining must be anticipated. If procedures for the resolution of impasses without recourse to work stoppages are to be successful, these procedures too must be the result of agreement between public employees and managers. If organized public employees share in the creation of the settlement machinery they are far more likely to abide by the established procedures and accept the results.[6]

What Weisenfeld suggests is that public employee groups *voluntarily* agree to give up the strike as a weapon and in return be given full participation in the decision-making process that determines wages, hours, and conditions of employment. This participation should not be an intermittent, *ad hoc* proposition, but should continue on a year-round basis. Weisenfeld recognizes that, even with this type of arrangement, disagreements will still arise occasionally. The processes used to resolve these disagreements must then be a product of the parties themselves, and must include voluntary *ad hoc* agreements to call in a neutral third party to arbitrate interest disputes (the terms and conditions of the agreement itself).

The value of this proposal is its emphasis on the requirement that the parties themselves voluntarily arrive at creative solutions rather than follow rigid procedures and dicta imposed by the government. It seems to me that this procedure has particular appeal to the professional—teacher and administrator alike.[7]

Weisenfeld's analysis also serves to emphasize another very important point too often missed in a discussion of this nature. Collective bargaining, whether public or private, is never strictly an exercise in either "raw power" or "rational problem solving." Rather, it is almost universally a combination of both, and the appropriate use of either and the overall mix is determined by whatever issues, circumstances, and limitations of time are pertinent and by the skill and personalities of the negotiating parties.

The Structure of the Bargaining Relationship

Basically, two rather distinct bargaining structures have emerged within the first year and one-half of bargaining in Michigan education. These structures have several common features, the most visible of which is the designation of the kindergarten through twelfth grade (K-12) as the appropriate bargaining unit for teachers. Almost all determinations made by the Michigan Labor Mediation Board have made this designation. Similarly, the designation that certified classroom teachers have a peculiar community of interest that *usually* excludes other employees within the school system is common to both structures. (The Mediation Board has departed from this rationale in some cases by including other professional employees in the teacher unit, however.) Finally, all "units," throughout the State, are limited to individual school districts.

Departures from either the K-12 designation or the inclusion of non-teaching personnel in units of teachers have occurred most frequently when the parties themselves agree that a particular unit is appropriate and do not go through the process of a hearing or election conducted by the Mediation Board. The figures defining the number of these atypical units are not readily available and are the subject of some ongoing research efforts. However, we expect that the number will be small.

OTHER STRUCTURAL CONSIDERATIONS

Although the negotiation units all are restricted to one individual school district, this characteristic does not completely define the realities of the bargaining structure. The state-level organizations of both the Michigan Education Association and the Michigan Federation of Teachers play extremely important roles that directly affect the nature of the negotiations structure. The Michigan Association of School Boards and the Michigan Association of School Administrators are also influential but, at this time, to a much smaller degree. Even though their influence is great, the MEA and the MFT exert different kinds of influence on their local groups, primarily because the local organizations are related to the parent state organization in different ways. The vast majority of the MFT's membership is concentrated in one local union, the Detroit Federation of Teachers (DFT); hence, a substantial portion of the MFT's resources and efforts are directed there. This does not say that the MFT and the DFT are structurally synonymous; however, the influence of the DFT on other smaller MFT locals regarding contract proposals and settlements may be considerable. Yet in some situations, the reverse is also true. Where a small MFT local is in a district that is favored by either financial or locational considerations, it may be able to expand on the DFT contract settlement and thus become an important "pace setter" that the DFT must recognize.

On the other hand, the MEA operates throughout the state in a strong advisory capacity in its relationships with its local organizations. For example, in the first two years of negotiations, the state organization circulated a "suggested" master agreement to all local organizations, assisted in the local bargaining when asked or where a "target" district had been selected, and attempted to have all local units submit their negotiated agreements to MEA headquarters for review and comments *before the agreements were signed and ratified.* Additionally, field representatives are assigned throughout the state from central MEA headquarters to assist the local organizations in a variety of ways, including bargaining. Finally, the similarity of many of the local MEA agreements strongly suggests that centralized rather than local control may be the chief characteristic of the MEA bargaining structure.

Similar efforts at centralized "consultation" by school board and administrative organizations have been proposed and implemented to a degree. Although the impact of these efforts has not been readily visible and has not altered the bargaining structure in any discernible way, it may just be too early in the development of structural relationships to ascertain the results of these efforts.

STRUCTURAL DANGERS TO CONSIDER

Some of the trends (they certainly are nothing more at this time) accompanying the evolution of the bargaining structure are *potentially* dangerous and should at least be carefully considered before organizational structures, attitudes, and practices become fixed. The high level of involvement by state organizations in the bargaining activities of the local units may very well have been necessary in the early stages of the development of the bargaining relationship, merely to activate the local groups and to provide some of the information and assistance necessary to begin the process of collective bargaining. However, to continue this high level of involvement and inevitably to increase it can sap the vitality, imagination, and organizational effectiveness of the local organizations so that they may become uninterested in or unsupportive of the agreements that are negotiated. This type of alienation is all too common in private industry. I do not deny that a state organization has a legitimate interest in the agreements negotiated by local units. But the extent of the involvement and the degree of toleration for local autonomy and democracy should be examined constantly. Without a high degree of local autonomy, the purpose of collective bargaining—an agreement adapted to the needs and requirements of those directly involved in the working relationship—may not be achieved.

Another structural danger concerns the uneven distribution of power: a paucity of members in the employee group or the limitation of resources available to the school district. A corollary danger is the situation in which neither the school district nor the employee group has adequate financial or administrative resources to truly enter into a bargaining relationship.

In these situations, I feel that it is entirely appropriate for the parties to explore other possibilities to alter the structure of the bargaining relationship as defined by the Labor Mediation Board and state legislation. One possibility might be for the Mediation Board to experiment with another definition of the appropriate unit. Thus, an appropriate unit might include more than one school district where the individual districts are very small. In this way, a form of coalition bargaining that would include perhaps three to five local teacher groups bargaining with three to five local school boards could develop. This scheme obviously is patterned after the bargaining structure in some of the construction trades, where a number of small contractors will band together in an association-type of organization to bargain with either one large local union or a coalition of small locals. This type of experimentation in the schools—on a very restricted basis—may very well allow for effective collective bargaining where it might not otherwise develop.

It would also have the advantage of reducing "whip sawing" tactics practiced by some employee groups: the settlement price of one district in a small geographical area is based not on needs or even bargaining power within that district, but rather on a settlement extracted from another district within the area, often a district whose bargaining power is weak or whose financial base is superior to other area districts. In either case, a higher settlement than otherwise might have been achieved is potentially exacted from all of the districts in the area almost by fiat; and no actual bargaining takes place. It is difficult to regard agreements arrived at in this manner as meeting the individual needs and requirements of the two parties directly involved.

The multi-district structure has obvious difficulties and dangers, particularly given the requirement that the bargaining be related directly to the circumstances and financial structure within the local units. However, I believe that adaptations can be made to accomplish this objective if the proper controls are applied to insure that these arrangements and determinations are allowed only when serious study indicates that meaningful bargaining cannot occur under the normal structural designation. Even then, the Mediation Board should proceed on a case-by-case basis, and should assess the results of each experimentation before attempting others. The most apparent advantages of implementing this type of structural change is that meaningful bargaining will have a far better chance of succeeding if (1) the power of both sides is evenly distributed or (2) both sides have the ability to provide the necessary manpower, resources, and expertise that they simply cannot afford individually. However, the Mediation Board has never been asked to consider this type of unit nor if asked is it likely to be favorably disposed to do so under the present statutory limitations. Nonetheless, I feel that controlled experimentation with the determination of appropriate units is highly desirable.

Conclusion

A remarkably good experience was achieved during the first year's bargaining in Michigan education. In no sense, however, does this first year's experience predict rigid patterns for the future. Frankly, the first year's successes will probably be hard to duplicate.

Serious problems will develop over the next few years, and there may be failures in bargaining. Both sides will be testing each other to determine the limits of a particular advantage or their general power, and in this exercise, mistakes will inevitably be made. The parties' faith and trust in each other and in the collective bargaining process itself, and changes in attitudes and roles will take time to develop.

But, in public employment—as well as private—no other institution for the resolution of employee-employer conflicts and disputes over wages, hours, and working conditions is as compatible with a free, open, democratic society as the institution of collective bargaining.

NOTES

1. See report, *School Employee-Management Relations Information Program—1966–67*, Charles T. Schmidt, Jr., Project Director. The report is available from the School of Labor and Industrial Relations, Kedzie Hall, Michigan State University, East Lansing, Michigan.

2. See the "Report to Governor Romney," Advisory Committee on Public Employee Relations, Russell A. Smith, Chairman, February 15, 1967.

3. Vernon Jensen, "The Process of Collective Bargaining and the Question of Its Obsolescence," reprinted from the *Industrial and Labor Relations Review*, Vol. 16, No. 4 (July, 1963), pp. 549–550. (Copyright © 1963 by Cornell University. All rights reserved.) No assumption is made that Dr. Jensen would agree that his postulates apply as redefined here.

4. A trial examiner's decision becomes final unless exceptions are filed within twenty days of the service of the trial examiner's decision on the parties. In this case, exceptions were filed, but the withdrawal was prior to the Board's consideration of the case. The Board granted the withdrawal and therefore did not review the trial examiner's decision on the merits. Accordingly, it is speculative whether the Board would have agreed or disagreed with the trial examiner.

5. Allen Weisenfeld, "The Philosophy of Bargaining for Municipal Employees," *The Arbitration Journal*, Vol. 22, No. 1 (1967), p. 46. (Reprinted by permission of the publisher.)

6. *Ibid.*, pp. 46–47.

7. On May 26, 1967, the Michigan Attorney General issued Opinion No. 4578, which stated that:

. . . boards of education are without lawful authority to include in their master contracts with representatives of their employees a provision for compulsory arbitration.

This opinion, however, is strictly an advisory opinion and has not been tested in the courts. Furthermore, the opinion is not clear on at least these specific points: (1) It makes no distinction between arbitration of interest disputes and arbitration of grievances, (2) it does not differentiate between compulsory arbitration and voluntary arbitration, and (3) its usage of the term "compulsory arbitration" is not consistent with the usage as currently understood in either the theory or practice of industrial relations.

VI

SOME ISSUES AND CHALLENGES— OLD AND NEW

At this early stage in the development of public employee bargaining, the issues and challenges have not been fully identified. The appropriate bargaining unit, the subject matter of bargaining, the relationship to civil service systems, and the resolution of disputes are among the issues that need clarification. Although experiences are limited, public employment collective bargaining affords unique opportunities for research.

The following three selections call attention to three important issues in public employment collective bargaining: (1) compulsory arbitration, (2) the right to strike, and (3) the role of state agencies that administer collective bargaining legislation. Two of the readings recommend the need for creativity in arriving at solutions to the issues posed. Creative approaches will also be needed in defining and debating other issues. There is the tendency to transfer experience gained in one kind of institutional setting to another different setting. To put it another way, the experiences of collective bargaining in the private sector may not be fully applicable to collective bargaining in the public sector.

David Shenton's "Compulsory Arbitration in the Public Service" and Marc Somerhausen's, "The Right to Strike in the Public Service" focus on alternatives available to the parties when collective bargaining fails. Professor Somerhausen's contribution is especially valuable because it provides an international frame of reference. Jean T. McKelvey's "The Role of State Agencies in Public Employee Labor Relations" is a brilliant and complete exploratory analysis of the administrative and quasi-judicial roles of state labor relations boards, commissions, and agencies that are becoming more extensively involved in public employment collective bargaining.

Compulsory Arbitration in the Public Service

DAVID G. SHENTON

Compulsory arbitration has sometimes been suggested as the answer to one of the basic problems of union-management relations in the public service: how to insure bargaining power to unions, while denying them their strike privilege.[1] And yet this proposed solution is itself engulfed in a tangle of legal, historical, and emotional problems—so much so that its implementation would be extremely difficult.

Legal Obstacles

The basic dilemma stems from the firmly entrenched policy that government employees may not strike. There are several reasons for this policy. The first involves the doctrine that the people are sovereign: that a strike against the government is in actuality a strike against the entire nation.[2] Another reason for the government's immunity from strikes is the vital nature of government services. The oft-cited example of this is policemen and firemen. It is pointed out that the public could never be ex-

Reprinted from *Labor Law Journal*, XVII (March 1966), 138–147, by permission of the author and publisher. Copyright © 1966 Commerce Clearing House, Inc.

David G. Shenton is a research assistant at the New York State School of Industrial and Labor Relations.

pected to forego these services in the event of a strike; thus, the answer is to outlaw the strike. This reasoning has simply been extended to include all government personnel.

Proponents of compulsory arbitration argue that this loss of the strike weapon places the union in public service in a disadvantaged position. It has no foundation of power from which to press its demands. Thus, compulsory arbitration is advocated as a compromise to compensate for the loss of the right to strike. It provides the union with an avenue of recourse in the event of an unfair administrative decision. This is its main advantage —that it compensates for the loss of the union's right to strike.

There are, however, disadvantages to a compulsory arbitration law. This paper will focus mainly on the legal problems, but there are a host of other problems that would greatly hinder the implementation of such a law. These problems (that is, the acceptability of the decision to the parties, a collapse of the collective bargaining machinery as the parties simply rely on the arbitrators, decisions founded on compromise instead of principle, etc.) are not within the scope of this paper. One should realize, however, that in addition to the legal problems to be discussed, these other problems would further complicate any attempts to introduce compulsory arbitration.

The main constitutional problem involves the doctrine that the people comprise a sovereign entity. Can the elected representatives of the people delegate to others, either inside or outside the government, the exercise of authority or discretion confided in them by law? The position of the New York City administration during the recent welfare strike is a perfect illustration: "The unions said they opposed the advisory panel . . . because its decision would be binding on them but not the city. The city has contended it cannot commit itself to binding arbitration, because only the Mayor and the Board of Estimate can legally dispose of municipal funds." [3]

Another constitutional problem revolves around the question of government liability. "Opposition to arbitration in the public service is based on the broader question of whether or not the nature of public employment is such as to permit the adjudication of issues between the employing authorities and their staffs by 'outsiders.' " [4]

To be added to these problems are some basic differences between public and private employment. In private industry an arbitration system is voluntarily established between an employer and a union which is the employees' exclusive bargaining representative.

This arrangement basically rests on a rather elaborate structure of law and practice protecting the right of employees to join unions of their own choice, providing for designation by public authority of the appropriate bargaining unit, and guaranteeing to the union chosen by the majority in that unit, the right to serve as the exclusive representatives of the employees.[5]

It is important to recognize that the essential elements of this institutional framework are almost entirely absent from public employment.

It should be fairly obvious from the foregoing description of differences and problems that any law calling for compulsory arbitration for government employees would run into stiff opposition. Still, there have been efforts made along this line.

Early Cases and Experience

So far back as the late 1800s, cases arose concerning the problem of compulsory arbitration and the public service. Illustrative is *Mann v. Richardson*,[6] which in 1873 concerned the right of public officials in Illinois to submit discretionary matters to arbitration. A commissioner of highways and a homeowner were unable to agree on a price for the disposed owner's home. They asked that the matter go to arbitration. The Circuit Court of Illinois, however, ruled that this question could not go to arbitration, and thus bind the town. The court, in addressing the public official said:

Where the law imposes a personal duty upon an officer in relation to a matter of public interest, he can not delegate it to others, and, therefore, such officer can not submit such matters to arbitration.

During the 1940s, two decisions were handed down which serve to illustrate the prevailing thought on compulsory arbitration for government employees. The leading case, *Mugford, et al. v. Mayor and City Council of Baltimore*,[7] involved a taxpayer's suit to enjoin the enforcement of a contract between the City of Baltimore and Local 825 of the Teamsters. The contract provided for, among other things, binding arbitration of disputes between the city and the union.

The actual decision in this case turned on the authority of the municipality to grant exclusive recognition for collective bargaining to one labor union, and on its authority to enter into an agreement fixing the terms and conditions of employment.[8] The court did, however, discuss the clause which called for binding arbitration. It pointed out that the same reasoning which nullified the entire contract also applied to the arbitration provision; governmental authority may not be delegated to others, since this authority is public property; the public officer does not have the same freedom as the private employer and his authority is limited by law. Specifically the court said, "The authority of municipal officers may not be diminished or impaired by agreement to arbitration or by any other device."

A year later the Ohio Court of Common Pleas faced the same basic question in *City of Cleveland v. Division 268, Amalgamated Assn. of Street, Electric Railway and Motor Coach Employees of America.* This case concerned the authority of the Cleveland Transit Board to enter into a collective bargaining agreement designating the union as exclusive bargaining agent. The agreement was similar to the one cited in the *Mugford* case and provided that "the finding of the said Board of Arbitration shall be final and binding on both parties hereunto when made in accordance with the agreement." [9] The court dealt with the exclusive bargaining agent question by citing the *Mugford* decision and thus holding that the Transit Board did not have the power to enter into such an agreement in the absence of an express grant of authority to do so. The court further held that the provision calling for compulsory arbitration was illegal as an improper delegation of authority. It cited *Mugford* and *8 Ohio Jurisprudence,* Section 218, which states: "The principle is fundamental and of universal application, that public powers conferred upon a municipal corporation and its officers or agents cannot be surrendered or delegated to others."

This then was the state of affairs prior to 1950. Compulsory arbitration was deemed to be an unlawful delegation of legislative authority. "As a matter of principle, government is not in a position to permit its relations with its employees to be fixed by arbitration." [10]

The first major decision in favor of some form of arbitration of public employment disputes was handed down in 1951 by the Supreme Court of Errors of Connecticut. The court, in *Norwalk Teacher Assn. v. Board of Education*,[11] was asked for a declaratory judgment on several questions. The plaintiff was an independent labor union representing all but two of the 300 employees in the Norwalk school system. After a salary dispute, 250 union members refused the individual contracts offered them by the Board and refused to return to work. Negotiations were begun which resulted in a master contract between the union and the School Board. The union nevertheless brought the action because a teacher was discharged.

Among the several questions posed to the court was the following: "Is arbitration a permissible method under Connecticut law to settle or adjust disputes between the plaintiff and the defendant?" The court replied:

The power of a town to enter into an agreement of arbitration was originally denied on the ground that it was an unlawful delegation of authority. *Griswold v. North Stonington*, 5 Conn. 367, 371. It was later held that not only the amount of damages but liability could be submitted to arbitration. *Hine v. Stephens*, 33 Conn. 497, 504; *Mallory v. Hunington*, 64 Conn. 88, 96, 29 A. 245. The principle applies to the case at bar. If it is borne in mind that arbitration is the result of mutual agreement, there is no reason to deny the power of the defendant to enter voluntarily into a contract to arbitrate a specific dispute. On a proposal for a submission, the defendant would have the opportunity of deciding whether it would arbitrate as to any question within its power. Its power to submit to arbitration would not extend to questions of policy but might extend to questions of liability. Arbitration as a method of settling disputes is growing in importance and, in a proper case, "deserves the enthusiastic support of the courts." *International Brotherhood of Teamsters, Local 145 v. Shapiro*, 138 Conn. 57, 69, 82 A. 2d 345, 20 LC ¶ 66,446 (1951). Agreement to submit all disputes to arbitration, commonly found in ordinary union contracts, are in a different category. If the defendant entered into a general agreement of that kind, it might find itself committed to surrender broad discretion and responsibility reposed in it by law. For example, it could not commit to an arbitrator the decision of a proceeding to discharge a teacher for cause. So, the matter of certification of teachers is committed to the State Board of Education. Gen. Stat., 1432, 1433, 1435. The best answer we can give to (the) question . . . is, "Yes, arbitration may be a permissible method as to certain specific, arbitrable disputes."

Thus, where the previous cases had been of the opinion that arbitration in any form constituted an unlawful delegation of authority, this decision said arbitration is a legal device to handle certain, specific, narrowly defined disputes.

Although the legality of arbitration in the public service has been questionable at best, there are instances where arbitration has been used to settle public service disputes. There are well over 70 cities which now have contracts specifying grievance arbitration.[12] Illustrative is the 1956 contract between the City of New Haven, Connecticut and Local 713 of the American Federation of State, County and Municipal Employees, AFL-CIO, which provided for the last step in the grievance procedure to be arbitration. And in 1957, Local 713 became the first AFSCME union to use the services of the American Arbitration Association.[13] The grievance in question evolved from a conflict between the contract's "full eight-hour day" clause and a "present benefits" clause which declared that "all benefits enjoyed by city employees affected shall be contained and considered a part of this agreement." The city's refuse collectors had traditionally stopped work after the completion of their routes which took from six to six and one-half hours; when the city made them complete a full eight-hour day upon finishing their routes, the workers staged a work stoppage. The city and union, after failing to reach an agreement, finally agreed to let the issue be resolved by a single arbitrator.

The fact that the arbitrator ruled against the union is of little importance; that both parties agreed to accept arbitration is important. The Local President declared after the decision:

The union's members are satisfied with the decision. The Local's contract with the City of New Haven represents the first agreement with a city of its size in Connecticut. In addition to winning seniority and sick leave under the contract, the Local established the right to submit problems to arbitration. This is certainly an important step in gaining full union rights for government employees.[14]

In summary, although several courts have banned compulsory arbitration of grievances in the public service, at least one court has given qualified approval and there are several contracts in existence which call for arbitration.

Arbitration by a Government Body

One possible avenue for the handling of government-union disputes would be the statutory establishment of a "Labor Court" with authority broad enough to successfully discharge its responsibilities. There is already precedent for such a legislative enactment—the many Civil Service Commissions. While some states have established civil service arrangements by means of state constitutional mandates, many states and the federal government have done so by means of statutory provisions.[15] Illustrative is the Civil Service Act originally adopted in 1883.[16]

An analogy can be drawn, at least arguably, between the Civil Service Commission and an arbitrator. The Commission is a governmental body; yet, it does have some autonomous control over its function. It can review dismissals, set wage rates, establish conditions of work, etc. Thus, if a governmental body exists which already has this kind of authority, why not extend the principle one step further? Why not enable a "Court" or "Commission" to have the power to settle these questions for all government service employees?

Critics will immediately charge that this is an improper delegation of legislative power and authority; that broad questions will undoubtedly be raised that can only be handled legally by the legislature. Yet, the Civil Service Commission has never been restricted on such a charge.

The Civil Service Commissions were among the earliest administrative agencies empowered to adopt rules and regulations to implement application and enforcement of the enabling statute, the civil service laws. Such authority to make rules and regulations carrying out the purposes and intent of the civil service statute has been held not to be a delegation of legislative power.[17]

In fact, the doctrine of nondelegation is entirely judge made, and its history is, therefore, riddled with inconsistencies and contradictions. The [U.S.] Constitution merely provides: "All legislative Powers herein granted shall be vested in a Congress of the

United States . . . (and the power) . . . to make all Laws which shall be necessary and proper for carrying into Execution the Foregoing Powers. . . ." [18] That Congress must delegate some powers is, of course, clear. Such powers as "to raise and collect taxes," "to coin and borrow money," etc. must be delegated. To this day, however, people still believe that legislative power cannot be delegated. Yet, according to Davis (see footnote 21), the Supreme Court has invalidated only three laws as being unlawful delegations of legislative power; they were New Deal cases handed down in 1935–1936.[19]

Sovereign Immunity Doctrine

The establishment of a "Labor Court" would not only call into focus questions of legislative delegation, but also governmental immunity. Can the government surrender its long tradition of immunity to accept a court's decision against it?

The one major area in which the government has surrendered immunity has been tort liability. In 1907 Mr. Justice Holmes said:

A sovereign is exempt from suit, not because of any formal conception or obsolete theory, but on the logical and practical ground that there can be no legal right as against the authority that makes the law on which the right depends.[20]

Since this statement, however, the sovereign immunity doctrine has become quite limited. In 1966, New York and Illinois are only two among many states which impose broad tort liability upon themselves.[21]

Following this lead the federal government enacted the Federal Tort Claims Act in 1948. The Act does not go so far as to abolish the sovereign immunity doctrine. It merely imposes liability upon the federal government for "damages to or loss of property or . . . personal injury or death caused by negligent or wrongful act or omission of any employee of the Government while acting within the scope of his office or employment, under circumstances where the United States, if a private person, would be liable." [22] Further, the Act does not impose liability for intentional torts; such things as assault, false arrest, battery, libel, slander, etc. are excluded from the Act. The government is immune from liability in tort for the exercise of discretionary powers by its officers—even if the discretion is abused.

Thus, although the federal government has surrendered its immunity, it has done so only in a limited degree. Actions of subordinates, discretionary, and intended acts cannot be the basis for tort action. The fact remains, however, that to some extent the federal government *has* surrendered its immunity; the legislature has surrendered immunity to the judiciary.

Currently, Civil Service decisions are subject to judicial review. This feature would be unnecessary for a labor court to function properly, but the right of appeal on certain major questions could be provided for.

A labor court may be a possible answer to the perplexing problems created by the loss of the strike weapon. There is precedent for having a government agency handle disputes. The principles expounded in founding the Civil Service system (that is, the delegation of legislative authority) and enacting the Torts Act (surrendering governmental immunity) are the blocks of the foundation upon which to build. Expanding the principles from this foundation would be a difficult, but not insurmountable task.

Arbitration by Nongovernmental Personnel

Another possible solution would be the arbitration of disputes by nongovernmental personnel in a manner similar to that of private industry. Arbitrators could be used on an *ad hoc* basis or for the life of the contract depending upon the uniqueness of the situation.

It would also be possible to expand the scope of arbitration to include substantive or contract as well as grievance issues. There is very little material on this aspect of the problem, but one state case does provide some insight into problems that might arise.

Since 1947, the Minnesota Labor Relations Act has outlawed strikes and provided for compulsory arbitration in charitable, nonprofit hospitals, a "charitable hospital" being defined as "all *state,* university, *county* and *municipal* hospitals or any hospital no part of the net income of which inures to the benefit of any private member, stockholder, or individual." [23] Section 179.38 of the Act states:

> If such dispute is not settled within ten days after submission to conciliation, *any unsettled issue of maximum hours of work and minimum hourly wage rates* shall, upon service of written notice by either party upon the other party and the State Labor Conciliator, be submitted to the determination of a board of abritrators whose determination shall be *final and binding* upon the parties. The board of arbitrators shall be selected and proceed in the following manner, unless otherwise agreed upon by the parties: the employees shall appoint one arbitrator, the employers shall appoint one arbitrator, and the two arbitrators so chosen shall appoint a third arbitrator who shall act as chairman. . . .[24]

Although not stated explicitly, this section is important in that it does provide the avenue through which to bring in outside arbitrators. Further, the arbitrators are selected in a manner similar to that often used in private employment.

Needless to say, the clause has been challenged in the courts. In 1954 the *Fairview Hospital Ass'n v. Public Building Service and Hospital Employees Union, Local 113* [25] decision was handed down. The case was brought by nine charitable hospitals to enjoin the union from "causing, promoting, or participating in a strike or other work stoppage affecting plaintiffs' employees, pursuant to the union's strike notice filed with the Minnesota Labor Conciliator, April 1, 1953."

As stated above, the Minnesota Act calls for binding arbitration of questions involving "maximum hours of work and minimum hourly wage rates." This wording seems to leave many important collective bargaining issues beyond the scope of the arbitration provision, but the Minnesota Court in the *Fairview* case gave this clause a very broad interpretation. It said this clause would seem to cover "matters relating to daily hours of work; work days per week; days of sick leave; holidays and vacation days; health and welfare matters; and numerous other issues bearing most directly upon the defendants' welfare." [26] In short, the court included as arbitrable issues almost everything except union security. Thus, this is one of the first attempts at including contract or substantive issues in the arbitration procedure for public service employees.

The union's defense was to challenge the constitutionality of several of the Act's sections, including the compulsory arbitration provision. The union asserted that: (1) the sections deny equal protection to hospital employees and deprive them of commonlaw rights without due process; (2) they constitute an unlawful delegation of legislative power to boards of arbitration without providing standards for their decisions; and (3) they are vague and indefinite and hence not susceptible to judicial construction.[27]

The court answered the first argument by stating that the equal protection clause of the Constitution does not require that an enactment operate with rigid sameness upon all persons. The legislature, under its police power, may prescribe rules respecting rights, duties, and obligations of employers and employees as separate groups. The compulsory arbitration section, which limits the bargaining power of both parties (the union cannot strike and the hospitals must submit issues to arbitration), is not arbitrary and unreasonable legislation that discriminates against employees. The union must show this section's arbitrariness and unreasonableness to make its enactment invalid under the equal protection clause.

The court handled the unlawful delegation question by stating that basic standard policy (as set forth in Section 179.40) and rules of action (Sections 179.35–179.39) were established for the guidance of the "agency" in exercising its power. Sections 179.35–179.38, respectively, give definitions to the terminology, prohibit strikes, prohibit lockouts, and provide for compulsory arbitration. The court felt that when this was coupled with the broad policy guidelines enumerated in Section 179.40, sufficient guidance was provided for the just and equitable determination of the issues. Thus, this was not an unlawful delegation of legislative power.

The last constitutional problem faced was the vague and indefinite nature of the sections and their insusceptibility to judicial construction. Here the Minnesota Court pointed to the National Labor Relations Act which does not define wages or hours to a more specific degree than the Minnesota Act and has never been challenged on this ground. It also cited *New Jersey Bell Company v. Communication Workers,* which stated:

It is . . . requisite that the delegation of legislative power prescribe the standards that are to govern the administrative agency in the exercise of such delegated power, but it is only necessary that the statute establish a sufficient basic standard—a definite and certain policy and rule of action for the guidance of the agency created to administer the law.[28]

Since the Minnesota Act provided specific standards and policy to follow, it could not be declared unlawful by reason of its vagueness.

This is an extremely important case to keep in mind, for although the case is obviously not controlling over any other state or federal court, it is evident that a law was upheld which called for the arbitration of some key new contract terms. It is also important because nongovernmental personnel are used on the arbitration panels and present awards that are binding on the government. While the compulsory arbitration principle has been applied only to an extremely narrow segment of the government of Minnesota, nonetheless, it has been applied and upheld.

There have been no attempts at the federal level to provide compulsory arbitration. The strongest parallel that can be drawn is a case which upheld a delegation of legislative power to private individuals. In *St. Louis, I. M. & S. R. Co. v. Taylor*,[29] a statute was challenged which provided that the American Railway Association should certify to the Interstate Commerce Commission a standard height for drawbars on all freight cars; the Commission had no discretion to reject or modify the height that was certified. Congress, furthermore, did not prescribe any standards in the statute. All action was brought by the small railroads who were forced to abide by the will of the larger lines. The Supreme Court, undaunted, upheld the delegation as a proper use of the legislative function.

Whether the Supreme Court would be as willing to allow legislative power to be delegated to nongovernmental arbitrators would be only speculation. It has been the contention of this section that nongovernmental personnel could be used on arbitration panels to fix contract terms and adjust grievances. A federal law calling for such a panel would undoubtedly be challenged on grounds very similar to those used by the union in the *Fairview* case. What this section has attempted to show is that these problems have been met and surmounted on the state level and in a different form at the federal level.

Conclusions

The conclusions of this paper are basically the same as those of Blaine, Hagburg and Zeller. Because of the union's loss of the right to strike in public service, compulsory arbitration must be included in the collective bargaining procedure if it is to be at all meaningful. Whether this is done by means of a government "Labor Court" or by nongovernmental personnel, the legal problems faced will be substantially the same. Problems of surrendering governmental immunity, unlawful delegations of legislative power and authority, denying equal protection, etc., must be faced.

The area of government-labor relations is not static; creative approaches are needed to solve the many perplexing problems. Compulsory arbitration could be the answer to these problems. It compensates for the loss of the union's right to strike. At the same time, a carefully drawn statute (as illustrated by the Minnesota Act) would still safeguard the government's final authority. While compulsory arbitration certainly will not be the panacea for all government-labor relation problems, it deserves a more intensive examination into its merits as a possible solution.

NOTES

1. During the recent welfare strike in New York City, for example, Welfare Commissioner James R. Dumpson said: "I believe people dealing in human services should not strike. I believe arbitration should be mandatory." *New York Times,* Jan. 5, 1965, p. 21, col. 3.
2. Herbert Hoover stated: "If civil servants are to strike, they are striking against the entire people, and there is no right or justification for that." National Civil Service League, *Employee Organization in the Public Service,* New York, 1946, p. 22.
3. *New York Times,* January 5, 1965, p. 21, col. 3.
4. Sterling D. Spero, *Government as Employer,* New York, Remsen Press, 1948, p. 407.
5. Charles C. Killingsworth, "Grievance Adjudication in Public Employment," *The Arbitration Journal,* Vol. 13, No. 1 (1955), p. 5.
6. 66 Ill. 481.
7. Cir. Ct. No. 2 of Baltimore, April 13, 1944. 8 LC ¶ 62,137.

8. The court did not declare all agreements with labor organizations unlawful, but simply said, "preferential ?nd exclusive features common to labor union contracts must in the field of government be altogether avoided. . . ."

9. Agreement between the Transit Board of Cleveland and the Union, as quoted in Rhyne, p. 189.

10. Report of the Second Industrial Conference called by the President, March 6, 1921, p. 42, as quoted in Spero, cited in footnote 4, p. 408.

11. 83 A. 2d 482, 20 LC ¶ 66,543 (1951).

12. Killingsworth, cited at footnote 5, at p. 9. Among cities included in this category are New Haven and Norwalk, Connecticut; Niagara Falls and Troy, New York; Dayton, Ohio; and Racine, Wisconsin.

13. "Arbitration in Action," *The Public Employee*, Vol. 22, No. 2, February 1957, p. 13.

14. *The Public Employee*, cited at footnote 13, at p. 13.

15. H. Eliot Kaplan, *The Law of Civil Service*, New York, Matthew Bender & Co. Inc., 1958, p. 33.

16. 22 Stat. 403, 5 U.S.C.A. 633.

17. Kaplan, cited at footnote 15, at p. 35.

18. The Constitution of the United States of America, Art. I, Sec. 1, and Sec. 8.

19. *Panama Refining Co. v. Ryan*, 293 U. S. 388, (1935); *Schechter Poultry Corp. v. United States*, 295 U. S. 495 (1935); *Carter v. Carter Coal Co.*, 298 U. S. 238 (1936).

20. *Kawananakoa v. Polybank*, 205 U. S. 349.

21. Kenneth Culp Davis, *Administrative Law*, St. Paul, Minnesota, West Publishing Co., 1951, p. 97.

22. 62 Stat. 982 (1948), Sec. 2672.

23. Minn. Stat. Ann., Sec. 179.35. West Supp. (1964), p. 164. (Italics added.)

24. Minn. Stat. Ann., Sec. 179.38, p. 166. (Italics added.)

25. 241 Minn. 523, 64 N. W. 2d 16, 25 LC ¶ 68,285 (1954).

26. See footnote 25: *Fairview*, cited at footnote 24, at p. 541.

27. See footnote 25: *Fairview*, cited at footnote 24, at p. 528.

28. 5 N. J. 354, 370, 75 A. 2d 721, 729, 18 LC ¶ 65,997 (1950).

29. 211 U. S. 281 (1908).

The Right to Strike in the Public Service

MARC SOMERHAUSEN

If the right to strike in the free world is at present generally admitted in the private sector of economic activity, there is no

Reprinted from *Free Labour World*, CLXXVI (February 1965), 3–8, by permission of the author and publisher.

Marc Somerhausen is Professor of Law at Brussels University.

such general recognition so far as the public services are concerned. The evolution is ohly just beginning in the public sector. Most political scientists would probably deny that there was any such evolution at' all; they would consider those countries where the right of civil servants to strike is admitted as exceptions proving the rule.

Indeed, in most countries the very notion of civil service implies the prohibition of any concerted stoppage of work. In some cases, however, distinctions are made between different branches or various levels of the public services.

When governments and municipalities started to engage in industrial activities, it became clear that the rules applying to the traditional functions of the state should not necessarily apply to the economic activities of the state, local authorities or public corporations. If a bricklayer or a coal miner in private enterprise was allowed to strike, why should the bricklayer or the coal miner in a nationalised industry be forbidden to do so?

A distinction was thus drawn between public officials who are intimately connected with the machinery of government, who exert a measure of public authority, who are entitled to command or to transmit commands to their fellow citizens, on the one hand, and, on the other, workers who, though paid by the state, the municipalities or an official corporation, are otherwise indistinguishable from ordinary private employees.

This distinction takes different forms in different countries.

In Great Britain different rules apply to non-industrial civil servants and government industrial employees.

In Sweden, train drivers and conductors, station masters, railway clerks and station staff are all civil servants, whilst modern state-owned industries, some iron ore mines, some pulp and saw mills, a commercial bank, etc., are run as private enterprises.

In Germany, a distinction exists between officials (*Beamte*), whose status is governed by a special law, and salaried employees (*Angestellte*) and workers (*Arbeiter*), to both of whom the law of the private labour market applies. Government functions in a wide sense are entrusted to *Beamte,* whilst clerical work is done by *Angestellte* and manual work by *Arbeiter.* The terms of employment of the two last categories are laid down in collective agreements.

In theory, the distinction between authority over subordinate staff or over the public at large, on the one hand, and service to the public on the other, may seem convincing, but in practice the line is difficult to draw. And even when the legislator himself draws the line or empowers the government to do so, the distinction is sometimes blurred by the efforts of officials themselves, who strive for regrading in what they consider as a higher category, even if this promotion deprives them of the right to strike.

Obedience, Respect, Discipline, Devotion

Let us look again at the traditional concept of the civil servant.

We still find this in its purest form in the German civil service. There the civil servant is required conscientiously to discharge all the duties directly appertaining to his office, to obey the official orders of his superiors in so far as they do not contravene the law, and to behave in a manner fitting the dignity of his office. Without entailing a legal claim to extra pay, existing functions may be extended or altered, so long as the new work corresponds to the training and capacity of the official. When special help is demanded during a strike to do the work the strikers would normally have done, all officials have to obey —even higher officials are obliged, where necessary, to do purely physical labour.

Respect for ,superiors is demanded outside as well as inside the office, even when the superior is objectionable in character and demeanour. Officials must not allow insults to pass unnoticed, lest the service suffer degradation. They must order their general way of life to conform to prevalent opinions on virtue, manners and morals.

This discipline is especially strict in relation to school teachers, and marriages must be notified as soon as they take place, including the name and profession of the father-in-law. Police officials have especially severe obligations as to sobriety. In the matter of contracting debts, not only is the official himself watched, reprimanded and fined when the matter becomes serious and damaging enough, but he is expected to stop his wife from frivolous domestic expenditure. Games of chance may be played in good company so long as one's economic independence is not thereby jeopardised.

No official may take on any additional offices or employments other than those for which he has asked and obtained permission of the appropriate departmental authority. It is an axiom that all the official's time and energy must be devoted to the proper fulfilment of official duties and that he must observe official secrecy.

Similar rules to those of the German civil service exist in other countries, but are not always as precisely codified. These rules are ubiquitous and ever-present threats and the essence of their purpose is subordination and devotion. They constitute a kind of state religion. If one accepts this religious attitude towards the state it is obvious that a strike of civil servants is absolutely out of the question.

Another aspect of civil service which is often stressed is disinterestedness: the public welfare is supposed to be the civil servant's sole aim in life.

There is also a political argument advanced against strikes in public services. Any strike for better conditions or higher wages is tantamount to insurrection against the overriding power of the legislator, because any increase in remuneration or change in the hours of work is bound to affect the budget which has been voted by parliament and the ordinances which have been legitimately made by the government. Any strike of public servants is therefore illegal. It is the negation of democratic rule.

A similar reasoning prevails in communist countries. Here it is said that the strike is an aspect of the class struggle. In a communist state, where the state is the instrument of the working class, the class struggle has been abolished. A section of the working class may not impose its will upon the legitimate organs of the whole working class. A strike is in essence counter-revolutionary, it is a survival of the capitalist system and as such should be ruthlessly suppressed.

The Sanctity-of-Continuity Theory

Another point is made against strikes in public services from a purely legalistic point of view. Railroads, postal services, hospitals as well as prisons, courts and police have been established because they were deemed indispensable to the public. Therefore nobody can interfere with their operation. Strikes are illegal because they impede the continuity of public services.

Whatever the theory may be, the fact is that in most countries clauses have been inserted in the statute books in order to prevent strikes in the public services. These clauses may apply to all persons engaged in public services or connected with them, or only to some branches of the civil services. They may provide penal sanctions or only disciplinary sanctions.

The French penal code of 1810 includes a chapter on "coalitions of civil servants." Article 123 provides for prison sentences of between two and six months on persons entrusted with any part of public authority who take concerted action contrary to the laws. Article 126 is aimed at civil servants who have jointly decided to resign with the aim, or with the effect, of impeding or interrupting either the administration of justice or the provision of any service whatever.

Similar clauses are found in the Belgian penal code (art. 233 to 236), but they have never been applied to strikes of civil servants. As a matter of fact civil servants who go on strike do not resign and have no intention of doing so, neither do they break any formal law. In France, however, these clauses have been applied to strikers in public services.

The Italian penal code inflicts penalities for the collective abandonment of their jobs by civil servants (art. 330) and considers strikes as offences against "public economy" (art. 502 to 505). Lawyers discuss the problem whether these clauses have been abolished by article 40 of the constitution of 1947 which proclaims the right to strike within the limits determined by law. A physician who refused his services to a patient because he was taking part in a strike was punished and his conviction was upheld by the supreme court. So was a striking level-crossing keeper.

In the Netherlands the penalty for strikes of civil servants or railway servants or railway workers is jail up to two years (law of 1903, art. 358). However, it seems that these clauses have rarely been applied.

In Great Britain the Conspiracy and Protection of Property

Act of 1875 contains a clause making strikers in the gas and water supply industries "liable either to pay a penalty not exceeding twenty pounds or to be imprisoned for a term not exceeding three months." This clause has been extended to persons employed in the electricity supply industry.

In Great Britain, there is no law forbidding civil servants to strike, but it is clear that striking, even if not illegal, is a disciplinary offence on the part of a civil servant.

In the United States of America, the Taft-Hartley Labor Management Relations Act of June 1947 (section 305) made it unlawful for any person employed by the United States or any agency thereof (including any wholly-owned government corporation) to participate in any strike. The penalty is immediate discharge, the forfeit of civil service status and a three-year ineligibility for re-employment.

In Belgium, the prime minister, Mr. Theodore Lefevre, declared in the Senate on 13 July 1961: "The statute of the personnel of the state does not exclude the right to strike. I believe everybody agrees on this point." The government and the local authorities, however, may consider a strike as a breach of discipline, and inflict penalties on civil servants who take part in one. Such disciplinary measures have been upheld on appeal.

Remarkable Evolution

The situation in France deserves closer study, because the evolution in this country has been most remarkable.

At the beginning of the century, the right of association itself was expressly denied to civil servants for the same reasons that the right to strike was denied later. When civil servants were supposed to be bound to the state by contract, the government held that they broke that contract if they went on strike. No disciplinary procedure was necessary to discharge them and no hearing of the culprit was required prior to discharge. Later, the notion of contract was discarded and the government considered that the legal position of the civil servant was unilaterally decided by law or regulations. The penalty for striking remained the same: automatic discharge without any hearing.

Then after the second world war came the constitution of the

Fourth Republic whose preamble stated that the right to strike was recognized within the limits determined by law. Laws were passed which forbade any strike in the police forces, but for the great majority of the civil service there was no legislation about the right to strike at all. What was the position for these other branches of government?

A heated controversy then developed as to whether the clause in the preamble meant nothing so long as specific legislation did not exist, or whether it had legal force and could be invoked in a court of law.

The argument was finally settled when the Conseil d'Etat (the constitutional court) ruled that the preamble of the constitution was not merely a piece of literature, but contained general principles of law which had to be applied by the courts.

Since there was no statutory limitation of the right to strike, it was within the powers of the government or of individual ministers to prescribe limits with due consideration for the essential character of the various government services and of the degree of authority of the various ranks of the civil service. The government may not outlaw strikes altogether for a particular class of civil servants, but it may forbid higher officials to strike or even minor officials whose activity is essential for the protection of life and property. Thus departmental heads may be restrained from joining a strike of the staff of the department. But the minister exceeds his powers if he suspends for a month the janitor of a state factory who, as shop steward, has organised a strike in his plant. And in any case, disciplinary sanctions cannot be applied without giving a hearing to the civil servant and applying all the rules of due disciplinary procedure.

A further step was taken with a new law in July 1963.

Article 3 of that law states: "Whenever the staff mentioned in Article 1 make use of the right to strike, the concerted cessation of work must be preceded by a notice. The notice must be given by the trade union organisation or organisations most representative at the national level, in the craft or in the enterprise, establishment or service concerned. The notice mentions the reasons for resorting to a strike.

"The notice must reach the hierarchic authority, the management of the establishment, enterprise or corporation concerned five clear days before the beginning of the strike. It mentions the place, the date and the hour of the planned strike as well as its duration, limited or unlimited.

"The notice does not impede negotiations with a view to the settlement of the conflict."

This act is important. True, it outlaws "creeping" and "lightning" strikes, but whatever one may think of this limitation of trade union practice, one fact appears paramount to a political scientist: for the first time in modern history, the right of public servants to strike is unequivocally proclaimed by statute and it is admitted in all branches of the public service—administrative and industrial, national, regional and local. It is also important because it discards the sacrosanct theory of the continuity of public services hitherto upheld by leading jurists and political scientists.

Steady Progress in Scandinavia

The evolution evidenced by recent Scandinavian laws is less sensational than the French, but is perhaps deeper and has wider implications.

In Norway it is generally accepted that higher civil servants are not entitled to strike by reason of their constitutional position, nor are members of the armed forces or the police. But for the remaining civil servants there was no prohibition of strikes under the act of 1918.

An act of 1933 introduced the right of negotiation for organisations of civil servants and the duty to negotiate for the state authorities on matters of wages and working conditions. However, the authorities retained the right to take the final decision.

The act on public service disputes of 1958 went a step further. Wages and working conditions are established by agreement between the parties on an equal footing, just as in private employment. The agreement is binding for the civil servants and for the state. The similarity between the public sector and the private sector is further enhanced by the fact that the state may resort to a lockout.

In Sweden, too, the relationship between employees in the public service and the public authority is now seen as an agreement between the latter and the organisations representing civil servants.

This new relationship was first initiated in respect of municipal employees. In 1945 the Confederation of Boroughs and a number of employees' organisations signed an agreement on standard service regulations for established employees. Innovations have also been made in Swedish government service. Bills affecting the salaries of government employees are now regarded as the outcome of negotiations and are approved by parliament without detailed examination on the presumption that, upon the whole, the results are reasonable. But however smoothly these arrangements have usually worked in practice, the legal position could hardly be considered as satisfactory. The minister for civil service affairs has therefore agreed with the unions on the terms of a bill on collective negotiations for state officials. This bill includes precise rules governing strikes of government employees and lockouts by state authorities. It is now before parliament and is expected to be passed very shortly and to take effect from 1 January 1966.

In Sweden as in Norway, the legal status of civil servants is thus being remodelled so as to entitle them to the methods of collective bargaining applied in the private sector, and strikes and lockouts are included in those methods.

The Change in Public Service

How can one explain that the state should enact laws which allow its servants "to turn against it, equal to equal, in an imperious and menacing manner," as the French minister Barthou put it 60 years ago?

To my mind, the explanation is to be found in economic evolution.

Originally, civil servants were a small and privileged minority within the nation. They accepted special rules and submitted to a strict discipline because they enjoyed material advantages and social prestige.

Public employees had stable employment, in a society where unemployment was a constant threat to workers in private enterprise. They retired with a pension whilst the workers had to rely on their savings or, if they had been unable to save, to fall back on their children or public charity. Public servants often wore a uniform and were better dressed than people who had to buy their own clothing.

Yet, at the beginning of this century, they were often badly paid. The workmen in municipal gas plants were sometimes worse off than in similar private undertakings. It was therefore logical that the first congress of the Public Services International in 1907 should have passed a resolution protesting "against the limitation of the right to organise and strike on the part of public service employees."

In the course of this century, owing to the pressure of organised labour, the situation of the workers in private enterprise has been constantly improving. Social security has provided protection against the risks of accidents, illness, unemployment and old age. In many countries job security has increased in the private sector.

On the other hand, this century has witnessed an extraordinary growth of public services. The number of civil servants in the direct employ of the state has increased considerably and, at the same time, the state has taken over an increasing number of industries through the mechanism of public corporations. These public corporations have hundreds of thousands of employees who serve the state and are under the ultimate control of the government as to general policy. The more people the state employs directly or indirectly, the less capable it becomes of giving them the privileged status formerly attached to public employment. In fact, in many countries public servants are now lagging behind the workers of private enterprise in periods of rising living costs and of rising productivity.

There is a third factor. Outlawing strikes is one thing. But applying penal or disciplinary sanctions in a period of full employment is another. Very often when the government decides to punish its servants who go on strike they are induced to cancel the disciplinary sanctions which have been inflicted. When fines or prison terms are imposed by the courts, parliament has to vote an amnesty. Sometimes the courts themselves evade the strict application of laws carrying harsh penalties for striking.

If these various factors lead to the recognition of the right to strike in public services, it does not mean that such strikes are a desirable method of settling disputes. In public service as in private industry the strike is the last resort when all other methods have failed. Consultation, collective bargaining, conciliation, mediation, voluntary or compulsory arbitration are certainly to be preferred to strikes.

But highly developed countries as different as France, Norway and Sweden have nevertheless come to the conclusion that public servants should not, as a group, be denied a last recourse which is available to all the other social groups they serve.

The Role of State Agencies in Public Employee Labor Relations

JEAN T. MC KELVEY

State and Local Agencies

The agencies or administrative bodies responsible for the administration of public employee relations at the state and local level can be classified as follows: (1) existing *labor* relations agencies, such as labor relations and mediation boards; (2) new public agencies, for example, Office of Collective Bargaining for New York City and the Public Employee Relations Board suggested by Governor Rockefeller's blue-ribbon panel for New York State; (3) professional agencies, such as civil service commissions and commissioners of education; and (4) private agencies, such as the American Arbitration Association or the Honest Ballot Association.

In any analysis of the current role of state labor agencies, as distinguished from the other arrangements outlined above, it

Reprinted from *Industrial and Labor Relations Review*, XX (January 1967), 182–197, by permission of the publisher. Copyright © 1966 by Cornell University. All rights reserved.

Jean T. McKelvey is a professor at the New York State School of Industrial and Labor Relations, Cornell University, Ithaca, New York.

should be noted at the outset that the states have been laggards in this field. Unlike the situation in private industry, where the states rushed to enact baby Wagner Acts in the late 1930's and 1940's and where only a few municipalities created their own mediation agencies, in the public sector the cities have been innovators and the states, until recently, have been slow to enact constructive, as opposed to restrictive, legislation governing public employees. New York City, Philadelphia, and Cincinnati were the pioneers in developing new models of public employee negotiations through executive orders, local ordinances, and agreements without the benefit, or as some might say, the hindrance of state guidance or guidelines.[1]

A number of reasons account for the rapid development of municipal bargaining arrangements. One is the fact that the great bulk of government employees, 6,000,000 out of a total of 10,000,000 are employed at the local level. Over one half of these 6,000,000 are employed in local education, which thus accounts for almost one third of total public employment at all levels, federal, state, and local.[2] And as we shall presently relate, it has been the rivalry between the two major teacher organizations, the National Education Association and the American Federation of Teachers, which has been primarily responsible for the diverse patterns which are shaping the role of state agencies in the public employment arena. Another reason for the greater activity at the municipal level lies in certain features of the urban environment. Unlike their counterparts at the federal and state levels, municipal employers are more accessible to their employees, as well as more susceptible to political pressures and alliances.[3] Still a third factor accounting for the more rapid growth of municipal bargaining has been the surge in union organization of government workers led by the American Federation of State, County and Municipal Employees, which is currently sixteenth in size within the AFL-CIO, with 275,000 members.[4]

Almost all of these developments at the municipal level have occurred without the encouragement or protection of state legislation and, with the exception of Wisconsin, until recently have been outside the jurisdiction of existing state labor relations and mediation agencies. As a result, the cities have had an opportunity to experiment with a diversity of procedures and to create their own administrative arrangements, which in some important instances have provided barriers to the extension of state jurisdiction over their activities. Moreover, the fact that at the state level influence is wielded by professional organizations such as civil service associations, nurses associations, and education associations has meant that strong opposition has developed to the regulation of public employee labor relations by state labor agencies. The reasons for this antipathy to state labor agencies can best be illustrated by tracing briefly the activities of the National Education Association in this area.

The NEA and Teacher Representation

The attempts of the National Education Association to stimulate professional negotiations by school teachers began in 1960 at its national convention, when a resolution giving mild and cautious endorsement to the principle of "representative negotiations by teachers with their governing boards" and calling for the appointment of mediators drawn from members of the profession was debated, but failed to pass. Two years later at its Denver convention, the NEA adopted Resolution 18, which marked its first official endorsement of professional negotiations. What is noteworthy about Resolution 18 is its strongly negative stand against the use of labor agencies in teacher negotiations.

Under no circumstances should the resolution of differences between professional associations and boards of education be sought through channels set up for handling industrial disputes. The teacher's situation is completely unlike that of an industrial employee. A board of education is not a private employer, and a teacher is not a private employee. Both are public servants. . . . Industrial disputes conciliation machinery, which assumes a conflict of interest and a diversity of purpose between persons and groups, is not appropriate to professional negotiation.[5]

Subsequently this negative statement was removed, so that the Denver resolution as last amended in New York in 1965 now reads in part as follows.

The Association believes that procedures should be established which provide for an orderly method of reaching mutually satisfactory agreements and that these procedures should include provisions for appeal [6] through designated educational channels when agreement cannot be reached. . . .

The National Education Association calls upon its members and affiliates and upon boards of education to seek state legislation and local board action which clearly and firmly establishes these rights for the teaching profession.[7]

Following the 1962 NEA convention, the National School Boards Association rejected both the principle of negotiations and the procedure of "mandated mediation against school districts" on the ground that Boards of Education could not delegate authority to outsiders, that is, mediators.[8] The American Association of School Administrators, however, adopted a more moderate view, endorsing mediation by mediators who were drawn from the ranks of the profession. Its views are worth a brief quotation:

In those few, highly unusual instances where major controversy threatens to disrupt the schools, an appeal to an unbiased body should be available to either the board or the teachers, or both. The function of this third party should be limited to fact finding and to advisory assistance. Its identity might vary from state to state, but it should always be an agency which has responsibility for some segment of public education in the state. Included among such organizations might be a state board of education, a state department of education, a state university, or a state public college.[9]

It is worth pausing at this point to ask why the NEA and the AASA were so firmly committed to procedures which were divorced from the operations of labor laws and labor precedent. The answer, I believe, is twofold. In the first place, as a professional organization the NEA includes supervisors in its ranks. It was therefore feared that state labor relations agencies, such as the Wisconsin Employment Relations Board, the only state agency operating in the public employment field until 1965, would, if they had jurisdiction over teachers, exclude supervisory teachers from the bargaining unit and thereby make it more difficult for NEA units to win certification in contests with the American Federation of Teachers. In the second place, the alleged emphasis of the labor movement on class conflict and strikes seemed to the NEA to be foreign to an association which stressed the mutual interests of teachers and school boards in education, and which therefore sought the assistance of professional educators rather than labor mediators in resolving differences of opinion.[10]

One might ask, however, why the NEA by 1965 had committed itself to a policy of seeking the enactment of state legislation rather than relying upon the ad hoc and flexible procedures through which a number of its affiliates had won recognition and agreements in such cities as New Rochelle, Rochester, Newark, and Denver. The answer was, in part, supplied by its national counsel, Donald H. Wollett, at the American Bar Association Section of Labor Relations Law meeting in 1964. Commenting on the section of the *Report of the Committee on Law of Government Employee Relations* which dealt with local policy determination, Mr. Wollett said:

> Perhaps the most striking aspect of these local policy determinations has been their remarkable diversity. What has emerged and what seems likely to emerge, is a crazy-quilt pattern which, in my judgment at least, defies rational analysis and understanding.

As examples of this remarkable, and in Mr. Wollett's view, deplorable diversity, he cited the wide variations in the criteria employed for unit determination; the administration of policies and procedures in some instances by interested parties, such as school boards, or by inexperienced groups like the League of Women Voters; the unilateral establishment of policies and procedures by boards of education and the consequent lack of elementary due process; the variations in election rules, definitions of majority and extent of recognition; and the broad divergences in the scope of bargaining.[11] In conclusion Mr. Wollett said:

> I have cited these examples because it seems to me that no matter how much we may be attached to notions of local autonomy, it is very doubtful that such important matters of public concern, whether they happen to involve education, . . . or whether they involve other types of governmental enterprise, should be decided in such a willy-nilly, haphazard fashion.[12]

State Experience

The drive for specialized laws at the state level, so far as teachers are concerned, has produced mixed results. The Wisconsin model of conferring jurisdiction over the public sector upon the state labor agencies operating in the private sector[13] was followed by Michigan[14] and Massachusetts[15] in 1965. Jurisdiction over public employee labor relations is conferred on the Labor Mediation Board in Michigan,[16] while in Massachusetts jurisdiction is divided between the State Labor Relations Commission and the State Board of Conciliation and Arbitration.[17] All of these statutes cover unit determination, representation elections, unfair labor practices, the settlement of grievances by arbitration and the provision of fact-finding procedures for impasses which may arise in negotiations.

On the other hand, the states of Connecticut,[18] Oregon,[19] Washington,[20] and California[21] have enacted laws for teachers which provide educational, rather than labor, channels for dispute settlement. A New Jersey bill which was vetoed by Governor Hughes in 1966 would have entrusted jurisdiction over educational disputes to the state commissioner of education with the proviso that mediators were to be selected from a list of ten persons experienced in public education.

According to spokesmen for the NEA, the reason for the adoption of the labor model in Wisconsin, Massachusetts, and Michigan was the fact that the legislation was initiated by the state AFL-CIO, whereas the adoption of the education model in Connecticut, California, Oregon, and Washington was the result of intensive lobbying by the respective state NEA affiliates.[22]

The most unusual state effort to reconcile the conflicting positions of the NEA and the AFT is the law recently enacted in Rhode Island, the "School Teachers' Arbitration Act," which attempts to accommodate both groups by vesting jurisdiction over elections, unit determination, and unfair labor practices in the State Labor Relations Board, but provides that in the event of a bargaining or negotiating impasse either side may request mediation and conciliation from the State Department of Education, the Director of Labor, or "from any other source." [23]

Connecticut,[24] Delaware,[25] and Rhode Island,[26] however, have enacted legislation covering public employees other than teachers which confers administrative jurisdiction on the state labor relations and mediation agencies.

Minnesota vests jurisdiction over questions of representation in the labor conciliator but provides that in the event of an impasse which has not been successfully mediated by the labor conciliator, either party may initiate the establishment of a tripartite Adjustment Panel. If there is no agreement upon the neutral member, the presiding judge of the district court in the area in which the dispute occurs is to make the appointment, providing he first gives the labor conciliator a chance to suggest the names of neutrals. (The law stipulates that the neutral shall be paid $50 a day.) One other point of interest in the Minnesota law is that the recommendations of the Adjustmental Panel are to be presented by the government employer or agency involved to the government body or official having authority to implement them. What the experience has been, under the Minnesota statute, has not been, apparently, a subject of research or report.[27]

The Oregon statute covering all employees of the state and all units of local government, which was adopted in 1963 and amended in 1965, is something of a hybrid.[28] It vests control over representation procedures in the appropriate civil service commissions, but lodges the mediation function in the state conciliation service. In May 1966 the constitutionality of the Oregon law was challenged by the Oregon AFL-CIO, which objected to the authority lodged in the civil service commission and sought instead to have the state labor commission supervise collective bargaining. The Oregon State Employees Association, however, appeared in defense of the jurisdiction of the civil service commissions. The suit was dismissed by the county court.[29]

What we have then by way of design, so far as state legislation in this field is concerned, is not so much a crazy quilt, perhaps, as a choice of two patterns, one a labor and the other a commission model.

New York State

It is only when we turn to the recent experiences in New York State that something resembling a crazy-quilt pattern of administrative agencies begins to emerge. Since 1947, New York has provided no procedures at the state level for solving public employee labor relations problems other than the repressive

Condon-Wadlin Act,[30] the executive orders establishing grievance procedures for state employees,[31] and the legislation mandating grievance procedures for employees of local governments, including school boards.[32] This vacuum has left New York City free to design its own labor relations procedures and has also enabled other cities and school boards to enter into collective relationships with employee organizations. The City of Rochester, for example, has recently negotiated new agreements with the Firefighters, the Police Locust Club, and Local 1635 of the American Federation of State, County and Municipal Employees which provide in the first two instances for the agency shop, and in the latter, for a union shop for non-civil service employees. Paradoxically, this emulation of the labor model has occurred in a city which, for its size, is probably the largest unorganized city, so far as the private sector is concerned, in the United States. Although there is not space here to develop the reasons for this paradox, it should be pointed out that in the absence of state legislation, the city has been free to develop its own procedures based on the enactment of a local collective bargaining ordinance which vests jurisdiction over labor relations policy in the city manager and which has successfully withstood challenge in the courts.[33]

The Rochester Board of Education has likewise developed its own recognition and negotiating procedures. After an election run by the American Arbitration Association, with Professor Walter Oberer of the Cornell Law School as hearing officer and Cornell students as election officials, the Rochester Teachers Association emerged as victor. This past spring when negotiations for a second agreement reached an impasse, the parties created a three man blue-ribbon fact-finding board [34] which obtained in advance the consent of the parties to be bound by their recommendations—a form of voluntary arbitration which is most exceptional in the area of public employment.[35]

Meanwhile, New York City, which is the largest municipal employer in the country, has embarked on a second experiment in public employee relations.[36] As a result of negotiations between the city and its employee organizations held under the aegis of the Labor-Management Institute of the American Arbitration Association, with the assistance of four distinguished neutrals who served as mediators,[37] the parties have agreed upon legislation which establishes a timetable for bargaining, provides for mediation, grievance arbitration and fact-finding, and most important of all for our purposes, establishes a new independent and tripartite administrative agency, the Office of Collective Bargaining, consisting of seven members, two appointed by the mayor, two by the Municipal Labor Committee, and three impartial members selected by the other four, one of whom is to be a full-time chairman and the other two per diem members.[38] It should be obvious that New York City has patterned its administrative agency upon the arbitration model prevalent in private industry. This model perhaps explains in part the paradox that whereas government usually provides free labor relations services to the private sector, in New York City the employees of government are to share with the municipal employer the costs of the administrative agency. This arrangement, it should be noted, has its parallel in the federal service, where the determination of bargaining units is made by privately employed arbitrators and where mediation, if agreed upon, is usually available only at a fee.[39] These arrangements suggest that where government is the employer, some neutral and independent private body may be preferred as an administrative agency, one to which no suspicion of employer interference is attached.

New York City and the State Legislature

The relationship of these proposed municipal arrangements in New York City to the conflict which has been raging in the New York legislature during the past few years, most intensely in 1966, will become clearer if we first examine the types of bills which were introduced. If we ignore the major political controversy over strike sanctions and concentrate only on the dispute over administrative agencies, we shall perhaps gain a clearer understanding of some of the forces which will determine whether the existing agencies or new agencies will have jurisdiction.

In the first effort to amend the Condon-Wadlin Act in 1963, the New York State Joint Legislative Committee on Industrial and Labor Relations drafted a bill which would have given the New York State Labor Relations Board jurisdiction over questions of representation and unit determination in public employment and would have made impasses subject to mediation by the New York State Board of Mediation.[40] These provisions were dropped and only the strike sanctions were modified.

In 1965 as these interim modifications of Condon-Wadlin approached their two-year expiration date, four bills containing three different administrative arrangements for regulating public employee relations were made the subject of a public hearing. Two of these, the Dominick-Kingston and the Thaler bills, would have vested jurisdiction in the state Labor Relations and Mediation Boards. The Laverne bill proposed the expansion of the Labor Relations Board from three to four members, with one of the four named as vice-chairman to direct a separate public employment unit within the board. This unit was to deal with questions of representation involving public employees. The fourth bill, the Lentol-Rossetti bill, and the one which eventually passed but was vetoed by Governor Rockefeller, carried decentralization even further by calling for the establishment of separate labor relations agencies by each public employer.[41] A labor relations agency was defined as "a public agency, department or board or any other person or group of persons which has been designated by the public employer to aid and assist in adjustment of the differences and issues between employers and employees. . . ." The bill further provided that in the event no labor relations agency was in existence at the time a dispute arose, one was to be appointed by the presiding justice of the appellate division in the judicial department where either party was located.[42]

One may as well ask at this point why the Lentol-Rossetti bill contained these rather novel provisions for the creation of local labor relations agencies in a state which has long prided itself on the possession of two distinguished state agencies. One answer, and perhaps the most important is that the bill was drafted to assure the continued operation of the ten-year-old New York City program of municipal labor relations free from regulation by state agencies.[43] Another is that in New York State at both state and New York City levels, union leadership was opposed to vesting jurisdiction over public employees in state agencies appointed by a governor who was of an opposite political faith. Whether this mistrust of the existing agencies was justifiable or fancied is unimportant. What is important is that in New York State, the labor movement and the professional organizations, such as the Civil Service Employees Association and the New York State Teachers Association, were in agreement in rejecting the use of the state Labor Relations and Mediation Boards as administrative agencies in the area of public employment. One further point should also be noted. Unlike the agencies in Wisconsin, Connecticut, Massachusetts, and Michigan,[44] which had themselves taken an active role in endorsing legislation which expanded their jurisdiction to include the public sector, the New York State Board of Mediation took the position that it wanted no enlargement of its jurisdiction to cover this area. Indeed, even before any legislation had been proposed, the New York State Board of Mediation instructed its staff not to intervene in public employee disputes. Whether this negative attitude reflected a praiseworthy exercise in self-restraint or a timid and unimaginative leadership which shied away from new challenges and responsibilities is an open question. In any event, it can be concluded that there is little support from any quarter in New York State for the proposition that existing state labor agencies should have jurisdiction over the public sector.

The Governor's Panel

It is therefore not surprising that the blue-ribbon panel appointed by Governor Rockefeller on January 15, 1966, in the midst of the New York City transit strike, to make a thorough study of a legislative framework for public employee relations,[45] should have recommended the creation of a new state agency, a Public Employment Relations Board, and at the same time have accommodated the desire for autonomy and local regulation on the part of New York City and its public employee unions by providing for the creation of local government procedures as an alternative to the use of the new state board.[46] Another reason for bypassing the existing state agencies can be found in the basic premise of the report that " 'collective negotiation' in the public services is unlike collective bargaining in the private enterprise sector. . . . It cannot be achieved by transferring collective bargaining as practiced in the private enterprise sector into the governmental sector. New procedures have to be created." [47] New procedures and, one should add, *new agencies*. As we have noted earlier in analyzing Executive Order 10988, an emphasis on the dissimilarities between public and private employment creates an implicit recognition of the need for keeping jurisdiction out of the hands of those bodies which regulate the private sector. In addition, the fact that the proposed legislation covers state employees, as well as those of subordinate units of state government, adds even greater impetus to the proposal for new agencies, given the distaste expressed by employee professional organizations operating at the state level, such as the Civil Service Employees Association, New York State Teachers Association, and New York Nurses Association, for being lumped together with trade unions in matters involving recognition and negotiation. [48]

A bill introduced in the 1966 legislature with the strong support of the governor embodied the administrative arrangements contained in the committee report. [49] It provided for the creation in the State Department of Civil Service of a Public Employment Relations Board consisting of three members to be appointed by the governor, two to work on a per diem basis and one to be a fulltime salaried chairman. [50] The board was to be charged with a variety of functions: the resolution of disputes over representation and contract terms; the provision of mediation and fact-finding personnel and services; the conduct of studies of public employment conditions, exclusive recognition and the scope of negotiations; and finally, the administration of the strike penalty provisions of the statute. The proposed board was thus to be a labor relations agency, a mediation board, a court, and a research institute—all wrapped into one package!

The bill also incorporated the decentralization of procedures recommended by the committee. It provided that

every government (other than the state or a state public authority), acting through its legislative body, is hereby empowered to establish procedures not inconsistent with the provisions of section two hundred seven of this article and after consultation with interested employee organizations and administrators of public services, to resolve disputes concerning the representation status of employee organizations of employees of such government.[51]

The bill further empowered public employers "to enter into written agreements with recognized or certified employee organizations setting forth procedures to be invoked in the event of disputes which reach an impasse in the course of collective negotiations." [52]

It would appear that the Rockefeller bill skillfully made provision for accommodating the autonomous procedures of New York City agreed to under the Lindsay plan. But appearances here, as elsewhere, may be deceptive. The fact that the Rockefeller bill conditioned recognition and certification upon "the affirmation by [an employee] organization that it does not assert the right to strike against any government. . . ." [53] might mean the doom of the Lindsay plan, which is silent on the question of strikes, should the state bill become law. Although the issue is not altogether free from doubt, both the state AFL-CIO and the major New York City employee unions strenuously opposed the state bill because it threatened the New York City plan. Once again, as in the past, the interests of New York City and the rest of the state were in conflict.

In opposition to the Rockefeller plan, the Democrats again rallied behind the Lentol-Rossetti bill, which was enacted in 1965 and which contained the same provisions as its predecessor for local labor relations agencies.[54] Both the Rockefeller and the Lentol-Rossetti bills perished in the closing hours of the 1966 legislature, despite last-minute efforts to reach a compromise. [The reader is reminded that legislation was enacted in New York State in 1967.]

Some Hypotheses

After this long journey, it is time to return to a question posed at the outset: how can these variations in the role of state labor agencies in the public employment field be explained? Under what circumstances will state labor agencies be vested with jurisdiction; or, conversely, under what circumstances will new agencies or other administrative arrangements be created?

There seems to be general agreement on the need for some

state legislation in order to reduce strikes, curb court litigation and destroy the "crazy-quilt" pattern which has emerged in those states which lack a framework for public employee representation and negotiation. As the Interim Commission Report in Connecticut observed, after reviewing the accelerated collective bargaining activity in Connecticut cities and towns after 1958:

> In the absence of any standards for the conduct of collective bargaining by municipalities, the process has developed in diverse directions, varying all the way from refusal of city officials even to discuss representation rights with union representatives to full-fledged contract bargaining. The statute which is being recommended . . . is intended to eliminate the uncertainties and to clarify the rights and responsibilities of municipal employers, municipal employees, and municipal employee organizations.[55]

This is the same position which, as set forth earlier, the NEA has adopted.

But if there is agreement on the need for statutes, there is disagreement on their contents. Should they follow the model of the private sector or be newly designed? The conditions favoring the adoption of the private model, particularly the conferring of jurisdiction on existing state labor agencies, seem to be the following.

(1) The exclusion of state civil service employees from coverage. This is the situation in Connecticut and Michigan, and in Wisconsin until recently.[56] Since state employees generally have strong civil service associations, they are more likely to object to the assumption of jurisdiction by state labor agencies.

(2) The exclusion of teachers from coverage. This situation exists in Connecticut and Rhode Island. As we have seen, the NEA has taken a strong position in opposition to sending disputes through labor, rather than educational, channels.

(3) The support of the state labor agencies by the trade union movement in the state. Michigan, Wisconsin, Connecticut, and Massachusetts all enjoyed this support. This condition, as we have noted, however, was not met in New York State.

(4) The support of an expansion of their jurisdiction by the state labor agencies themselves. Again Michigan, Wisconsin, Connecticut, and Massachusetts provide examples.

(5) The absence of established urban public employee rela-

tions programs which can, as in New York City and perhaps Philadelphia, block a state threat to their autonomy.

(6) An assumption on the part of the legislature, or the executive, that labor relations in the public sector are more like, than unlike, labor relations in the private sector. An emphasis on dissimilarities will, as we have seen in our examination of the Executive Order 10988 and in the Rockefeller report, lead to the creation of new agencies or ad hoc administrative devices. This may be traced in part to the fact that a preoccupation with anti-strike controls will tend to create a bias against the use of state labor agencies which have developed methods for settling legal disputes in the private sector.

Advantages and Disadvantages of State Labor Agency Jurisdiction over Public Employee Relations

It may be helpful to list briefly what seem to be the advantages and disadvantages of state labor agency jurisdiction in the field of public employee relations. One is reminded in this connection, however, of one of the less frequently quoted passages from Alice in Wonderland: "Alice began to get rather sleepy and kept on saying to herself in a dreamy sort of way 'do cats eat bats? do cats eat bats?' and sometimes, 'do bats eat cats?' for, as she couldn't answer either question, it didn't much matter which way she put it." [57]

The advantages of using existing labor agencies can be enumerated as follows. (1) The experience and expertise which the states have developed in the private sector in such matters as unit determination, mediation, arbitration, and fact-finding are easily transferrable to the public sector. (2) It is more economical and efficient in terms of overhead, administration, personnel, etc., to use the same agency or agencies in both the private and public sectors. (3) The familiarity of unions in the state with existing agencies and their procedures and services should facilitate recourse to these agencies, unless the familiarity has bred contempt! (4) The extension of their activities to the public sector should not only provide a new lease on life for those agencies which may be stranded in the no-man's land between federal and state jurisdiction in the private sector; it should also stimulate new energy and interest on the part of boards and staffs in exploring a new and challenging frontier.[58]

The arguments against conferring jurisdiction on state labor agencies may be summarized as follows.

(1) Problems of unit determination and the resolution of impasses in the public sector are sufficiently different from those encountered in the private sector as to warrant the creation of new agencies which will not be bound by past practice and "labor" precedent. (2) Public employers and most professional organizations are suspicious of collective bargaining. Whatever negotiations they may be prepared to undertake will be aided if they have confidence in neutrals who are familiar with the unique problems of public employment. (3) Existing state agencies have little experience with delegating jurisdiction to local agencies. In the interests of flexibility, autonomy, and experimentation it would be advisable to create a new agency empowered to delegate authority.[59] (4) Existing agencies are underbudgeted and understaffed and therefore unable to provide adequate service in a rapidly expanding field. This criticism was expressed by the Michigan Federation of Teachers during the epidemic of teacher strikes around Detroit in 1966.

Conclusions

The task of striking a balance between these two positions is left to the reader. Perhaps it is not necessary to reach a judgment one way or the other, for in this field as in so many others, it may be desirable to encourage diversity and experimentation in the laboratories of the fifty states. If the states do not perform well, however, they may face the prospect of federal legislation in this field. One will recall the threat of President Johnson a year ago to deal with the New York City transit strike through federal legislation. A number of unions in public employment such as the Teachers and the State, County and Municipal Workers have begun to grumble about the diversity or "crazy quilt" of state laws, complaining that it is difficult to adjust their organizing techniques and negotiating strategies to the different patterns of laws and regulations.[60] These may indeed be only straws in the wind. But one should perhaps heed the ominous warning sounded by James Reston in an editorial article, "Detroit: Power and the Governors," where, after noting the declining influence of governors in American society with Washington dealing more and more directly with cities in such areas as poverty and education, he commented:

The Governors of the American states almost sound these days as if they were going the way of the modern kings.[61]

NOTES

1. For an interesting account of early municipal experiences, see American Bar Association, Section of Labor Relations Law, 1961, *Report of the Committee on Law of Government Employee Relations,* pp. 95–114. In addition to surveying developments in New York City and Philadelphia, the report noted the passage of ordinances granting city employees the right to organize and bargain collectively in Oregon City and Sacramento in 1961. It also reported the findings of a survey by the Michigan Municipal League which showed that 25 cities in 1961 had working agreements or contracts with one or more unions of municipal employees.

2. *1964–1965 Statistical Supplement—Monthly Labor Review,* Table I-7, p. 19. The employment figures cited above are for December 1965.

3. For an excellent analysis of the emerging patterns at the federal, state, and local levels, see Ronald Donovan, "Labor Relations in the Public Service: A Survey," *Report Card* (Ithaca, N.Y.: New York State School of Industrial and Labor Relations, Cornell University), Vol. 14, No. 3 (March 1966). Jesse Simons points out that in our major cities a large and enlarging proportion of the electorate consists of public employees themselves.

Employees bargaining with public officials are simultaneously an organized and powerful segment of that same official's constituency, exercising an influence which is growing rapidly and constantly. Thus, the official who is employer-surrogate, negotiates with employees who are also a part of his constituency, and who simultaneously are, in part, the employer. The elected official can ignore this, but at his peril. Industrial Relations Research Association, *Proceedings of the 1966 Annual Spring Meeting,* pp. 108–109.

4. The number of union members employed at all levels of government has increased from 915,000 in 1956 to 1,453,000 in 1964, and has risen from 5.9% of all union members in 1962 to 8.1% in 1964. Although the federal service shows a higher intensity of union membership because of Executive Order 10988, with 40% of all federal employees belonging to unions or associations, the state and local area is showing marked growth. Without the benefit of state law or executive order (with the exception of Wisconsin), some 550,000 out of 7,673,000 state and local government employees were organized in 1964, or a little over 7%, and the percentage is undoubtedly much higher today. See "Trends and Changes in Union Membership," *Monthly Labor Review,* May 1966, pp. 510–513. In 1962, 80% of American cities with populations of over 10,000 reported the presence of one or more employee organizations among their employees.

5. *Addresses and Proceedings,* 100th Annual Meeting of NEA, Denver (Washington: National Education Association, 1962), Vol. 100, pp. 174–183.

6. It should be noted, parenthetically, that in the lexicon of the NEA which has tried hard to create a semantic difference between its activities and those of the labor movement, the word "appeal" means "mediation." There are other terminological distinctions, to give only a few illustrations: professional negotiations for collective bargaining; sanctions for boycott; recess for strikes; and urban project for organizing.

7. T. M. Stinnett, Jack H. Kleinmann, and Martha L. Ware, *Professional Negotiations in Public Education* (New York: Macmillan, 1966), p. 209.

8. *Ibid.,* p. 271. Cf. the recent reaction of the mayor of Kansas City to the offer of the governor to have the State Mediation Board help settle a dispute between the city and its firefighters. The mayor said in an interview that elected city officials could not delegate their authority in such matters to mediators. *New York Times,* July 12, 1966.

9. *Roles, Responsibilities, Relationships of the School Board, Superintendent, and Staff* (Washington: American Association of School Administrators, 1963), p. 14.

10. See Stinnett, Kleinmann, and Ware, *op. cit.,* pp. 16–17, for an interesting and candid analysis of the differences between professional negotiations and collective bargaining. For a comprehensive study of the two organizations and their respective attitudes toward "collective negotiations," see Michael H. Moskow, *Teachers and Unions* (Philadelphia: University of Pennsylvania, Wharton School, 1966), Industrial Research Unit Study No. 42.

11. For documentary examples of some of the ad hoc determinations of bargaining units and election procedures in New Rochelle, Rochester, Newark, and Philadelphia, see Robert E. Doherty, "Determination of Bargaining Units and Election Procedures in Public School Teacher Representation Elections," *Industrial and Labor Relations Review,* Vol. 19, No. 4 (July 1966), pp. 573–595.

12. American Bar Association, Section of Labor Relations Law, 1964, *Proceedings,* pp. 19–21. It is interesting to note, however, that in an address given by Mr. Wollett that same summer to the Joint Annual Meeting of the Association of State Mediation Agencies and the National Association of State Labor Relations Agencies he commented: "You will note that I have said nothing about the role of state laws and state agencies in implementing these suggestions and guidelines. My silence on this point reflects my feeling that extensive and formalized legislation is premature." Wollett, "The Public Employee at the Bargaining Table: Promise or Illusion?," *Labor Law Journal,* Vol. 15, No. 1 (January 1964), p. 8.

13. *West's Wisconsin Statutes Annotated,* Title XIII, Chap. III, subchap. IV, sec. 111.70. The original Wisconsin statute covering public employees was enacted in 1959. It imposed a duty on municipalities to recognize the chosen representatives of their employees, but did not provide any machinery for determining questions of representation. The bill originally granted jurisdiction to the Wisconsin Employee Relations Board, but this was deleted before passage. As a result, the law did little more than protect employees against discrimination for union activity. In 1962, however, the law was amended to give jurisdiction to the WERB over questions of repre-

sentation, unfair labor practices, and bargaining impasses. Evaluating this experience in 1964, the Section of Labor Relations Law of the American Bar Association reported through its Committee on Law of Government Employee Relations that the Wisconsin statute revealed "an integrated system of labor-relations policies and practices much like that prevailing in the state for private employment relationships." See American Bar Association, Section of Labor Relations Law, 1964, *Report of Committee on Law of Government Employee Relations,* pp. 373–374.

The Committee also stated that Wisconsin provided a laboratory experiment which should permit a judgment of the effectiveness of these procedures elsewhere. *Ibid.,* p. 381. Recent developments under the Wisconsin statute are noted in the American Bar Association, Section of Labor Relations Law, 1966, *Report of the Committee on Law of Government Employee Relations,* pp. 154–158 and 176–185. For an excellent account of the Wisconsin Public Employee Fact-Finding Procedure, see James L. Stern, "The Wisconsin Public Employee Fact-finding Procedure," *Industrial and Labor Relations Review,* Vol. 20, No. 1 (October 1966), p. 3 ff. See also the Note, "Municipal Employment in Wisconsin," *Wisconsin Law Review,* Summer 1965, pp. 652 ff.

14. *Michigan Statutes Annotated,* Title 17, Chap. 154, sec. 17.454 (7).

15. *Annotated Laws of Massachusetts,* Chap. 149, sec. 178 G.

16. For developments under the Michigan law, see the American Bar Association, Section of Labor Relations Law, 1966, *Report of the Committee on Law of Government Employee Relations,* pp. 142–148 and 162–165.

17. See *ibid.,* pp. 153–154, for an analysis of the new Massachusetts statute.

18. Connecticut Public Act 298, 1965, *Connecticut General Statutes Annotated,* Title 10, Chap. 166, Part I, secs. 10-153a–10-153f. The Connecticut Act, which mandates Globe type elections for supervisors, vests mediation jurisdiction in the Secretary of the State Board of Education and provides also for tripartite advisory arbitration of disputes over contract terms. Representation elections are conducted by an "impartial person or agency" mutually selected by the parties on an ad hoc basis. The first year's experience under the statue is set forth in the American Bar Association, Section of Labor Relations Law, 1966, *Report of the Committee on Law of Government Employee Relations,* pp. 158–162.

19. *Oregon Revised Statutes,* Title 30, Chap. 342, sec. 342.470. The Oregon law vests jurisdiction over unit determination in the School Board and provides for tripartite "consultation" on impasses.

20. *Laws of Washington,* 1965, Chap. 143. The state superintendent of public instruction is authorized to appoint fact-finding commissions composed of educators and school board members.

21. *West's Annotated California Education Code,* Part 2, Div. 10, Chap. 1, Art. 5, secs. 13080–13088. This law, which was approved by the governor on July 17, 1965, lodges the administration of the statute in the hands of the public school employer. Similarly, the California statute conferring bargaining rights on state and local government employees vests administration in the employing agencies. *California Government Code,* secs. 3500–3508.

22. See Stinnett, Kleinmann, and Ware, *op. cit.,* pp. 185–186.

23. *Rhode Island General Laws,* Title 28, Chap. 9.3. The full text may also be found in BNA, *Government Employee Relations Report,* No. 141, May 23,

1966, p. B-2. The Rhode Island statute is also unique in providing for binding arbitration (with the AAA or the State Board of Education as the designating agency) on all matters not involving money.

24. *Connecticut Laws of 1965,* Public Act No. 159, *Connecticut General Statutes Annotated,* Title 7, Chap. 113, Part III, secs. 467–477. This statute covers local government employees except teachers.

25. *Delaware Code,* Title 19, secs. 1301–1313. This law, enacted in 1965, grants state and local government employees the right to organize and at the option of the local government, the right to bargain collectively. Representation matters are handled by the State Department of Labor and Industrial Relations, and impasses over any matters in dispute except wages or salaries may be submitted by either party to the State Mediation Service.

26. For the text of the new Rhode Island statute, "Organization of State Employees," S. 292 (as amended), enacted in April 1966, vetoed by Governor Chafee, with the veto overridden in May 1966, see BNA, *Government Employee Relations Report,* No. 140, May 16, 1966, pp. B-2–B-3. (*General Laws of Rhode Island,* Title 36, Chap. 11, secs. 36-117–36-118). All state employees except the state police are covered.

27. *Minnesota Statutes Annotated,* Chap. 179, secs. 179.51–179.57; Chap. 146 as last amended by Chap. 839, L.1965, effective May 27, 1965.

28. *Oregon Revised Statutes,* Title 22, Chap. 243; *Oregon Laws of 1965,* Chap. 543.

29. BNA, *Government Employee Relations Report,* No. 139, May 9, 1966, p. B-5. A comprehensive bill entitled the Public Employees Collective Bargaining Act which vests jurisdiction in the commissioner of labor was introduced in the General Assembly of Kentucky by Mr. Norbert Blume on Feb. 14, 1966—House Bill No. 345. Its fate is not known to the author at this time.

30. *New York Civil Service Law,* sec. 108.

31. Executive Order Relating to Procedures for the Submission and Settlement of Grievances of State Employees, Public Papers of Governor Harriman 1955, Aug. 6, 1955, p. 679. This Order, which superseded an earlier order issued by Governor Dewey on Feb. 23, 1950, established a Grievance Board composed of two impartial members and the secretary of the State Civil Service Commission. Aside from the fact that the tribunal was under the control of the employer, the Board had little authority to implement its decisions. A detailed study of its operations is not available.

32. *New York General Municipal Law,* Art. 16. To the best of my knowledge, no study of the operation of this law has been made.

33. Lipsett v. Gillette, 12 N.Y. 2d 162; 187 N.E. (2d) 782 (N.Y. 1962). The local ordinance authorizing the city to recognize unions and bargain collectively was not held invalid for lack of prescribed standards.

34. The members of the board were Marion Folsom, former Secretary of Health, Education and Welfare and Treasurer of the Eastman Kodak Company; C. Peter McColough, president of the Xerox Corporation; and Professor Walter Oberer who served as chairman.

35. At the 1966 national convention of the NEA the executive secretary praised the Rochester Teachers' Association and the Board of Education for their skill and ingenuity in resolving their differences through ad hoc ar-

rangements, but he went on to stress the need for state legislation to provide machinery for settling disputes under law. *Rochester Democrat and Chronicle*, June 29, 1966. Professor Oberer's account of the Rochester experience appears in the American Bar Association, Section of Labor Relations Law, 1966, *Report of Committee on Law of Government Employee Relations*, pp. 168–169.

36. The first, of course, was Executive Order No. 49 of 1958, entrusting the administration of municipal labor relations to the New York City Department of Labor. For an excellent analysis of the evolution of labor relations in public employment in New York City, see the address by Ida Klaus, "The Emerging Relationship," delivered before the Conference on Public Employment and Collective Bargaining held at the University of Chicago, Feb. 5, 1965. See p. 3.

37. Saul Wallen, chairman, Philip Carey, S.J., Vern Countryman, and Peter Seitz.

38. See *Report of the Tri-Partite Panel on Collective Bargaining Procedures in Public Employment*, March 31, 1966. The text of the statute was introduced into the Council of the City of New York on May 17, 1966 by Mr. F. Smith. No. 134, Int. No. 129. The bill proposes to amend the Charter of the City of New York by adding thereto a new chapter, Chapter 54, entitled "Office of Collective Bargaining." The bill also provides that, upon the request of the mayor, the mediation, impasse, and arbitration services of the Office of Collective Bargaining may be made available to private employers and unions.

39. See U.S. Bureau of Labor Statistics, *Collective Bargaining Agreements in the Federal Service, Late Summer 1964* (Washington: G.P.O., 1964), Bulletin No. 1451, p. 55.

40. Staff report to the New York State Joint Legislative Committee on Industrial and Labor Conditions, *Proposed Bill and Supporting Report on Employee-Management Relations in the Public Service*, December 1962. It is interesting to note that the report anticipated the conflict which has since developed over the appropriate administrative agencies in this field. Mr. Anthony P. Savarese, Jr., who served as chairman of the Joint Legislative Committee, noted in his preface:

Understandably the Committee was not in full agreement with all provisions of the staff bill. As to the machinery provided for mediation and advisory arbitration of disputes *there were misgivings as to its adaptability to New York City* and the State's great variety of other subdivisions. (Emphasis added.)

41. The term "public employer" was defined as:

The State of New York, any city, county, town or village, any other political or civil division of the State, and municipality, any governmental agency operating any public school or college, any school district or any other public special district, any public authority, commission or board or any other public agency or instrumentality or unit of government which exercises governmental powers under the laws of the State.

42. For a more detailed account of these bills and their legislative history, see Kurt L. Hanslowe, "Labor Relations Law," *Syracuse Law Review*, Vol. 17, Winter 1965, p. 183.

43. *Ibid.*, pp. 190–191.

44. In Connecticut, the chairman of the state Board of Mediation and Arbitration, Robert Stutz, also served as chairman of the commission whose recommendations were subsequently enacted. See State of Connecticut, *Report of the Interim Commission to Study Collective Bargaining by Municipalities* (as provided by Public Act No. 495 of the 1963 Session of the General Assembly), February 1965. In Michigan, the state Labor Mediation Board was also active in pushing the bill which was enacted in 1965. See West State edition of the *Detroit Free Press*, June 18, 1965.

45. The Governor requested the Committee "to make legislative proposals for protecting the public against the disruption of vital public services by illegal strikes, while at the same time protecting the rights of public employees."

46. State of New York, Governor's Committee on Public Employee Relations, *Final Report*, March 31, 1966. The members of the committee were E. Wight Bakke, David L. Cole, John T. Dunlop, Frederick H. Harbison, and George W. Taylor, chairman. None of them was a resident of the state.

47. *Ibid.*, pp. 12 and 16.

48. For example, in the recent jurisdictional dispute over representation of licensed practical nurses in New York City hospitals, between District Council 37, AFSCME, and a professional nurses' association, many of the pickets were reported as saying they wanted the association, not a union, as their bargaining agent. "We're not laborers," said one nurse. "Unions are for non-professional people." *New York Times*, July 12, 1966.

49. S. Int. No. 4781 (May 5, 1966); and A. Int. No. 6042, Pr. No. 7088 (May 5, 1966). Rockefeller termed the report "a milestone in the development of the theory and practice of collective bargaining."

50. *Ibid.*, sec. 205.

51. *Ibid.*, sec. 206.1.

52. *Ibid.*, sec. 209.2. In the absence of established local procedures for resolving disputes over recognition, or impasses, either side might request the services of the PERB.

53. *Ibid.*, sec. 207.3.

54. S. Int. No. 745, Pr. No. 748 (Jan. 11, 1966); A. Int. No. 4078, Pr. No. 4199 (Feb. 9, 1966).

55. State of Connecticut, *Report of the Interim Commission to Study Collective Bargaining by Municipalities*, February 1965, pp. 9–10.

56. On June 1, 1966, the Wisconsin Legislature enacted a comprehensive collective bargaining bill for state employees to become effective Jan. 1, 1967. Jurisdiction is vested in the Wisconsin Employment Relations Board.

57. *Alice's Adventures Underground* (Ann Arbor, Mich.: University Microfilms, Inc., 1964), pp. 4–5.

58. A summary of the first year of experience under the Connecticut Municipal Employees Bargaining Act, prepared by the Connecticut Labor Department, attributes the success of the statute in promoting orderly municipal collective bargaining relationships to the wisdom shown in entrusting its administration to the state Labor Relations Board. The survey points out that while there are some major differences between the private and public labor relations statutes, "the procedural similarities found the staff

of the Board prepared for the case load which grew rapidly following the passage of the Act." BNA, *Government Employee Relations Report*, No. 148, July 11, 1966, pp. B-1–B-2.

59. It should be noted, however, that the Wisconsin Employment Relations Board has power to cede fact-finding jurisdiction to local agencies which meet the standards of the statute. In three important decisions this past year the Board has held that the local ordinances did not meet the standards set forth in the state law. Litigation over some of these decisions is still pending. See American Bar Association, Section of Labor Relations Law, 1966, *Report of the Committee on Law of Government Employee Relations*, pp. 181–182. The fact-finding commission set up to make recommendations in Milwaukee's dispute with its unions, under the chairmanship of Professor Feinsinger, recommended that Milwaukee establish its own Labor Peace Agency. See BNA, *Government Employee Relations Report*, No. 69, Jan. 4, 1965, p. D-1, for the full text of this proposal.

60. In a recent talk, Al Bilik, assistant to the president of AFSCME, said: "We need uniform legislative standards regarding the basic rights of public workers in order to dispel the jungle atmosphere which still persists in most of the nation. . . . The National Labor Relations Act should be made available to all levels of the public service." "The Other Fourteen Percent," n.d., p. 8. Recently, the Chicago Teachers Union requested the NLRB to conduct a representation election for Chicago school teachers. The Board declined, saying it had neither funds nor authority to conduct "outside elections." Consequently, the union suggested that the vote be conducted by the Chicago Bar Association! BNA, *Government Employee Relations Report*, No. 139, May 9, 1966, p. B-4.

61. *New York Times,* June 24, 1966.

VII

A LOOK AHEAD

Collective bargaining for public employees was given a powerful stimulus by Executive Order 10988, signed by President John F. Kennedy in 1962. This order provided federal employees with the right to engage in collective bargaining and demonstrated that either administrative or legislative action is required for the growth of collective bargaining in the public sector. Such a legal framework is crucial for the existence of collective bargaining by public employees; as soon as proper legislation has been enacted, employee organizations can begin to exercise their legal right to engage in collective bargaining. For example, in Michigan, the growth of collective bargaining in public employment was a direct result of the Public Employment Relations Act of 1965. This emerging pattern parallels, in many instances, the growth of collective bargaining in the private sector that followed the enactment of the National Labor Relations Act in 1935. As soon as the legal right was established by public policy, employee organizations began to use the law to obtain collective bargaining rights for their members.

Thus, the growth of collective bargaining in public employment will be affected by the enactment of appropriate state legislation and by the willingness of employee organizations to take advantage of such legislation. We believe that in the next few years, additional states will

237

enact legislation providing for collective bargaining by public employees. Pressure for such legislation will come primarily from teacher organizations, state nurses' associations, the American Federation of State, County and Municipal Employees (AFL-CIO), and other unions representing employees in public jurisdictions. Furthermore, some state employee associations are likewise seeking the legal right to negotiate for wages and benefits for their members. For example, in 1967, the California State Employees Association, representing 115,000 civil service workers, voted to ask the state legislature to set up formal collective bargaining procedures between employees and the state. This request marks a radical change in the association's former position and could well influence the legislature to enact legislation providing for collective bargaining for state employees in California.* Furthermore, pressure for legislation can be exerted by the growing number of public employees of state and local governments. In 1967, these governmental units employed approximately 8 million persons.

The expansion of collective bargaining in public employment will have a significant impact on civil service and merit systems. In many jurisdictions, the civil service administers examinations for classified positions, establishes wage and salary structures, and promulgates rules and regulations with regard to hours of work and other conditions of employment. With the introduction of collective bargaining, the civil service or merit system will have to share the decision-making process with employee organizations in matters dealing with wages, hours, and conditions of employment. Even in the absence of formal procedures for collective bargaining, employee organizations are being consulted increasingly on matters pertaining to conditions of employment. Exactly what role the civil service will play in collective bargaining remains to be seen. The traditional role and concept of civil service systems will undoubtedly change as the result of the advent of collective bargaining for public employees.

Collective bargaining in public employment thus raises the question: What constitutes the appropriate subject matter of

---

* Six states in 1967—Connecticut, Delaware, Massachusetts, New York, Oregon, and Washington—had legislation providing for bargaining with state employees.

collective bargaining? Collective bargaining, as generally understood, involves joint decision-making between the employer and
employee organizations that have obtained bargaining rights on
such matters as wages, hours, and conditions of employment.
The broad concept of wages, hours, and conditions of employment covers an array of subjects over which the parties can
bargain. In collective bargaining agreements involving school-
teachers, for example, teacher organizations are concerned about
improving the quality of education as well as the professional
and economic status of teachers. Thus, teachers appear to want
a voice in a myriad of decisions that include curriculum, text-
book selection, size of class, teaching load, and teaching assignments, in addition to improvements in salary and fringe benefits.
In public collective bargaining, especially that involving professional groups, the subject matter will cover both professional
concerns and economic issues.

Collective bargaining in public employment will be shaped by
the role of the chief executives of the public jurisdictions (governors, mayors, and superintendents). These chief executives
will become increasingly involved in the bargaining process.
Political considerations cannot be ignored, either in the size of
the wage bill for employee groups with bargaining rights or
in the disruption of services in the event of a strike. The strike
of New York sanitation workers in February 1968 dramatized
the involvement of the chief executives at both local and state
levels. In this instance, there were sharp differences between the
mayor and the governor in their efforts to bring about a resolution of the strike. It may be argued that the New York City
situation was a special case, but in our judgment, it was not.
In Michigan, for example, the large number of impasses between local school boards and teacher organizations in the late
summer and early fall of 1967 caused the Office of the Governor
to become involved in trying to hasten the resolution of differences to permit the schools to open on schedule. There are
several reasons why the elected chief officials cannot stand idly
by in labor disputes involving groups of workers employed in
their jurisdiction. These officials may want to run for reelection
or may have other political ambitions, or there may be public
pressure for them to intervene.

The state legislatures will also become increasingly involved in collective bargaining for public employees, especially in view of the growing number of strikes in public employment. There were 146 work stoppages in government in 1966—more than three times the number in 1965. The thorniest issue in collective bargaining in the public sector is what to do about strikes, which are illegal for public employees in most jurisdictions. The sanitation workers' strike in New York City pointed out another special aspect of collective bargaining in the public sector. The pressure to end the strike on the part of the governor vitiated the existing law passed in 1967, commonly called the Taylor Act. Legislatures in states with public collective bargaining are exploring ways to resolve differences arising out of the collective bargaining process without resorting to strikes. Placing union officials in prison does not seem to deter employee organizations from engaging in work stoppages. Furthermore, as collective bargaining spreads in the public sector, we will see legislatures seeking to restrict the rights of the parties to walk out, especially if the number of walk-outs among public employees continues to increase. The public will probably pressure the legislatures for some kind of action to restrict strikes. One possibility is to provide, in addition to fact-finding and mediation, arbitration not only as the final step in the grievance procedure but also as a means of resolving impasses over contract terms.

As we have noted, collective bargaining in the public sector will expand through the enactment of appropriate legislation. Equally important is the acceptance of this public policy by the parties themselves and by the general community. What will be the acceptance of such public policy? Given the history of collective bargaining in the private sector, the acceptance will probably vary. The attitudes of public employers toward sharing decision-making with employee organizations can be catalogued according to (1) resistance, (2) reluctant acceptance, and (3) genuine acceptance. A brief comment will be made on each of these attitudes.

There are and will be public employers who are opposed to the concept of joint decision-making. They argue that sovereignty, authority, and responsibilities established by law cannot be shared with other groups. By sharing statutory decision-making authority, the public employer, in this view, may not be able to respond to the wishes of the citizens.

There are public employers whose attitude toward collective bargaining can and will be characterized as reluctant acceptance. In this kind of situation collective bargaining is only tolerated, perhaps grudgingly. The position of these employers is that because the employee organization has legally obtained bargaining rights, the employer must at least sit down at the bargaining table. Depending on the provisions of the law, failure to do so can result in an unfair labor practice charge against the employer. At the bargaining table, their strategy can proceed in the direction of either delay or containment. The objective of the former tactic is to meet frequently or infrequently to discuss items but not to reach agreement on specifics. The containment approach limits the subject of negotiations to a narrow and strict interpretation of the law. The public employer meets the legal requirements and no more.

The public employer who takes a position of genuine acceptance looks to the collective bargaining mechanism as a means to forge constructive relationships with the employee organizations that have bargaining rights. The joint making of decisions is viewed as being mutually advantageous. It represents participative public administration through the involvement of employee groups.

In a way, the involvement of employees in the decision-making process is a natural outgrowth of modern organizational theory. An examination of current literature on the management process reveals extensive usage of such words as cooperation, consultation, communication, involvement, participation, democratic work environment, and consent. Modern organizational theory has its philosophical roots in the concept of the dignity of the human being. The organization is viewed as a social organism in which individuals interact with one another. The job, in addition to providing income, is viewed in terms of providing satisfaction to the individuals. In the traditional hierarchical approach, decisions were highly centralized. In modern organizational theory, decision-making involves participation and involvement by the individuals in the organization. Collective bargaining, therefore, formalizes the participative process.

With an attitude of genuine acceptance, the parties seek diligently to work out their problems and to reach agreements that are acceptable to both sides. In the final analysis, the test of a good agreement is its acceptance by both parties.

The range of attitudes toward decision-making (resistance, reluctant acceptance, and genuine acceptance) is not fixed or immutable; positions do change over time. The experience of business and industry has demonstrated that the parties in a collective bargaining relationship can accommodate themselves to each other's needs without destroying the enterprise or the employee organizations. Although generalizations can be made about collective bargaining, each and every collective bargaining relationship has its own history. The parties develop a *modus operandi* to fit the uniqueness of their relationship.

There is another development emerging out of public collective bargaining that has implications for the future. The professional associations (education associations and nurses' associations, to mention two) are assuming functions historically ascribed to labor unions. They are concerned not only with improving the professional status of their group but with negotiating wages, hours, and conditions of employment. The differences between such professional organizations and unions are becoming blurred. This situation could well bring about a merger of the American Federation of Teachers (AFL-CIO) and the National Education Association. Furthermore, the growth of teacher collective bargaining may well stimulate other professional associations to enter collective bargaining relationships on behalf of their members.

In summary, the windows of change are open and we shall see a significant increase in the growth of collective bargaining among public employees in the years immediately ahead. The effectiveness of this relationship will depend primarily upon the parties themselves. Elected officials in both the executive and legislative branches of state and local government will become increasingly involved in the collective bargaining process, especially as it relates to a resolution of differences. Finally, the public will be watching closely the developments emerging out of these relationships. The people will make their voices heard, if need be, through their elected representatives.

BIBLIOGRAPHY

Agger, Carol. "The Government and Its Employees," *Yale Law Journal,* XLVII (May 1938), 1109–1135.

Alaska Railroad, Board of Arbitration. "A Wage Award on the Alaska Railroad," *Monthly Labor Review,* LXXXI (September 1958), 965–973.

Allen, Roy B., and John Schmid (eds.). *Collective Negotiations and Educational Administration.* Fayetteville: University of Arkansas, College of Education, and the University Council of Educational Administration, 1966.

American Federation of Teachers. *Collective Bargaining Contracts.* Chicago: American Federation of Teachers, 1962.

———. *A Sample Study of Coercion by School Administrators in America.* Chicago: American Federation of Teachers, no date.

Amidon, Beulah. "Strikes in Public Employment," *Survey Graphic,* XXXV (May 1946), 153–155, 182–184.

Anderson, Arvid. "The Developing State of Collective Bargaining for Public Employees." Address presented at the Conference on Public Employment and Collective Bargaining, University of Chicago, February 5, 1965.

———. "Disputes Affecting Government Employees," *Labor Law Journal,* X (October 1959), 701–711.

———. "Evolving Patterns of Labor Relations in Public Employment: Labor Law Developments," *Proceedings of the 11th Annual Institute of Labor Law.* Washington, D.C.: Bureau of National Affairs, 1965, pp. 209–224.

———. "Labor Relations in the Public Service," *Wisconsin Law Review,* IV (July 1961), 601–635.

Anrod, Charles W. "Postwar Labor Relations," *American Economic Review,* XXXVI (May 1946), 375–378. (A discussion of Joseph Mire's "Collective Bargaining in the Public Service," included in same issue.)

"Anti-Strike Legislation in Operation," *Civil Service Law Reporter,* I (August 1951), 36–39.

Baldwin, Roger N. "Have Public Employees the Right to Strike?—

Yes," *National Municipal Review,* XXX (September 1941), 515–517.

Bambrick, James J., Jr., and Albert A. Blum. *Labor Relations in the Atomic Energy Field.* ("Studies in Personnel Policy," No. 158.) New York City: National Industrial Conference Board, 1957.

Barbash, Jack. "Bargaining for Professionals and Public Employees," *American Teacher Magazine,* XLIII (April 1959), 7–8.

Baughman, J. D. "Bargaining with Employee Groups," *Public Management,* XXXVIII (January 1956), 4–5.

Bean, George E. "Organized Labor and the Council-Manager Plan. Part I: Views of a City Manager," *Public Management,* XXXIX (June 1957), 122–125.

Becker, Harry A. "Role of School Administrators in Professional Negotiations," *American School Board Journal,* CL (May 1965), 9–10.

Belasco, James A. *American Association of University Professors: A Private Dispute Agency.* (Reprint Series No. 174.) Ithaca: Cornell University, New York State School of Industrial and Labor Relations, 1966, pp. 535–553.

———. *Public Employee Dispute Settlement: The Wisconsin Experience: Collective Bargaining in City X.* (Reprint Series No. 188.) Ithaca: Cornell University, New York State School of Industrial and Labor Relations, 1966.

———. "Resolving Disputes Over Contract Terms in the State Public Service: An Analysis," *Labor Law Journal,* XVI (September 1965), 533–544.

Belinker, Jerry. "Binding Arbitration for Government Employees," *Labor Law Journal,* XVI (April 1965), 234–236.

Betchkal, J. "N.E.A. and Teacher Unions Bicker and Battle for Recognition," *Nation's Schools,* LXXIV (August 1964), 35–41.

Beyer, Otto S. "Bonneville Power and Labor," *Survey Graphic,* XXXV (October 1946), 344–348, 373–374.

———. "Employee Relations in the Public Service—Present and Future," *Public Personnel Review,* VII (January 1946), 20.

Bilik, A. "Problems and Prospects for Organizing and Representing Public Employees." Address presented at the Conference on Public Employment and Collective Bargaining, University of Chicago, February 5, 1965.

Birnbaum, Elliot. "Who Speaks for Teachers?" *I.U.D. Digest,* VII (Summer 1962), 42–47.

Bishop, Edward. "Present Position of Collective Bargaining in the Local Government Services," *Public Administration,* XI (January 1933), 79–85.

Blaine, Harry R. "The Grievance Procedure and Its Application in the United States Postal Service," *Labor Law Journal,* XV (November 1964), 725–734.

———, et al. "Discipline and Discharge in the United States Postal

Service: Adverse Action and Appeal," *Industrial and Labor Relations Review*, XIX (October 1965), 92–98.

Blankenship, A. H. "Role of the Superintendent in Teacher Negotiations," *Theory into Practice*, IV (April 1965), 70–74.

Block, Joseph W. "The Collection and Analysis of Collective Bargaining Agreements," *Monthly Labor Review*, LXXVIII (June 1955), 673–678.

Blum, Albert A. *Management and the White-Collar Union*. (Research Study No. 63.) New York: American Management Association, 1964.

Bradley, Phillips. "Local Government Is News. Part XX: City Hall, Strikes, and Collective Bargaining: Front Page Stuff," *American City*, LVII (December 1942), 73, 75.

———. "Local Government Is News. Part XXV: City Hall, Strikes, and Collective Bargaining: 2," *American City*, LVIII (January 1943), 73, 75.

———. "Local Government Is News. Part XXVI: City Hall, Strikes, and Collective Bargaining: 3," *American City*, LVIII (February 1943), 64–65.

———. "The Human Side of City Hall: Collective Bargaining Again," *American City*, LIX (March 1944), 67, 69.

Brinker, Paul A. "Recent Trends of Labor Unions in Government," *Labor Law Journal*, XII (January 1961), 12–22, and 77–88.

Brooks, George. "A Case for Teachers' Unions," *Industrial and Labor Relations Report Card for Social Science Teachers*, XII (November 1963), 5–7.

———. *Report and Findings of the Conference on Employee-Management Relations in the Public Service with Emphasis on New York State and Municipal Employees*. Ithaca: Cornell University, New York State School of Industrial and Labor Relations, October 1964.

Buder, L. "Teachers Revolt," *Phi Delta Kappan*, XLIII (June 1962), 370–376.

Bureau of Labor Statistics. *Collective Bargaining Agreements in the Federal Service*. (Late Summer, 1964) (Bulletin No. 1451.) Washington, D.C.: Government Printing Office, 1965.

———. "Labor-Management Relations in TVA," *Monthly Labor Review*, LXIX (July 1949), 41–42.

———. Division of Wages and Industrial Relations. "Strike-Control Provisions in Union Constitutions," *Monthly Labor Review*, LXXVII (May 1954), 497–500.

Bureau of National Affairs. "Bar Association Report on Bargaining by Teachers," *Government Employee Relations Report*. Washington, D.C.: Bureau of National Affairs, August 15, 1966, pp. D-1–D-14.

———. "NEA Seeks Clear Right to Negotiate for Teachers," *Government Employee Relations Report*. Washington, D.C.: Bureau of National Affairs, July 13, 1964, p. 2.

Burns, John E. "The Professional Employee Dilemma and the Appropriate Bargaining Unit," *Labor Law Journal*, XII (April 1961), 303–307.

Burton, Donald B. *Personnel Welfare Provisions for Public School Teachers.* Chicago: American Federation of Teachers (AFL-CIO), March 1966.

Caliguri, Joseph. "The Relationships of Teachers' Organizations to the Superintendent and the School Board." Unpublished Ph.D. dissertation, University of Chicago, 1962.

Campfield, William L. "Motivating the Professional Employee: A Reconciliation of Organizational Constraints and Incentives," *Personnel Journal*, XLIV (September 1965), 425–428.

Carpenter, Richard. "Collective Bargaining in Public Employment," *Local Government Law Service Letter,* XII (October 1962), 1–5.

————. "Organizing the Municipal Employee," *Western City*, XXXVI (January 1960), 21–22, 26.

Case, Harry L. "Cornerstones of Personnel Administration," *Personnel Administration,* XI (January 1949), 10–12.

————. "Past, Present, and Future Studies of Federal Personnel Administration," *Public Administration Review*, XV (Spring 1955), 96–101.

————. "Wage Negotiation in the Tennessee Valley Authority," *Public Personnel Review*, VIII (July 1947), 132–138.

Caskey, Clark C. "White Collar Employees—A Union Dilemma and a Management Challenge," *Management of Personnel Quarterly,* I (Spring 1962), 10–13.

Centner, James L. "Hospitals and Collective Bargaining," *Personnel Journal*, XXXVIII (November 1959), 203–205.

Cherry, Howard L. "Negotiations between Boards and Teacher Organizations," *American School Board Journal,* CXLVI (March 1963), 7–9.

Christoph, James B. "Political Rights and Administrative Impartiality in the British Civil Service," *American Political Science Review,* LI (March 1957), 67–87.

Civil Service Assembly of the United States and Canada. "Appendix 9: Progress Report of the Technical Committee on the Part of Organized and Unorganized Employees in Administering a Well-Rounded Personnel System Submitted by the Chairman, Mr. Oliver C. Short," *Public Personnel Studies,* VIII (October–November 1930), 147–148.

Clapp, Gordon R. "Problems of Union Relations in Public Agencies," *American Economic Review,* XXXIII (March 1943), 184–196.

Clemens, Eli W. "The Interdependence of Wages and Price Determination in the Regulated Industries," *American Economic Review,* XLII (May 1952), 674–685.

Citizens' League of Cleveland. "Public Employees and the Right to Strike," *Public Personnel Studies,* X (February 1942), 242–245.

Cogen, Charles. "Collective Bargaining: The AFT Way." Address given at the National Institute on Collective Negotiations in Public Education, Rhode Island College, Providence, R.I., July 8, 1965. Chicago: American Federation of Teachers, 1965 (mimeographed).
———. "Teachers on the March." *I.U.D. Digest,* VII (Winter 1962), 45–60.
Cohany, Harry P. "Trends and Changes in Union Membership," *Monthly Labor Review,* LXXXIX (May 1966), 510–513.
———, and James H. Neary. "Collective Bargaining Agreements in the Federal Service," *Monthly Labor Review,* LXXXVIII (August 1965), 944–950.
Cohen, Fredrick. "Legal Aspects of Unionization Among Public Employees," *Temple Law Quarterly,* XXX (Winter 1957), 187–198.
Cole, G. D. H. "Labor and Staff Problems under Nationalization," *Political Quarterly,* XXI (April–June 1950), 160–170.
Cole, Taylor. "Reform of the Italian Bureaucracy," *Public Administration Review,* XIII (Autumn 1953), 247–256.
———. "Wartime Trends in the Dominion Civil Service in Canada," *Public Administration Review,* VI (Spring 1946), 157–167.
"Collective Bargaining and the Closed Shop in Cities," *Public Management,* XXIV (September 1942), 277–278.
Collective Bargaining for Professional and Technical Employees. Urbana: University of Illinois, Institute of Labor and Industrial Relations, 1965, pp. 22–45.
"Collective Bargaining in the Public Service: A Symposium." *Public Administration Review,* XXII (Winter 1962), 1–23.
"Collective Bargaining Right of Government Employees: Check-off," *University of Pennsylvania Law Review,* XCIV (July 1946), 427–431.
Collett, Merrill J. "Personnel Management in the Bonneville Power Administration," *Personnel Administration,* XI (September 1948), 5–10.
Colter, E. Royden. "Effects of Industrial Wage Contracts," *Public Management,* XXXVIII (January 1956), 3–4.
Conlon, Alice Y. "Bargaining Rights for Nurses: Convincing the Legislature," *American Journal of Nursing,* LXVI (March 1966), 544–548.
Cook, Alice H. "Adaptations of Union Structure for Municipal Collective Bargaining," *Proceedings of the Annual Spring Meeting.* Milwaukee, Wisconsin: Industrial Relations Research Association, 1966, pp. 81–90.
———. "Union Structure in Municipal Collective Bargaining," *Monthly Labor Review,* LXXXIX (June 1966), 606–608.
Cooper, Alfred M. "Does Labor Favor Government as an Employer?" *Public Utilities Fortnightly,* XXXII (November 25, 1943), 671–676.
Cooper, Leon. "Municipal Government Labor Unions. Part I: Col-

lective Bargaining," *Michigan Municipal Review,* XXII (May 1949), 72–73, 78.

———. "Municipal Government Labor Unions. Part II: Some Union Security Measures," *Michigan Municipal Review,* XXII (July 1949), 105–106, 108–109.

Cornell, Herbert W. "Civil Service Benchmark Decisions," *Public Personnel Review,* XVII (October 1956), 215–224.

———. "Collective Bargaining by Public Employee Groups," *University of Pennsylvania Law Review,* CVII (November 1958), 43–64.

Corson, John J., and Ilse M. Smith. "Federal Policies on Employee Relations," *Personnel Journal,* XVIII (October 1939), 151–159.

Corwin, Donald G. "Militant Professionalism, Initiative and Compliance in Public Education," *Sociology of Education,* 38 (Summer 1965), 310–330.

Crawford, Robert C. "Government Intervention in Emergency Labor Disputes in Atomic Energy," *Labor Law Journal,* X (June 1959), 414–429.

Crispo, John H. G. (ed.). *Collective Bargaining and the Professional Employee.* Toronto: University of Toronto, Centre for Industrial Relations, 1966.

Cron, Theodore O. "Inside the Teachers' Union." *American School and University,* 38 (November 1965), 42–46.

Cross, Elmer. "Experience with the Union Shop," *Public Management,* XXXVIII (January 1956), 7.

Crowley, John C. "How Practical Are Cost-of-Living Salary Plans for Cities?" *Western City,* XXV (April 1949), 22–24.

Cullerton, John. "Public Policy for Public Employees." Address presented at the Conference on Public Employment and Collective Bargaining, University of Chicago, February 5, 1965.

Cunningham, Robert J. "Legal Notes: Limitation on Labor Contracts by Municipalities," *Municipality,* XLV (May 1950), 102, 104.

Dahl, Robert A. "Workers' Control of Industry and the British Labor Party," *American Political Science Review,* XLI (October 1947), 875–900.

Daly, Ronald O. "New Directions for Professional Negotiation," *National Education Association Journal,* LV (October 1966), 27–29.

David, Paul T. "Training for Work in Federal Employee Relations," *Personnel Administration,* VI (April 1944), 6–9.

Davies, Audrey M. "History and Legality of Police Unions," *GRA Reporter,* V (July–August 1953), 40–42, 46–47.

Davis, Jerome. "The Teacher's Struggle for Democracy," *New Republic,* XCVII (March 15, 1939), 161–163.

Davis, Richard G. "Governmental Employees and the Right to Strike," *Social Forces,* XXVIII (March 1950), 322–329.

Dawson, G. G. "Doctoral Studies on the Relationship Between the Labor Movement and Public Education," *Journal of Educational Sociology,* XXXIV (February 1961), 260–269.

Dewey, Allen C. "Right or Power of Municipalities to Engage in Collective Bargaining," *Michigan Law Review*, LVI (February 1958), 645–648.

Diggin, Thomas E. "Executive Order 10988: A New Concept in Federal Labor-Management Relations," *Personnel Journal*, XLII (September 1963), 383–388.

Dishman, Robert B. "The Public Interest in Emergency Labor Disputes," *American Political Science Review*, XLV (December 1951), 1100–1114.

"Dismissal for Union Participation." *Civil Service Law Reporter*, I (December 1951), 118–120.

"Disputes between Local Authorities and Their Employees in the United States," *International Labour Review*, XLVII (March 1943), 370–371.

Doherty, Robert E. *Attitudes Toward Labor When Blue-Collar Children Become Teachers*. (Reprint Series No. 135.) Ithaca: Cornell University, New York State School of Industrial and Labor Relations, 1963.

————. "Determination of Bargaining Units and Election Procedures in Public School Teachers Representation Elections," *Industrial and Labor Relations Review*, XIX (July 1966), 573–576.

————, *et al.* "Collective Bargaining vs. Professional Negotiations," *School Management*, IX (November 1965), 68–75.

Doherty, William C. "Government Workers and Organizations," *American Federationist*, LXIII (June 1956), 9–10, 30–31.

Donovan, B. E., *et al.* "Collective Bargaining vs. Professional Negotiations," *School Management*, IX (November 1965), 68–75.

Doolan, Richard J. *Attitudes of White Collar Workers Toward Unionization*. Ann Arbor: University of Michigan, Bureau of Industrial Relations, Bulletin 27, 1959.

Dorros, Sidney. "The Case for Independent Professional Teachers' Associations," *Monthly Labor Review*, LXXXVIII (May 1964), 543.

Dotson, Arch. "The Emerging Doctrine of Privilege in Public Employment," *Public Administration Review*, XV (Spring 1955), 77–78.

————. "A General Theory of Public Employment," *Public Administration Review*, XVI (Summer 1956), 197–211.

Douty, H. M. "New Agreement for Review of Salaries of White-Collar Civil Servants in Great Britain," *Monthly Labor Review*, LXXXIV (May 1961), 487–488.

————. "Salary Determination for White-Collar Civil Servants in Great Britain," *Monthly Labor Review*, LXXXIII (November 1960), 1158–1165.

Dufty, N. F. "The White Collar Unionist," *The Journal of Industrial Relations*, III (October 1961), 151–156.

Eastman, George D. "Seattle Policemen Paid Less Than Laborers," *American City*, LXV (April 1950), 83.

Eby, Kermit. "Unionization of Government Workers," *Public Administration Review,* IX (Spring, 1949), 132–134.

Edenfield, Newell. "Strikes Against the State," *Law Notes,* XLV (September 1941), 9–13.

Educational Policies Commission, *The Public Interest in How Teachers Organize.* Washington, D.C.: National Educational Association, 1964.

Elam, Stanley. "Teachers' Unions: Rift without Differences," *Nation,* CCI (October 18, 1965), 247–249.

Epstein, Benjamin. *The Principal's Role in Collective Negotiations Between Teachers and School Boards.* Washington, D.C.: National Association of Secondary School Principals, 1965.

―――. "What Status and Voice for Principals and Administrators in Collective Bargaining and 'Professional Negotiation' by Teacher Organizations?" *The Bulletin of the National Association of Secondary School Principals,* XLIX (March 1965), 226–259.

Epstein, Leon D. "Political Sterilization of Civil Servants: The United States and Great Britain," *Public Administration Review,* X (Autumn 1950), 281–290.

Errant, James W., *et al.* "Labor Unions and Collective Bargaining in Government Agencies: A Panel Discussion," *Public Administration Review,* V (Autumn 1945), 373–379.

Exton, Elaine. "NSBA Opposes Teachers' Strikes and Sanctions," *The American School Board Journal,* CXLVI (June 1963), 41, 44–46.

―――. "Teacher Groups Challenge Lay School Board Control," *The American School Board Journal,* CXLVII (August 1964), 28–29.

Faricy, John J. "Use of Cost of Living Index in a Municipal Salary Plan," *Municipal Finance,* XXIV (August 1951), 43–44.

Fitch, Edwin M. "The Government and Bargaining on the Alaska Railroad," *Monthly Labor Review,* LXXXIV (May 1961), 459–462.

Flaxer, Abram. "Collective Bargaining in the Civil Service," *Survey Midmonthly,* LXXVIII (April 1942), 111–113.

―――. "Government's Major Personnel Problems Today," *Personnel Administration,* X (March 1948), 19–23.

―――. "Public Employee Unions: State, County and Municipal Workers of America," *Public Management,* XIX (September 1937), 262–264.

Flexner, Jean A. "British Labor under the Labor Government. Part II: Position and Role of Trade-Unions," *Monthly Labor Review,* LXVII (October 1948), 366–372.

―――. "Great Britain: Coal Mining Since Nationalization," *Monthly Labor Review,* LXX (January 1950), 19–25.

Frankel, Saul J. "Employee Organization in the Public Service of Canada," *Public Personnel Review,* XVII (October 1956), 246–252.

―――. *A Model for Negotiation and Arbitration Between the Canadian Government and Its Civil Servants.* Montreal: McGill University Press, 1962.

French, Wendell L. and Richard Robinson. "Collective Bargaining by Nurses and Other Professionals: Anomaly or Trend?" *Labor Law Journal,* XI (October 1960), 903–910.

Friedman, Clara H. "Education of New York City Public School Teachers: An Economic Analysis," *Industrial and Labor Relations Review,* XVII (October 1964), 20–31.

Frischknecht, Reed L. "Federal Employee Unions and the First Session, Eightieth Congress," *Western Political Quarterly,* I (June 1948), 183–185.

Gabel, George H. "Legal Problems Involved in Municipal Labor Relations," *Municipality,* XL (February 1945), 23–24, 36.

Gagliardo, Domenico. "Strikes in a Democracy," *American Economic Review,* XXXI (March 1941), 47–55.

Gambs, John S. "Hospitals and the Unions," *Survey Graphic,* XXVI (August 1937), 435–439.

————. "Relief Workers' Unions," *Survey,* LXXII (January 1936), 11–13.

Garber, L. O. "When Your Teachers Want to Elect a Bargaining Agent," *Nation's Schools,* LXX (July 1962), 62–63.

————. "These Ten Legal Principles Control Collective Bargaining," *Nation's Schools,* LXXVI (September 1965), 67.

Gardner, Howard. "Two Years' Pay Experience in 43 [California] Cities." *Western City,* XIX (June 1943), 23–24.

Gendron, U. J. "Labor Management Cooperation in Government," *Public Personnel Review,* XVIII (January 1957), 45–47.

Gibbons, Harold J., et al. *Developments in White Collar Unionism.* (Occasional Papers No. 24.) Chicago: University of Chicago, Industrial Relations Center, 1962.

Giorgi, Andrew V., and Donald John Tufts. "Unionization of Municipal Police Forces," *Notre Dame Lawyer,* XXVII (Fall 1951), 88–97.

Godine, Morton R. "Collective Negotiations and Public Policy in Public Education." Paper presented at the National Institute on Collective Negotiations in Public Education, Rhode Island College, Providence, R.I., on July 9, 1965.

Goldberg, Joseph P. "Constructive Employee Relations in Government," *Labor Law Journal,* VIII (August 1957), 551–556.

————. "Consultation, Bargaining, and Wage Determination," *Monthly Labor Review,* LXXVII (March 1954), 249–256.

————. "Extent of Employment, Status, Organization," *Monthly Labor Review,* LXXVII (January 1954), 1–6.

Golden, Clinton S. "Employee-Management Cooperation in Public Work," *Advanced Management,* VII (October–December 1942), 161–164.

Goldstein, Bernard. *The Perspective of Unionized Professionals.* (Reprint No. 7.) New Brunswick, N.J.: Rutgers, The State University, Institute of Management and Labor Relations, 1959.

Goode, Cecil E. "Personnel Opinions: What Do You Think Is a Reasonable, Enforceable Policy Regarding Restrictions on Political Activities by Civil Service Employees?" *Public Personnel Review*, XXI (January 1960), 65–71.

"Government Employees and Unionism," *Harvard Law Review*, LIV (June 1941), 1360–1368.

Green, Sedgwick. "The Effect of a Labor Dispute on the Administration of a Government Contract," *Harvard Law Review*, LXX (March 1957), 793–811.

Greene, Lee S. "Personnel Administration in the Tennessee Valley Authority," *Journal of Politics*, I (May 1939), 171–194.

Gross, Calvin. "Ways to Deal with the New Teacher Militancy," *Phi Delta Kappan*, XLVI (December 1964), 147–151.

Guidelines for Professional Negotiation. Rev. ed. New York: National Education Association, Office of Professional Development and Welfare, July 2, 1965.

Hagburg, Eugene C. (ed.). *Problems Confront Union Organizations in Public Employment.* Columbus: Ohio State University, Labor Education and Research Service, 1966.

Hall, Edith Dee. "Negotiations End and Nurses Accept New Contract," *Hospital Management*, CII (July 1966), 90.

Haller, George D. "Policemen in Politics," *American City*, LXXIII (August 1958), 100.

Hamilton, David. "Will the College Teacher Organize?" *I.U.D. Digest*, VII (Spring 1962), 121–128.

Harper, Dean. "Labor Relations in the Postal Service," *Industrial and Labor Relations Review*, XVII (April 1964), 443–454.

Harris, Herbert. "Collective Bargaining in the Local Public Service," *American City*, LXI (January 1946), 89–90, 127.

Hart, Wilson R. *Collective Bargaining in the Federal Civil Service.* New York: Harper & Row, 1961.

————. "The Impasse in Labor Relations in the Federal Civil Service," *Industrial and Labor Relations Review*, XIX (January 1966), 175–189.

————. "The U. S. Civil Service Learns to Live with Executive Order 10988: An Interim Appraisal," *Industrial and Labor Relations Review*, XVII (January 1964), 203–221.

Heady, Ferrel. "American Government and Politics: The Hatch Act Decisions," *American Political Science Review*, XLI (August 1947), 687–699.

Hedges, Marion H. "Labor Problems," *American Economic Review*, XXXIII, No. 1, Part II (March 1943), 202–204.

Heisel, W. D., and J. P. Santa-Emma. "Unions in City Government: The Cincinnati Story," *Public Personnel Review*, XXII (January 1961), 35–38.

Hepbron, James M. "Police Unionization Means Disorganization," *American City*, LXXIII (November 1958), 131–132.

Herrick, Elinore M. "Unions: Partners or Adversaries?" *Good Government*, LXXI (July–August 1954), 40–43.

Herrick, H. T. "Unions for Government Employees: Their Implications," *Proceedings of the Conference on Labor*. New York: New York University Press, 1962, pp. 129–136.

Hetter, Frederick L. "A University Local," *I.U.D. Digest*, VII (Winter 1962), 101–109.

Hewes, George R. "How Toledo's Municipal Job Classification System Works," *American City*, LXII (November 1947), 85.

Holland, Ann. *Unions Are Here to Stay: A Guide for Employee-Management Relations in the Federal Service*. (Pamphlet No. 17.) Washington, D.C.: Society for Personnel Administration, 1962.

Holt, John Fox. "Labor Rights of Public Employees," *Southwestern Journal*, II (Spring 1948), 226–237.

Hopkins, J. "Review of Events in Professional Negotiations," *Theory into Practice*, IV (April 1965), 1–4.

Houghton, A. L. N. D. "Collective Bargaining in the Civil Service," *Public Administration*, XI (January 1933), 86–97.

Hughes, Helen and D. W. Rawson. "Collective Bargaining and the White-Collar Pay Structure," *Journal of Industrial Relations*, II (October 1960), 75–89.

Humphrey, Hubert H. "A Community Program for Labor Management Peace," *American City*, LXII (May 1947), 92–94.

International City Managers' Association. "Cities Establish Arbitration Boards to Settle Labor Disputes," *American City*, LXVI (November 1951), 103.

Irons, Warren B. *State of the Art in Employee-Management Cooperation*. (Government Employee Relations Report No. 83.) Washington, D.C.: Bureau of National Affairs, 1965, p. A3.

Irwin, James W., *et al.* "Labor Relations in the Public Water Supply Field," *Journal of the American Water Works Association*, XXXV (December 1943), 1565–1573.

Jacoby, Robert. "Collective Bargaining Rights for Federal Employees," *Intramural Law Report*, XVIII (May 1963), 287–310.

Johnson, David B. "Dispute Settlement in Atomic Energy Plants," *Industrial and Labor Relations Review*, XIII (October 1959), 38–53.

Johnson, Eldon L. "General Unions in the Federal Service," *Journal of Politics*, II (February 1940), 23–56.

————. "Joint Consultation in Britain's Nationalized Industries," *Public Administration Review*, XII (Summer 1952), 181–189.

Johnson, Richard B. "Administrative Problems of Government Seizure in Labor Disputes," *Public Administration Review*, XI (Summer 1951), 189–198.

Jones, Roger W. "The Federal Civil Service Today," *Public Personnel Review*, XXI (April 1960), 114–120.

Kahn, Mark L. "Regulatory Agencies and Industrial Relations: The

Airlines Case," *American Economic Review*, XLII (May 1952), 686–698.

Kammerer, Gladys M. "An Evaluation of Wartime Personnel Administration," *Journal of Politics*, X (February 1948), 49–72.

Kaplan, H. Eliot. "Concepts of Public Employee Relations," *Industrial and Labor Relations Review*, I (January 1948), 206–230.

——. "Have Public Employees the Right to Strike?—No," *National Municipal Review*, XXX (September 1941), 518–523.

——. "Public Employee Relationships," *Civil Service Law Reporter*, I (October 1951), 92–98.

——. "What Rights Have Public Employees?" *Good Government*, LXIV (January–February 1947), 1–4.

——, et al. "How Can Strikes by Municipal Employees Be Avoided?" *American City*, LXII (February 1947), 83–85.

Kassalow, Everett M. "New Union Frontier: White-Collar Workers," *Harvard Business Review*, XL (January–February 1962), 41–52.

——. "Occupational Frontiers of Trade Unionism in the U.S.," *Proceedings of the Fourteenth Annual Winter Meeting*. St. Louis, Missouri: Industrial Relations Research Association, 1960, pp. 183–203.

——. "Organization of White Collar Workers," *Monthly Labor Review*, LXXXIV (March 1961), 234–238.

——. "The Prospects for White-Collar Union Growth," *Industrial Relations*, V (October 1965), 37–47.

Kelly, George A. "Civil Servants: Government Workers and the Right to Strike," *Commonweal*, XLVI (May 9, 1947), 87–89.

Kennedy, Stephen P. "No Union for New York City Police," *American City*, LXXIII (October 1958), 179, 181.

Keppel, F. "Use Strike Only as Last Resort, Keppel Urges A.F.T. Members," *Nation's Schools*, LXXVI (October 1965), 92.

Keresman, Peter. "Constructive Employee Relations in Police Departments," *Labor Law Journal*, VIII (August 1957), 556–558.

Khanna, B. S. "Whitleyism: A Feature of Democratic Administration," *Indian Journal of Public Administration*, V (April–June 1959), 207–222.

Killingsworth, Charles T. "Grievance Adjudication in Public Employment," *American Arbitration Journal*, XIII (Spring 1958), 3–15.

King, Oren L. "How Riverside, California Benefits by . . . Labor Council Support for the City Manager," *American City*, LXXIII (March 1958), 129, 145, 147.

Kite, Robert H. "A Study to Determine the Degree of Influence Selected Factors Had in Causing Teacher Strikes and to Determine the Degree to Which These Factors Were Present in School Districts in Which Teacher Strikes Were Averted," *Dissertation Abstracts*, XXVI (October 1965), 2017.

Klass, Irwin. "The New Breed of Teacher," *American Federationist*, LXIX (November 1962), 1–5.

Klaus, Ida. *Collective Bargaining Will Help Staff Morale.* New York: Society for the Experimental Study of Education, 1963.

―――. "The Emerging Relationship." Address presented at the Conference on Public Employment and Collective Bargaining, University of Chicago, February 5, 1965.

Klein, Lawrence R. "The NEA Convention and the Organizing of Teachers," *Monthly Labor Review,* LXXXVIII (August 1965), 883–885.

Kline, Clarice. "The Professional Pattern in Teachers' Organizations," *Teachers College Record,* 63 (November 1961), 121–127.

Knapp, Daniel C. "Administering Federal Grievance Procedures," *Public Personnel Review,* VIII (April 1947), 96–101.

Knowlton, Thomas A. "Is Collective Bargaining the Answer?" *Arbitration Journal,* No. 21 (July 1966), pp. 93–97.

Kooken, Don L. and Loren D. Ayres. "Police Unions and the Public Safety," *Annals,* CCXCI (January 1954), 152–158.

Krislov, Joseph. "The Cleveland Transit Strike of 1949," *Personnel Administration,* XIV (November 1950), 25–30.

―――. "The Independent Public Employee Association: Characteristics and Functions," *Industrial and Labor Relations Review,* XV (July 1962), 510–520.

―――. "Prospects for the Use of Advisory Grievance Arbitration in Federal Service," *Industrial and Labor Relations Review,* XVIII (April 1965), 420–422.

―――. "The Union Quest for Recognition in Government Service," *Labor Law Journal,* IX (June 1958), 421–424, 461.

―――. "The Union Shop, Employment Security, and Municipal Workers" *Industrial and Labor Relations Review,* XII (January 1959), 256.

"Labor Committee [Wisconsin Legislative Council, Labor Relations Committee] Opposes Interference in Municipal Employer-Employee Relations," *Municipality,* LII (February 1957), 35, 49.

Labor Management Institute of the American Arbitration Association. *Memorandum of Agreement.* New York: City Administrator's Office, March 31, 1966.

La Due, Wendell R. "Significance of Legislation Forbidding Strikes by Public Employees," *Journal of the American Water Works Association,* XXXIX (September 1947), 844–854.

―――. "Union Relations with Public Ownership," *Journal of the American Water Works Association,* XXXVIII (August 1946), 914–920.

Lang, William. *The Development and Techniques of Collective Bargaining in the Municipal Service.* Washington, D.C.: International Association of Fire Fighters, 1966.

Law, Kenneth L., *et al. The Manual for Teacher Negotiators.* Windsor, Ontario: Educational Consultative Service, Inc., 1966.

Lawton, Esther C. (ed.). "Viewpoints: Should Personnel Staff Members Belong to Unions?" *Personnel Administration,* XIX (March–April 1956), 46–50.

Leich, Harold H. "The Hoover Commission's Personnel Recommendations: A Progress Report," *American Political Science Review,* XLVII (March 1953), 100–125.

Levitan, David M. "The Employee and the Government," *Journal of Politics,* VII (August 1945), 295–313.

Lieberman, Myron. "Influences of Teachers' Organization upon American Education," in Nelson B. Henry (ed.), *Social Forces Influencing American Education.* Chicago: National Society for the Study of Education, 1961, pp. 182–202.

————. "Teachers Choose a Union," *Nation,* 193 (December 2, 1961), 443–447.

————. "Teachers on the March." *Nation,* 200 (February 1, 1965), 107–110.

————. "Teachers' Strikes: Acceptable Strategy?" *Phi Delta Kappan,* XLVI (January 1965), 237–240.

————. "Who Speaks for Teachers?" *Saturday Review,* 48 (June 19, 1965), 65–66, 74–75.

————, and Michael H. Moskow. *Collective Negotiations for Teachers.* Chicago: Rand McNally, 1966.

Lowe, William T. "Who Joins Which Teachers' Group?" *Teachers College Record,* LXVI (April 1965), 614–619.

McCafferty, Bart. "Unionized Municipal Employees: Financial Aspects," *Municipal Finance,* XXXIII (November 1960), 98–103.

McCaffree, Kenneth M. "Collective Bargaining in Atomic-Energy Construction," *Journal of Political Economy,* LXV (August 1957), 322–337.

McCutchen, Duval T. "Seniority and the Democratic Crisis," *Social Forces,* XXI (March 1943), 351–358.

McDermott, F. Arnold. "The Denver Lay-Off Formula: Seniority Plus Merit," *Public Personnel Review,* XXI (July 1960), 179–182.

McGlothlin, William J. "The Apprentice Program of TVA," *Personnel Administration,* VIII (April 1946), 5–8.

————. "Union-Management Administration of Employee Training: The Experience of TVA," *Advanced Management,* VIII (April–June 1943), 38–44.

McIntosh, Marjorie. "The Negotiation of Wages and Conditions for Local Authority Employees in England and Wales. Part I: Structure and Scope," *Public Administration,* XXXIII (Summer 1955), 149–162.

————. "The Negotiation of Wages and Conditions for Local Authority Employees in England and Wales. Part II: The Process of Negotiation and Settlement," *Public Administration,* XXXIII (Autumn 1955), 307–323.

————. "The Negotiation of Wages and Conditions for Local Authority Employees in England and Wales. Part III: Some Results of

Joint Negotiation," *Public Administration,* XXXIII (Winter 1955), 401–417.

McKelvey, Jean T. "The American City and Its Public Employee Unions," *Proceedings of the Annual Spring Meeting.* Milwaukee, Wisconsin: Industrial Relations Research Association, 1966, 68–69.

———. "The Role of State Agencies in Public Employee Labor Relations," *Industrial and Labor Relations Review,* XX (January 1967), 179–197.

Macmahon, Arthur W. "A Balanced Approach to Unionization," *Public Administration Review,* II (Spring 1942), 168–171.

———. "Collective Labor Action in City Government," *Public Management,* XXIII (November 1941), 328–334.

———. "The Mexican Railways under Workers' Administration," *Public Administration Review,* I (Autumn 1941), 458–471.

———. "The New York City Transit System: Public Ownership, Civil Service, and Collective Bargaining," *Political Science Quarterly,* LVI (June 1941), 161–198.

Macy, John W., Jr. "The Federal Employee-Management Cooperation Program," *Industrial and Labor Relations Review,* XIX (July 1966), 549–561.

———. "Personnel Developments on the Federal Level," *Public Personnel Review,* XXV (January 1964), 7–12.

Mahoney, Anne. "Bargaining Rights for Nurses: Convincing the Membership," *American Journal of Nursing,* LXVI (March 1966), 544.

Mailick, Sidney. "Organization for Personnel Management in Israel," *Public Personnel Review,* XIII (January 1952), 28–34.

Martin, Richard. "Municipal Recognition of Employees," *Public Management,* XXXVIII (January 1956), 2–3.

Martin, T. D., *et al.* "Compulsory Membership in Teachers' Associations?" *Phi Delta Kappan,* XXXIII (September 1951), 56–61.

Mathewson, Stanley B. "Labor, Management and the Public," *Survey Graphic,* XXVI (July 1937), 388–391.

Megel, Carl J. "The Union Patterns in Teachers' Organizations," *Teachers College Record,* 63 (November 1961), 115–120.

Melton, Presley W. "Employee Relations in Federal Service," *Personnel Journal,* XVII (September 1938), 96–101.

Miller, Glen W. *Collective Bargaining by Public Employees.* Columbus: Ohio State University, Ohio State Labor Education and Research Services, College of Commerce and Administration, 1966.

Mire, Joseph. "Collective Bargaining in the Public Service," *American Economic Review,* XXXVI (May 1946), 347–358.

———. "Freedom of Assembly, Speech and Petition," *Wisconsin Law Review,* MXMXLVII (July 1947), 693–696.

———. *Labor Organizations in German Public Administration and Services.* (United States Expert Series No. 8.) Washington, D.C.: United States Office of Military Government for Germany, 1949.

Moffitt, J. C. "Sanctions Do What?" *American School Board Journal,* CXLIX (September 1964), 25–26.

Moore, John Bassett. "Restrictions on the Civil Rights of Federal Employees," *Columbia Law Review,* XLVII (November 1947), 1161–1189.

Morgan, Arthur E. "Bench-Marks in the Tennessee Valley. Part VI: Building a Labor Policy," *Survey Graphic,* XXIV (November 1935), 529–532, 575–576.

Mosher, William E. "Implications of an Enlightened Personnel Policy," *Library Journal,* LXII (November 15, 1937), 849–852.

———. "The Profession of Public Service," *American Political Science Review,* XXXII (April 1938), 332–342.

Moskow, Michael H. "Collective Bargaining for Public School Teachers," *Labor Law Journal,* XV (December 1964), 784–794.

———. "Recent Legislation Affecting Collective Negotiations for Teachers," *Phi Delta Kappan,* XLVII (November 1965), 136–141.

———. "Teacher Organizations: An Analysis of the Issues," *Teachers College Record,* LXVI (February 1965), 453–463.

———. *Teachers and Unions.* Philadelphia: University of Pennsylvania Press, 1966.

"Municipal Employee Labor Relations Practices," *Municipality,* LI (March 1956), 65, 76.

National Civil Service Reform League, Special Committee on Government Employee Relationships. "Employer and Employee Relationships in Government," *Public Personnel Studies,* X (August 1941), 74–75.

National Civil Service League. "Anti-Strike Laws Won't Work: Can Public Employee Strikes Be Avoided?" *Good Government,* LXVIII (May–June 1951), 29–30.

———. "Little Hatch Acts Provide Election-Time Do's and Don'ts for Public Servants," *Good Government,* LXX (September–October 1953), 42–46.

National Education Association. *Classroom Teachers Speak on Professional Negotiations.* Washington, D.C.: National Education Association, 1963.

———. *Professional Negotiation with School Boards: A Legal Analysis and Review.* Washington, D.C.: National Education Association, Research Division, 1965.

———. *Public School Teachers and Collective Bargaining.* (Special Memo.) Washington, D.C.: National Education Association, Research Division, May 1955 and March 1958.

"NEA's New Alternatives." *I.U.D. Digest,* VIII (Spring 1963), 38–46.

"Negotiating with Teachers." *School Management,* IX (May 1965), 81–87.

Nesbitt, Murray B. "League Studying Employee Organizations in Government," *Good Government,* LXXVIII (June 1960), 1–3.

[New York State] Governor's Committee on Public Employee Relations. *Final Report*. Albany, New York: Office of the Governor, March 31, 1966.

Newland, Chester A. *Public Employee Unionization in Texas*. Austin: University of Texas, Institute of Public Affairs, 1962.

Nolan, Loretta R., and James T. Hall, Jr. "Strikes of Government Employees, 1942–1961," *Monthly Labor Review*, LXXXVI (January 1963), 52–54.

Nolte, M. C. "Teacher Militancy May Be Counter-Pressure," *American School Board Journal*, CLI (October 1965), 7–8.

———. "Teachers Face Board of Education Across the Bargaining Table Legally," *American School Board Journal*, CL (June 1965), 10–12.

Nolting, Orin F. "Management Policy on Employee Relations," *Public Management*, XXIX (January 1947), 5–10.

Northrup, Herbert R., and Richard L. Rowan. "Arbitration and Collective Bargaining: An Analysis of State Experience," *Labor Law Journal*, XIV (February 1963), 178–191.

Oakes, R. C. "Should Teachers Strike? An Unanswered Question," *Journal of Educational Sociology*, XXXIII (March 1960), 339–344.

Office of Education. *Teachers Negotiate with Their School Boards*. (Bulletin No. 1964.) Washington, D.C.: Government Printing Office, 1964.

Office of Professional Development and Welfare. *Guidelines for Professional Negotiation*. Rev. ed. Washington, D.C.: National Education Association, July 2, 1965.

———. "Professional Negotiations: Selected Statements of School Board Administrator-Teacher Relationships." Washington, D.C.: National Education Association, 1965.

Ohm, Robert E., and Oliver D. Johns. *Negotiations in the Schools: The Superintendent Confronts Collective Action*. Norman: University of Oklahoma, College of Education, 1965.

Olmstead, H. M. "Controversies between Cities: Organized Labor Causes Critical Situations." *National Municipal Review*, XXXIII (April 1944), 195–197.

———. "Organizing by Public Employees: Civil Service League Makes Policy Statement," *National Civic Review*, L (February 1961), 86–87.

Orzack, Louis H. *Work as a Central Life Interest of Professionals*. (Reprint Series No. 3.) Madison: University of Wisconsin, Industrial Relations Research Center, 1959.

Padway, Joseph A. "Collective Bargaining in Government Enterprise," *Lawyers Guild Review*, II (March 1942), 1–7.

Parker, Hyman. "Role of the Michigan Labor Mediation Board in Public Employee Labor Disputes," *Labor Law Journal*, X (September 1959), 633–642.

Perlman, David. "Government Employees and Unions," *The American Federationist*, LXVIII (September 1961), 4–7.

Perry, Charles R., and Wesley Wildman. "A Survey of Collective Activity among Public School Teachers," *Educational Administration Quarterly,* II (Spring 1966).

Phelps, Orme W. "Compulsory Arbitration: Some Perspectives," *Industrial and Labor Relations Review,* 18 (October 1964), 81–91.

Plunkett, Thomas J. "Collective Bargaining and the Municipal Personnel Officers [Canada]," *Public Personnel Review,* XVI (July 1955), 139–142.

"A Policy for Employee-Management Cooperation in the Federal Service," *Report of the President's Task Force.* Washington, D.C.: Government Printing Office, 1962, p. 19.

"Political Activity of Public Employees," *Civil Service Law Reporter,* V (July–August 1955), 67–68.

Posey, Rollin B. "Analysis of City Employee Strikes," *Public Management,* XXXIV (June 1952), 122–127.

———. "Employee Organization in the United States Public Service," *Public Personnel Review,* XVII (October 1956), 238–245.

———. "Handling City Employee Grievances," *Public Management,* XXXV (March 1953), 54–58.

———. "How to Negotiate with Labor Unions," *Public Personnel Review,* XIV (January 1953), 11–17.

———. "Organized Labor and the Council-Manager Plan. Part III: Views of an Observer," *Public Management,* XXXIX (June 1957), 129–132.

———. "Recognition of Unions in Municipal Employment," *Public Management,* XXXI (February 1949), 40–43.

———. "Union Agreements in Municipal Employment," *Public Management,* XXX (February 1948), 35–40.

Potts, Georgena R. "A Summer School Short Course in Teacher Negotiations," *Monthly Labor Review,* LXXXIX (August 1966), 847–850.

"Power of a Municipal Corporation to Enter into a Check-off Agreement with a Labor Union: Mugford v. Mayor and City Council of Baltimore," *Maryland Law Review,* IX (Winter 1948), 70–73.

President's Commission on Labor Relations in the Atomic Energy Installations. "Panel to Handle Atomic Energy Plant Disputes," *Monthly Labor Review,* LXVIII (June 1949), 661–662.

Presthus, R. Vance. "British Public Administration: The National Coal Board," *Public Administration Review,* IX (Summer 1949), 200–210.

Public Employee Labor Relations. (Publication 132.) Springfield: Illinois State Legislative Council, 1958.

The Public Interest in How Teachers Organize. National Education Association, and American Association of School Administrators, Educational Policies Commission, Washington, D.C.: The Commission, 1964.

Radke, Mrs. Fred A. "Real Significance of Collective Bargaining for

Teachers," *Labor Law Journal,* XV (December 1964), 795–801.

Rains, Harry H. "Collective Bargaining in Public Employment," *Labor Law Journal,* VIII (August 1957), 548–550.

Ranen, Ellis. "Bargaining Rights in Civil Service," *Survey Midmonthly,* LXXVIII (February 1942), 42–45.

Raskin, A. H. "Do Public Strikes Violate Public Trust?" *The New York Times Magazine,* CX (January 8, 1961), 12.

Rawn, A. M. "Employee Organization in the Professional Field and the Public Services," *Journal of the American Water Works Association,* XXXVI (July 1944), 762–770.

"Recognition of Representatives of Federal Employee Organizations in Grievance Procedures," *Hearings before House Committee on Post Office and Civil Service on H. R. 554 and H. R. 571.* 82d Cong., 2d sess. (August 1951 and March 1952).

Repas, Robert. "Collective Bargaining Problems in Public Employment." East Lansing: Michigan State University, University Labor Education Association, March 31, 1966 (mimeographed).

Report on a Program of Labor Relations for New York City Employees. New York: [City] Department of Labor, 1957.

Rhyne, Charles S. *Labor Unions and Municipal Employee Law.* National Institute of Municipal Law Officers, 1946. See also: *Supplemental Report,* No. 129.

————. "Public Employees Have No Right to Strike: Municipal Relations with Unions Representing Municipal Employees," *American City,* LVIII (January 1943), 89, 91.

————. "Public Workers and the Right to Strike," *Engineering News-Record,* CXXXVII (September 5, 1946), 80–83.

————. "Recent Decisions on Labor Union Contracts and Municipalities," *American City,* LXI (February 1946), 139, 143.

Rich, J. M. "Civil Disobedience and Teacher Strikes," *Phi Delta Kappan,* XLV (December 1965), 151–154.

————. "Teacher Unrest Has Damaged School Public Relations," *Nation's Schools,* LXXV (March 1965), 46–47.

Richardson, George J. "Labor Unions in Fire Departments," *Public Management,* XIX (January 1937), 6–9.

"Right of Municipal Employee's Union to Strike and to Bargain Collectively," *Minnesota Law Review,* XXXIV (February 1950), 260–266.

"Right of Municipality to Enter into Collective Bargaining Agreements on Behalf of Civil Service Employees," *New York University Law Quarterly Review,* XVIII (January 1941), 247–261.

Roach, S. P. "Collective Bargaining," *School Management,* X (March 1966), 66.

Rock, Eli. "Municipal Collective Bargaining: New Areas for Research," *Proceedings of the Annual Spring Meeting.* Milwaukee, Wisconsin: Industrial Relations Research Association, 1966, pp. 70–80.

————. "The Process and Procedures of the Long-Standing Relationship." Address presented before the Conference on Public Employment and Collective Bargaining, University of Chicago, February 5, 1965.

Ross, N. S. "Joint Consultation and Workers' Control," *Political Quarterly,* XXVII (January–March 1956), 82–100.

Ross, Philip. *The Government as a Source of Union Power.* Providence, R.I.: Brown University Press, 1965.

Rowlands, David D. "Labor Relations in the City Government," *Public Management,* XL (February 1958), 30–32.

Roy, Walter. "Membership Participation in the National Union of Teachers," *British Journal of Industrial Relations,* II (July 1964), 189–203.

————. "Reaction of Organized British Teachers to Crises," *Monthly Labor Review,* LXXXVII (September 1964), 1022–1025.

Rushin, Emmett R. "A New Frontier for Employee-Management Cooperation in Government," *Public Administration Review,* III (Spring 1943), 158–163.

Samuel, Edwin. "The Israel Civil Service," *Indian Journal of Public Administration,* VI (July–September 1960), 267–271.

Sanford, William V. "Strikes by Government Employees," *Vanderbilt Law Review,* II (April 1949), 441–450.

Scanlon, John. "Strikes, Sanctions, and the Schools," *Saturday Review,* XLVI (October 19, 1965), 51–55, 70–74.

Schmidt, Charles T., Jr. "Organizing for Collective Bargaining in Michigan Education, 1965–1967." Unpublished Ph.D. dissertation, Michigan State University, 1968.

————. "The Process of Fact-Finding in Michigan Public Education Teacher-School Board Contract Disputes," *Proceedings of the Joint Conference of the Association of Labor Mediation Agencies and National Association of State Labor Relations Agencies.* Dorado, Puerto Rico, August 1968, BNA, 1968.

————. "The Question of the Recognition of Principal and Other Supervisory Units in Public Education Collective Bargaining," *Labor Law Journal,* 19 (May 1968), 238–291.

————. "Representation of Classroom Teachers" (Case Studies of Detroit and Grand Rapids), *Monthly Labor Review,* 91 (July 1968), 27–36.

————, et al. *A Guide to Collective Negotiations in Education.* Social Science Research Bureau, Michigan State University, 1967.

Schnaufer, Pete. "Representing the Teacher's Interest. Response from the AFT." *Monthly Labor Review,* LXXXIX (June 1966), 620–621.

————. *The Uses of Teacher Power.* Chicago: American Federation of Teachers, 1966.

Schneider, B. V. H. "Collective Bargaining and the Federal Civil Service," *Industrial Relations,* III (May 1964), 97–120.

Schneider, Carl J. "The Revival of Whitleyism in British Local Government," *Public Administration Review,* XIII (Spring 1953), 97–105.

Schnoor, Howard. "Employee Participation in Management in the German Civil Service," *Personnel Administration,* XV (September 1952), 11–18, 22.

Schoemann, Peter T. "The Right of Teachers to Organize," *The American Federationist, LXX* (March 1963), 23–24.

Schwartz, Murray L. "Notes: Industrial Nationalization and Industrial Relations in Great Britain," *University of Pennsylvania Law Review,* XCVII (March 1949), 543–558.

Seasongood, Murray, and Roscoe L. Barrow. "Unionization of Public Employees," *University of Cincinnati Law Review,* XXI (November 1952), 327–392.

Seeman, Melvin. "Role Conflict and Ambivalence in Leadership," *American Sociological Review,* XVIII (August 1953), 373–380.

Segal, Melvin J. "Grievance Procedures for Public Employees," *Labor Law Journal,* IX (December 1958), 921–924.

Seitz, Reynolds C. "Rights of School Teachers to Engage in Labor Organizational Activities," *Marquette Law Review,* XLIV (Summer 1960), 36–44.

———. "School Board and Teacher Unions," *American School Board Journal,* CXLI (August 1960), 11–13, 38.

Selden, David. "American Federation of Teachers: What It Wants, How It Bargains, Where It's Headed," *School Management,* VIII (February 1964), 56–58.

———. "Class Size and the New York Contract," *Phi Delta Kappan,* XLVI (March 1964), 283–287.

———. "Teacher Collective Bargaining Today," in Eugene C. Hagburg (ed.), *Problems Confronting Union Organizations in Public Employment.* Columbus: Ohio State University, Labor Education and Research Service, 1966, pp. 39–52.

———. *Winning Collective Bargaining.* Chicago: American Federation of Teachers, 1963.

Seligson, Harry. "A New Look at Employee Relations in Public and Private Services," *Labor Law Journal,* XV (May 1964), 287–299.

Sessions, Jack. "Who Runs the Public Schools?" *The American Federationist,* LXX (July 1963), 21–22.

"Settlement of Disputes in Public Employment," *Monthly Labor Review,* LXXXIX (April 1966), iii–iv.

Seymour, Harold, "Divided, the [Teaching] Profession Weighs the Pros and Cons of Unionism," *Industrial Bulletin,* XLI (January 1962), 17–20.

Shenton, David G. "Compulsory Arbitration in the Public Service," *Labor Law Journal,* XVII (March 1966), 138–147.

Shestack, Jerome J. "The Public Employee and His Government:

Conditions and Disabilities of Public Employment," *Vanderbilt Law Review,* VIII (June 1955), 816–837.

Shils, Edward B. "Philadelphia Streamlines Personnel Plan," *National Municipal Review,* XXII (July 1943), 367–372.

Shoben, E. J. "When Teachers Strike," *Teachers College Record,* LXV (November 1963), 164–167.

Short, Lloyd M. "Unions of Municipal Employees," *Minnesota Municipalities,* XXIX (July 1944), 219–225.

Siciliano, Rocco C. "Employee-Management Relations in the Federal Government," *Good Government,* LXXVII (January 1960), 3–4.

Silver, Jonas. "Labor Relations of Public Employees," *American Labor Legislation Review,* XXX (December 1940), 169–170.

———. "Union Agreements with Municipalities," *Monthly Labor Review,* LVI (June 1943), 1165–1170.

Silver, Richard A. "Collective Bargaining with Public Employees," *Personnel Administration,* XXII (January–February 1959), 27–34.

Smith, M. Mead. "Labor and the Savannah River AEC Project. Part I: Manpower, Wages, and Recruitment," *Monthly Labor Review,* LXXIV (June 1952), 629–639.

———. "Labor and the Savannah River AEC Project. Part II: Unionization and Industrial Relations," *Monthly Labor Review,* LXXV (July 1952), 12–21.

Smith, Oscar S. "Are Public Service Strikes Necessary?" *Public Personnel Review,* XXI (July 1960), 169–173.

———. "The Effect of the Public Interest on the Right to Strike and to Bargain Collectively," *North Carolina Law Review,* XXVII (February 1949), 204–212.

———. "Implications for Collective Bargaining in Quasi-Public Work," *Monthly Labor Review,* LXXIV (March 1952), 257–262.

———. "Obligations of Government as Owner, Financier and Consumer in Relation to Collective Bargaining," *Labor Law Journal,* VII (November 1956), 684–689.

Smith, Russell A., and Doris B. McLaughlin. "Public Employment Research: A Neglected Area of Research and Training in Labor Relations," *Industrial and Labor Relations Review,* XVI (October 1962), 30–44.

Smythe, Cyrus. "Collective Bargaining Under Executive Order 10988: Trends and Prospects," *Public Personnel Review,* XXVI (October 1965), 199–202.

Snyder, Eleanor M. "Cost-of-Living Adjustment of State and Municipal Wages," *Monthly Labor Review,* LVII (November 1953), 885–894.

Solberg, James G. "Representing the Teachers' Interest. Response from a School Board Member," *Monthly Labor Review,* LXXXIX (June 1966), 622–623.

Solomon, Benjamin. *The Role of the Teacher in Educational Deci-*

sion Making. (Reprint Series No. 125.) Chicago: University of Chicago, Industrial Relations Center, 1966.

Somens, Gerald G. (ed.). "Collective Bargaining in the Public Service," *Proceedings of the 1966 Annual Spring Meeting.* Milwaukee, Wisconsin: Industrial Relations Research Association, May 6–7, 1966.

Sommers, William A. "Municipal Wage Policy for Unionized Employees," *American City,* LXX (November 1955), 141, 143.

"Sound Off: Teachers Should Have the Right to Strike," *The Instructor,* LXXII (March 1963), 10–11.

Spencer, V. "Nurse and Her Employee Labor Relations," *Hospital Management,* XCVII (April–May 1964), 44–48.

Spero, Sterling D. "Arbitration in the American Public Service," *Arbitration Journal,* II (October 1938), 347–351.

———. "Collective Bargaining in the Public Service," *Annals,* CCXLVIII (November 1946), 146–153.

———. *Government as Employer.* New York: Chemical Publishing Co., 1948.

———. "Have Public Employees the Right to Strike?—Maybe," *National Municipal Review,* XXX (September 1941), 524–528, 551.

———. "Whitleyism and Collective Bargaining," *Public Administration Review,* IV (Spring 1944), 164–167.

Srivastava, Anand K. "Public Service Unions in the United States," *Indian Journal of Public Administration,* I (October–December 1955), 335–343.

Starie, John H., and Jack Spatafora. "Union or Professional Membership: A Matter of Philosophy and Program," *Industrial and Labor Relations Report Card for Social Science Teachers,* XII (November 1963), 2–5.

Steet, Marion L. "Professional Associations: More than Unions," *Teachers College Record,* LXVI (December 1964), 203–218.

Steffensen, James P. "Board-Staff Negotiations," *School Life,* XLVII (October 1964), 6–8.

———. *Teachers Negotiate with Their School Boards.* (Bulletin 40.) Washington, D.C.: U.S. Office of Education, 1964.

Stephens, Kenton E. "Collective Relationships Between Teachers' Organizations and Boards of Education." Unpublished Ph.D. dissertation, University of Chicago, 1964.

Steward, Luther C. "The Part of Organized Employees in Developing and Administering a Personnel System," *Public Personnel Studies,* VIII (October–November 1930), 141–143.

Stinnett, T. M. "Professional Negotiation, Collective Bargaining, Sanctions and Strikes," *The Bulletin of the National Association of Secondary School Principals,* XLVIII (April 1964), 93–105.

———, Jack H. Kleinman, and Martha L. Ware. *Professional Negotiation in Public Education.* New York: Macmillan, 1966.

Story, H. W. "Collective Bargaining with Teachers Under Wisconsin Law," *Theory into Practice,* IV (April 1965), 61–65.

Stout, Dorman L. "Public Employees: Rights to Strike and to Bargain Collectively," *Tennessee Law Review*, XXV (Summer 1958), 511–515.

Straus, Donald B. "The Atomic Energy Program and Collective Bargaining," *Monthly Labor Review*, LXXI (November 1950), 587–588.

Strauss, George. "The AAUP as a Professional Occupational Association," *Industrial Relations*, V (October 1965), 128–140.

———. "Professionalism and Occupational Associations," *Industrial Relations*, II (May 1963), 7–31.

Strickland, Jack F. "The 49th Convention of the Federation of Teachers," *Monthly Labor Review*, CXXXVIII (October 1965), 1204–1205.

Stumpf, W. A. "New World of Educational Administration: Teacher Militancy," *American School Board Journal*, CLVIII (February 1966), 10.

Sturmthal, Adolph. "Nationalization and Workers' Control in Britain and France," *Journal of Political Economy*, LXI (February 1953), 43–79.

Stutz, Robert L. "Collective Bargaining by City Employees," *Labor Law Journal*, XV (November 1964), 696–701.

———. *Collective Dealings by Units of Local Government in Connecticut*. Storrs: University of Connecticut, May 1960.

Sublette, Donald J., and Charles A. Meyer. "Detroit Does Not Experiment in Arbitrating Labor Disputes," *Public Personnel Review*, XIII (June 1952), 134–136.

Sunby, Robert D. "Municipal Employee Labor Relations: Discussion of Legal Aspects of Municipal Labor Relations," *Municipality*, XLVIII (April 1953), 80–81, 89–94.

Sussna, Edward. "Collective Bargaining on the New York City Transit System, 1940–1957," *Industrial and Labor Relations Review*, XI (July 1958), 518–533.

Thompson, Arthur A. "Collective Bargaining in the Public Service," *Labor Law Journal*, XVII (February 1966), 89–98.

Thompson, Peter M. "Negotiating with Unions: The Canadian Experience," *Public Personnel Review*, XXIII (October 1962), 235.

Thorne, Irene. "Collective Negotiation: A Survey and Analysis of Teacher Group Collective Negotiation Contracts with School Boards." Unpublished Ph.D. dissertation, Teachers College, Columbia University, 1961.

Torpey, William G. "They Shall Not Strike," *Minnesota Municipalities*, XXXII (January 1947), 16–19.

Torres Braschi, Ramon, *et al.* "Personnel Opinions: What Policies and Rules, If Any, Should Govern Supplementary Outside Employment by Public Employees?" *Public Personnel Review*, XV (April 1954), 93–99.

"Tripartite Panel to Improve Municipal Collective Bargaining Procedures," *Memorandum of Agreement*. New York: City Administrator's Office, March 31, 1966.

"Union Activity in Public Employment," *Columbia Law Review*, LV (March 1955), 343–366.

"Union Labor and the Municipal Employer," *Illinois Law Review*, XLV (July–August 1950), 364–377.

"Unions Eye Municipal Employees," *Business Week*, 1542 (March 21, 1959), pp. 116–122.

Unruh, A. "Negotiations and the Role of the Superintendent," *Educational Forum*, XXIX (January 1965), 165–169.

Upton, C. D., LeRoy Miller, and John E. Erickson. "Minnesota State Employees Train for Unionism," *American Federationist*, XLVII (May 1940), 496–501.

Vietheer, George C. "The Government Seizure Stratagem in Labor Disputes," *Public Administration Review*, VI (Spring 1946), 149–156.

Vogel, Isadore, "What About the Rights of the Public Employee?" *Labor Law Journal*, I (May 1950), 604–618.

Vosloo, William B. *Collective Bargaining in the United States Federal Civil Service*. Chicago: Public Personnel Association, 1966.

Warner, Kenneth O. (ed.). *Developments in Public Employee Relations: Legislative, Judicial, Administrative*. Chicago: Public Personnel Association, 1965.

————. *Management Relations with Organized Public Employees: Theory, Policies, Programs*. Chicago: Public Personnel Association, 1963.

Washington Education Association. *Guidelines for Professional Negotiations*. Seattle: Washington Education Association, 1965.

Weber, F. W. "The Federal Personnel Officer: Management or Employee?" *Personnel Administration*, XVIII (January 1955), 38–42.

Weiford, Douglas, and Wayne Burggraaff. "The Future for Public Employee Unions," *Public Management*, XLV (May 1963), 102.

Weisenfeld, Allan. "Collective Bargaining by Public Employees in the U.S.," *Proceedings of the Annual Spring Meeting*. Milwaukee, Wisconsin: Industrial Relations Research Association, 1966, pp. 1–10.

————. "Public Employees: First or Second Class Citizens?" *Labor Law Journal*, XVI (November 1965), 685–704.

Welsh, James T. "Employee Participation in Personnel Procedures," *Public Management*, XXXVIII (January 1956), 5–6.

Wermel, Michael T. "A Look Ahead at Personnel and Salaries," *Western City*, XXXIV (May 1958), 27–30.

"What Impacts Will the Trend Towards Unionization and Collective Bargaining with Public Employee Organizations Have on the Merit System?" *Public Personnel Review*, XXVII (January 1966), 52–59.

"When Teachers Organize," *Monthly Labor Review*, LXXXVII (November 1964), 1295–1298.

White, Leonard D. "Strikes in the Public Service," *Public Personnel Review,* X (January 1949), 3–10.

Wilbern, York. "Professionalization in the Public Service: Too Little or Too Much?" *Public Administration Review,* XIV (Winter 1954), 13–21.

Wildman, Wesley A. "Collective Action by Public School Teachers," *Industrial and Labor Relations Review,* XVIII (October 1964), 3–19.

————. *Implications of Teacher Bargaining for School Administration.* (Reprint Series No. 120.) Chicago: University of Chicago, Industrial Relations Center, 1965.

————. *Legal Aspects of Teacher Collective Action.* (Reprint Series No. 124.) Chicago: University of Chicago, Industrial Relations Center, 1966.

————. "Representing the Teachers' Interest," *Proceedings of the Nineteenth Annual Winter Meeting.* Madison, Wisconsin: Industrial Relations Research Association, 1966, pp. 113–123.

————, and Charles R. Perry. *Group Conflict and School Organization.* (Reprint Series No. 124.) Chicago: University of Chicago, Industrial Relations Center, 1966.

Wirth, Richard M. "Sane About the Union," *Michigan Education Journal,* XL (October 1, 1962), 205, 223.

Wollett, Donald H. "Professional Negotiations: What Is This Thing?" Washington, D.C.: National Education Association, 1964 (mimeographed).

————. "The Public Employee at the Bargaining Table: Promise or Illusion?" *Labor Law Journal,* XV (January 1964), 8–15.

Wolpert, Arnold W. "Representing the Teachers' Interests. Response from the NEA," *Monthly Labor Review,* LXXXIX (June 1966), 621–622.

Woodcock, George. "Trade Unions under Nationalization," *Labor and Industry in Britain,* V (June 1947), 123–125.

"Work Stoppages, Government Employees, 1942–1961," *Monthly Labor Review,* LXXXVI (January 1963), 52–54.

Work Stoppages Involving Teachers, 1940–1962, Summary Release. Washington, D.C.: Government Printing Office, 1963.

Wormuth, Francis D. "The Hatch Act Cases," *Western Political Quarterly,* I (June 1948), 165–173.

Yabroff, Bernard, and Mary David Lily. "Collective Bargaining and Work Stoppages Involving Teachers," *Monthly Labor Review,* LXXVI (May 1953), 475–479.

————, and Daniel P. Willis, Jr. "Federal Seizures in Labor-Management Disputes, 1917–52," *Monthly Labor Review,* LXXVI (June 1953), 611–616.

Young, Dallas M. "Fifty Years of Labor Arbitration in Cleveland Transit," *Monthly Labor Review,* LXXXIII (May 1960), 464–471.

Zander, Arnold S. "Labor Problems," *American Economic Review,*

XXIII (March 1943), 205–206. (A discussion of Gordon R. Clapp's "Problems of Union Relations in Public Agencies, included in same issue.)

———. "Organized Labor and the Council-Manager Plan. Part II: Views of a Labor Official," *Public Management,* XXXIX (June 1957), 126–129.

———. "Public Employee Unions: The American Federation of State, County and Municipal Employees," *Public Management,* XIX (September 1937), 259–261.

———. "Trends in Labor Legislation for Public Employees," *Monthly Labor Review,* LXXXIII (December 1960), 1293–1296.

———. "Where Our Union Stands on Its Collective Bargaining Program," *Public Employee,* XXIV (July 1959), 3–6.

Zwackman, John E. "Municipal Employment Relations in Wisconsin: The Extension of Private Labor Relations Devices into Municipal Employment," *Wisconsin Law Review,* VIII (Summer 1965), 671–701.

INDEX